Giants on the Earth

Global Communications

GIANTS ON THE EARTH

This edition Copyright 2009 by Global Communications/Conspiracy Journal

If you are the legitimate copyright holder of any material inadvertently used in this book please send a notice to this effect and the "offending" material will be immediately removed from all future printings. The material utilized herein is reproduced for educational purposes and every effort has been made to verify that the material has been properly credited and is available in the public domain.
Otherwise:
All rights reserved. No part of these manuscripts may be copied or reproduced by any mechanical or digital methods and no exerpts or quotes may be used in any other book or manuscript without permission in writing by the Publisher, Global Communications/Conspiracy Journal, except by a reviewer who may quote brief passages in a review.

Revised Edition

ISBN 1-60611-066-7
978-1-60611-066-9

Published by Global Communications/Conspiracy Journal
Box 753 • New Brunswick, NJ 08903

Staff Members
Timothy G. Beckley, Publisher
Carol Ann Rodriguez, Assistant to the Publisher
Sean Casteel, General Associate Editor
Tim R. Swartz, Graphics and Editorial Consultant
William Kern, Editorial and Art Consultant

Sign Up On The Web For Our Free Weekly Newsletter
and Mail Order Versions of Conspiracy Journal and Bizarre Bazaar
www.conspiracyjournal.com

Credit Card Order Hot Line: 1-732-602-3407
PayPal: MrUFO8@hotmail.com

GIANTS ON THE EARTH

Scientists tell us there were giant reptiles, giant sea creatures, giant dinosaurs, giant plants, giant insects, giant proto-mammals and giant flying pterodons, but refuse to believe or reveal that there were also giant humans living on Earth at the same time.

Why is that?

In this book, you will learn that there is ample evidence to prove that early humans and giant humans lived during the age of dinosaurs and pterodactyls, and that the fossil evidence has been suppressed and even destroyed to prevent you from learning the true origins of human life on Earth.

THE NEPHILIM GIANTS

Museums, Government Agencies And Establishment Archeologists Have Hidden And Destroyed The Evidence Of Early Civilizations!

A CONSPIRACY OF SILENCE

Pterodactyls, particularly Quetzalcoatylus, were huge. Some fossilized bones show they may have grown as large as a DC-3. Although none were found, recent expeditions to New Guinea indicate from local legends that they may still exist there. Some photoluminescent flying creatures were filmed at night, however, the great distance of the objects or creatures precluded positive identification as pterodactyls.

Contents

Are Giants Returning to Israel?
Modern Anecdotal Accounts
Giant Creatures During The Age Of Dinosaurs
Giants May Live Today
Giants in Modern America
Giants in the Bible

A HISTORY OF GIANTS
Part 1
Introduction
Chapter 1: Creation
Chapter 2: Pre-Adamic Earth
Chapter 3: The Destruction of Angelic Civilization
Chapter 4: Pre-Adamic Science
Chapter 5: Angels and Giants
Chapter 6: Religions of Giants
Chapter 7: Once Were Giants
Chapter 8: Giants in the New World
Chapter 9: Giants in Europe
Chapter 10: Nothing New Under the Sun

Part 2
Chapter 11: Giants in North America
Chapter 12: Giants in South America
Chapter 13: Africa's Giants
Chapter 14: Asian Giants
Chapter 15: Australian Giants
Chapter 16: British Giants
Chapter 17: Giants in Europe
Chapter 18: Giants in the Middle East

- Book of Enoch
- Epic of Gilgamesh
- Ancient & Lost Civilizations
- Gilgamesh Tomb Found!
- Gog
- Floods Stories from Around the World
- The Book of Giants
- Ancient Egyptian Treasures in Grand Canyon
- The Karankawa

GIANTS ON THE EARTH

FROM OUT OF THE SKY
By Timothy Green Beckley

There once were giants living on the earth.

We know this because the Bible and other early texts tell us so.

We know it because the bones remain for us to see-bones of beings that could have stood upwards of fifteen feet tall.

Where did these giants come from? Were they born on earth? Did they come from a vast underworld that could exist beneath our feet? Or is it possible they came straight down out of the sky, down from "Heaven" above?

There are numerous theories to "explain" the giants of the earth and it is possible that all theories explored may have some basis in reality.

When I was editing UFO UNIVERSE magazine, one of our regular contributors was a freelance writer from Israel named Barry Chamish . A reporter worth every grain of salt, Chamish kept our readers abreast of all the latest UFO/alien stories.

And while I would not consider this to be a book that postulates Biblical explanations for giants existing on the earth, certainly such accounts need to be considered-past, present and maybe even into the future (i.e. the return of the Nephilim as written about in Zacharia Sitchin's works).

So before I go onto my own writings involving stories of giants dropping down from above, we should make a humble presentation of Barry Chamish's claim that such space giants are a representation of Biblical beings returning at this critical period in earth's time line.

Are Giants Returning to the Holy Land?
by Barry Chamish

Are the Anakim or the Refaim, the giants of the Bible, returning to Israel today? There are only two periods of recorded history when giants were reported in Israel: in Biblical days from the time of the Flood to the ascension of King David and since 1993 in modern Israel.

The case for the return of the giants to Israel is strong. In fact, what characterizes the current Israeli UFO wave from others in the world is the sheer abundance of physical evidence left behind by the visitors. Consider the first incident to usher Israel into the UFO age.

On the evening of Sept. 28, 1987, a 27 year old auto mechanic, Ami Achrai, was driving

GIANTS ON THE EARTH

just south of Haifa when he saw what he thought might be a helicopter in distress hovering just above the sands of Shikmona Beach on the Mediterranean Sea. He stopped his car and to his utter amazement saw a disc-shaped craft which emitted a bright red flash before disappearing.

Two days later he returned to the site with a ufologist the police referred him to, Hadassah Arbel. What they discovered remains one of the most lasting proofs ever left by a UFO of its physical existence. The flash emitted by the craft burned its image into the sands of Shikmona Beach. A fifteen-meter ellipsoid disk was burnt black into the sand, but what was more interesting was what wasn't burned. In the vegetation which wasn't burned was a clear image of the pilot of the craft facing a control board.

Examining the Shikmona Beach burnt image

Seven years later I sent samples of the burnt sand to the television show Sightings which subjected it to laboratory tests. The sand seemed to melt in the heat of the camera light. The reason later discovered was the sand particles were covered by a low melting hydrocarbon material. The laboratory could find no natural or human explanation for the phenomenon.

Ami Achrai's incident was followed by a repeat performance on June 6, 1988, when a similarly shaped craft was once again burned into the sands of Shikmona Beach, about 100 yards north of the first site. This was followed by the most spectacular display of all. On April 27, 1989, two teenagers witnessed a UFO explode into thousands of shards over Shikmona Beach.

By now, Israeli ufologists were prepared to handle the latest incident more scientifi-

GIANTS ON THE EARTH

cally. The beach was strewn with burning white metal which was cool to the touch. The metal even glowed in water. When picked up, the shards turned into a white ash. Scientists from the Technion Institute of Technology tested the site and found that magnetism was 6000 times higher than the surrounding area. The shards were found to be very pure magnesium.

Two hundred yards above Shikmona Beach is a biblical shrine called Elijah's cave. Here Elijah preached and here or somewhere nearby in the Carmel Mountains, Elijah challenged the Canaanites to a duel of Gods. Two bulls were tethered and the gods were beseeched to roast them. Naturally, Baal failed the Canaanites but Elijah's God sent a ray of light from heaven which cooked the bull on the spot. This ray must have been similar to the kind of beam which burned the sands of Shikmona Beach into a saucer shape.

Within the Cave of Elijah is an ancient drawing of something that was the spitting image of the craft burned into the sands below. The Sightings team decided the image "was a coincidence. Maybe it was a bat." When Michael Hesemann filmed the drawing he left certain it was a match for the burned sand pictures.

Although the cave drawing's meaning is in dispute, the fact of the modern UFO-burned inscriptions is not. Something unique occurred at Shikmona Beach. Alien craft decided to leave souvenirs there at least three times. By doing so, they revealed the dimensions of their craft and apparently its pilot, as well as their construction material. These were not crop circles nor were they formed the same way. A very different message was left on Shikmona Beach's sands.

After the UFO explosion, there was a hiatus of UFO activity until 1993, broken only once in late 1991 over the village of Sde Moshe, some five miles from Kadima. There, after two straight nights of having the inside of his house lit up by an unexplained craft hovering above it, Eli Cohen captured the responsible UFO on videotape. Several minutes of the tape were filmed after daybreak making the result a most clear and convincing record of a UFO.

It seems the visitors were merely scouting the Kadima area in 1991 but they returned in force in 1993. And this time, the occupants of the crafts did more than merely hover in the sky.

In the early morning of April 20, Tsiporet Carmel's house glowed from within. She stepped outside and saw what she thought was a new fruit silo built outside her backyard. But then she saw the silo add a second storey to itself. Ten yards to the side of this magical silo, Tsiporet saw a seven-foot-tall being wearing metallic overalls. Its head was covered in what looked like a beekeeper's hat. Tsiporet said, "Why don't you take off your hat so I can see your face?" The being answered her telepathically, "That's the way it is."

This was Israel's first publicized close encounter with an alien being. Tsiporet could easily have been made an object of ridicule but for the fact that a crop circle 4.5 meters in diameter was found exactly where she had seen the craft. Within the circle were shards of a material later found to be a very pure silicon. I add, Israel's ufologists are divided over the veracity of the silicon because there was a prankster loose in Kadima.

However, within ten days, two more circles were found just outside Tsiporet's backyard. This time, they were soaked with a red liquid and this fluid would be a constant feature of upcoming landing circles. It was tested by the National Biological Laboratory

GIANTS ON THE EARTH

in Ness Tziona and found to be composed mostly of cadmium.

This was the end of Tsiporet's incidents. Now the visitors concentrated on two other women in their late thirties living on Hapalmach Street. The first was a Russian immigrant, Mara. Strange forces shook her house so hard they caused the outside air conditioning unit to fall out of its casing into the house. Voices called to Mara in her childhood nickname. Eventually she decided the house was haunted and she moved far from Kadima.

Shosh Yahud is the treasurer of the town of Kadima. She is down to earth and wants as little to do with her UFO experience as possible. In May, she awoke to see a seven foot, round faced being in silvery overalls circling her bed as if "floating on his shoes." The creature assured her he was not there to harm her and she became relaxed. After a few minutes the being floated through her wall outside.

Shosh thought she had dreamed the incident until she looked out her window in the morning and saw a 4.5 meter crop circle in her backyard. The ufologists descended on her home and discovered the silicon and cadmium within the circle.

Next, in June, it was Hannah Somech's turn to be visited by a giant. Hannah lives in Burgata, three miles from Kadima. She was startled to see her dog go flying across the kitchen into a wall. She stepped outside to investigate and her way was stopped by an invisible force. She then saw a seven foot, round-faced being in metallic overalls examining her pickup truck. She said to it, "What did you do to my dog?" It answered telepathically, "Go away. I'm busy. I could crush you like an ant if I wanted to. Go back to your husband."

Needless to say, a 4.5 meter circle crushed out of the grass was later found in Hannah's back yard. Within, the grass was soaked with red liquid cadmium.

By the end of the summer, the credible reports of giants roaming the land persuaded the normally staid television station Channel One to broadcast a one hour program on the subject. Tsiporet and Shosh appeared as well as the ufologists who had examined the circles of Kadima. To the apparent shock of the host, the viewing audience believed the advocates of alien landings. The result was two more witnesses coming out into the open.

Both were women in their late thirties who lived within ten miles of each other south of Tel Aviv. Clara Kahonov of Holon was most reluctant to be quoted but acknowledged that she had seen a giant being.

Batya Shimon of Rishon Letzion saw far more than one. In early July, two seven foot tall, bald creatures beamed themselves into her seventh floor apartment. They told her telepathically not to be frightened and she immediately relaxed. She then felt they had "friendly faces." They roamed her home, "floating on their shoes" and dusting her shelves with a yellow, foul-smelling powder. One being saw her son's aquarium and became very excited and called his colleague over. After a few minutes, they beamed themselves outside. The next night at 3 a.m., a dozen giants visited Batya arriving and leaving the same way.

I have had extensive conversations with the contactees and there is much in common with their stories. That is a fit subject for a separate lecture. In short, all were the same age, all were white collar workers, three have been haunted since their encounters telepathically, all their men slept through the encounters, two had mysterious pregnancies, etc. But the core commonality is that these women did not know each other and sepa-

GIANTS ON THE EARTH

rately described the same seven foot tall, bald, round-faced giants.

And if absolute proof that giants were about in Israel was needed, it came in December in the village of Yatzitz, twelve miles east of Rishon Letzion. The giants had opened a new axis after Kadima, a triangle of twenty miles linking Rishon Letzion, Holon and Yatzitz.

Herzl Casatini, the village security chief, and his friend Danny Ezra were sharing conversation when they heard an explosion and felt Ezra's house shake. Herzl opened the door and stood face to face with a nine foot tall creature in metallic clothes whose face was hidden in "a haze." He shut the door and called the police. They arrived and discovered deep boot tracks in the hard mud. The tracks sank 35 centimeters into the ground, meaning whoever made them had to have weighed, literally, a ton. Thinking there might have been a terrorist incursion, the army was called in.

Military trackers were totally stumped. The tracks carried on for 8 kilometers. The heel dug in only 5 cm. meaning whatever made the tracks was walking almost on tiptoes. If you can call it walking. Sometimes the distance between tracks was twelve feet, meaning the intruder was a world-record-holding broad jumper weighing about a ton.

The Yatzitz incident confirmed, even to the deepest skeptics, that giants were indeed sighted and they left proof that was nearly impossible to dispute. The best the Israeli authorities could come up with to explain the tracks was they were left by an unknown cult. It would have to be a very unknown one, for records of cults whose ceremonies include dressing as giants and leaving miles of unidentifiable tracks are undoubtedly quite rare.

After Yatitz, giant sightings were reported in Ramat Hasharon, Rehovot and Afula. And 1996 became a vintage year for UFO evidence gathering with a good dozen craft filmed. Two incidents stand out. In August, a UFO was filmed over three nights with professional equipment at Kibbutz Hatzor. The results include a close-up of what appear to be rows of square-shaped vents on the craft. In December, a Netanya household reported constant contact with small grays, the first such report from Israel. The witnesses backed up their claims with an abundance of physical evidence, including stones that melt ice immediately without a known energy source.

The Israeli UFO experience is unique and very complicated. I have touched on just one aspect of it, but it is vital to understanding the Israeli puzzle. Of the seven best documented close encounters with alien beings provably connected to UFOs, six involved giants. These giants were determined to leave evidence of their arrival in the form of cadmium-imbued landing circles, miles of impossible boot tracks and deliberate communication with witnesses. Indeed, the abundant evidence more than indicates that there are giants roaming Israel today.

As they were 5,000 years ago when they also left proof of their existence. The giants were descended from the Nephilim, literally "the fallen ones." In ancient times, entities fell on Israel from the heavens and later became the mortal enemies of the Hebrew nations.

GIANTS ON THE EARTH

The Circle of the Giants - Gilgal Refaim. 5200-year-old monument believed by some to have been built by the biblical giants, also called Nephilim.

One giant king was Og of Bashan. The Bible records that his bed was thirteen feet long. Bashan's territory included the Golan Heights. Sitting on the Golan Heights is the Israeli version of Stonehenge. Called Gilgal Refaim, the Circle of the Refaim or giants in English, this site consists of five concentric rings whose beauty can only be appreciated from above. Unfortunately, there was supposedly no way for the simple nomads of 5000 years ago to see the circles from above.

The site is enormous. The outside circle has a diameter of 159 meters and over 37,000 tons of rock went into the construction of the complex. Two openings in the circles may have been used to measure the solar solstice and the rising of Sirius in 3000 BCE.

The fact remains that Israeli archaeologists are totally mystified by the Gilgal Refaim. No other complex built in the Middle East resembles it and it predates the pyramids by over 500 years. The indigenous nomads of the time did not engage in this kind of megalith building, so outsiders were probably the builders. According to the Bible, the only outsiders living on the Golan Heights back then were giants.

Maybe it's a long shot, but no one has come up with a better explanation for Israel's current UFO wave. I believe the ancient giants may be coming home. I conclude on a somber note. The biblical giants were God's enemy and Israel's armies were the means to their utter destruction. There is a legitimate reason to contemplate the recent re-arrival of giants in Israel with a good measure of dread.

(This material Copyright (c) by Barry Chamish, for a full list of available titles by this writer visit www.thebarrychamishwebsite.com)

GIANTS ON THE EARTH

Invasion of the Space Giants

Authorities around the world have been flooded with reports of giant aliens whose mysterious actions have left them completely baffled.

By Timothy Green Beckley

It was a humid evening in late August 1963. The moon was full and the stars twinkled brilliantly. Near the town of Sagrada Famila, Brazil, the Eustagulo family lived in a modest home in a rural area. They never heard of flying saucers.

On this particular evening, the two Eustagulo boys, Fernando, 11, and Ronaldo, 9, were told to go to the well in the garden and clean the family coffee filter. The two went down the little stone stairway that led to the well with their friend Marcos. The night was so clear and luminous, they didn't immediately recognize the sphere that was floating in front of them as they stood in front of the well cranking the pulley to bring up a bucketful of water.

When they first saw the object, it was above the trees, practically touching the branches. The boys could make out people sitting one behind the other in four or five rows inside the craft. Then suddenly a door popped open, making a humming noise. Two luminous parallel bands speared the ground near a flower bed and a slender being, about 10-feet-tall, glided on the two bands of light to the ground, landing near the foot of the stone stairway.

The being rode down the beams, with his arms outstretched, in a slow sliding movement. Once he reached the ground, he walked about 20 feet, with his back stiff, legs open, and arms stretched out, balancing himself. He moved, swinging his body from left to right continuously until he reached a rock in the yard and proceeded to sit down. All three boys agreed that the being wore a transparent helmet over his head and had only one visible eye of dark color in the middle of his forehead. It was actually a giant-sized saucerian Cyclops! The ufonaut was wearing high boots, which had long, thick triangular spikes protruding from each other. The spikes made strange impressions in the soft earth, which could be seen for days following the sighting.

The trousers the being wore seemed to be fastened to the boots in a ring fashion. The moment the being hit the ground, his suit seemed to inflate as if it filled with air. His garment was very shiny and similar to leather. Fernando said that the being had a copper colored box on his back, and a square pack that covered part of his chest. He said

GIANTS ON THE EARTH

this pack gave off flashes of light and he thought it was either a camera or flashlight. In the craft's open doorway, the boys could plainly see the other occupants sitting behind control panels turning knobs and flicking switches.

Frozen in their tracks, the boys said the being reached for one of them as if he meant to sweep him up in his giant hands and carry him to the waiting ship. Fearing the worst, Fernando picked up a brick and was about to heave it at the spaceman, who was seated on the rock, when the being stood up and stared at the youth. Fernando was unable to move or throw the brick. It was as if the being had gained control over his body and his movements.

As if surprised by the boy's hostile action, the "spaceman" took a few steps back, his mouth opening in a vertical fashion, showing a row of white teeth with two larger ones at the corners of the mouth-one directed downward, the other up. The being proceeded to enter the ship, gliding up the shafts of light still beaming down. This time, however, the Cyclops floated skyward with his hands pressed against his body and not outstretched as before.

Looking through the door of the open ship, the boys saw that all the crew members were about the same size and stature and wore the same transparent helmet. The youngsters also felt that one of the beings on board was a female, since it had long hair pulled tightly in a bun, while all the others appeared to be bald.

As in many cases already reported, the boys felt that the occupant was not really attempting to hurt them. They could not explain how they got this impression, but their fear had disappeared. The boys were also quite certain that he would return again. When asked how they knew this, they answered that it was just a feeling, as if someone was talking to them. A local Brazilian UFO researcher explained this as a telepathic suggestion and claimed that others in the vicinity had also reported strange objects in the skies that evening.

Another of the many cases of giant ufonauts was reported in the Australian Flying Saucer Review. It was raining heavily at dawn on October 18, 1963. Eugenio Douglas was driving with a truckload of coal, between Monte Maix and Isla Verde, in Argentina, when a brilliant headlight, apparently from an approaching car, blinded him. As another "auto" approached, Douglas realized that the vehicle had only one headlight. He slowed down to avoid a collision, and as he did the light became so bright he could not look at it any longer. He stepped on the brakes and put his head on the steering wheel. The truck was now on the edge of the road. Douglas got out of the truck and through the veil of rain saw a circular metallic craft about 35 feet high in front of him.

Douglas told an investigator from the Review that, "Suddenly another light of lesser intensity appeared in the vehicle. It passed through the opening. They were humanlike, but extremely tall." He estimated their height at approximately 13 feet and they were dressed in tight-fitting metallic suits.

According to the filed report, the occupants wore strange headgear with protrusions that looked like small antennae. Douglas said there was nothing repulsive about the big men, yet he was terribly frightened.

The moment his presence was discovered by the aliens, a ray of red light flashed, burning his skin. Eugenio Douglas was in such a state of fright that he could think of nothing but grabbing his revolver and firing three shots at the tall being. Then he started

GIANTS ON THE EARTH

to run on the road toward the town of Monte Maix.

But the "burning light" from the ship followed him wherever he went. When he reached the village, Douglas noticed that as the red beam touched electric lights in the street, they turned violet and then green. A strong smell of gas immediately spread all around the area.

As he came to the nearest home he began to shout for help. This was the house of a Mr. Ribas, who had died the night before. Unexpectedly, the candles around the casket and all the electric lights in the house turned green. A strange smell instantly filled the room.

Hearing the shouts outside and seeing the weird happenings inside, the Ribas family rushed out of their house to find Douglas with an overcoat over his head and a gun in his hand. Neighbors appeared on the scene to stare at the green streetlights. In the meantime, the ufonauts had disappeared into the night.

Douglas was taken to the police station where he showed the burns on his face and hands and again related his weird experience. The police officer then remembered that he had received a number of calls about the electric lights changing color throughout the town, which was attributed to irregularities at the local power plant. Douglas was examined by a Dr. Dabolas, who stated that the burns had been caused by radiations similar to those from an overexposure to ultraviolet rays.

The following day the villagers went to the site where Douglas met the strange machine with the giants and found large footprints (19 and a half inches long) partially washed away by the rain. Burnt out cables were also found in the truck.

There had been many observations of flying saucer "giants" in South America, but sightings of these beings seem to abound in Argentina. Saucer News (September 1965) contains a brief report concerning an incredible incident which occurred in the town of Torren. During February of that year, a UFO landed in full view of a group of extremely excited and frightened farmers. Two strange beings, towering over seven feet tall, emerged from the craft and walked toward the villagers. As in the Douglas case, they had an apparatus on their foreheads which gave off small rays of many-colored light. The beings then went into one of the nearby houses and attempted to kidnap the farmer who lived there. They were unsuccessful, due to the combined efforts of his friends who came to his rescue.

On the same evening, the craft landed again, and this time the farmers opened fire on the giants. To their horror and dismay, the bullets had no effect. Despite the ability to withstand the fussilade, the spacemen were easily discouraged from their kidnap mission. Interestingly, one of the farmers who fought the spacemen hand-to-hand later came down with a strange skin disease.

Brazil has also had its share of visits by these giants. In August, 1958, three men on the outskirts of Mindui reportedly observed a pair of eight-foot-tall beings dressed in brilliant red clothing. They watched the spacemen walk up a hill to their UFO and take off.

On February 14, 1965, on a beach near Guarani, Brazil, five local residents observed the landing of an unusually large object. Three of those present went back to a nearby motel to get additional witnesses. While they were gone, the two remaining UFO witnesses cautiously approached the ship from behind sand dunes until they managed to maneuver within 60 feet of the craft. From this position, they noticed that three beings had alighted from the ship. The ufonauts were thin, tall creatures about eight feet tall,

GIANTS ON THE EARTH

wearing a dark, one-piece suit which fit very tightly around their bodies.

Before anyone else could arrive at the site, the craft took off. However, those who did return could see traces of footprints and unusual circles where the object had rested.

Several hours later, on the same evening, Nilo Domingues, while resting on a beach in Atlandia, Brazil, saw a UFO land and immediately turn on what appeared to be a bright spotlight that moved about on the sand. A porthole could be seen on the craft and from a door on its underside came another strong light. Suddenly the object took off rapidly and disappeared. Half an hour later, Domingues returned to the beach with his son and found strange markings in the sand, which looked like the ship and its crew had returned during his brief absence.

From Vilovi, Spain, comes a sighting of an enormous hairy monster seen on February 27, 1968. The "animal" reportedly left huge footprints in the ground and walked the countryside at night scaring animals. Several horses were reportedly attacked by the beast. There have been frequent reports of UFOs in the area.

A Rumanian migrant in Australia reportedly saw three giant creatures in purple and yellow clothing about 200 miles north of Brisbane. This sighting was carried in The News of January 17, 1969: "Mr. George Vas, a repairman, his wife Malanka, and daughters Olga, 14, and Maria, 13, all say they watched the spacemen collecting sugar cane and other plant specimens for 10 minutes. Mr. Vas said he and his family were asleep in their caravan at the edge of the road. About 4:30 a.m. they were awakened by the barking of their dog, Ica. He heard a loud buzzing noise like a big swarm of wasps, and said he saw an object land; it was between 25 and 30 yards in diameter and looked like a Mexican sombrero. It gave off a brilliant violet color. Mr. Vas said he had his family watched as three spacemen-about three times larger than human beings-descended from the ship. They had blocky arms and legs and shapeless bodies. They gave off a purplish glow. After gathering specimens for about 10 minutes, the spacemen returned to their ship. The craft went straight up, traveling very quickly. As it took off, the hair on everyone's body stood up as if affected by a form of magnetism. Mr. Vas said this was his third sighting of 'spacemen.' He saw one as a child in Rumania in 1918, and another near Belgrade in 1946."

Although the appearances of these giant ufonauts have been less frequent in North America, information has been obtained of at least 25 reports centering around sightings of these creatures. Mary Lou Guenther, a Canadian researcher, reports that on September 19, 1963, about 8 p.m., a UFO hovered over a field across from a school yard in Saskatoon, Canada. As the UFO passed over the vacant lot, it dropped a large container of some type. After the UFO took off, the young witnesses, including 11-year-old Brian Whitehead, started walking in the direction of the "box." When they were within 15 feet of the object, someone or something stood up. The being was about 10 feet tall and suddenly started moving toward the children, moaning and holding his hands out as he came at them.

Brian described the alien as being dressed in clothes which "were like a cloak worn by a monk." The "suit" was white like a huge crayon. When questioned whether he saw pants legs, Brian seemed puzzled and said, "I don't know. Sometimes I could see right through him."

After the children were calmed down, the police were summoned, and they arrived

GIANTS ON THE EARTH

about 45 minutes after the incident took place. The investigation centered around the field for several days, and details of it were sketchy. The boys were questioned separately and asked to draw sketches, which apparently matched. According to Mrs. Guenther: "The following evening, some boys, while in the playground, saw the same UFO return and again hover above the lot. They thought they saw an extremely large man lying on the ground because they saw 'arms and legs move.' The object then disappeared and they saw nothing else."

During a widespread wave of saucer sightings in Mexico in 1965 there were several cases involving giants. In September, a group of saucer occupants estimated to be 10 feet in height, with brilliant red eyes and no mouths or noses, were seen by three women who claim they popped out in front of them during a stroll through a suburb of Mexico City. The beings were dressed in shiny gray suits and boots "just like out of the comic strips." After seeing the beings, the women said they ran away in panic and when they eventually decided to return to the site the ufonauts had departed.

Not to be outdone, the U.S. has had its share of this type of creature.

On the evening of September 14, 1952, seven witnesses, including a National Guardsman, climbed a hill in Flatwoods, West Virginia, after watching a flaming fireball land in the immediate area. When they reached the top of the hill, they were startled to see a dull orange globe resting on the ground. From the glow surrounding the object emerged a 15-foot-tall being which towered over the witnesses. Its face, everyone agreed, was round and blood red. No one noticed a nose or mouth, only eyes, or eye-like openings, which projected "greenish-orange" beams of light. Around the red "face" and reaching upward to a point was a dark hood-like shape, which could have been a helmet.

Watching the "monster" gliding over the ground in their direction, the witnesses took off, running back down the hill and clearing a four-foot gate without opening it.

Later, questioned by researcher Gray Barker, the witnesses stated that an awful odor, like rotten eggs, covered the entire area. This stench was so horrible that they were sick to their stomachs for hours afterward.

Returning to the area with Gene Lemon, the Guardsman, Barker found the site covered with mysterious "ski marks." The impressions were about 10 feet apart in the tall grass and led from the tree, where the "monster" was last seen standing, to the location of the alleged "fireball."

Oddly enough, at the exact same time of these seven witnesses' experience, residents from surrounding states were calling local police departments, TV and radio stations, and military installations to report peculiar aerial observations, which were generally interpreted as meteorites.

The Air Force sent an investigator to Flatwoods a few weeks later and convinced at least one witness that what they had seen was a top secret government rocket, propelled by an ammonia-like fuel. No answer has been offered to explain the appearance of the 15-foot-tall monster. Thus it must be listed as another appearance made by giant saucerians!

A young Van Nuys, California, electrician, Ted Kittredge, came forward in June 1956 with his account of meeting three seven-foot-tall "visitors" who appeared quite friendly and, had long flowing hair, and spoke English, "as if they had memorized thousands of conversations and were repeating the words on tape."

GIANTS ON THE EARTH

Kittredge said his stepmother, with whom he shared his home, slept through the entire episode. Kittredge himself was awakened by the barking of his dogs and upon stepping out to investigate saw a huge golden colored ball in his yard.

"Three men approached me without hesitation and told me not be frightened," he said. "I was really scared. In fact, the whole thing seemed like a dream. Only I know it wasn't. Several other people in the Valley had seen the same thing, even talked with the men. I just hope I never see it again, that's all."

Kittredge also appears to have had a brush with a mysterious group who try to silence saucer witnesses. After appearing on a TV show in Van Nuys, he got a phone call in the middle of the night warning him that it would be wise not to talk about his contact. "I was told to stop worrying and stop talking," Kittredge said. "I could hear machines clicking in the background and the voice said, 'We know all about what's going on. You just keep your mouth shut and forget about it.'" This type of phone call has been received by many people after a close sighting or contact.

While going for a late walk on the sand near Riis Park, New York, in September 1961, Stan Suban, of Brooklyn, claims that he saw a creature at least seven feet in height near a burning fire. The young Columbia University student maintains that his sighting occurred around 2:30 a.m.: "A sphere of white light hung suspended around the fire. Near the water I could see five or six persons whom I took to be skin divers. I could see the black 'wet' suits with the white strings drawn at their arms. They were all about six and a half feet tall and well built. I was about 50 yards from the fire and was attempting to get a closer look at what was going on. Then a figure, much larger than the rest, approached from the direction of the water. It came up to the fire and bent over it and remained in that position for some time. Then he walked around the fire several times, stopped and took off what appeared to be sweat pants. What then terrified me was the appearance of this figure. He was white as snow, seven to seven and a half feet tall and had no distinguishable facial features.

"I couldn't believe my eyes, but stared at him in fascination and terror. At this time, I hid behind a concrete block which was about seven feet high." The "alien" even towered above this structure. "After looking at the creature for several minutes I knew he was not of this world. He walked with an animated gait. I was impressed with the massive power it seemed to have within itself. I do not believe the 'person' was human."

Minutes later, the creature disappeared as it moved out of the firelight toward the ocean. Because of the constant shifting of the sand, no impressions were found to confirm Stan Suban's tale, but he is very definite about what he saw.

One of the strangest encounters involving giant-sized saucer occupants occurred to six teenagers in Daniels Park just south of Denver, Colorado, on the evening of April 8, 1966.

The group of teenagers consisted of Alan Scrivner, Donald Otis, Michael Simington, all 17 years old, and Patricia Retherford, Kaye Hurly, both 16, and Mary Zolar, 18. At about 5:30 p.m. they drove to Daniels Park, which is a short ride from the heart of Denver. They parked their car and walked, joking as they went, a distance of some 350 feet to an old dugout shelter where they proceeded to build a fire and have a picnic.

About 9:30, Scrivner told reporter William Logan of the Rocky Mountain News, "We were all inside the shelter and thought we heard a sound like someone walking on top of

GIANTS ON THE EARTH

the roof." Scrivner and Donald Otis took a flashlight and went out to have a look. "We couldn't see anything. It seemed real quiet outside, and then we noticed this buzzing sound. There was something out there rustling and it would stop when Don and I would stop. Up near my car we looked out into a nearby field and saw something that looked like another car with big round tail lights. The lights moved around and then were gone. We went back to the shelter, where the others (were waiting), and they told us they had seen a big figure or something pass in the light outside. They said it was a lot taller than me, and I'm six feet one inch." Scrivner estimated that the being was seven feet tall.

"We decided to leave and as we walked to the car, Don yelled about a light. There was a white light that shot out real bright across from us, and two blue lights, dimmer, and a brighter one below us."

Four of the teenagers stood on the hood of the car to get a better view. They saw four objects that looked like "footballs with domes on them, sort of squashed spheres. This strange sound was all around us. It didn't come from one direction. It was pulsating."

Scrivner told reporter Logan that three of the objects were off to the right. "Two that hovered and one that went up and down-and the fourth came around from the left. The last one changed its color to red after it got close to us."

Red rays seemed to be coming out of the bottom of the object "on and off" as if the object was trying to blast off unsuccessfully. Scrivner continued: "We decided to drive out of there. My car wouldn't work right. It's a 1954 Ford, but has a new engine and works fine, but the engine kept (conking out) like the ignition was going on and off. There was nothing but static on the radio."

After Scrivner finally managed to get the car started, he reported that the others all saw a huge light on the road behind them. "It was 30 feet behind us and came up right behind our car and then it went out. The strange thing is I couldn't see the light in the rearview mirror."

Police Chief John C. MacLvor said the teenagers seemed quite sincere and "two of the girls were really frightened." The chief commented, "I'm inclined to think they really saw something."

Emil Slaboda, Wire News Editor of The Trentorian, has been one of the few dedicated newsmen who has tried to get the facts about flying saucers across to the public. His investigations of several sightings which have taken place in New Jersey have turned out to be valuable contributions to UFO research.

In his Across the Board column of February 5, 1967, Slaboda wrote: "The following two stories are true to the best of my knowledge. They happened in the Trenton area and both cases were reported to the police. The principals, however, wanted to remain anonymous and for good reason . . . monsters and flying saucer stories often bring ridicule to the tellers! Although only a select group of people know it, a monster, presumably from a saucer, visited Washington Crossing Park, New Jersey, and scared the daylights out of four nocturnal visitors to the park some five weeks ago."

Slaboda reported that two men and two women were driving through the park when they noticed an unusual shadow pass over their car. "Although there was no sound of engines, the four passed off the shadow as that of an airplane heading for nearby Mercer Airport. They stopped the car moments later and two of the group left the car for a short walk." Suddenly, there was an alarming roar, "as if some animal were nearby." Hurrying

GIANTS ON THE EARTH

back to their parked auto, the couple saw an eight-foot-tall creature gliding toward them over a grassy knoll. "It definitely did not walk like an animal or anything human," one of the witnesses explained.

Slaboda interviewed a brother of one of the witnesses who told the newsman, "I don't know what they saw out there, but I do know that whatever it was, it certainly scared the heck out of them."

The second encounter reported by Emil Slaboda occurred on Friday, March 3, 1967, not far from the same Washington Crossing Park. "Two 19-year-old girls were driving down Bear Tavern Road, in Ewing Township. They were in the vicinity of the Mountain View Golf Course when the UFO put in its appearance." The girls told the Ewing Police that the craft was about 20 feet long, cigar shaped, and was lit up along its entire length. When the object dipped down in front of their car, the girl driving slammed on the brakes and began to scream.

It has been suggested by the late Ivan Anderson, the late John Keel, and many others that many UFO occupants are actually "androids"-manufactured creations. This would mean we are dealing with non-thinking, non-feeling beings and are faced with the task of trying to understand machines which are merely "programmed."

So what of these "extraterrestrial" giants? First off, who can prove that they are extraterrestrial? These ships that transport them could be vehicles that transported the original Gods down and around the Earth from their Heavenly homes upon Mount Olympus. All we can be certain of is that, as it states in Genesis, "There were giants in the earth in those days," and apparently they came and went as they saw fit. Some-perhaps different groups-decided to stay and took on different tasks. Some blended in easily with those they discovered here, going so far as to mate with the daughters of men whom they found so fair. Could it be that the giants carved up the Earth, establishing a sphere of influence for themselves?

Again, we should not throw caution to the wind and declare all-or any-giants to be extraterrestrial.

They could have developed as a separate species. Remember all giants, just like all "ordinary" humans, are not the same. They come in all sizes from say 8 or 9 feet up to 13, possibly even 15 feet tall. Some groups of giants may have come from inside the earth. There is still a widespread belief that the interior of the earth might be inhabited. I recall the author of The Hollow Earth, Dr Raymond Bernard, writing me one time and telling about a group of giants he met in the jungles of Brazil. And then there are the stories repeated by different explorers, including Admiral Richard Byrd, who exposed a secret society of giants that are still around but keep to themselves.

It remains a puzzle that science wishes to ignore. All I can say for certain is that this book offers abundant proof that we humans are not by ourselves here on Earth and that some of the monstrous beasts that flew through the sky and roamed the planet may not be extinct yet as the scientific community would want us to believe in service to their own pesky reasons and resources.

GIANTS ON THE EARTH

GIANTS ON THE EARTH

Introduction

Believers in the Thunderbird tell of a fantastic, reptilian creature which, years ago, glided across the skies of the American southwest with glory and power. It was an animal the Indians sometimes feared, sometimes respected, and sometimes destroyed. Whatever it was, it was real.

Skeptics of the Thunderbird tell of the over imagination of native Americans. Or, if it was an animal, it was a large condor, vulture, or other known species of bird. Whatever it was, it was insignificant.

Yankee soldiers pose with a pteranodon Quetzalcoatalus they killed during the civil war. With a wingspan of 18 meters (60 feet), it was the largest creature ever to fly. A few smaller specimens have been seen in and near Papua, New Guinea, but may be rhamphoryncoids.

In the next few moments, let us take you on a journey into the heart of the Native Americans. Learn of their stories and legends, and then logically deduce for yourself whether all, when put together, are lucky coincidences, or the legitimate writings of people who were actual living witnesses of a thought-to-be extinct flying reptile.

We Begin

While exploring the Sonora Desert on February 12th, 1699, Captain Juan Mateo Manje, accompanied by Jesuits Eusebio Francisco Kino and Adam Gil, was told by the Pima Indians that a giant monster lived in a cave nearby in days past. The creature was a horror to the people, for it would fly around and catch as many Indians as it could eat.

One day, they continued to tell him, after the creature had eaten its fill, some of the men followed it back to its cave. While sound asleep, they closed the entrance to the cave with wood collected specifically for this occasion. They set it on fire, and as the creature couldn't escape, it growled fiercely, dying from asphyxiation by the flames and smoke.

Another Pima recalled a story of killing a similar animal in the pueblo of Oposura by using the same tactic. We are told the actual bones were found during the pacification of Mexico by General Don Hernando Cortes and were sent to Spain.

Stories of such incidents are prevalent among many other Indian tribes of the American Southwest, suggesting that they had a long history of encounters with creatures reminiscent of pterosaurs, especially the gigantic pteranodon. The standard long-age scenario of evolution, of course, does not easily fall in line with the belief of living dinosaurs

GIANTS ON THE EARTH

in recent history (or for those who wish to be technical, "flying reptiles"). After all, they died some 65 million years before monkey had yet turned to man.

What about the Yaqui Indians?

They also spoke of a giant bird that lived on the hill of Otan Kawi. Every morning it flew out to capture human prey, and then return. A young boy who had lost his entire family to the monster finally killed it with a bow and arrows.

What about the Sioux Indians?

They told of a story about an experience some of their warriors had with a Thunderbird that fits near perfectly with the description of the pteranodon.

"One day, long long ago, before the white man came to America, a party of Sioux Indian warriors were out hunting. They had left their village far behind. Before they realized it, the group of braves found themselves alone in the bare and rocky badlands of the West.

"Suddenly the sky darkened . . . There was a clap of thunder that shook the earth. Looking up in terror, the Indians thought they saw the shape of a giant bird falling to earth . . .

"The band of hunters traveled over the badlands for days until they came at last to the spot where they thought the giant bird had fallen. Nothing was left of the terrible creature but its bones . . .

"The Indians shuddered as they looked at the monster's skeleton. The bird had fallen so hard, they thought, that its bones were partly sunk in the rock. But the braves could see that its wingspread was as big as four tall men standing on top of one another. The strange creature had fierce claws on its wings, as well as on its feet, and the beak was long and sharp. There was a long, bony crest on its head. The Indians knew that they had never seen a bird like it before."

What about the Illini Indians?

The Indians of Illionois, called the Illini, were once terrorized by a large bird they called the "Piasa", which means "bird that devours man". So large was the Piasa that it could allegedly carry off a full-grown deer. Every Indian tribe in the area greatly feared the Piasa and sought to destroy it.

One day the Illini were said to have tricked the creature by hiding 20 armed warriors in a certain spot, while the Chief himself chose to stand in the open as a victim for the Piasa. As the bird neared to attack him, the men in hiding leapt out and speared it to death.

What was the Piasa? Many speculate it to be the imagination of superstitious natives, while others believe it to have been a large condor, while still others believe it to have been an actual flying reptile. In 1848, John Russell, a writer from Illinois who was interested in the Piasa, explored the caves where the creature was said to live. After his exploration, one cave, particularly difficult to access, gave evidence for the Illini's story. Russell stated:

"The shape of the cave was irregular, but so far as I could judge the bottom would average twenty by thirty feet. The floor of the cave throughout its whole extent was one mass of human bones."

GIANTS ON THE EARTH

In Alton, Illinois, a painting existed high upon a cliff. Though destroyed in the 1850s when the face of the cliff collapsed into the river, a number of explorers during the seventeenth and eighteenth centuries saw the painting and described what it looked like in great detail in their journals. The description? A bird-like animal with many reptilian characteristics.

According to some, the first account of the Piasa paintings came late in the 17th century when Father Marquette recorded in his journal strange observations he made during an exploratory trip by canoe down the Mississippi. That he was a reliable observer is not open to question. His writings have remained to the present time as important and credible references to scholars studying customs and culture of the Indians when white men first arrived. His account states:

"While skirting some rocks which by their height and length inspired awe, we saw upon one of them two painted monsters which at first made us afraid, and upon which the boldest savages dare not long rest their eyes. They are as large as a calf, have horns on their heads like those of a deer, a horrible look, red eyes, a beard like a tiger's, a face somewhat like a man's, a body covered with scales, and a tail so long that it winds all around the body, passing above the head and going back between the legs, ending in a fish's tail. Green, red and black are the three colors composing the picture. Moreover, these two monsters are so well painted that we cannot believe that any savage is their author, for good painters in France would find it difficult to do so well. And besides, they are so high up on the rock that it is difficult to reach that place conveniently to paint them."

What about the Hoh and Quileute Indians?

They tell of a Thunderbird so large that its wingspan was twice the size of their war canoes. It possessed great claws, a long beak, and the ability to pluck some types of whales out of the sea. They attributed the lack of trees in Beaver Prairie to a terrific battle between a whale and thunderbird:

Thought to have gone extinct during the K2 event, this great flying reptile has been seen right up to modern times.

"One time Thunderbird got a big whale in his talons and carried him to Beaver Prairie and ate him there. The whale fought very hard before he was killed. Thunderbird and whale fought so very hard that they pulled up the trees by their roots. And no trees have ever grown in that place to this day."

What about the Indians of Mexico and South America?

A Mexican archaeologist named Jose Diaz-Bolio came upon an ancient Mayan relief sculpture in Veracruz, Mexico, depicting an animal very similar to the pteranodon. In Science Digest (November, 1968), an article was published on this "evolutionary oddity", called "Serpent-bird of the Mayans". According to Bolio, the bird:

" . . . is not merely the product of Mayan flights of fancy, but a realistic representation of an animal that lived during the period of the ancients Mayans - 1,000 to 5,000 years

GIANTS ON THE EARTH

ago."

Missionaries have also come out of South America with stories from Indians of "birds" that closley resemble pterosaurs. In Venezuela, the Yek's have a story centuries old of a giant man-eating bat. The creature lived at the headwaters of the river in a cave on a large mountain, and would periodically attack canoes and carry off people. Eventually, men were chosen to go to its lair and kill it, which they did. Also, because it was said to defecate in the river (Erebato), the Indians would not drink from it.

While some cryptozoologists believe el Chupacabra might be a pterosaur, others believe it is a velociraptor!

Another tribe, the Corentyn, also tell of an enormous gliding serpent.

The Thunderbird: What Was It?

Some argue that the Thunderbird was an actual bird. When conducting a thorough investigation, this conclusion should not be met. Rather, when all is said and heard, the animals could very well have been a Quetzalcoatlus.

This huge pterosaur was the largest flying creature to have lived. Its wingspan was equivalent to modern jet fighter planes, and it weighed up to 220 lbs (100 kg). Fossils suggest that it lacked proper anchor points for the powerful flapping down strokes of which most birds are capable. So, as the theory goes, the animal was a glider.

Conclusion

Could it have carried off humans as the legends tell? Yes, it physically could have, but it is more likely that the accounts are the result of legendary accretion, inspired by its terrifying size. As with all legends, events are exaggerated over time.

No, we shouldn't believe every account or every detail relating to the Thunderbird. What we should believe, however, and must believe is that an animal did exist in recent past that very well could have been a "living fossil." Evolutionary thinking tells us otherwise, but it is this bias that we must rid ourselves of. Can all these sightings be easily written off as coincidental? Absolutely not. To think so borders absurdity. Even if one does not believe the Thunderbird to have been a species of pterosaur, one should consider whether the animal was another unknown species that tragically went extinct.

We may never know. As with most cryptozoological studies, we are simply left to wonder.

Reports from South America, Mexico's Sonora Desert and Papua, New Guinea claim sightings of a pteranodon with a wingspread of 27 meters (89 feet) but those claims are probably great exaggerations spawned by fear of the unknown or the superstitions of the native claimants.

The Douglas DC-3 Dakota had a wingspread of about 95 feet, or only slightly more than six feet greater than the claimed sighting of P. Quetzalcoatalus, as shown by the following composite graphic.

It seems unlikely that a creature so large as this could remain hidden from modern

GIANTS ON THE EARTH

adventurers or satellite surveillance, even if the areas in which it was reportedly sighted are extremely remote.

Still, stranger things have happened, have they not?

In the early part of the last century, two cowboys, out looking for stray cattle, observed a large pteranodon gliding down towards them. As it prepared to land, they shot and killed it. To prove they had seen the creature, they cut off one of its wings and took it back to town.

Excavations in the Big Bend National Park in Texas in 1972 have unearthed the fossil remains of large specimens of P. Quetzalcoatalus, providing confirmation that the large pteranodons lived in that area and may have been at that time (if not still) contemporaries of modern humans.

In South Africa, natives report that large, rather aggressive pteranodons often attack men who are fishing in shallow waters in an attempt to steal their catch.

From "Dinosaurs by Design" by Dr. Duane Gish

They call this large creature, "Kongamato" (see below).

Some of these flying creatures are pteranodons (wings-no teeth) while others may be gnathosaurs (toothed) and others may be Dimorphodons or Ramphoryncoids.

Additionally, several of the pteranodons are said to be bioluminescent, appearing as glowing balls of lights as they glide silently through the night skies!!! (photos available from the Papua, New Guinea expedition)

More details follow.

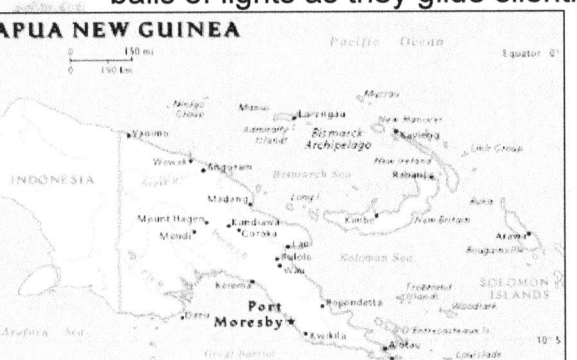

GIANTS ON THE EARTH

WHAT'S THE DIFFERENCE?

< VELOCIRAPTOR—2 to 3 meter reptile, probably covered with feathers and having rudimentary wings as front limbs.

> CEARADACTYLUS—long curved beaks with plenty of teeth for catching and holding fish and other prey.

PTEROSAURS— shorter beak with no teeth; usually sporting a large bony head-crest. Fragments of several species have been unearthed.

< ANHA— heavy, long beak, teeth pointing outward; body and inner wings may have been covered with hair (specialized scales) or proto-feathers (specialized scales).

< DIMORPHODON—small, feathered bird-like creature with a short, thick beak much like present day Puffin; a rather long rigid tail with a feathered vertical rudder at the tip. About 18 to 24 inch span.

< RAMPHORYNCUS—smaller, toothed beak reptilian, having a long, rigid tail with a leathery rudder at the tip. One meter and larger.

P. QUETZALCOATALUS— clearly the largest of the flying reptiles, with wingspread reaching up to 15 meters or greater. It was strong enough to carry off prey the size of a modern day adult sheep, young calves or even a human; especially children.

GNATHOSAURS—large, powerful reptilians with a long, toothed beak. It skimmed the crests of ocean waves and waters of shallow lakes searching for fish, snakes and other marine prey. It may also have been a carrion eater. Several species.

ALL OF THESE CREATURES, except Velociraptor and Dimorphodon, flew on long, narrow wings of thin but strong skin formed by elongation of the fourth finger of the "claw" which appeared at the end of the wrist about mid way along the length of the wing's leading edge. They ranged in span from 18 inches to 15 meters or greater.

GIANTS ON THE EARTH

Pterosaurs, Pteranodons, Pterodactyls, Ramphoryncoids, Gnathosaurs and Dimorpodons lived during the Jurrasic and Cretaceous periods.

Researchers and Cryptozoologists believe some may still live in remote areas of the world.

GIANTS ON THE EARTH

Modern seabirds, particularly Pelicans, may be pterosaurs evolved. Pterosaurs and others may also have dived into the oceans and lakes to catch prey by spearing them or swimming after them under water as some modern birds do. The proportions of wing to body are the same as most pteranodons.

A magnificent modern female Frigate bird with long, narrow wings designed for soaring. (right) >

People who have never seen the oceans or Pelicans may mistake these birds for prehistoric pteranodons. I once found a badly dehydrated Brown Pelican in the desert in the Imperial Valley, California. Fortunately, I was able to save it and release it. It had strayed 125 miles from the ocean.

GIANTS ON THE EARTH

Because some Pteranodons were as large as humans and their bodies resembled human beings with outstretched arms, they are sometimes referred to as "flying men," or "winged men," and they are and were depicted as flying giant humans (or gods) in cliff and cave paintings and on ornaments and pottery. It is easy to see why.

Most paleantologists today believe the wings were not attached to the legs but to the short, rigid tail which was an extension of the rigid, fused spine. Having the wings attached to the lower portion of the legs would have made it nearly impossible for the creatures to walk on land, to build nests or to care for their young.

The legs, like those of modern birds and other fowl, were free and separate from the wings, and the wings were probably somewhat narrower in cord than are shown in most modern illustrations and graphics.

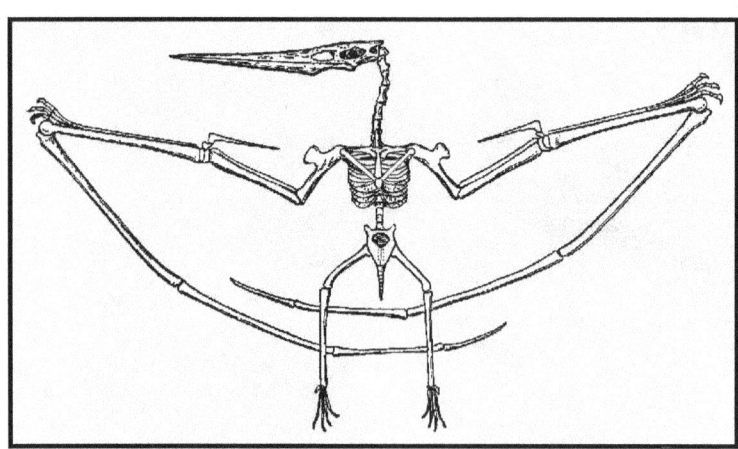

Skelton of P. Nyctosaurus as reconstructed from fossil fragments. Note the false "thumb" at the end of the humerus returns toward the scapula to form a thick leading edge of the inner wing, with the radius, ulna and the fingers of the "hand" or "claw" with the elongated fourth finger forming the leading edge of the outer wing. The trailing edge of the wing was attached to the fused rigid "tail"; not to the lower leg.

GIANTS ON THE EARTH

Pterosaurs in the Bible

Sauropods and Plesiosaurs are not the only dinosaurs / reptiles mentioned in Scripture.

Isaiah 30:6 tells of a flying reptile like the pteranodon or Rhamphorhynchus.

Isaiah 30:6 (King James Version)

"The burden of the beast of the south: into the land of trouble and anguish, from whence come the young and old lion, the viper and fiery flying serpent..."

What is a flying serpent? - The only known reptiles with the ability to fly are the Pterosaurs. In this verse we see them described as living alongside the other animals. The flying serpents are used in the text with other animals we readily recognize. They are not set apart in any way as to conclude they are fictitious. In fact, the verse continues and speaks of men carrying their riches "upon the bunches of camels". This makes it clear that these flying dinosaurs lived alongside mammals, and man.

God created flying creatures such as birds and pterosaurs on the fifth day of Creation. Man and other mammals were created on the 6th day.

This creature in Isaiah is described as a "fiery flying serpent".

The description of them as being "fiery" may be in reference to their color, or as some have suggested a burning sensation left from one of their bites.

Personally I think it may actually have been bioluminescent, this is particularly true of the "Ropen" (see below).

bioluminescent

"Emission of visible light by living organisms such as the firefly and various fish, fungi, and bacteria."

Did Pterosaurs live with man?

According to the Bible, they were created on the 5th day with the fish and the birds. If this were true, we would expect to find some stories of them living with man.

Guess what we find?

Accounts of Pterosaurs living alongside humans are recorded all throughout history.

Herodotus, the Greek historian wrote about "winged serpents" living in Arabia in the 5th century Before Christ. ("The Great Dinosaur Mystery and the Bible" by Paul S. Taylor)

Reports of Pterosaurs still alive are recorded in Ethiopia, India and the jungles of Africa. Some of the flying dinosaurs are said be nocturnal, and have a phosphorescent quality about them. These could be the fiery flying serpents described in the book of Isaiah.

A flying reptile the Natives call "Kongamato" is often seen in the jungles of South Af-

GIANTS ON THE EARTH

rica. Still alive today, and unchanged by Evolution.

There are many different flying reptiles. The Pteranodon which means: "winged-without teeth" is one of the most common. There is also one called "Rhamphorhynchus".

The Ropen

Here is a letter that I recieved from Paul G. Nation on January 18, 2002

"I just wanted to add to your thoughts about the fiery flying serpent. You see I have been to Papua New Guinea looking for the Dewas - Ropen creature. What I wanted to say is as I told with many eyewitness of this pterosaur type creature an interesting obsevation by the nationals was made consistently. This creature can generate it's own bioluminence. In short it glows! On eyewitness described the glow as " when an iron is pulled from the fire" People always said it was burnt red glow to a bright orange. This "glow" is what really terrifies them when they see this creature at night. They also describe it as haveing a long beak with teeth and a long "snake like tail" Makes you wonder what they are seeing. I am trying to return and search for this creatue in April the Lord willing will try to keep you informed."

Pterosaur sighting

Here is a pterosaur sighting I recieved recently:

"It was around 9am on a Sunday morning in Oct. of 2005. I was in Mount Vernon, Ohio. I was coming to preach at a church out in the country (the same church I will soon be the church plant pastor of). This had been my first visit there to preach.

There were many times in the trip that I slowed down because I wasn't sure I was still on the correct road or didn't want to pass the church (i.e., blink and you miss it). At one of those times I happen to notice a creature in the sky. Having no one behind me I took a moment to slow the car down and take a look at it. To my estimation it appeared to have no feathers. It was a leathery grayish color. The beak seemed to protrude from its face not like a separate part of the head, but looking to be the same color, etc. It's wings did not look like bird wings, but also appeared leathery and bat-like (I have seen actual bats in caves and zoos). The kicker, for me, was the tail: longer than most bird tails I am used to, no feathers, and with a diamond-shaped point at the end.

I know how people can have a stigma about persons who have stories like mine, so I have been careful not to tell many people. I also have made it a point to look at the birds in Mount Vernon, Ohio. They are larger--many of the them--than in the lower central and southern areas of Ohio where I lived before, or grew up. However, all of the others birds I have seen have clearly had feathers on the body, wings, and tails, with beaks that look different from the rest of their facial make up (and certainly none with a diamond-shape point at the end of a long tail or bat-like wings)."

God bless you,

Mark 3/06

I am not very good at judging the size of animals in the air. I will say this, he was high up and yet I could tell everything about him/her that I told you. Easily larger than a bald eagle.

Possible pterosaur sighting

Dear Jesus,dinosaurs and more,

My name is Phillip O'Donnell. We live in Oregon. I really enjoy this website. The info

GIANTS ON THE EARTH

about living dinosaurs is great! I just thought that you might like to know that in 2003 my brother and I saw a strange bird. It was perched in a tree for about 1 minute. It was about three feet tall with a white chest and black spots. I looked at through the binoculars and so did my brother. It had a horn-like thing protruding out of the back of it's head that was pointing upwards and was not like a heron's tuff of hair. As it flew away we guessed the wingspan to be about 9 feet.

I have seen many Great Blue Herons and I enjoy to watch them, but this bird was different. The wings were long and pointy. It returned the next year and we saw it in the same field. The sighting only lasted about 5 seconds. We briefly saw a long and very large pair of wings that had red streaks on them. They were also very bright like a mirror reflecting on sunlight. I have recently talked on the phone with Charlie Knight in Washington. He said that when he was a boy, he saw two pterosaurs that had a horn on back of their head.

Here is my sketch. Please note that the body is not the right size compared to the head.

The Thunderbird

The Sioux Indians have long told the story of the huge "thunderbird". They gave it this nickname because this flying reptile was hit by lightning and fell from the sky during a thunderstorm.

They searched for this creature and when they found it they described it as having wings almost 20 foot across. It had a long sharp bill and a large bony knob-like protrusion on the back of its head.

There are no birds that fit this description. The similarity between the "thunderbird" and the pteranodon is striking. Flying dinosaurs like the pteranodon have been found fossilized with a wingspan of 23 feet!

Pteranodon also have a large bony crest jotting off of the backs of their heads. Just as the Indians described.

I believe the creature the Indians saw was a pteranodon. A creature that many people have mistakenly thought to have gone extinct long ago.

The Indians have made many paintings and carvings of this dinosaur with accuracy that can only come from seeing the creature first hand.

I will be adding pictures of these carvings and paintings soon!

They have also found perfect pictographs of a pterodactyl in Utah. About 200 years ago, the Fremont Indians drew these. This was at a time when pterodactyl fossils had not yet been discovered.

Pictographs always show the dinosaurs "fleshed out", living creatures. They are not drawings of bones or dead animals. These pictographs accurately show what many of these dinosaurs looked like. When many scholars debate on what a dinosaur looked like, they should close their books and listen to the eyewitnesses.

When dinosaurs are shown in pictographs they are usually shown interacting with man.

Dinosaur petroglyphs were also found in the area of the Natural Bridges Monument. The Anasazis drew these dinosaurs in perfect detail. They were covered and protected by an accumulation of what is known as "desert varnish". This is a coating formed natu-

GIANTS ON THE EARTH

rally by pollens and various components of desert air. - This coverage can not be duplicated by artificial means which rules out the possibility of a hoax or fraud.

These drawings on the cliff wall are dinosaurs we know today by the name "Tenontosaurus", a sauropod much like the long necked Apatosaurus.

The idea of pterosaurs living in caves is also supported by an account recorded in David Untred's book: "Dinosaurs and the Bible"

This eyewitness account tells of workmen digging a railroad tunnel in France in 1856. These men were using gunpowder to remove a large boulder. After the dust from the explosion settled, the men found a large bat-like creature out of the cave.

The creature was barely alive, and described as being black and shiny. It had a long neck and a beak like mouth filled with sharp teeth.

On being exposed to the light the creature shrieked and beat its wings. Its wings were measured giving a wingspan of 9 feet!

The helpless creature soon died. Upon being examined by a Scientist, the animal was determined to be a pterosaur. ("Dinosaurs and the Bible" by David Untred)

(*Please note that the above information should not be taken as a fact without having pictures, or the specimen to analyze)

There is another account of a living Pterosaur from April of 1890.

This time the eyewitness were two men riding horses across the hot Arizona desert (just outside of Tombstone). They noticed a large flying reptile with a six foot wing span and long slender body. As it was about to land the men shot and killed the creature.

Knowing this was a significant find, the men are said to have cut off part of the wing and brought it back to town with them.

In his book "Dinosaurs by Design" Duane Gish speaks of the above pterosaur and believes it is a Quetzalcoatlus (ket-sol-ko-AT-lus). He bases this on the fossil Quetzalcoatlus found in 1972 at Big Bend National Park, Texas. This confirms they did indeed live in the general area.

With a 48-foot wingspan the Quetzalcoatlus is the largest flying creature ever found.

It is possible for a pterosaur to survive for 6,000 years from the creation of the earth, and the fall of man. But with the climate changes and loss of atmospheric pressure they would not likely grow to be as large as they once were.

The recent existence of pterosaurs is much harder to believe if you've been brainwashed into believing that dinosaurs lived millions of years ago.

But if you believe the Biblical account of Creation, then these creatures did live alongside man and their survival makes perfect sense.

Bill Cooper has an excellent book called "After the flood"

This book traces the post flood history of Europe back to the descendants of Noah. Bill Cooper tells of many pterosaur encounters that were a common feature in Welsh life, even as late as the beginning of this century.

A colony of these winged serpents lived in the woods nearby Penllin Castle, Glamorgan. Eyewitnesses describe them as very beautiful. Their bodies were covered with bright colors as if "covered in jewels".

In 1793 the flying serpents were included in official Government reports. These were not the creatures of fairy tales or fables, but real live breathing creatures.

GIANTS ON THE EARTH

They, along with their behavioral traits and migrating patterns were so familiar to the people that they predicted the weather based upon their migration patterns.

Pterodactyls have extremely fragile wings. They would easily be damaged in high winds. Consequently, they were often seen fleeing prior to bad weather coming off of the Atlantic. Such reports span the years 793 to 1532 AD

This was one thousand and seven years before present day Americans knew these creatures even existed, let alone had reached near extinction.

Thunderbirds

In Jurassic Park III, the most exciting part of the movie for me was the sudden introduction of the pteranodons. I was on the edge of my seat as these monstrous bird-like pterosaurs hotly pursued the search team working their way out of the birdcage.

Of course, the standard long-age scenario of our evolution-riddled culture says that such encounters between pterosaurs and man have never happened, because all flying reptiles, along with the dinosaurs, allegedly became extinct some 65 million years before man came on the scene.

However, my research on the Indians of North and South America permits a different conclusion. There are many stories and related lines of evidence suggesting that the American Indians may have a long history of encountering creatures reminiscent of pterosaurs, especially the huge Pteranodon or the even larger Quetzalcoatlus (see aside below). The following stories, all on similar themes (even though they generally have obvious legendary aspects, presumably accumulated through retelling), raise the intriguing possibility of a common basis in historical reality.

American Southwest

While exploring the Sonora Desert on 12 February 1699, Captain Juan Mateo Manje, accompanied by Jesuits Eusebio Francisco Kino and Adamo Gil, was told by the Pima Indians that a giant monster lived in a nearby cave in days past. It was a menace to the Pima because it would fly around and catch as many Indians as it could eat.

One day, after the creature had eaten its fill, some Indians followed it back to its cave. When it was sound asleep they closed the entrance of the cave with wood collected for this occasion; then set it on fire. The creature couldn't escape and, growling fiercely, died as it was asphyxiated by the flames and smoke.1

The Pima recalled another story of killing a similar creature in the pueblo of Oposura by using the same strategy. We are told the bones of this creature were found during the pacification of Mexico by General Don Hernándo Cortés and were sent to Spain.1

Stories of giant man-eating birds are common among many other Indian tribes of the American Southwest.2 The Yaqui Indians spoke of a giant bird that lived on the hill of Otan Kawi. Every morning it would fly out to capture its human prey. After many deaths, a young boy who lost his family to this bird killed the creature with a bow and arrows.3

In Utah's San Raphael Swell there is other suggestive evidence for man's coexistence with pterosaurs. In the Black Dragon Canyon there is a beautiful pictograph of a pterosaur. The Indians of the Swell apparently saw a bird-like creature with enormous wings, a tail, a long neck and beak, and a vertical head crest, which some flying reptiles sported.

GIANTS ON THE EARTH

Thunderbirds

One creature in Indian mythology that has long puzzled anthropologists is the thunderbird. Stories of thunderbirds are widespread, extending from Alaska all the way down to South America. Indians attributed thunder and lightning to these birds: the thunder resulted from the flapping of their wings, while bolts of lightning proceeded from their mouths. The impressive size of the thunderbirds meant that during midday flight they would cast strikingly large shadows upon the ground.

The thunderbirds' description, albeit distorted by time and retelling, so much fits that of pterosaurs that even some evolutionists have conceded on that point: 'The thunderbird appears in many Indian tales and Indian art work. Its description is very much like one of the prehistoric flying reptiles that flapped its way through the skies in the days of the dinosaurs.'4

The Sioux Indians tell a story about an experience some of their warriors had with a thunderbird that perfectly fits the description of the pteranodon.

'One day, long long ago, before the white man came to America, a party of Sioux Indian warriors were out hunting. They had left their village far behind. Before they realized it, the group of braves found themselves alone in the bare and rocky badlands of the West.

'Suddenly the sky darkened ... . There was a clap of thunder that shook the earth. Looking up in terror, the Indians thought they saw the shape of a giant bird falling to earth ... .

'The band of hunters traveled over the badlands for days until they came at last to the spot where they thought the giant bird had fallen. Nothing was left of the terrible creature but its bones ... .

'The Indians shuddered as they looked at the monster's skeleton. The bird had fallen so hard they thought, that its bones were partly sunk in the rock. But the braves could see that its wingspread was as big as four tall men standing on top of one another. The strange creature had fierce claws on its wings, as well as on its feet, and the beak was long and sharp. There was a long, bony crest on its head. The Indians knew that they had never seen a bird like it before.'5

The Hoh and Quileute of western Washington boast of a thunderbird so large that its wingspan was twice as long as their war canoes. This immense 'bird' also had a long beak, great claws, and the alleged ability to pluck some types of whales out of the sea (see aside below). Their mythology, again with obvious elements of exaggeration, attributes the lack of trees in Beaver Prairie to a fight between Whale and Thunderbird:

'One time Thunderbird got a big whale in his talons and carried him to Beaver Prairie and ate him there. The whale fought very hard before he was killed. Thunderbird and Whale fought so very hard that they pulled up the trees by their roots. And no trees have ever grown in that place to this day.'6

The Indians of Vancouver Island say that they feared being in the presence of killer whales when they were plentiful, because of their frail canoes. Knowing thunderbirds to be their enemy, the Indians painted these birds on their bodies and homes to try to secure protection.7

GIANTS ON THE EARTH

Piasa

In the Midwest, the Illini Indians of Illinois were once terrorized by a creature they called 'Piasa', which means 'bird that devours man'. The Piasa was so large that it could allegedly carry off a full-grown deer. When it finally acquired a taste for human flesh, no Indian was safe. The Illini, as well as other Indian tribes in the area, greatly feared the Piasa and sought to destroy it.

One day the Illini were said to have tricked the Piasa by hiding 20 armed warriors in a designated spot, while the Chief chose to stand in open view as a victim for the Piasa. When the bird was about to pounce upon the Chief, the warriors leapt out and speared it to death.

John Russell was a writer from Illinois who had a great interest in the Piasa. In 1848, Mr Russell explored the caves where this creature was said to live. One cave that was extremely difficult to access yielded evidence for the Illini's story. Russell stated, 'The shape of the cave was irregular, but so far as I could judge the bottom would average twenty by thirty feet. The floor of the cave throughout its whole extent was one mass of human bones.'8

So, what kind of creature was the Piasa? High upon a cliff in Alton, Illinois, the Indians made a painting of the Piasa. The painting was destroyed in the 1850s when the face of the cliff collapsed into the river. However, many explorers during the seventeenth and eighteenth centuries saw the painting and described it in great detail in their journals. These explorers describe a bird-like creature with many reptilian characteristics.

Mexico and South America

Controversy has raged over the authenticity of the Ica Stones (above) since their discovery in South America. Skeptics have claimed, though without proof, that they are modern forgeries, based on the premise that it is impossible for humans to have seen a living dinosaur. The stones remain a mystery, and reinforce the intriguing possibility that the ancient Amerindians knew of such creatures. [For an updated report, see reference 17 of Bishop Bell's brass behemoths!.]

There is similar evidence, suggesting possible coexistence with pterosaurs, among the Indians of Mexico and South America, too. Jose Diaz-Bolio, a Mexican archaeologist, discovered an ancient Mayan relief sculpture in Veracruz, Mexico, of a bird with some features of the Pteranodon. The November 1968 edition of Science Digest published an article on this 'evolutionary oddity', called 'Serpent-bird of the Mayans'. The serpent-bird, says Bolio, 'is not merely the product of Mayan flights of fancy, but a realistic representation of an animal that lived during the period of the ancient Mayans—1,000 to 5,000 years ago.'9

Two of the most controversial discoveries in the 20th century are the ceramic and clay figurines of Acambaro, Mexico, and the Ica stones of Peru [for an updated report of the Ica stones, see reference 17 of Bishop Bell's brass behemoths!]. The reason why there is so much controversy regarding these artifacts is that a large number of them are of the dinosaur type.

The figurines of Acambaro were discovered in the 1940s by a German archaeologist named Waldamar Julsrud. One day, while on the outskirts of Acambaro, Julsrud discovered a figurine protruding half out of the ground. He had one of his employees dig in the

GIANTS ON THE EARTH

area and bring the artifacts back to his home. Not long after, over 33,000 figurines filled nearly every square inch of his mansion.

The controversial Acambaro figurines (above, top and middle) include, among representations of other living animals, creatures which could only be decribed as dinosaurs and similar extinct reptiles. Some are recognizable as known types, others not. The above images depict a creature with a tipped tail, bat-like wings and long head. Though clearly artistically exaggerated, some small 'rhamphorhynchoid' pterosaurs such as Dimorphodon (lower image) share some of these features, especially the unique tail. The Ica stones of Peru were brought to light in the first half of the 20th century as a result of the overflowing of the Ica River. This flood caused the eroding of a mountainside, thus exposing a cave. The cave proved to be a repository of the stones. There are a total of 16,000 stones in existence. 11,000 were amassed by Dr Javier Cabrera, former professor of medicine at the University of Lima, and displayed in his museum.

These artifacts from Mexico and South America depict dinosaurs and flying reptiles of all types and sizes. Unless both discoveries are elaborate hoaxes (always a possibility in this sinful world, as both evolutionists and creationists have been 'taken' by manufactured artefacts supporting their particular cause), they demonstrate once more that the American Indian was well acquainted with the pterosaur.

In recent years, missionaries have come out of South America's interior with stories from Indians of 'birds' that are also suggestive of pterosaurs. In Southern Venezuela, about 150 km (100) miles from the Brazilian border, the Yek'wana have a story of a giant man-eating bat. This story has been with them for several centuries. Clint Vernoy, a missionary to these Indians, told me the following:

'The legend is told that a few generations ago there was a large bat that lived at the headwaters of the river in a cave on a large mountain. Periodically it would attack canoes and carry off people as its prey. After quite a few deaths men were chosen to go to the animal's lair and kill it, which they did. I asked them which mountain it was but there is no consensus, even though I would love to know where that was.

'Because it was seen to defecate in the river after carrying off humans the Indians would not drink from the Erebato River, they will cross a river 100 yards wide just to get to a small stream that feeds into the river for their drinking water.

'We showed the Indians pictures of pterodactyls and such and they said, "Yes", that had to be the giant bat. For them it is not a myth or legend, but a true story of their past that has been handed down through the years.'

The Indians of the Corentyn, according to missionary W.H. Brett, also tell of an enormous gliding serpent.10

Conclusion

Space has prevented giving more than a fraction of the evidence available for man coexisting with pterosaurs—not just in the Americas. There are even some reported sightings, from remote regions in the world, over the last 120 years.

Can all these sightings and stories be easily written off as 'coincidentally' having a pterosaur-like common thread? It seems easier to believe that the evolutionary/long-age notion that these reptiles became extinct 65 million years ago is flawed—people have indeed encountered some of the terrifyingly large birdlike creatures we know to-

GIANTS ON THE EARTH

day from the fossil record.

Bill Johnson works for the US postal service and is a student at Moody Northwest in Spokane, Washington. His interests are theology and apologetics. Return to top.

References and notes

1. Karns, H.J., Unknown Arizona and Sonora 1693-1721, Arizona Silhouttes, Arizona, pp. 105-106, 1954. This book is a translation of Manje's Luz De Tierra Incognita.
2. As they are in many cultures; the Arabs have their roc, New Zealand's Maoris the pouakai.
3. Giddings, R.W., 'Yaqui Myths and Legends' in Anthropological Papers of the University of Arizona, Tucson, pp. 36-38, 1959.
4. Geis, D., Dinosaurs and other prehistoric animals, Grosset & Dunlap, New York, p. 10, 1972.
5. Ref. 4, p. 9.
6. 'Tales From the Hoh and Quileute' in Journal of American Folklore 46:320, 1933.
7. 'The Thunderbird' in American Anthropologist II, p. 333, Oct. 1889.
8. The Piasa, or The Devil Among the Indians, E.B. Fletcher, p. 31, 1887.
9. 'Serpent-bird of the Mayans' in Science Digest, p. 1, Nov. 1968.
10. Clay, R., Indian Tribes of Guiana, Taylor and Son Printers, p. 375, 1868.

Quetzalcoatlus

An average-sized man compared to the gigantic Quetzalcoatlus

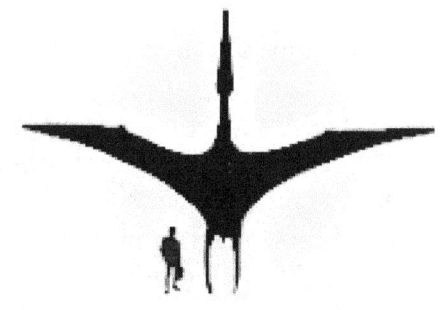

This huge pterosaur (as all the flying reptiles are collectively known) was the largest flying creature ever known to have lived—a distinction previously held by the Pteranodon. At up to 15 m (50 ft) its wingspan was equivalent to many modern jet fighter planes. It weighed up to 100 kg (220 lbs), which, proportional to its size, was actually rather light.

A more recent unsubstantiated claim from a paleontologist in South America suggests that reconstructed "bones" (no suggestion of fossil remains) of a Quetzalcoatl pteranodon shows the creature had a wingspan of 27 meters, or slightly less than 89 feet. To give you an idea how large it would have been, compare it to a Douglas C-47 Dakota with a wingspan of 95 feet and 8 inches, about nine feet greater than the huge flying reptile!

Reconstructions from its fossils have suggested that Quetzalcoatl lacked appropriate anchor points for the powerful flapping downstrokes of which many birds are capable. Thus it would have been predominantly a glider; though it still may have been able to carry off a human, it is likely that many of the fearsome accounts are the result of legendary accretion, perhaps inspired by its terrifying size. This would have been more so in times when they were becoming rarer—close familiarity with the creatures would presumably have indicated that their threat to man was less than their intimidating size suggested.

Secular scientists have suggested that Quetzalcoatlus may have plucked fish from the sea. Though the idea of it scooping up the average whale (see main text) is clearly an

GIANTS ON THE EARTH

exaggeration, it is not hard to see where such a notion might have come from. Anyone who witnessed firsthand the sight of such an awesome creature, the size of a jet fighter (or even as large as a two-engined transport aircraft), swooping down to pluck a large struggling fish (possibly even a dolphin frolicking at the surface) from the sea would have sparked a story retold down the generations.

What About Thunderbird?

There is a Native American legend that says a thunderbird saved a tribe from starvation by bringing it a whale to eat.
A deep whirring sound, like giant wings beating, came from the place of the setting sun. All of the people turned to gaze toward the sky above the ocean as a huge, bird-shaped creature flew toward them.
This bird was larger than any they had ever seen. Its wings, from tip to tip, were twice as long as a war canoe. It had a huge, curving beak, and its eyes glowed like fire. The people saw that its great claws held a living, giant whale.
In silence, they watched while Thunderbird-for so the bird was named by everyone- carefully lowered the whale to the ground before them.
...
Thunderbird's home is a cave in the Olympic Mountains, and he wants no one to come near it. If hunters get close enough so he can smell them, he makes thunder noise, and he rolls ice out of his cave.
...
Thunderbird keeps his food in a dark hole at the edge of a big field of ice and snow. His food is the whale. Thunderbird flies out to the ocean, catches a whale, and hurries back to the mountains to eat it. 1
Is the thunderbird an imaginary, mythical creature? Or did it really exist? Let's use the "unicorn test". Has anyone ever found any bones that would match the description of thunderbird? Yes, two pterodactyls (pteranodon and quetzalcoatlus 2) match the description very well.
In fact, the picture under the heading "What About Thunderbird?" shows a reconstruction of a pterodactyl 3 , not a Native American sculpture of a thunderbird.
Pterodactyl fossils have been discovered in North America where Native Americans lived. (Pterodactyl fossils have also been found in Europe, Africa, and Australia.) Nobody claims these bones are phony. There aren't any pterodactyl deniers. The fossils are real. Based on those fossils, scientists have produced the reproductions shown on this page and the previous page. They look just like a thunderbird.
One might dismiss the Native American legends about animals because they are fictional stories designed to teach moral lessons. But the fiction is based on fact. These legends take familiar animal characteristics and exaggerate them, giving the animals human emotions and motivations. We do the same thing today. Garfield would not be funny if cats did not exhibit the traits that are so overblown in the Garfield comic strip. But everyone has seen cats acting like Garfield, and that's what makes the comic strip funny. In the same way, the Indian legends were able to teach moral lessons because the animals in the legends have humanized characteristics consistent with their behavior.

GIANTS ON THE EARTH

Suppose you wanted to teach a lesson about cleanliness. You might concoct a story about a raccoon that always washed his food before eating. You wouldn't tell a story about a pig that always washed his food, unless you were trying to be funny. We have certain preconceived notions about the cleanliness of raccoons and pigs that are based, to some extent, on actual observation. You can use those notions to help you teach your lesson. You could not teach your lesson using an animal that didn't exist, or was so rare nobody knew anything about it, because your audience would not know how the animal acts.

Native American legends taught moral lessons effectively for centuries because the animals in them were familiar, and those animals acted the way the students would expect them to act. Every other animal in Native American legends really existed. Why would an ancient medicine man make up a story about a thunderbird if nobody had ever seen a thunderbird or knew how it acted? The medicine man always used actual, common animals to make his point.

There is no question that the greatest North American naturalists in the 17th, 18th, and 19th centuries were the Indians. Pilgrims, explorers, and fur traders learned that any arrogant pale face who wouldn't take the advice of an "ignorant savage" either froze or starved to death. The study of nature wasn't just a hobby for the Indians. Their lives depended upon knowing when and where the deer fed, and which caves the bears lived in. If pterodactyls still lived in North America before the coming of the white man, Indians certainly would know where they lived, what they ate, and what made them mad.

The fictional stories about thunderbird are base on plausible facts. It isn't unreasonable to think pterodactyls could swoop down and catch really large fish. Certainly it would be an exaggeration to say they caught whales, but pterodactyls could certainly handle more than a rainbow trout. It isn't outside the realm of possibility that they caught large salmon. It is reasonable to believe that they lived among the rocks on high mountains. Some of the spaces under large rocks might be described as caves. Isn't it possible that pterodactyls instinctively pushed small rocks, or snowballs, at predators approaching their lairs from below?

There is no question that the fossil record shows that creatures that fit the description of a thunderbird once lived. It is certainly true that those creatures are extinct now. Therefore, the last one must have died at some time in the past. The question is, "When did the last one die?" Evolutionists claim that the rocks say they died out 65 million years ago.[4] But Native Americans apparently saw some within the past few hundred years. Who should a reasonable person believe? A rock or an eye witness?

The Thunderbird. Image from Deities & Demigods (Lake Geneva: TSR Games, 1980), 16.

The legend of the Thunderbird is an ancient myth that survives even to the present day in some Native American cultures. Though the Thunderbird myth varied from region to region and tribe to tribe, the Thunderbird was, in the eyes of the ancient Native Americans, a magical animal that was sent by their gods to protect them from the powers of evil. Riding on the wings of the storm, the Thunderbird embodied the power of the storm. Its eyes flashed fire, its cry was like the crack of lightning, and its mighty wings beat with the sound of rolling thunder, ever protecting its people from the powers of evil.

GIANTS ON THE EARTH

There are at least three different legends of the Thunderbird available to us today, that can give us some information about what this creature was like. The first comes from the Winnebago Indians of the northern Midwest and Plains states, a second comes from the Passamaquoddy Indians of Maine, and a third comes from the Quillayute, a Chimakoan tribe living along the Quillayute River, a six-mile river on the Olympic Peninsula, near Seattle, Washington.

The Winnebago were an ancient and powerful people that once spread out from Wisconsin all across the northern Midwest and Plains states to Nebraska. They believed that the Thunderbirds were powerful, eagle-like divine creatures that were able to affect the winds and created storms, lightning, thunder, and rain. They also believed that they could take the form of humans, and that some humans, though not actually Thunderbirds, shared their characteristics and were considered to be semi-divine.

Thunderbird figures from Washington County, Minnesota (top left), and from the Three Maldena Area in the Pipestone National Monument, also in Minnesota.

This thought is reminiscent of the "bird-man" concept prevalent at Cahokia , and it is believed that the Cahokians were related to the Winnebago peoples. Richard L. Dieterle explains in The Short Encyclopedia of Hotcâk (Winnebago) Myth, Legend, and Folklore,

Thunderbirds are powerful and warlike avian spirits who animate the gray clouds with thunder and lightning. Together with the Waterspirits, they were the first spirits that Earthmaker created. Their name, Wak'âdja, means, "Divine Ones." On the model of other tribes, they are conventionally called "Thunderbirds," since they alone possess lightning. Their basic somatic form runs the gamut of several species of birds, the hawk and the eagle being the most common. However, they are far stronger in build and have polychrome plumage that gives them a magnificent appearance unrivaled by the birds of earth. Their voices are like the sounds of flutes, recalling both the whistle of wind and the voices of raptors. 1

The enemies of the Thunderbirds in Winnebago legend are the "Water Spirits". These became the enemies of the Thunderbirds in primordial times, when the Thunderbirds shot their lightnings everywhere, including the waters. The Thunderbirds still use their lightning when crossing the waters, as that helps protect them from the waterspirits. The Winnebago believed that all lightning was directed at Waterspirits, which lived in bodies of water, or in streams of water beneath the surface of the Earth. The waterspirits were the favorite food of the Thunderbirds, though they usually ate animals and sometimes even humans.

Another primary source is from the legends of the Passamaquoddy Indians, who lived in the northeast, in the Quoddy Loop area of Maine and New Brunswick. In this story, two Passamaquoddy Indians went on a quest to find the origin of thunder:

This is a legend of long, long ago times. Two Indians desired to find the origin of thunder. They travelled north and came to a high mountain. These mountains performed magically. They drew apart, back and forth, then closed together very quickly. One Indian said, "I will leap through the cleft before it closes. If I am caught, you continue to find the origin of thunder." The first one succeeded in going through the cleft before it closed, but the second one was caught and squashed. On the other side, the first Indian saw a large plain with a group of wigwams, and a number of Indians playing a ball game. After a little while, these players said to each other, "It is time to go." They disappeared into

GIANTS ON THE EARTH

their wigwams to put on wings, and came out with their bows and arrows and flew away over the mountains to the south. This was how the Passamaquoddy Indian discovered the homes of the thunderbirds.

The surviving Passamaquoddy Indian brave had discovered the home of the Thunderbirds, but the intrepid Indians who had set out on a quest for the source of thunder had gotten more than they had bargained for. One Indian had died already, and his companion was about to undergo a transformation:

The remaining old men of that tribe asked the Passamaquoddy Indian, "What do you want? Who are you?" He replied with the story of his mission. The old men deliberated how they could help him. They decided to put the lone Indian into a large mortar, and they pounded him until all of his bones were broken. They moulded him into a new body with wings like thunderbird, and gave him a bow and some arrows and sent him away in flight. They warned him not to fly close to trees, as he would fly so fast he could not stop in time to avoid them, and he would be killed.

The Thunderbirds, according to the Passamaquoddy, were men who could transform themselves into flying creatures. These men were also able to transform the Passamaquoddy Indian brave into a bird like themselves. However, this brave now had a new enemy: Wochowsen, "great bird from the south", who had control of the south wind, and made it blow so hard that the Passamaquoddy brave could not return to his homeland.

The lone Indian could not reach his home because the huge enemy bird, Wochowsen, at that time made such a damaging wind. Thunderbird is an Indian and he or his lightning would never harm another Indian. But Wochowsen, great bird from the south, tried hard to rival Thunderbird. So Passamaquoddies feared Wochowsen, whose wings Glooscap once had broken, because he used too much power. A result was that for a long time air became stagnant, the sea was full of slime, and all of the fish died. But Glooscap saw what was happening to his people and repaired the wings of Wochowsen to the extent of controlling and alternating strong winds with calm. Legend tells us this is how the new Passamaquoddy thunderbird, the lone Indian who passed through the cleft, in time became the great and powerful Thunderbird, who always has kept a watchful eye upon the good Indians. 2

A belief in the magic of the Thunderbird is held by the Passamaquoddy, because he can tame the winds alternating between calm and storms. In this way the Thunderbird was not merely seen as a large, natural flying creature, but as at least a semi-supernatural creature with ties to the divine world above.

Another Thunderbird story can be found in the myths and legends of the Quillayute Indians of the Pacific Northwest. In this story, disaster had struck the Quillayute - rain and hail had fallen for many days, destroying all of the edible plants and making it impossible to fish. Many of their people had been killed by the hail, which was followed by sleet and snow. Out of food, the Quillayute were desperate, and the Great Chief was forced to call upon the Great Spirit for help. The Great Spirit answered, sending them the Thunderbird:

The people waited. No one spoke. There was nothing but silence and darkness. Suddenly, there came a great noise, and flashes of lightning cut the darkness. A deep whirring sound, like giant wings beating, came from the place of the setting sun. All of the

GIANTS ON THE EARTH

people turned to gaze toward the sky above the ocean as a huge, bird-shaped creature flew toward them. This bird was larger than any they had ever seen. Its wings, from tip to tip, were twice as long as a war canoe. It had a huge, curving beak, and its eyes glowed like fire. The people saw that its great claws held a living, giant whale. In silence, they watched while Thunderbird - for so the bird was named by everyone - carefully lowered the whale to the ground before them. Thunderbird then flew high in the sky, and went back to the thunder and lightning it had come from. Perhaps it flew back to its perch in the hunting grounds of the Great Spirit. Thunderbird and Whale saved the Quillayute from dying. The people knew that the Great Spirit had heard their prayer. Even today they never forget that visit from Thunderbird, never forget that it ended long days of hunger and death. For on the prairie near their village are big, round stones that the grandfathers say are the hardened hailstones of that storm long ago.

    The Quillayute described the Thunderbird as essentially a very large bird, though no bird in history was ever as big as the type of bird they described, and of course no other bird ever had the same supernatural powers:

    Thunderbird is a very large bird, with feathers as long as a canoe paddle. When he flaps his wings, he makes thunder and the great winds. When he opens and shuts his eyes, he makes lightning. In stormy weather, he flies through the skies, flapping his wings and opening and closing his eyes. Thunderbird's home is a cave in the Olympic Mountains, and he wants no one to come near it. If hunters get close enough so he can smell them, he makes thunder noise, and he rolls ice out of his cave. The ice rolls down the mountainside, and when it reaches a rocky place, it breaks into many pieces. The pieces rattle as they roll farther down into the valley. All the hunters are so afraid of Thunderbird and his noise and rolling ice that they never stay long near his home. No one ever sleeps near his cave. Thunderbird keeps his food in a dark hole at the edge of a big field of ice and snow. His food is the whale. Thunderbird flies out of the ocean, catches a whale and hurries back to the mountains to eat it. One time Whale fought Thunderbird so hard that during the battle, trees were torn up by their roots. To this day there are no trees in Beaver Prairie because of the fight Whale and Thunderbird had that day.

    The battle between Thunderbird and Whale appears to be primarily symbolic of the battle between the air and the sea, as imagined by the Quillayute in their attempt to interpret the forces of nature. Like most ancient peoples, the Quillayute interpreted the forces of nature in symbolic forms, inventing gods and goddesses, deities, and demigods as causes of these phenomena.

    At the time of the Great Flood, Thunderbird fought a long, long battle with Killer Whale. He would catch Killer Whale in his claws and start with him to the cave in the mountains. Killer Whale would escape and return to the water. Thunderbird would catch him again, all the time flashing lightning from his eyes and flapping his wings to create thunder. Mountains were shaken by the noise, and trees were uprooted in their struggle. Again and again Killer Whale escaped. Again and again Thunderbird seized him. Many times they fought, in different places in the mountains. At last Killer Whale escaped to the middle of the ocean, and Thunderbird gave up the fight. That is why Killer Whales live in the deep oceans today. That is why there are many prairies in the midst of the forests on the Olympic Peninsula. [3]

    It is interesting that the Quillayute mention the "Great Flood" in their description of the

GIANTS ON THE EARTH

battle between Thunderbird and whale. The story of a Great Flood that covered the Earth at one time is nearly universal throughout the ancient world - but that is a story for another time.

The Quillayute legend describes the Thunderbird as a giant flying creature with feathers. According to the geologic record, no avian (bird) was ever as large as the creature that the Quillayute described. However, there were flying creatures that were that large - the giant pterosaur Quetzalcoatlus Northropi, native to the Mesozoic Period (65 million - 230 million years ago). With a wingspan of 33 feet, Quetzalcoatlus Northropi was possibly the largest flying creature on earth in any period. A fully grown Quetzalcoatlus was also quite capable of catching and carrying

An artist's rendition of the controversial Thunderbird photo, allegedly taken in Tombstone, Arizona in 1890. The creature shown here is essentially a pteranodon with feathers, though the oral account makes no mention of feathers, and describes the creature as being much larger. Image from Wierd Predators Petting Zoo: Thunderbird.

off a small whale like the Killer Whale. Absurd as this might seem, there have been sightings of similar creatures all the way up to the present day in various parts of the world (see The Mysterious Piasa Creature Part II).

One problem with this theory is the fact that the Thunderbird is described as having feathers. However, recent evidence out of China suggests that at least some dinosaurs may have had feathers. One controversial photo, which has now been lost (if it ever truly existed), shows a pterodactyl-like creature with feathered wings being displayed by a group of men as a sort of hunting trophy. This controversial photo, some believe was a sort of urban legend, a thing that never happened but was believed by many to be true, despite the fact that large-scale searches have been made for the photo without success.

The most celebrated Thunderbird encounter took place in 1890, on the desert sands of what was then the Arizona Territory. Two cowboys had a bizarre confrontation which has varied widely in the telling, but the gist of the story is this: they saw a giant flying bird, shot and killed it with their rifles, and carried its spectacular carcass into town. A report in the April 26, 1890 Tombstone Epigraph listed the creature's wingspan as an alarming 160 feet, and noted that the bird was about 92 feet long, about 50 inches around at the middle, and had a head about eight feet long. The beast was said to have no feathers, but a smooth skin and wingflaps "composed of a thick and nearly transparent membrane... easily penetrated by a bullet." Perhaps the hardest part of this story to swallow is that two horses could manage to haul a dead behemoth like this for any distance. The Tombstone newspaper printed its highly embroidered version of the cowboy's sighting, which was spared from fading into obscurity by its inclusion in a 1930 book on the Old West.

In 1963, the story came to the attention of writer Jack Pearl, who revived the tale for an article in a pulpy men's adventure magazine called Saga. As if the Epigraph report hadn't spiced up the facts enough already, Pearl liberally embellished the encounter into a dramatic rip-snorter entitled "Monster Bird That Carries Off Human Beings!" Pearl pushed the date of the encounter back to 1886, and he described the witnesses as two prospectors who killed the bird and proudly showed off their trophy in Tombstone. Pearl also added some extra conflict by telling of a how a second Thunderbird snatched up a heckler who had ridiculed the prospectors and flew away with him in its talons. But Pearl's

GIANTS ON THE EARTH

most significant editorialization was this: he said that the Epigraph newspaper story had run with a photograph of the giant bird's carcass, nailed up to a wall with its mighty wingspan unfurled, and a number of men posing next to it for scale. 4

So, despite the existence of plenty of secondary evidence, the quest for an actual photo or other decisive evidence for the existence of a Thunderbird continues on. Like the quest for Piasa, dragons, and other mythical monsters, the Thunderbird and its paranormal ilk continue to live on the fringes of human perception, waiting for the lucky snapshot to snap them into focus.

Reports of strange flying reptiles, some quite large, have continued well into modern times. As we shall see, reports of pteranodons, dragons, thunderbirds, and other similar monsters, are relatively common. Could the sudden rash of Chupacabras attacks and sightings be related to the occasional rash of pteranodon sightings?

Many of the aspects of the Chupacabras and living pteranodons seem to match. They are both monsters and flesh eaters. Pteranodons may well drink blood and gorge themselves on internal organs, which are easy to eat.

Carrion birds such as vultures and condors eat the exposed softer flesh first, lips, eyes, underbelly, etc. It would seem natural for pteranodons to do this as well.

Admittedly, the Chupacabras' supposed habit of draining all the blood from two small holes on the neck, similar to the familiar vampires of lore, seems more fiction than reality.

In Chile, animals were actually disappearing or being half eaten. Pteranodons are vicious meat eaters with very sharp teeth and claws to rip open victims. They apparently feed at night, much like owls. Their survival in the mountains of northern Mexico and the southern Andes has been theorized for decades by cryptozoologists.

Giant bats, huge super—eagles called "pteratorns" and weird "mothmen" have all been put forward as explanations of these various reports. Now I come forward to state, unequivocally, that I believe these legends and sightings can be attributed to still—living flying dinosaurs-to pterodactyls or, more precisely, pteranodons.

We know that these creatures once existed because of the fossil record. Sightings have continued to this day, and legends abound, but where is the physical evidence that these creatures still exist?

One thing that must be first understood is that fossils are anomalous geological artifacts, typically made because of some cataclysm or volcanic disaster. Most animals when they die, naturally or by a predator, simply decay and return to dust.

The point here is that a pterodactyl that died in a desert or jungle or mountain crag 1,000 years ago (or even 10) would not have left a fossil behind for us to prove to us that it had been there.

The second thing that must be understood about these amazing flying animals is that they are nocturnal and live only in extremely remote and uninhabited areas of the earth. Even so, there are literally hundreds of reports of giant birds and flying lizards showing up around the world.

The most amazing pteranodon fossil ever discovered was at Big Bend National Park in Texas. The park was the site of the discovery of the skeleton of a giant pteranodon in 1975. It had a wingspan of 51 feet and is the largest fossil of a flying reptile so far discovered. Other pterodactyls were much smaller and had wingspans from 8 to 20 feet.

GIANTS ON THE EARTH

Though pteranodons are believed to have become extinct about 65 million years ago, this may not necessarily be the case. Many creatures which lived at that time are still alive, such as crocodiles, turtles, and the famous coelacanth prehistoric fish.

Even the date of the fossil of the giant pteranodon found at Big Bend is in question. Since fossils cannot be dated by any known technical method, their age is guessed at from the geological strata around them, and since the current dating of geological strata is based on the prevailing Uniformitarian theory of slow geological change, the date of many fossils may be radically closer to our own than 65 million years.

Legends of Flying Reptiles

(This "dragon" pictured looks very much like a plant eating dinosaur-click here to read more about it.)

The Chinese have had legends for thousands of years of flying reptiles called dragons, and flying snakes as well- something apparently different. Flying reptile dragon images in China are so prevalent, they can easily be considered amongst the most common of motifs. Are they stylized depictions of real flying animals? The ancient Chinese certainly thought they were.

Similarly, most countries of Europe and the Mediterranean have myths and legends of heroes battling flying reptiles-or dragons. Often depicted as winged snakes or winged alligators, these dragons were a common image as well, and are still used in the crests of royal families.

Did dragons-flying reptiles-pterodactyls-still exist in small numbers, even up to the Middle Ages?

Almost every Indian tribe from Alaska to Tierro del Fuego has legends of a gigantic flying monster so large that, ". . . it darkened the sun." The clapping of these giants' wings created thunder, so they were known as "Thunderbirds."

The Navajo Indians still perform their Thunderbird dance, and tell the legends of the "cliff monster" which lived in a high craggy roost, descending to carry people off to feed to its young.

The Haida natives of the Queen Charlotte Islands of British Columbia believe that some Thunderbirds were so large that they could literally pick up small whales from the sea. Much of their art and woodcarving depicts exactly such a capture by a Thunderbird.

Some South American Indians believed that the bird was constantly at war with the powers living beneath the sea, particularly a horned serpent, and that it tore open large trees in search of a giant grub which was its favorite food.

It has been suggested that the Thunderbird is in fact a living fossil-a pteranodon. Though few in number, especially these days, pterosaurs may have survived in small numbers in remote desert and mountain areas. Though it seems incredible, as I have stated, reports of "giant birds" and pteranodons continue to this day from around the world.

Pterodactyls in South America

Persistent legends and stories abound in South America of giant winged creatures. These stories have been told since before the Conquistadors arrived, and some seem to be based on far more recent sightings.

The following article appeared in a magazine called The Zoologist in July, 1868, dateline Copiapo, Chile, April 1868:

GIANTS ON THE EARTH

"Yesterday, at about five o'clock in the afternoon when the daily labours in this mine were over, and all the workmen were together awaiting their supper, we saw coming through the air, from the side of the ternera a gigantic bird, which at first sight we took for one of the clouds then partially darkening the atmosphere, supposing it to have been separated from the rest by the wind.

Its course was from north—west to south—east; its flight was rapid and in a straight line. As it was passing a short distance above our heads we could mark the strange formation of its body.

Its immense wings were clothed with something resembling the thick and stout bristles of a boar, while on its body, elongated like that of a serpent, we could only see brilliant scales which clashed together with metallic sound as the strange animal turned its body in its flight."

Also in South America, a Mr. J. Harrison of Liverpool said that when he was navigating an estuary of the Amazon in 1947 called Manuos, he and others observed from the boat's deck a flight of five huge birds passing overhead and down the river in a V—formation. But they were no ordinary birds, said Mr. Harrison in a letter:

"The wingspan must have been at least twelve feet from tip to tip. They were brown in colour like brown leather, with no visible signs of feathers. The head was flat on top, with a long beak and a long neck. The wings were ribbed." He said that the creatures "were just like those large prehistoric birds."

Airplane—Pterodactyl Encounter?

A similar incident in South America was published in 1992 by the Australian weekly magazine People. In this encounter, a small commuter aircraft nearly crashed into a giant flying lizard over the mountain jungles of Brazil.

A U.S. anthropologist named Dr. George Biles was supposedly aboard the plane of 24 passengers and was quoted as saying, "This was a classic case of a white pterodactyl with a giant wingspan.

Of course, I've heard the rumors for many years that these prehistoric creatures still roamed the Amazon. But I was skeptical like everybody else. But that wasn't an airplane or a UFO flying beside us. It was a pterodactyl."

The People story says that the pterodactyl was flying alongside the plane as it was preparing to land and that the pilot veered away to avoid colliding with the "giant bird."

A stewardess named Maya Cabon is quoted as saying, "Here was this giant monster flying right next to the plane. He was only a few feet away from the window-and he looked right at me.

I thought we were all going to die." No actual size is given in the story, and tales like this start becoming suspect when the pilot is quoted as saying ". . . he was coming straight at us and he was mighty big!". . .

The Feathered Serpent

In the mythology and religion of Central America there is the very real tradition of Quetzalcoatl, of the Feathered Serpent (While Quetzalcoatl was a man, or series of men, he was named after the "feathered serpent.").

Was there such an animal at one time-a flying reptile? Biologists say yes, pterosaurs or pteranodons, but they have been extinct for millions of years. Or have they? And could they be one possible explanation for some of the Chupacabras sightings?

GIANTS ON THE EARTH

Film of a pterodactyl flying over the Yucatan was widely viewed in the early 1970s, according to famous cryptozoologist Loren Coleman in his book, Mysterious America.

Carvings of what appear to be pteranodons can be found in Mayan ruins at Tajin, located in northeastern Vera Cruz state in Mexico.

Under the title "Serpent—Bird of the Mayans," Science Digest published a brief article in its November, 1968 issue on the subject of a pteranodon being possibly carved into a wall at the pyramid of Tajin.

Says the article, "An ancient Mayan relief sculpture of a peculiar bird with reptilian characteristics has been discovered in Totonacapan, in northeastern section of Veracruz, Mexico.

Jose Diaz—Bolio, a Mexican archaeologist—journalist responsible for the discovery, says there is evidence that the serpent—bird sculpture, located in the ruins of Tajin, is not merely the product of Mayan flights of fancy, but a realistic representation of an animal that lived during the period of the ancient Mayans- 1,000 to 5,000 years ago.

"If indeed such serpent—birds were contemporary with the ancient Mayan culture, the relief sculpture represents a startling evolutionary oddity. Animals with such characteristics are believed to have disappeared 130 million years ago. The acrhaeornis and the archaeopteryx, to which the sculpture bears a vague resemblance, were flying reptiles that became extinct during the Mesozoic age of dinosaurs.

"And since man did not appear, according to current geological charts, until about one million years ago, there appears to be a 129—million—year discrepancy. The twain (Mayan and serpent bird) never should have met. But Jose Diaz—Bolio is continuing his investigation, and he says that he knows of the existence of a serpent—bird skull that may hold a clue to the mystery once it has been identified."

The idea that the "feathered serpent" of the Mayas was a real animal has been a popular subject over the years. The concept that the Mayan feathered serpent was a long—necked flying reptile was used in the 1946 film The Flying Serpent starring George Zucco (featured in the Adventures Unlimited video Dinosaurs Alive!) and more recently in the 1982 David Carradine film Q-The Winged Serpent.

The "Q" stands for the Mayan word Quetzalcoatl, or "feathered serpent." While these grade—B movies have made little impact on audiences, they do show that the idea of flying serpents- also called pteranodons-are a popular belief along the Mexican border.

The Lost Pterodactyl Photo

According to the Fortean investigator John Keel, more than 20 people have written to him claiming to have seen a photo of a dead pterodactyl nailed to the side of a building in Tombstone, Arizona. Keel claims that he has seen this photo, too, but no one can remember where!

In his column "Beyond the Known" in the March 1991 issue of Fate magazine, Keel discusses this intriguing photograph at length. He also quotes from a letter from the son of a Pennsylvania man named Robert Lyman who had written numerous articles and books about the weird and the unknown. Lyman wrote about Thunderbirds in one of his books entitled Amazing Indeed:

"About 1900, two prospectors shot and carried into Tombstone, Arizona, one of these birds. When nailed against the wall of the Tombstone Epitaph building its wingspread measured 36 feet. A photograph showed six men standing under the bird with out-

GIANTS ON THE EARTH

stretched arms touching. One of them said: 'Shucks, there is no such bird, never was and never will be.'

I saw that picture in a daily paper. Many other persons remember seeing it. No one has been able to find it in recent years. Two copies were at Hammersley Fork only a few years ago. One burned in a home. The other was taken away by strangers.". . .

"Officer, There's a Pterodactyl in My Backyard!"

That there were sightings of pterodactyls in the 1800s, I have no doubt. In fact the sightings in the Sonora Desert continue to this day. In the early months of 1976, a rash of "flying reptile" sightings were reported in the Rio Grande River Valley along the Mexican—American border.

One of the first encounters was in the early hours of December 26, 1975 when a rancher named Joe Suárez discovered that a goat he had tied up in a corral in Raymondville, Texas (about 30 miles north of the Rio Grande in southeastern Texas), had been ripped to pieces and partially eaten by some unknown assailant.

The goat had been mauled from the right side and was lying in a pool of blood with the heart and lungs missing with the snout bitten away. The blood was still wet and warm when police officers examined the carcass.

They could find no footprints around the goat and concluded that a flying creature of unknown origin had caused the death.

Then, in the same town, on January 14, 1976 at about 10:30 in the evening on the north side of Raymondville, a young man named Armando Grimaldo was sitting in the backyard of his mother—in—law's house when he was attacked by a strange winged creature.

"As I was turning to go look over on the other side of the house," said Armando to the Raymondville press, "I felt something grab me, something with big claws. I looked back and saw it and started running. I've never been scared of nothing before but this time I really was. That was the most scared I've ever been in my whole life."

This strange flying attacker had dived out of the sky-and it was something Grimaldo described as being about six feet tall with a wingspread he estimated as being from ten to twelve feet. Its skin was blackish—brown, leathery and featherless. It had huge red eyes.

Grimaldo was terrified. He screamed and tried to run but tripped and fell face first into the dirt. As he struggled up to continue running for his mother—in—law's house, the beast's claws continued to attempt to grasp him securely, tearing his clothes, which were now virtually ripped to shreds.

He managed to dive under a bush and the attacking animal, now breathing heavily, flew away into the sky.

Grimaldo then crashed into the house, collapsing on the floor, muttering "pájaro" (Spanish for bird) over and over again. He was taken to the hospital, treated for shock and minor wounds, and released.

Blazing Red Eyes

A short time later, in nearby Brownsville, on the Rio Grande, a similar creature slammed into the mobile home of Alverico Guajardo on the outskirts of town. Alverico went outside his trailer to investigate the crash into his house.

When he noticed a large animal next to the crash site, he got into his station wagon

GIANTS ON THE EARTH

and turned the lights on to see the creature, which he later described as "something from another planet."

As soon as the lights hit it, the thing rose up and glared at him with blazing red eyes. Alverico, paralyzed with fear, could only stare back at the creature whose long, batlike wings were wrapped around its shoulders.

All the while it was making a "horrible—sounding noise in its throat." Finally, after two or three minutes of staring into the headlights of the station wagon, it backed away to a dirt road a few feet behind it and disappeared in the darkness.

These were just the first of a number of bizarre encounters with seemingly prehistoric "birds." Also in January of 1976, two sisters, Libby and Deany Ford, spotted a huge and strange "big black bird" by a pond near Brownsville.

The creature was as tall as they were and had a "face like a bat." They later identified it out of a book of prehistoric animals as a pteranodon.

The San Antonio Light newspaper reported on February 26, 1976, that three local school teachers were driving to work on an isolated road to the south of the city on February 24 when they saw an enormous bird sweeping low over cars on the road.

It had a wingspan of 15-20 feet and leathery wings. It did not so much fly, as glide. They said that it was flying so low that when it swooped over the cars its shadow covered the entire road.

As the three watched this huge flying creature, they saw another flying creature off in the distance circling a herd of cattle. It looked, they thought, like an "oversized seagull." They later scanned encyclopedias at their school, and identified the creature as a pteranodon.

The sightings of flying reptiles over Texas subsided for a while, but then on September 14, 1982, James Thompson, an ambulance technician from Harlingen, saw a "birdlike object" pass over Highway 100 at a distance of 150 feet or more above the pavement. The time was 3:55 in the morning, and this huge flying creature was obviously a night hunter.

"I expected him to land like a model airplane," Thompson told the Valley Morning Star, the local Rio Grande newspaper. "That's what I thought he was, but he flapped his wings enough to get above the grass.

It had a black or grayish rough texture. It wasn't feathers. I'm quite sure it was a hide—type covering. I just watched him fly away." It was as the others had described the same flying creature: a "pterodactyl—like bird."

Diving "Big Bird"?

Fortean writers Loren Coleman and Jerome Clark made extensive investigations of the "Big Bird" sightings in Texas and later published their results in the book Creatures of the Goblin World.

They chronicle all of the above incidents, and a number of others. They even obtained fecal matter from what was thought to be a pterodactyl. Although they report that the fecal matter was being analyzed, they do not give the results.

Coleman and Clark also tell the strange story of James Rowe, a retired Corpus Christi newsman, who recalled the story of a man who ran a grocery store along Corpus Christi Beach. The unnamed man was fishing along the Nueces River before the Wesley Seale Dam was built (1958) when something grabbed his hook and took off downstream.

The thing almost took all of his line before he got it turned around, then it headed

GIANTS ON THE EARTH

upstream just as far. "He fought it and fought. Then finally the thing just climbed out of the water on a sandbar across the river from where he was standing. It was this creature with fur and feathers and it just took the hook out of its mouth. Then it climbed up a tree.

"The fellow had a pistol in his tackle box, so he took it out and started to shoot at the animal. Then as he took aim, the thing just flew away."

While this may sound like a Texas tall tale, it is curious to note here that tales of the Kongamato in Zaire/Congo/Angola also mention that the animal goes underwater and can fly as well, similar to loons, grebes, pelicans and other birds. It sounds bizarre, but then, why would people make up this unusual bit of information concerning these "monsters"?

Strange Tracks

The above stories aside, other tales were taken more seriously, even by the police. Unlike most of the others, one incident took place in daylight hours on January 1, 1976, near Harlingen, Texas. Two children, Tracey Lawson, 11, and her cousin Jackie Davies, 14, were playing in the Lawsons' backyard while their parents slept off the excesses of New Year's Eve. The two children were playing in a large backyard that faced a plowed field five miles south of Harlingen along Ed Carey Road.

Suddenly, Tracey noticed something standing a hundred yards away. Dashing inside, she picked up a pair of binoculars and returned to focus on a "horrible—looking" huge black bird.

She described it as over five feet tall with big, dark red eyes, with wings bunched up at its shoulders, which were three feet wide. Its face was grey in color and "gorilla—like."

It had a beak, however, that was sharp, thick, and at least six inches long. The head was bald. On one occasion during the sighting the thing made a loud, shrill "eeeee" sound.

The children were amazed and frightened. The creature suddenly disappeared, apparently flying low over a quarry or "borrow pit" along an irrigation canal, and then reappeared on the northeast corner of the property, its head poking above a small clump of trees.

The children, more and more frightened, went inside the house and stayed. Later, the parents were disinclined to believe the story they were told upon awakening, but the next day Jackie's stepfather, Tom Waldon, went to the Lawson property to look for tracks to satisfy his stepson. To his surprise, he found several three—toed tracks from some unknown creature.

The first three tracks were close to the fence behind the house. The fourth print was 20 yards out into the field, and the fifth 20 yards beyond that. The tracks were three—toed, eight inches across, square at the head, and were pressed an inch and a half into the hard ground. Later, after the police and Stan Lawson arrived, the entire group examined the prints and decided that the children had been telling the bizarre truth.

Stan Lawson, who weighed 170 pounds, pressed his own foot down alongside the bird print and found it made practically no impression. "That thing must have been pretty heavy," he said later.

Coleman and Clark also mention that Stan Lawson had noticed something strange about their dog's behavior. All day it cowered inside the doghouse leaving it only once, at suppertime, when Lawson went to feed it and it bolted through the door into the main

GIANTS ON THE EARTH

house.

It had to be dragged back outside. And that night, around 10:00, Lawson heard something like large wings scraping across his bedroom window screen, but he saw nothing. In the morning he found that the screen was torn.

One puzzling part of the information is the frequent report that these strange, flying creatures have a face like a gorilla, monkey or a man. Even with a beak, it seems to have a short, flat face, rather than a long narrow pointed head as we typically associate with pterodactyls.

However, some pteranodons had short, flat faces, and some had no beak whatsoever. For instance, a pterosaur known as the Anurognathus had a stubby face and sharp teeth; the Batrachognathus had a flat face, forward claws and extremely sharp teeth. Such a creature was perfectly suited for eating a goat, or even a larger animal. It would also have the appearance of a gorilla with a beak. . . .

Remote Nests in the Desert?

It seems likely that if Thunderbirds/pterodactyls live in this day and age, they must be nesting in some pretty remote and probably mountainous area. The most likely area for any concentration of flying lizards still surviving would have to be in the Sonora Desert in Mexico, just south of Arizona and New Mexico.

From this area it would be quite possible for pterodactyls to still live largely undisturbed and unseen by civilization.

Mexico's Sierra Madre Oriental, only 200 miles east of the Rio Grande sightings, is one of the least explored regions of North America. Flying reptiles or huge birds could still live in such a region, especially if they were mainly nocturnal.

Bibliography

Creatures of the Goblin World, Jerome Clark and Loren Coleman, 1978, Clark Publications, Chicago.

Lost Cities of North and Central America, David Hatcher Childress, 1994, Adventures Unlimited Press, Kempton, IL.

Megagods, Jim Woodman, 1987, Pocket Books, New York. The Mothman Prophecies, John Keel, 1975, Signet Books, New York.

Mysterious America, Jerome Clark and Loren Coleman, 1983, Faber & Faber, Boston.

Mystery in Acambaro, Charles Hapgood, 2000, Adventures Unlimited Press, Kempton, IL.

GIANTS ON THE EARTH

THE LAND OF THE GIANTS

There were giants in the earth in those days; and also after that, when the sons of God came in unto the daughters of men, and they bare children to them, the same became mighty men which were of old, men of renown. Genesis 6:4.

Stretch your mind back to childhood. What giants do you remember? Jack and the Beanstalk? Hercules? Paul Bunyan? Goliath? What were you told and what did you read? With the exception of Goliath and an occasional ornery cyclops, legends emphasized their innate goodness, eye-popping feats accomplished with unparalleled strength, victories over the bad guys and all performed by "gentle giants". What if it were all a lie? What if the truth were something much MUCH more sinister?

I have invested over 30 years researching the vast history of giants. It has, for the most part, been kept from the public. Proof of giants' existence - their skeletal remains - has been quickly secreted away in obscure museums, when not destroyed outright. Additionally, time has cloaked and sugar-coated these creatures' true perverse nature, the majority too vile, too demonic for bedtime stories. However, history is replete with their tales of unimaginable cruelty, sexual perversity, cannibalism and pagan rituals. This is only the beginning. Some things are best forgotten. . . or are they?

Where did these giants come from and what was their connection with ordinary humans? Just who were they? What happened to these extraordinary creatures? Is it possible they could ever return? The last question I will answer right now - YES, they most definitely could return! And they have something much worse in mind for mankind.

GIANTS ON THE EARTH

INTRODUCTION

I ask you to do only one thing when reading this book: Read it with an open mind. And by open, I mean that you will for a time suspend the notions (and — as I will prove to you in this book — propaganda) that you have been taught in school, by news magazines, and the majority of other outlets for the "facts" of science and history.

In doing this, you will discover that you are like the sleepers in the movie Matrix. You have been living a life in a dream world, where things are not as they seem. You are living in a place that has the truth hidden, substituting a series of carefully crafted lies to keep you permanently blinded, with the truth only having a chance to briefly surface from time to time.

This book will be your chance to see the truth, to learn what is going on behind the scenes and the many telling facts that have been carefully hidden from your view. If you will read it with an open mind, you will be able to take the first step toward seeing what is really going on, and see the monsters behind the scenes who are attempting to keep the truth from being revealed about them, as well as the ancient past and the ways it will effect the future.

Why must you keep an open mind as you read this?

Because like most of those reading this book, you have been hoodwinked by the education establishment which by intent or by accident, has become the prime purveyor of the lies that make up the "party line" that keeps the truth hidden. This education has been so deeply ingrained in almost every educated human being, so that responses and views are like thick sunglasses that prevent seeing in a dimly lit room. It is only by removing those glasses that one can see what's real, and in the process find the truth.

Because of this conditioning and training through the educational system as well as the entertainment and news media, those hiding the truth have a very powerful tool: Denial. And often they don't have to employ it directly; like rats trained by electrical shock, you jump to attention and deny the truth when it's presented to you. Years of conditioning with the electric shock of scorn and derision have taught you to do this. You not only do the work of hiding the truth, because of your conditioning you may even humiliate those who would bring the truth to you.

GIANTS ON THE EARTH

This conditioning has filtered through the educational system for centuries, so that today's scientists, doctors, and historians are likewise victims to it. As I will document in this book, when confronted with the truth of history, artifacts, or fossils, they have learned to shut out the facts from their minds through their educational conditioning.

Or if that truth is too strong to ignore, then they may hide it from site and attempt to forget. Because if they do not, they will quickly become the object of scorn and derision from their peers, with a quick trip to unemployment as one of the "kooks" or "nut cases" that are today full of similar men who attempted to have an open mind and register their second thoughts or reservations about the dogma of lies which they had been taught.

Thus denial is the first tool trotted out. It is the typical "educated response" when a researcher, newsman, or scientist is presented with anomalous evidence and findings that don't fit neatly into the category of "containment." And likewise today's academia is comprised of individuals living in intellectual boxes of dishonesty.

The Time of Change Is At Hand

For you and each person who will read this book with an open mind, that can change. Because for over 30 years now, I have been carefully tracing, finding, sleuthing the truth.

I started by investigating the origins of ancient civilizations: Their builders, their myths, their legends. Little by little what I discovered prompted and provoked me to seek answers beyond the party line. As Henry Ford, the automotive genius of the last century so aptly put it, "History is more or less bunk."

The Romanian–born French philosopher E. M. Cioran put it even more bluntly when he wrote, "History is nothing but a procession of false absolutes, a series of temples raised to pretexts, a degradation of the mind before the improbable."

As I will show you, these men are not far off the mark (perhaps because they were often rubbing shoulders with those working behind the scenes to hide the truth). As you'll see, past civilizations were not the primitive collectives they've been portrayed as being in textbooks and Hollywood. They were truly amazing, yes, even breath-taking. Because far from being the crude cultures they have been pictured as being, they held technology not only equal to today's, in many respects they were advanced beyond modern day technology, often to the point that they defy "modern man's" imagination in how they achieved their more remarkable accomplishments.

Modern historians, of course, play a game of deny, deny, deny, coming up with explanations for these accomplishments that are nearly as amazing as the artifacts they try to explain away. As you will see, the explanations and dismissals are full of holes. For there is truth to the many stories that are now denied. What you have been taught to scoff at and dismiss as myth more often than not may be truth.

This is not that hard to prove, either.

By simply looking at the ruins of the past, a person quickly discovers that the ancients constructed architecture that was so accurately positioned to "stellar and planetary coordinates" that only recently has modern science and computer technology been able to fathom the relevance of such positioning. (Indeed, some ancient constructions appear to have positioning that modern science does not yet understand.)

How the ancients were able to gain such knowledge with crude tools and the marginal math today's archeologists claim they had is impossible to explain. When not ignoring and denying, today's "modern sciences" develop very pathetic explanations and

GIANTS ON THE EARTH

theories. Yet these remain as "facts" because those scientists and researchers seldom dare to suggest otherwise, less they find their careers at an end.

Perhaps the most startling thing about the ancient wisdom and understanding which you'll be looking at throughout this book is that the calculations and knowledge behind them was, as is the case today, dependent on computers for such computations. Instead, it seems entirely possible (indeed probably since instrumentation that would permit such calculations has never been found) the work was done in the heads of those creating the monuments and machinery.

The conventional view of ancient peoples is that they are dumb brutes. And the farther back in time you go, the dumber they must be for the simple "reason" that human kind is supposed to be evolving into a better, wiser beast. Yet as you'll see, the exact opposite may have taken place. Because hidden in the truth is the fact that giants not only existed, they most likely ruled and controlled lesser men due to both their physical as well as their mental superiority.

Think about this: The skeletal remains of individuals up to 36 feet in height doesn't mean that giants were simply big. It also means that they were also smarter. Because with skulls (of which there are examples from South America and elsewhere) with three to six times the cranial mass of modern day humans, those ancient beings must have had mental abilities that would make Einstein seem retarded by comparison.

However, ancient people and giants aren't the only ones who created the artifacts and monuments of the past. Because, as I will show later in this book, there is conclusive evidence that many of these ancient artifacts were most likely made by non-human technology and hands.

Of course such things don't fit neatly into modern thinking that today's culture is the pinnacle of mental prowess, or that today's technologies are superior to those of the past. Thus they are denied and those who consider such possibilities quickly laughed out of the hall in which they present their facts.

Yet the truth remains: Those legends, myths, and oral traditions may not be so far fetched as you have been taught, and even would prefer to think. In fact they may have at least nuggets of truth in them. That truth points back to a period of time in the dateless past when great civilizations flourished with scientific and engineering achievements (which still challenge modern intellects) were the norm.

I don't want you to just take my word on this — it is, after all, a hard pill to swallow, especially after the propaganda you have been fed from the popular media as well as the "facts" found in almost any science or historic textbook. Instead I simply want you to read this book with an open mind. Do that, and I will provide you with enough evidence and background findings so as to challenge the official "scientific party line" and give you a set of mind-boggling exclamation points in place of question marks you have when approaching these with only the conventional party line.

Grant me this, and then in the next chapters I promise I'll give you the answers to history's puzzles instead of the denial and fabrications that you have heard from your youth until you picked up this book (and which you'll continue to hear — but be able to recognize for the lies they are).

Now... It's time to commence the journey that will lead to this amazing revelation of the truth.

GIANTS ON THE EARTH

Chapter 1: Creation

In the beginning God created the heaven and the earth. And the earth was without form, and void; and darkness was upon the face of the deep. And the Spirit of God moved upon the face of the waters. And God said, Let there be light: and there was light.— Genesis 1: 1-3.

In building any case, especially one that is counter to the lies that have been given as truth over the lifetime of a reader, it is essential that the "jury" reading the argument do so with an open mind. That said, what you read is going to at first seem outlandish but, as you continue and the premise I'm offering becomes fleshed out and buttressed with more and more facts, it will all fit together and make sense.

So please read thoughtfully and with an open mind. Doing so will reward you with the truth I have gleaned during my studies which have encompassed several decades.

Our journey toward discovering the truth must begin with the first-hand accounts of what happened. And as you'll see as I present the archeological evidence, there's every indication that these amount to first-hand accounts of very ancient events. Some of these have been passed down through myths long distorted by retelling and oral tradition, while others have come down almost verbatim from the ancients. While I've examined all these sources, I have been careful to concentrate on the most accurate accounts first and then work my way back through those that are less accurate, but still contain gems of truth hidden in the often distorted story line.

The most accurate of these sources can be found in the books that have been canonized into today's Bible. The reason for this accuracy is important to note as I start detailing the various clues that can be pieced together. Where ancient writers of Greek myths, for example, freely embellished and crated new features in any given story, the Bible was handed down from ancient times in a very different way.

The scribes copying the various books of the Old and New Testament did so with strict supervision and careful checking by the scribe as well as those working with him to avoid errors. Where many cultures rewarded the embellishment of stories, the Jewish writers worked in the opposite direction: The stories were never to be altered even by punctuation. Not the proverbial "jot or tittle" were changed, added, or deleted.

GIANTS ON THE EARTH

This extreme care to avoid altering the text means that these books have come through time to the present age almost exactly as they were when first penned. And one can assume that the oral traditions in which some of the older stories were first seen and handed down were likewise carefully recited and memorized to avoid any changes of the story.

This means that the Bible is a key source of detail that can't be found anywhere else. For this reason, it is the perfect place to begin the journey into the past to discover the true history and to see what really has lead to this present age.

In the Beginning

The very first verses of the Bible give key clues that will become more and more important as this book unfolds and will bring into sharp focus what has happened through the Earth's history as well as the human history that has comprised the last six thousand years.

You read that right. As I'll show later, all the evidence points to the fact that the Earth is much older than many conservative Christians who have embraced the young Earth theory would hold. It also shows that while human civilization only extends back about 6,000 years and that before that time, there was a vastly older and more developed planet that has a history which expanded back from the 6,000 years during which modern man and his ancestors have existed.

Perhaps the big surprise here is that it is possible to decipher this from the first few verses of the Bible provided a person actually sees what the original Hebrew language conveys to the reader. Unfortunately most readers of the Genesis account of creation read it in a native tongue other than Hebrew, and because of the imprecision and differences in languages, such translations lose much of their meaning and even allow for slight misinterpretations.

In this case, reading the passage only in the English translation causes such confusion can all be obscure the truth of this planet's past.

For starters you need to realize that when God went through the creation steps outlined in Genesis, they were a minor undertaking. Creation for human beings is a complicated and often agonizingly frustrating process. For the Heavenly Father, it is a simple task.

Thus the writers of the Bible in the words they select to tell about God forming the world and universe, describe the labor as an almost casual operation, a light bit of work. For example, Hebrews 11:3 makes perfect sense in this context when the writer tells that,

Through faith we understand that the worlds were framed by the word of God, so that things which are seen were not made of things which do appear.

In other words, God simply spoke and worlds were created. This also alludes to the "Word of God" that John wrote about in his gospel as well as the destroying sword that comes out of the mouth of the returning Messiah at the end of the Great Tribulation. This again presents the idea both of creation through arranging materials as well as the idea of a carpenter at work.

While it seems likely that this creation involved a change of spiritual things into physical, it once again isn't a matter of making something from nothing. When one continues to read the Hebrews passage, it also is found that "things which are seen were not made

GIANTS ON THE EARTH

of things which do appear." In other words the idea presented is that the worlds weren't created from nothingness, but rather from things which can not be seen: Immaterial forces, perhaps energy or forces of which most of mankind has no inkling.

Let's see how all this applies to the Genesis account. In the first verses of the Bible, the idea of creation is conveyed by the verb bara. This Hebrew word means to create, cut down, or dispatch. The overall feel is that of working with wood (an analogy that was undoubtedly purposeful since wood also represents mankind in many Biblical passages — with the fact that Jesus was a carpenter following this logic).

The Hebrew word bara also shows that God's creation of the world wasn't the work of creating it from nothing (as is often the mistaken notion people have); it connotes crafting an object into a finished form. The ease that is conveyed in the process of creating the universe is unfortunately, also lost in the translation into English. Bara suggests light work; this is reflected in Psalms 8:3 where the writer, praying to God, says,

When I consider thy heavens, the work of thy fingers, the moon and the stars, which thou hast ordained...

Notice that this passage tells that the heavens are works of God's fingers. The implication here is that the work was done simply by moving just his fingers, with hardly any effort at all. In an age when men pride themselves in what they create — from matter at that — it isn't hard to imagine how foolish the most creative of artists or scientists of today's culture might appear to the living God with such capabilities.

Beginning

It should also be noted that what is translated into English as "the beginning" in Genesis 1 is the Hebrew word reshiyth which denotes the first in a series of things or the first or principle thing. Thus, there isn't a specific starting of the heavens and the Earth, but a statement that they were part of the beginning period before the creation story that comes in subsequent verses. In other words, "in the beginning" really is closer to being a "beginning" than just the point at which things started. It tells that God made the heavens and the Earth, but doesn't give an inkling as to when or how.

This idea is bolstered by the fact that when Hebrew writers wanted to note the actual beginning of a time, as the time of day or week when a harvest commenced for example, the word employed was most often techillah. This word connotes an opening or commencement. And this passage avoids the use of this word. Techillah wasn't the word Moses chose to tell about the beginning of the heavens and the Earth. In other works, this opening passage of the Bible isn't necessarily telling about the start of things as is often thought but rather denotes that a period took place during which that first state of being took place and during which God created the heavens and the Earth.

This may seem like hair-splitting. But it has important ramifications, because it points to the idea that other events may have taken place before or during this beginning period, perhaps even outside the realm of time and space as most people know them. "In the beginning" was a period different from the subsequent events that come afterward in the rest of the Bible and may very well span a period of time many times longer than the time man has been on the Earth.

The mind-boggling complexity of this situation is reflected in the phenomenal logic of the beginning in the Gospel of John:

In the beginning was the Word, and the Word was with God, and the Word was God.

GIANTS ON THE EARTH

The same was in the beginning with God. All things were made by him; and without him was not any thing made that was made. In him was life; and the life was the light of men.

The parallels between these two views are interesting. But what about the "beginning" used by John? Being in the Greek, it presents a good opportunity to see how the New Testament writers viewed the idea of the first verse of Genesis as well. How does the Greek word John chose for "beginning" compare to that of the Hebrew?

The word chosen was arche. As can be seen, this is the same word that "arch" comes from and indicates not simply a beginning but a chief period of time, with the idea of a ruler's span of power behind it as well. John's "In the beginning" also conveys the idea of a period of time, not the commencement or creation of things.

The word translated into English as "made" in this passage is ginomai. This word conveys the idea of causing something to become something else or to assemble something into a whole. So, here again the idea is not of God (through Jesus Christ) creating the universe from nothing but rather assembling and forming it into a whole, much as a potter might form a pot or a carpenter frame and build a house.

A similar idea of the universe was conveyed by the ancient Greeks. Their word cosmos which is often translated to mean "world" or even universe, actually suggests a creation that is fabricated from other materials, becoming polished or adorned as it is fashioned; the word doesn't suggest something created from scratch.

Only during recent times has the notion that the Genesis passage here refers to the creation of the Earth from nothing caught on among theologians.

Cosmos to Chaos

With the realization that God created the heavens and Earth almost effortlessly and that verse one and two of the first chapter of the Bible aren't connected closely in time comes another revelation when the Hebrew wording of verse 2 is explored.

In the English translation, the tiny Hebrew word waw is translated "and". In the English translation, verse two starts out as if it has been coupled to verse one: "And the Earth was without form and void..."

However, waw doesn't necessarily always mean "and." It can also mean "but." The "and" was chosen simply because the translators felt it fit well there when reading it in the context of the two verses going together.

What happens if the translators were wrong?

When you substitute "but" in the passage, a different possibility can be seen. If the first verse marks a period during which the heavens and the Earth were created, and the second verse marks a second period, then the reading of that second verse as "But the Earth was without form or void," takes on a different meaning.

This alternate reader with "but" suggests that even though God had created the heavens and the Earth in a perfect form during the previous period (as described in verse one), an event took place before verse 2 that has caused the world to become chaotic. It can then be seen that something has changed, and that while this is a beginning for the saga of mankind, there was in every likelihood a previous existence of some sort.

What came before the "in the beginning" then? Is it possible to decipher what was before the first verses of the Bible?

In truth the answers to both are there to be found. But first it is necessary to dissect this first verse a bit more.

GIANTS ON THE EARTH

In the Beginning?

If the Earth was formed earlier, then what exactly does "in the beginning" mean? In the English translation the phrase seems straightforward; it means beginning at the first. But the Hebrew again conveys a lot more than just that.

When you study books written by Bible scholars, you realize that the phrase is much more complex than it might otherwise appear. In fact almost any commentary you pick up reveals that the scholar has struggled with what the phrase means or, in the case of translators, exactly what should be conveyed. This comes about because of the original Hebrew compound word used in this phrase: be-reshith).

The noun reshith always needs a modifier in order for its actual meaning to be seen. It can mean "beginning" but often it means something more akin to "previously" in English. For example in Job 42:12,

So the Lord blessed the latter end of Job more than his beginning [reshith].

To read this as the actual beginning of Job makes no sense. It obviously isn't talking about his conception or birth (at least unless one makes one very tortured argument for such), but it is obvious from the story that reshith is referring to the beginning of the story covered in the book of Job, prior to the misfortunate that Satan brought to the ancient saint.

Another such instance of the use of reshith can be found in Proverbs 8:22, where Wisdom tells the reader,

The LORD possessed me in the beginning [reshith] of his way, before his works of old.

Proverbs chapter 8 is considered a christophany of Jesus Christ appearing in the Old Testament — Wisdom is the person of Jesus who made man in his image. That aside that if one assumes that reshith means "beginning" here, it must also be assumed that God also had a beginning. Since it is a basic premise of the Bible that the Lord has no real beginning or end but is eternal, one must therefore assume that the beginning before his works means simply before what can be seen in this age was created, not before God.

It is also important to note that reshith is not the only word for "beginning" in Hebrew. And that when a true beginning is implied (such as Psalm 102:25), a different word is employed.

What this means is that "in the beginning" in Genesis 1 can be seen to mean not in the beginning of all time and things, but rather the start of (for human beings) the current frame of history. Thus the Earth was molded and reformed at a specific time.

But formed from what?

Something from Something

Undoubtedly the Universe itself was created by God. But this does not mean that this original event was anywhere close chronologically to the current world of today (or even that time flows in the same way as it now does, for that matter). A close reading of the Bible supports this idea.

For example Hebrews 11: 3 tells,

Through faith we understand that the worlds were framed by the word of God, so that things which are seen were not made of things which do appear.

This explains that the worlds were framed not from nothing, but rather (if this negative statement "not made" is unwrapped) made of invisible things. In other words re-

GIANTS ON THE EARTH

formed from some past materials.

Looking at the Genesis 1 passage, a similar idea is represented. The Hebrew word translated as "made" is asah This word is employed for appointing or designating things. For example elsewhere the word is employed when judges are appointed, when refuge cities are designated, or when evils are cataloged. The judges, cities, and evils weren't being created. Rather they were being appointed or modified to a new task.

Likewise it can be seen that when God "made" the Heavens and the Earth, he wasn't so much creating them from scratch as he was reforming and appointing them to a new task, that of a home for the new creatures and plants which he would populate it with as well as mankind.

It's interesting that the passage also hints as to what the past world that was reformed into the modern Earth had become before this re-creation. Because the "was without form and void" can just as easily be translated from the Hebrew to read "had become without form or void." This suggests that some cataclysmic event has taken place, causing the old world to be totally wasted and uninhabitable.

It should also be noted that many scholars suggest that there may be a grand "pause" between the first clause of Genesis 1 and the second half. Thus the first half points toward the actual creation of a perfect work, with the second telling that it had later become corrupt. This reading results in this:

In the beginning God created the Heavens and the Earth.... But [eventually much later] the Earth was without form, and void.

In fact this supposition is sustained in the original Hebrew through the use of the verb hayah (was). Hebrew doesn't employ "to be" unless it is necessary to denote a changing condition. This is shown in many translations such as the King James Bible where missing verbs which have been added by translators are in italics. Thus when you read something like "the Earth was without form, and void" you can tell whether the Hebrew writer was telling the reader that the Earth simply was that way or had become that way.

And if you look at a translation that conforms to these conventions, you'll discover that this is taking place in this passage with the verb hayah (was). In Genesis 1:2 the first "was" is ordinary type, meaning that it has come or has recently been transformed into a void, formlessness. The shows that it wasn't created this way, but rather than something terrible transformed it into this condition, and one that God was not satisfied with and, thankfully, would soon transform into the current Earth.

This is not the only argument for this, however. Because the normal order for the Hebrew sentence is conjunction, verb, subject object. This pattern is altered to given more power to a fact or otherwise make a point to the reader.

And this re-ordering of words to create such emphasis can be found in Genesis 1:2 to mean — "had become" (for those familiar with languages, this is given in the pluperfect form).

Thus it is apparent that the original creation which had been perfect had become desolate and void.

Why was the Earth this way? In fact there are also clues in this passage that help answer this question as well.

The Hebrew word tohuw is translated as "without form." This word appears elsewhere in the Bible and takes on some finer associations and meanings including formlessness,

GIANTS ON THE EARTH

confusion, unreality, and emptiness. It also is associated with the unreal as with an idol as well as wasteland and solitary wilderness. In its adverb form, tohuw means "wastefully" or "in vain" (points that will become important later in this book).

Thus while the word used here means primarily a wasteland, there are undercurrents and hints of idolatry, pride, and sin through the choice of this word. This is further reinforced by the "and void" phrase.

The Hebrew word bohuw is generally employed throughout the Bible in connection with the desolation of a city or nation. It also connotes an undercurrent of judgment from God (as in Isaiah 34:11 where the Lord's judgment results in the desolation).

Thus when the Earth was "void" (bohuw) it was desolate. That this is a judgment from God is further bolstered by the idea that darkness is upon the face of the Earth, since this is associated with evil in the Bible while God is associated with light.

Thus the "without form, and void" suggests not just physical desolation but spiritual a well, a point that will become very important as the story of ancient history is revealed.

Darkness Upon the Face of the Earth

The Hebrew word, choshek, employed for darkness in this passage also offers clues. Because this word not only means the absence of light, but rather a word that denotes an unnatural darkness (such as was seen during the plague of darkness which fell upon Egypt in Exodus 10:21). This argues that the darkness was more than the simple absence of light, or simply nighttime (the Hebrew word layilah).

"The deep" (tehom) further reinforces this feeling that things are under judgment. While this word is often associated with the sea or deep water, it has other shades of meaning as well, including the abyss and the grave. Thus tehom is employed in Genesis 7:11 where it is translated as "the great waters" of Noah's Flood and in Psalm 36:6 as "a great deep" associated with the Lord's judgment.

The deep does refer to the ocean. But it also is symbolic of a judgment against wrong doing and bolsters the overall feel that things are not right in creation as the opening passage of Genesis unfolds.

Furthermore the Greek equivalent of this word forms the "abyss" associated with the punishment reserved for Satan, the Great Serpent, and the Dragon — a point that will take on more importance throughout this book. In the ancient Greek version of the Old Testament, Jewish translators substituted the word abussos for the deep. This Greek word becomes "abyss" in English, a word often signifying Hades or Hell. Abussos was also the word John used in Revelation (9:11, 11:7, 17:8 and 20:1-3) for the final punishment and resting place for Satan and the evil Dragon.

It is not unreasonable, then, to see "the deep" in Genesis signifying something greater than simply deep water.

Let There Be Light

The "Let there be light" phrase in the opening chapter of Genesis does not appear to be a creative act when one studies the Hebrew words and their usage here. Instead, the Hebrew words suggest that the light was made to appear or made visible (most likely this is written from the viewpoint of someone on Earth). This fits well with the scientific ideas of today; the universe of stars, sun and moon were thus, created during the "in the beginning" period but not visible on the Earth, due to the darkness that apparently enveloped it.

GIANTS ON THE EARTH

This also explains why the Earth could be in existence during a long span of time without there being days and nights on its surface. For some reason (a thick cloud cover, perhaps) daylight didn't reach the surface of the planet. This, in turn, suggests that something evil might very well have changed the planet for the worse, if the darkness/evil idea is stretched just a bit.

Only when God was preparing to create man and living organisms on the face of the planet did he make days and nights appear on its surface. Time didn't start with the first day on Earth; but the separation of day and night on the surface of the planet made it possible to tell time as the first days started rolling around, marking God's creation of life on the planet.

There may be greater significance to these first days, however, because Moses employed the word combination that emphasizes the "to be" of the situation. In other words, this first day on Earth "had become" the first day. The evening and morning "were" the first day, to be followed by six more with very specific creations and a first Sabbath.

It should also be noted that the Hebrew word yom is employed in the first chapter of Genesis to mark each day in the account. As such, it can only be read to mean a 24-hour period. Had God aimed to convey a geological age, Moses undoubtedly would have employed the word 'olam which means an age or period of unspecified time.

While yom can be used to signify a longer period of time in a prophetic sense, it isn't utilized in this manner in Genesis and Biblical writers employing it to mean anything other than a day take pains to make note of the fact so there is no confusion. Likewise, when yom is employed with a specific number, it is always signifying a 24-hour period. It would appear, then, that Moses (arguably writing under the inspiration of God) meant these periods of time to be interpreted as normal, 24-hour days, not epochs of time.

Furthermore, if these days were geological ages (as some suggest in an effort to get Evolution to dovetail with Genesis), there is an immediate problem, because then there are days that must last so long one side of the planet is baked while nights last for thousands, if not millions, of years.

Life which is for the most part interdependent on other life forms for its continued existence would quickly vanish under such conditions. Plants that need to be pollinated being created thousands or millions of years before bees come onto the scene, for example, is not a viable model. Additionally, Adam and Eve would have to live for thousands, if not millions, of years (through the seventh day) before they could be cast out of the Garden of Eden. Since Adam dies at an age of 930 years (in Genesis 5:5), it's impossible to bend the truth to fit the need of Evolution.

While one might do mental gymnastics in an effort to somehow explain all this away, it makes more sense to simply assume that Moses penned the words the way the events actually happened. There is no need to "read into" the passage to make it work. All that is necessary is to believe in a God powerful enough to work miracles.

Furthermore, this reading of the past is not disproven by fossil records or the like. Because it's not only possible but almost a certainty that pre-historic, pre-Adamic life was on Earth before the Genesis 1:2 reforming of an Earth that had become formless and void. If anything, fossils buttress this reading of the Genesis account with its re-creation of the creatures that now inhabit it and the vanishing of vast hordes of creatures such as the dinosaurs.

GIANTS ON THE EARTH

Finally, this explanation fits perfectly with Biblical history which begins about 6,000 years ago — precisely when Adam and Eve would have been created if one figures back from now through the ages of various characters listed in the genealogies of the Bible. This is easily explained if mankind were created at that point. It is nearly impossible to explain if one assumes that mankind had evolved and then, suddenly, abruptly, and from one place, develops writing, metallurgy, and so forth.

As historian and Jewish scholar Noson Weisz put it:

About six thousand years ago, seemingly out of nowhere there is a record of a remarkable change in this stable Stone Age pattern of human remains in one particular area of the planet, Mesopotamia. Overnight in terms of historic time, we have the development of sophisticated architecture, advanced pottery, organized agriculture, the rise of major population centers akin to cities, the appearance of metallic weapons and ornaments, the development of writing and records, the appearance of sophisticated political structures and empires, traces of complex religions and the ceremonies associated with them.

The archeological record shows the spread of these trappings of advanced civilization from this one spot to the rest of the world in gradual stages. Thus the great leap forward was restricted to a single location and came out of nowhere.

This sudden explosion of knowledge and ability makes no sense — unless we're looking at a new creature that has suddenly come onto the scene. A creature of unbelievable intelligence, who is able to make profound leaps in technology. Then the line of history from 6,000 years ago to today makes perfect sense.

Marduk

It is interesting to see how other cultures that lacked the Hebrew technique of double-checking and carefully copying ancient stories have also had renditions of the same Genesis creation, warped, altered, and distorted through verbal changes distortions. While these often take outlandish forms on their face, careful examination reveals that they seem to have come from the same origins as those of the Bible.

A good example of this is the Babylonian story of creation. In this story a new world is created from a chaotic ancient time. The God of Order, Marduk, battles with the powerful Goddess of Chaos, Tiamat. During their battle to the death, Marduk seizes the goddess Tiamat in a giant net and then skewers her with his sword, splitting her body into two halves.

One half of the goddess becomes Heaven and the other an abyss of water which the Earth is hung upon.

Now notice: The goddess is associated with chaos and the abyss. Thus the god of order reforms her into a new, more ordered Earth. Not only that; her name, "Tiamat" is believed by many scholars to be related to the Hebrew word tohuw — translated "without form." Likewise again the abyss/deep is associated not just with water but also judgment and punishment.

There are also links between the Biblical view that associates the abyss with Satan's punishment. In some ancient Babylonian tablets Tiamat is referred to as "the Great Serpent."

Assyrian traditions have Tiamat dwelling in the sea with a kindred demon, Bahu, a being that brings disorder. What is interesting is that the demon's name is almost cer-

GIANTS ON THE EARTH

tainly related to the Hebrew word bohu found in Genesis 1:2. Thus these ancient myths appear to be reflections of an original story only hinted at by the first chapter of Genesis, even though the Hebrew passage far antedates the much later cuneiform texts in which the Assyrian and Babylonian stories have been found.

Likewise other ancient myths display the same sort of stories which occur over and over, with various deities having components or even the form of a serpent. The oldest deities of the Sumerians were all serpents or dragons of one sort or another with the serpent of the subterranean waters (again notice the abyss/deep connotations) being called Zu (and having an almost direct link to the Hebrew "Leviathan," a dragon-like creature). Again and again stories appear of a serpent representing primordial chaos from which an ordered world is formed.

In the Sumerian myths, the great serpent Zu, a universal watery chaos which is the originator of all life, is divided to become twin serpents. One becomes Anzu which lives in the constellation Orion, while the other half becomes his mate, Ki the Queen of the abyss. Again there's the theme of a powerful being in Heaven, and a dragon that is associated with the Abyss.

Perhaps equally thought-provoking is the fact that the Bible seems to be hinting at the same story in other passages. For example Amos 5: 7-9 reads:

Ye who turn judgment to wormwood, and leave off righteousness in the earth, seek him that maketh the seven stars and Orion, and turneth the shadow of death into the morning, and maketh the day dark with night: that calleth for the waters of the sea, and poureth them out upon the face of the earth: The LORD is his name: That strengtheneth the spoiled against the strong, so that the spoiled shall come against the fortress

Notice that the Lord is associated with the creation of Orion, that darkness, death, and punishment are also covered as well as the "waters of the sea" which we've seen can be associated with the Abyss. This passage suggests that those hearing it might have been familiar with stories not recorded in the Bible, and which might have become part of the distorted tales of Marduk and Tiamat

Likewise there are hints of this story in Job (which many consider to be one of the oldest books of the Bible). In Job 9: 9-10,

[The Lord] which alone spreadeth out the heavens, and treadeth upon the waves of the sea. Which maketh Arcturus, Orion, and Pleiades, and the chambers of the south. Which doeth great things past finding out; yea, and wonders without number.

Although one might suggest that this conjunction of the sea and Orion is happenstance, it actually happens several times in Job suggesting there's more to this. In Job 38: 5-31 the Lord speaks to Job about the creation of the Earth. Notice that the depths of the sea, light and darkness, as well as Orion are again part of the associations here. The Lord spoke:

Where wast thou when I laid the foundations of the earth? declare, if thou hast understanding. Who hath laid the measures thereof, if thou knowest? or who hath stretched the line upon it? Whereupon are the foundations thereof fastened? or who laid the corner stone thereof; when the morning stars sang together, and all the sons of God shouted for joy?

Or who shut up the sea with doors, when it brake forth, as if it had issued out of the womb? When I made the cloud the garment thereof, and thick darkness a swaddlingband

GIANTS ON THE EARTH

for it, and brake up for it my decreed place, and set bars and doors, and said, Hitherto shalt thou come, but no further: and here shall thy proud waves be stayed?

Hast thou commanded the morning since thy days; and caused the dayspring to know his place; that it might take hold of the ends of the earth, that the wicked might be shaken out of it? It is turned as clay to the seal; and they stand as a garment. And from the wicked their light is withholden, and the high arm shall be broken.

Hast thou entered into the springs of the sea? or hast thou walked in the search of the depth? Have the gates of death been opened unto thee? or hast thou seen the doors of the shadow of death?

Hast thou perceived the breadth of the earth? declare if thou knowest it all. Where is the way where light dwelleth? and as for darkness, where is the place thereof, That thou shouldest take it to the bound thereof, and that thou shouldest know the paths to the house thereof?

Knowest thou it, because thou wast then born? or because the number of thy days is great?

Hast thou entered into the treasures of the snow? or hast thou seen the treasures of the hail, which I have reserved against the time of trouble, against the day of battle and war?

By what way is the light parted, which scattereth the east wind upon the earth? Who hath divided a watercourse for the overflowing of waters, or a way for the lightning of thunder; to cause it to rain on the earth, where no man is; on the wilderness, wherein there is no man; to satisfy the desolate and waste ground; and to cause the bud of the tender herb to spring forth?

Hath the rain a father? or who hath begotten the drops of dew? Out of whose womb came the ice? and the hoary frost of heaven, who hath gendered it?

The waters are hid as with a stone, and the face of the deep is frozen. Canst thou bind the sweet influences of Pleiades, or loose the bands of Orion?

As one reads these passages it becomes apparent that the Bible is both hinting at the stories that came to be myths in other religions and also that it's perhaps mocking them. This also suggests that ancient man knew these stories which in the case of these other cultures was undoubtedly altered and distorted over time to become the mythology seen today.

The trick is sorting out the truth from the distortions. This is hard but not totally impossible to do as well be demonstrated later in this book.

In the meantime it is important to note that these common but lost stories manifest themselves in many different and far removed cultures. For example myths regarding dragons and deities that have components of dragons can be seen in very different and separated cultures all around the world from China to Central and South America; from Celtic peoples in Europe to the ancient Egyptians and Babylonians.

Suffice to say for now that the Hebrew story of creation can not be viewed as an isolated account known only to the ancient Jews. Rather it a story that has been mimicked and copied by very many other cultures, some of which could not have seen the Hebrew writings before developing their own versions of the basic story (and which were likewise not available to Jewish writers). That stories with similar elements sprang up in very different cultures around the world suggests that these stories have a common origin, with the Biblical account arguably the most accurate due to the unique pains that

GIANTS ON THE EARTH

were taken in keeping the stories true to the original.

As we'll see in a moment, the story as well as the clues given by other cultural versions of it, are key to understanding the truth about the ancient past as well as events that are being lied about and hidden today.

Even writers such as Zechariah Sitchin and others assume that the myths precede the Bible, when all historic evidence suggest that mythology was, and is, a distortion of the truth of the scripture!

The Forming of the Current Earth

Through a careful study of the first few verses of Genesis, several things become apparent, then. First, the universe could be very, very old. A lot could have happened during that time for the creation of the human race from the time of Adam until today — roughly 6,000 years.

It is also important to note that when the Bible refers to the "Earth," it is referring to the reformed Earth mankind presently inhabits, not the previous body that became without form or void. This must be kept in mind, otherwise one gets into some weird theology with verses like Romans 5:12:

Wherefore, as by one man sin entered into the world, and death by sin.

This "world" of course is today's present world, not its pre-existent form. To read it otherwise would have Adam's sin bringing death to the previous age — before he sinned. Obviously this can not be correct and therefore it is important to keep in mind that basically the reformed Earth is a new world in the sight of God.

Thus the high point of the current, early history was the creation of mankind in a perfect, sinless state. Genesis 1: 25-26 proclaims:

And God made the beast of the earth after his kind, and cattle after their kind, and every thing that creepeth upon the earth after his kind: and God saw that it was good. And God said, Let us make man in our image, after our likeness: and let them have dominion over the fish of the sea, and over the fowl of the air, and over the cattle, and over all the earth, and over every creeping thing that creepeth upon the earth.

Later, in Genesis 5:1, the fact that man has been created in the image of God is again emphasized:

This is the book of the generations of Adam, on the day the Lord created mankind, in the likeness of the Lord He made him.

The Hebrew word for "image" in all these passages is tzelem, a word derived from the word tzel, meaning "shadow" or "reflection." The word "likeness" in these verses is demus; this word is derived from domeh, meaning "similar." Human beings are not "little gods" or duplicates of a God that has no body nor form. But they are similar in their mastery of the spiritual and physical dimensions of the Maker.

This is an important point, as will later be detailed in this book. Mankind was made in the image of God. This begs the question of whether there are beings that are not created in God's image, or if that image can be defaced, profaned, or genetically altered! The terrifying answer to both these questions appears to be "yes." And the ramifications imperil modern man in many ways, making it essential that you learn to distinguish between the lies you have been taught and the truth that will be presented throughout this book.

But before you see how this defacement of God's image has and is taking place, you

GIANTS ON THE EARTH

must see why it comes about and who is behind it. To do that it is necessary to travel into the distant past, using the key secrets and hidden clues that will serve as stepping stones to that past.

So it is time for you to begin that journey to see just what came before the creation of this present Earth, what most likely lead to the "without form and void" state that resulted, and how that earlier, condemned age has invaded the present time and is, in fact, behind many of the falsehoods that have concealed the truth from you.

AFRICA
Chad's Giants

In 1936, two French archaeologists, Lebeuf and Griaule, led an expedition to Chad in North Central Africa. As they crossed the plains they saw some areas covered with small mounds. They also found large numbers of these mounds around Fort Lamy and Goulfeil. Deciding to investigate, they dug up several egg-shaped funeral jars that contained the remains of a gigantic race, along with pieces of their jewelry and their works of art.1 These giants, according to the natives, were called the Saos.

Scholars who traced their history say they came from Kheiber, located north of Mecca, to Bilma, which is situated about three hundred miles north of Lake Chad. A people with a "well-developed religion and culture," they grew in numbers and founded communities at Fort Lamy, Mahaya, Midigue, and Goulfeil. They lived in peace in their new land until the close of the ninth century when the Moslems made wars against them, intending to force their accep-tance of the Islamic faith. The Saos giants who converted to the faith lived to become servants of the Arabs. But those who steadfastly refused to convert were eventually wiped out. By the end of the sixteenth century not many Saos remained. (See Jericho's Giants; also see Curigueres; Ifrikish ibn Kais; Sudan's Giants; Watusi Giants; Zanzibar's Giants)

Moroccan Find

At Agadir in Morocco, reports Peter Kolosimo, the French captain Lafanechere "discovered a complete arsenal of hunting weapons including five hundred double-edged axes weighing seventeen and a half pounds, i.e. twenty times as heavy as would be convenient for modern man. Apart from the question of weight, to handle the axe at all one would need to have hands of a size appropriate to a giant with a stature of at least 13 feet."2 (See Australian Giants; La Tene; South American Giants)

Sudan's Giants

A tribe of giants survives in the Sudan, but apparently little has been written about them. In his Inside Africa, John Gunther de-scribes them as a Nilotic peoples who "have spread their virile blood far afield, as witness the Masai in Kenya and the giant Watutsi3 in Ruanda-Urundi, who are cousins to the Hamitic Sudanese."4 An example of their gigantic but very slender stature may be seen in Manute Bol, the seven-foot-seven-inch pro basketball giant, who hails from this region. Slim as he still looks, Bol has put on quite a bit of weight since his rookie year in the NBA. One sports writer jokingly wrote that he has now "added enough poundage to require at least two pinstripes on his pajamas."

GIANTS ON THE EARTH

Bol and his tall Sudanese kin may have the height of giants, but with such extremely slender builds they could hardly be reckoned among our other mighty men. (See Kreen Akrores; Watusi Giants; also see Chad's Giants; Curigueres; Ifrikish ibn Kais; Zanzibar's Giants)

Watusi Giants

Practically everyone has seen on film or at least heard about the very tall Watusi, who are famous for their dancing. For those who may never have seen them, Glenn D. Kittler offers the following superbly drawn word-picture: "For the most colorful and exciting dancing, you must go to Ruanda-Urundi... east of the Congo. Here the ruling tribe is the Watusi, the tallest people in the world. It has been said that these giants are born six feet tall, and when you walk among them you can believe it. Men towering seven or eight feet are a common sight. Women gain height by having their heads bound into conical shape in infancy, then training their thick hair to grow straight up to add a few inches. Beholding these lean, dignified, soft-spoken giants is quite overwhelming--and they know it.

"When they start dancing," continues Kittler, "the Watusi discard their usual reserve and become frenzied.... Twisting, bending, squirming, they leap into the air, breaking high-jump records with-out missing a beat. They carry spears, and when one jumper soars especially high the others throw down their spears in defeat. But the dance goes on. Ankle bracelets heavy with bells match the earth-trembling thunder of twenty royal drummers. First ten men dance, then fifty, then two hundred, their speed increasing with their number as they fly through intricate routines with thrilling precision and flair."[5]

The Watusi are black, but they are not Negroes. The spectacularly tall, slender, and statuesque tribesmen are a proud Hamitic or Nilotic people who migrated to Ruanda-Urundi country over four centuries ago. Many grow to heights of seven feet or more. John Gunther, who spent some time in Ruanda gathering material for his book, Inside Africa, found many things about the country fascinating, but what makes it the most distinctive, he writes, is the Watutsi[6] giants, who, because of their size, rule over the medium-size Bantu people and the Pygmies. "Outside the hotel in Astrida, next to a woman cupping a child's head to her naked breast," he recalls, "we ran into the tallest man I have seen except in a circus. He made the American playwright Robert E. Sherwood, who is six foot seven, look like a dwarf. He must have been at least seven and a half feet tall."[7]

Anthropologists are at a loss to explain the Watusi's tallness. One possible explanation is that they are offspring of the giants who fled before Joshua's legions and escaped to Africa (see Jericho's Giants), but, after many centuries of interbreeding with the aborigines, have been greatly reduced in bulk and might. "They do not look strong," adds Gunther, "and give the impression of being much inbred. They have small heads for their height, slim wrists, and delicate long thin arms."[8]

True, because of their great height, the Watusi can accomplish certain feats, like clearing a bar in the running high jump at more then eight feet, or rearing back and throwing a spear to an unbelievable distance. But they exhibit nowhere near enough strength to be reckoned among the other mighty men in this book. (See Kreen Akrores; Sudan's Giants; also see Chad's Giants; Curigueres; Ifrikish ibn Kais; Zanzibar's Giants)

GIANTS ON THE EARTH

Zanzibar's Giants

In recounting his travels, Marco Polo tells of running into a gigantic people in Zanzibar. Concerning them, he wrote:

"Zanzibar is situated off the coast of Tanganyika. Nearly 53 miles long and 24 miles wide, it is the largest coral island on the African coast.... Numerous bays, reefs, and islets are found along the western coast, while the eastern side is much more regular.

"Zanzibar is a very large and important island. It has a 2,000-mile coastline. All the people are idolaters, they have a king and a language of their own and pay tribute to no one. The men are large and fat, although they are not tall in proportion to their bulk. They are strong limbed and as hefty as giants. They are so strong that they can carry as many as four ordinary men. This is not altogether surprising because while they can carry as many as four men, they eat enough for five. They are quite black and go about completely naked but for a loincloth. Their hair is so curly that they can only comb it when it is wet. They have wide mouths and turned-up noses. . . .

"The natives live on dates, rice, meat and milk. They have grape wine but they also make an excellent wine from rice, sugar and spices. There is a great deal of trade on the island and ships arrive laden with every kind of cargo to be sold. The merchants take away other goods, in particular ivory from the elephant tusks. Because of the whales there is a lot of ambergris.

"The men on the island are excellent fighters and very courageous in battle. They are not afraid of death. Because there are no horses they use camels and elephants in war. They build little turrets on the elephants' backs which they cover carefully with the skin of wild animals. Between sixteen and twenty men get into these turrets from which they fight with lances, swords and pikes. Very bloody battles are fought on elephants. The only arms are leather shields, lances and swords, but the men can be cruelly killed. When the elephants have to charge, they are given as much wine and other drink as they want which makes them more aggressive and therefore more courageous in battle.

"Apart from the men, the animals and produce of Zanzibar, there is nothing more to discuss so we shall move on to the great province of Abyssinia."9 (See Chad's Giants; Curigueres; Ifrikish ibn Kais; Sudan's Giants; Watusi)

References

1 Lee, Giants: The Pictorial History, p. 44.
2 Peter Kolosimo, Timeless Earth (New Hyde Park, NY: University Books, 1968), p. 32.
3 A variant spelling of Watusi.
4 John Gunther, Inside Africa (New York: Harper & Bros., 1955), p. 229.
5 Glenn D. Kittler, Let's Travel in the Congo (Chicago: The Children's Press, 1961), p. 30.
6 A variant spelling.
7 Gunther, Inside Africa, p. 685.
8 Ibid., p. 686.
9 The Travels of Marco Polo (New York: Facts on File Publications, 1984), pp. 175-176.

GIANTS ON THE EARTH

Artist's rendering of the Grand Canyon Giants

NORTH AMERICA
Giants in Americas - Death Valley, California - Cavern Temple of Giants

Is there proof that giants once lived and raised families in North America? Stories and newspaper accounts attest to amazing discoveries of huge elaborate caves and mines, gold spears and polished granite inscribed with mystical symbols. Witnesses have reported their discoveries to the Smithsonian Institute and have been promised compensation. Yet, the Smithsonian, archaeologists and other scientists are silent as to the discoveries and have hidden all evidence that is contrary to Darwinian theory of evolution.

The following are actual accounts of giants in North America.

"Atlantis in the Colorado River Desert" - 1947 Nevada news: Near the Nevada - California - Arizona border area, 32 caves within a 180 square mile area were discovered to hold the remains of ancient, strangely costumed 8 -9 foot giants. They had been laid to rest wearing the skins of unknown animals similar to sheepskins fashioned into jackets with pants described as "prehistoric Zoot- suits". The same burial place had been found 10 - 15 years earlier by another man who made a deal with the Smithsonian. The evidence of his find was stolen and covered up by Darwinian scientists.

Dr. F. Bruce Russell had come to Death Valley from the east coast. He had taken up mining in the west for the sake of his health and was exploring across the Colorado River into Arizona. What he found he described as the burial place of a tribal hierarchy within the ritual hall of an ancient people. He felt that some unknown catastrophe had driven

GIANTS ON THE EARTH

them into these caves. All of the implements of their civilization were there, including household utensils and stoves. Dr. Russell reported seeing hieroglyphics chiseled on carefully polished granite within what appeared to be a cavern temple. Another cave led to their sacred hall which contained carvings of ritual devices and markings similar to those of the Masonic Order. A long tunnel from this temple led to a room where, Hill said, "Well-preserved remains of dinosaurs, saber-toothed tigers, imperial elephants, and other extinct beasts were paired off in niches as if on display."

Ten to fifteen years earlier the caves had been seen by another miner who had fallen from the bottom of a mineshaft. In his book, "Death Valley Men", Bourke Lee related a conversation among residents of Death Valley concerning the local Paiute Native American legends of an underground city at Wingate Pass. After falling through the ceiling of an unknown tunnel, the miner had followed it 20 miles north of the Panamint Mountains to discover a huge ancient underground city. He saw arching stone vaults with huge stone doors and a polished round table in the center of their council chamber which had once been lit by ingenious lights fueled by subterranean gases. Leaning against the walls were their tall gold spears. He said that the designs on their thick golden armbands resembled the work of the Egyptians. The tunnel ended at an exit overlooking Furnace Creek Ranch in California's Imperial Valley. He could see from there that the valley had once been underwater. The tunnel entrance had been a dock or a quay located halfway up the side of the mountain. A deal was made with the Smithsonian museum for the find, but the miner was betrayed by his partner. The evidence was stolen and the entrance concealed. In a 1940 a mining journal, another find was reported of much worked gold found in an 8 mile long cave near San Bernadino.

University of Arizona professor Vine Deloria, himself a Native American, made a similar accusation against the Smithsonian for covering up the remains found within the burial mounds of the Moundbuilder civilization. Surviving diaries from before the time Darwin attest to these discoveries. The Moundbuilders were a different civilization than that of the Indians, they said. The mounds contained the remains of hundreds of giants along with the bones of giant mastodons. In Cincinnati, Ohio the giant bones were found with large shields, swords, and engraved stone tablets. In Kentucky and Tennessee the bones of "powerful men of towering stature" were excavated. One of these 7 foot men was buried with an engraved copper plate beneath his head. A woman was also found. She was wearing a silver girdle with letters written on it. The Detroit Free Press reported in 1884 the discovery in Gartersville, Mississippi of the remains of a giant with waist-length jet-black hair. He was wearing a copper crown. With him in his timber burial vault were his children who wore garments decorated with bone beads. The tomb was covered with large flagstones engraved with inscriptions.

In Cayuga, Niagra there is a place called "The Cemetary of the Giants" which was discovered in 1880. Those giants were 9 feet tall and appear to have died violent deaths. Their axes were found with them. Giant bones were also unearthed from a rock fissure on Lake Erie Island. In some of the finds of giant bones, the bones lay in confusion as if left on a battlefield. The Smithsonian does display some artifacts of the Moundbuilders found with the bones of the giants - shell discs and carved stone beads. Many of the bones turned to powdery ash within a short time of being exposed to the air. The Smithsonian has been reluctant to test some less fragile finds. The late Vine Deloria said

GIANTS ON THE EARTH

that it is because they "Mightent find a really early date for the bones" and that it would be distressing - distressing to their Darwinian time-line.

By Mary Alice Bennett

Used with permission of Ufodigest.com

The Karankawa

The Karankawa Indian tribes played a pivotal part in early Texas history. The meaning of Karankawa is a bit misleading. The name Karankawa was the popular naming for various groups of Native Americans. The reason was because they all had a common dialect and culture. Those people were the Capoques (Coaques, Cocos), Kohanis, Kopanes (Copanes), and Karankawa (Carancaquacas) bands. They inhabited the Gulf Coast of Texas from Galveston Bay southwestward to Corpus Christi Bay. Their language, of which only about a hundred words are preserved, is also called Karankawa and is believed to have been related to the Coahuiltecan, but researchers cannot be certain as so little is known of languages in this region. The significance of the name Karankawa is not known, but it is generally held to mean "dog-lovers" or "dog-raisers." That rendering seems creditable, since the Karankawas had dogs that were a fox or coyote-like species. A nomadic-type culture existed and they seasonally migrated between the mainland and the barrier islands.

They were living that nomadic existence when Spaniards, lead by Alvarez de Piñeda, probed the coast in 1519. Governor Francisco de Garay of Jamaica had commissioned him to explore the Gulf Coast from Florida to Veracruz.

The heavily tattooed, pierced, and painted nomadic Karankawa tribe, held the islands for the most part in south Texas. The territory they held was from the west end of Galveston Island down the coast to the mouth of the Rio Grande perhaps, and inland about 25-65 miles depending on the region. Cannibalistic, superb hunters, fisherman, warriors and longbow archery experts, they were a powerful enemy to anyone wishing to take their prime hunting grounds away.

The impression they left on those that wrote of encounters with the tribes were monumental. The men were strikingly tall, described to be between six and almost seven feet. They were tattooed and wore shell ornaments and many greased themselves down with shark liver oil to ward off mosquitoes and other biting insects.

The true origins of this tribe of peoples is unknown to date. Some believed the Karankawa are related to a tribe of "giants Indians" located off the coast of California at the time. This is due to their strikingly tall appearance.

Still others are of the opinion they're related to an aborigine people from the Big Bend region thousands of years ago, linking them to the "Abilene Man," the most ancient known type of human in Texas. Most hold though, that the Karankawa were in relation with the Carib Tribes of the West Indies. The findings are grounded on the fact that both tribes had barkless dogs, on body sizes and on the fact that both are reputed to have participated in cannibalistic rituals. The belief is widely held they emigrated to the Florida peninsula, and when persecuted by other native tribes, struck out hugging the coast and reaching other lands, perhaps Louisiana or the extreme eastern Texas Coast, and likewise, driven from there till they reached the mostly uninhabited coast of Texas. The Karankawas, Coahuiltecan, Tonkawa, and the East Texas Caddoan peoples all had many

GIANTS ON THE EARTH

things in common. They (Karankawas) were known to be the arch enemy of the Comanches.

The Indian Tribes that lived along the Texas Coast from Galveston Island to a location southward far past Corpus Christi, Texas endured much hardship from the elements. The bays, back bays, lagoons and bayous along the Texas Coast, were the tribal hunting and harvesting grounds. The shallow waters in the bays allowed them to wade out into the deep pools with lances or bows and arrows, to spear fish as the older men, women and children harvested the waters for blue and stone crabs, oysters, mussels, sea turtles, shellfish, and other eatable crustaceans. There are accounts that some Karankawas were seen in Colorado County at Eagle Lake, close to 100 miles from the coastline, but no evidence shows they made permanent camps there.

A few of their campsites have been discovered in recent years, giving us better clues on daily life and activities. Disease, 'land acquisitions", troubles with the newcomers to the land, wars, and general genocide condemned them to extinction before 1860 arrived.

It is now known that they wintered around the coastal bays, eating oysters, clams, shellfish, Black Drum, Redfish, Sea Trout and the other abundant species of fish. During the summer months, and hot weather the oysters, clams and other shellfish are not safe to eat, and the fish make their yearly migration out the pass, which in turn would send the tribal bands migrating further inland as well. Undoubtedly summer tropical storms and hurricanes would have a impact on this decision to move further inland as well.

They would traverse the bays in dugouts and lived in round thatch huts. Some of the campsites show a population of several hundred. The discarded clam and oyster shells would make huge mounds around this camp site. Their most prized hunting tool was the long bow, some well over six foot long and arrow shafts as long as three foot, making it easier to spot and retrieve them from the shallow waters. Their major inland game was the deer and American Bison, as the many discarded remains of these animals has been found at these camp sites. They also harvested local roots, berries and nuts.

In 1768, a Spanish Padre gave detail to their ritual flesh eating ceremonies. The "savages" would lash a captive to a stake and then, dancing around the sacrifice, they would dart in, slice off a piece of flesh with a sharp blade, then roast it in front of the victim, in an already prepared campfire. Then they would devour it, as the victim watched in horror at consumption of himself, before his very eyes.

The Giants of Conneaut

WHEN the first European settlers came to North America they were not shy about digging up the graves of their Indian predecessors on the continent. As they generally found no great wealth in these burials, the motivation for their digging was probably mostly curiosity and a need to level their farmland. As the new Americans spread westward, into the states of New York and Pennsylvania, the peculiarity of the grave contents and the size of the tumuli thrown up over them increased. In the years following the conclusion of the Revolutionary war, the westward moving pioneers became less and less sure that the strange items they were finding preserved in the caves and artificial mounds of the west actually came from the Indians. Certainly, they rationalized, such huge and carefully designed earthworks could not have been built by the scanty Indian

GIANTS ON THE EARTH

population they were familiar with in the lands between the Great Lakes and the southern tributaries of the Ohio river.

In 1798 the first permanent settlers from the east arrived in the Western Reserve of Ohio. They began to clear the forests along the southern shore of Lake Erie, and in the process found numerous ancient earthen structures and almost everywhere the finely made spear points and other artifacts of a long forgotten and once populous native society, a people obviously quite different from the Massasauga Indians then living in that country. A generation before the first immigrant explorers of western Pennsylvania and southern Ohio had made similar discoveries -- the extensive earthworks of Circleville and Marietta Ohio were already well publicized by the time that settler Aaron Wright and his companions began to stake out their new homes along Conneaut Creek, in what would become Ashtabula Co., Ohio.

The Discoveries of Aaron Wright in 1800

Perhaps it was because he was a single young man with plenty of energy, or perhaps it was because his choice for a homestead included a large "mound-builder" burial ground -- whatever the reasons may have been, Aaron Wright has gone down in the history books as the discoverer of the "Conneaut Giants," the unusually large-boned ancient inhabitants of Ashtabula Co., Ohio. In an 1844 account, writer Harvey Nettleton reported that this "ancient burying grounds" of "about four acres" was situated in what soon became the village of New Salem (later renamed Conneaut), "extending northward from the bank of the creek... to Main street, in an oblong square" tract that "appeared to have been accurately surveyed into lots, running from the north to the south." Nettleton also said that the ancient "graves were distinguished by slight depressions in the surface of the earth disposed in straight rows, with the intervening spaces, or alleys, cover[ing] the whole area... estimated to contain from two to three thousand graves. These depressions, on a thorough examination made by Esq. Aaron Wright, as early as 1800, were found invariably to contain human bones, blackened with time, which on exposure to the air soon crumbled to dust."

The prehistoric cemetery on Aaron's Wright's land was remarkable enough, just in its size and the configuration of the graves -- but it was what was in those graves and in the adjacent burial mounds that captured Nettleton's attention:

The mounds that were situated in the eastern part of what is now the village of Conneaut and the extensive burying ground near the Presbyterian Church, appear to have had no connection with the burying places of the Indians. They doubtless refer to a more remote period and are the relics of an extinct race, of whom the Indians had no knowledge. These mounds were of comparatively small size, and of the same general character of those that are widely scattered over the country. What is most remarkable concerning them is that among the quantity of human bones they contain, there are found specimens belonging to men of large stature, and who must have been nearly allied to a race of giants. Skulls were taken from these mounds, the cavities of which were of sufficient capacity to admit the head of an ordinary man, and jaw-bones that might be fitted on over the face with equal facility. The bones of the arms and lower limbs were of the same proportions, exhibiting ocular proof of the degeneracy of the human race since the period in which these men occupied the soil which we now inhabit.

GIANTS ON THE EARTH

Circleville, Ohio antiquarian Caleb Atwater was the known first person to comment upon the earthworks at Conneaut (then New Salem) in a published text. In his 1820 report, Description of the Antiquities Discovered in the State of Ohio... Atwater describes the "work at Salem... on a hill near Coneaught river... having two parallel circular walls, and a ditch between them." Atwater says practically nothing about the burial mounds in the vicinity of this pre-Columbian fort "on a hill," but he does provide the following information on page 125 of his report: "My informant says, within this work are sometimes found skeletons of a people of small stature, which, if true, sufficiently identifies it to have belonged to that race of men who erected our tumuli." Thus, it was Caleb Atwater's opinion that the builders of the ancient mounds were a "people of small stature," and that reports of larger skeletons uncovered among their ruins were the exception, not the rule. To the above summary of Atwater's investigations it might also be added that many of the earthworks he described he never saw himself, relying upon information supplied by untrained observers living in the vicinity of these ancient remains.

What Nehemiah King Found in 1829

Nettleton's account was widely circulated when it was summarized in 1847 by historian Henry Howe in his Historical Collections of Ohio. Howe speaks of "Thomas Montgomery and Aron Wright" coming to Ohio "in the spring of 1798," and of the subsequent discovery of the "extensive burying ground" and of "the human bones found in the mounds" nearby. Howe repeats the report, that among these uncovered bones, "were some belonging to men of gigantic structure." He also tells how, in 1829, a tree was cut down next to the ancient "Fort Hill in Conneaut" and that the local land owner, "The Hon. Nehemiah King, with a magnifying glass, counted 350 annualer rings" beyond some cut marks near the tree's center. Howe concludes: "Deducting 350 firom 1829, leaves 1479, which must have been the year when these cuts were made. This was 13 years before the discovery of America, by Columbus. It perhaps was done by the race of the mounds, with an axe of copper, as that people had the art of hardening that metal so as to cut like steel."

The same year that Henry Howe's history of Ohio appeared another interesting book was published by the Smithsonian Institution, entitled, Ancient Monuments of the Mississippi Valley. On page 38 of that seminal report by E. G. Squier and E. H. Davis appears the first known published description of "Fort Hill," that strange pre-Columbian landmark situated on the property of Aaron Wright's neighbor, Nehemiah King.

Sketch of Fort Hill

Number 2. Ancient Work near Conneaut, Ashtabula county, Ohio. -- "This work is at present very slight, but distinctly traceable. The sketch is a mere coup d'aeil, without measurements. The elevation on the bluff upon which it stands is about seventy feet; and the banks of the aluminous state are, upon the north, very precipitous... Upon the south side... the wall which skirts the brow of the hill is accompanied by an outer ditch, while upon the north there is a simple embankment. The ascent (marked C-C in the cut), is gradual and easy. Within the enclosure the earth is very black and rich; outside of the wall it is a stiff clay. The adjacent bottoms are very fertile, and the creek is everywhere fordable. There can be no doubt that this was a fortified position." Near the village of

GIANTS ON THE EARTH

Conneaut are a number of mounds, and other traces of an ancient population, among which is an aboriginal cemetary regularly laid out, and of great extent.

The antiquarian who contributed the survey of "ancient works in Northern Ohio" to Squier and Davis was Charles Whittlesey (1808-1886) of Cleveland, Ohio, who had been sketching the ancient earthworks of his region since the mid 1830s. The archaeology and paleoanthropology pioneered by investigators like Squier, Davis and Whittlesey eventually revealed the fact that the builders of the mounds were, in fact, ancestors of some of the eastern woodland Indians. Whittlesey is remembered today in the application of his name to the "Whittlesey Culture" of late pre-Columbian Indians who inhabited northern Ohio and northwestern Pennsylvania at the time the "Fort Hill" and other Conneaut earthworks were constructed (c. 1000-1400 CE).

For a much more recent description of archaeological finds at this site, see David S. Brose et al., "Conneaut Fort: A Prehistoric Whittlesey Focus Village in Ashtabula County, Ohio" in Pennsylvania Archaeologist 46:4 (1976) pp. 29-77. Brose's 1971 excavations at Fort Hill were just one part of a wider archaeological survey conducted by Case Western Reserve University -- and his published report is merely a summary of a much more detailed "site plan." Brose found little of interest in his dig and concludes that "Conneaut Fort" was not so much a Mound-Builder fortification as it was "a base camp" from which migratory "hunting parties" went out into the surrounding woodlands to obtain food. Although he includes some brief comments regarding 19th century reports about the place, Brose says little about the other prehistoric earthworks in the area, and nothing at all about accounts of giant skeletons being found in the ancient cemetery just across the creek from the hill. However, his simply giving Whittlesey's name to a "focus" of these ancient Americans does not even begin to account for or explain the early discoveries of gigantic skeletons found along the banks of Conneaut Creek. It is obvious that the modern scientists, in their narrow investigations, have missed seeing the larger picture of the enigma the early settlers encountered at Conneaut -- the strange burial places, odd relics, and inexplicable remains of the previous inhabitants. To gain a useful perspective on these people the modern reader must turn the historical pages back to reports from the previous century.

Dr. Peet's 1878 Account of the Giants

In late 1878 or early 1879 William W. Williams' History of Ashtabula Co., Ohio appeared -- the first major publication devoted exclusively to the past years of that corner

GIANTS ON THE EARTH

of northeastern Ohio. In that volume various accounts of the first eastern settlers and their encounters with the remains of the "Conneaut Giants" are described in some detail. For example, on page 17 can be found the following description by the local (and later widely known) antiquarian, Stephen D. Peet:

... an impenetrable mystery still hangs over... a race preceding the various tribes of Indians which history has come in contact with, and may be regarded as strictly prehistoric.... Ohio gives numerous evidences of such. a race. Here, it would seem, was the chief seat of the ancient empire... in this State two classes of works have been discovered... [in] the southern counties the works are much more massive and distinct. They are also much more complicated and mysterious in their design... the works at the north, on the other hand, are much simpler in their character, and are mainly indicative of a military race.

Ashtabula County abounds in earthworks... These works are generally situated on the banks of streams, or in such locations as to have attracted attention... [some] are works of defense, and are well chosen for this purpose.... That at Conneaut is situated on the summit of a lofty hill... which has been left by some former change of the bed of the stream... A steep ascent protects it on all sides. The only approach is up a gradual slope to the eastward, formed by the narrow strip which has been left by the wash of the waters. The height of the eminence is... about seventy-five feet... The only mark of artificial defense is found on the summit. This consists of a simple earth-wall built on the very edge of the bluff, and following closely the very line of the bluff. A ditch was on the inside of the wall, and the height of the wall may have been at one time five feet. Possibly a stockade may have surmounted it, making the inclosure doubly secure both from the natural and artificial defense. The work has been described by those who visited it at an early date. The land thus inclosed was perfectly level, and embraced an area of about two acres, triangular in shape...

A single opening to the inclosure existed, and this was approached only from the level of the stream below by a narrow pathway... The work might have served for a defense to the various tribes of Indians which inhabited the region, or it may have been the residence of the ancient people called the mound-builders. There is on the bank opposite this work, but farther down the stream, a large burial-mound, which might indicate that the occupants of this spot were of the more ancient race of original mound-builders.

This mound is beautifully situated on the very summit of the point of land where the river turns to the northward... The location of this mound was favorable as a lookout, and connected with the defense. The defense itself might have served as a signal-station, to warn against the approach of an enemy from the lake below. There are also other mounds in this neighborhood, though they are of comparatively small size. They were situated in the eastern part of the village. It is not improbable that the Book of Mormon has some connection with these mounds, and possibly may have been suggested by them. Its author, Rev. Mr. Spalding, lived in Conneaut, and the story is based on the common sentiment that the descendants of the lost tribes buried their dead in large heaps, which caused the mounds so common in this country. Their arts and sciences and civilization account for all the curious antiquities found in North and South America. This theory of the lost tribes has long since been exploded.

Dr. Peet goes on to say a little about the "ancient burying-ground" which "was situated

GIANTS ON THE EARTH

a little west of the village" and repeats the story that it was "examined as early as 1800" by settlers like Aaron Wright. Peet only mentions in passing that these earthworks and burial ground "were found to contain human bones, some of which were of a large size." He provides no possible explanation for this necrological oddity, nor have the scientists of later years, who have described these ancient people and their "Whittlesey Culture" in some detail, provided the necessary explanations. It is obvious that the giantism evidenced in the "Whittlesey Culture" human remains was not an isolated phenomenon, occurring in a few, scattered individuals and then disappearing. This was an aspect of physical anthropology that appeared among several different late pre-Columbian "mound-builder" populations inhabiting the southern shores of lake Erie. The large boned trait continued through many generations -- probably for several hundred years -- among certain segments of those populations, at a rate seemingly far higher than what might be expected through natural, random processes. Nevertheless, there appears to be no firm evidence that the individuals who bore this strange physical trait were treated any differently in their own societies than other, less robust and tall members of their groups. The burials of these very large persons occurred among those of the less robust individuals without any recorded distinguishing features, as though they were all of a social status more or less equal.

On pages 18-19 of this history, Dr. Peet continues his article, telling a little about similar earthworks reported in neighboring Ashtabula by "Rev. Mr. Hall, the former, rector of St. Peter's church" in that town. Peet relays the following information: "In cultivating the soil in the vicinity implements have been found, and in excavating the ground for graves it is said that bones have been exhumed which seemed to have belonged to a race of giants... Mr. Peleg Sweet, who was a man of large size and full features... in digging, came upon a skull and jaw which were of such size that the skull would cover his head and the jaw could be easily slipped over his face, as though the head of a giant were enveloping his." Dr. Peet also examines the view of Charles Whittlesey, that a forgotten "white race" inhabited the region "long before the advent of the white settlers" in 1798 and thereafter. As an evidence for this theory he tells of "the discovery of an inscribed stone... near the burying-place upon the east side of the Ashtabula creek... found by the son of Peleg Sweet" in 1808, or perhaps shortly thereafter. "On turning it over it was discovered that its surface was covered with marks of inscribed letters... Roman capital letters," etc. Peet says, "It was too deeply planted in the ground to have belonged to any of the white settlers, as the discovery was within four or five years of the occupation" of Ashtabula by the pioneers.

In the 1878 history Dr. Peet also provides a lengthy and detailed account of the "Destruction of the Eries," the ancient foes of the Iroquois, who inhabited the southern shore of Lake Erie prior to the first settlement there by the Europeans. Although the writer does not specifically link the extinct Eries to their "Whittlesey Culture" predecessors, he tells of the later Indians' extermination in a romantic narrative reminiscent of some published conjectures regarding the fate of the "mound-builders" -- "A great battle was fought... in which the Eries were again defeated, and slain to a man. Their bones lie bleaching in the sun to the present day."

The 1878 history also provides some specific information on the first settlement of towns in Ashtabula county, partly contributed by the prolific pen of Stephen D. Peet. On

GIANTS ON THE EARTH

page 131, in discussing the early days of Ashtabula town, the writer again speaks of prehistoric "burying-places" and reports of "the bones of a gigantic people" having been "exhumed from these ancient sepulchres," adding, "of the people history knows nothing." In the section on Conneaut (beginning on page 154), the historian again takes up the subject of the ancient inhabitants of the area, providing the following interesting observations:

The banks of this river [Conneaut Creek] had long been the favorite resort of not only the red man of the forest but of a prehistoric people, who, without doubt, dwelt here in the remote past. The number and character of the mounds and burying-places, the exhumation of bodies from their ancient cemeteries, disclosing the fact that their bones belonged to a race of larger size than any known Indian tribe, are proofs of the fact that here in this delightful locality there lived, in the unknown past, a numerous people, and different from any Indian tribes of which the white man possesses any knowledge. There is no other spot in the county, and probably but few others anywhere, that abounds in such striking proofs of the existence of a powerful and populous people.... The ancient people disappeared, leaving no written record which might serve to enlighten us as to who they were, whence they came, and whither they have gone. Nevertheless they have left abundant proof in their burial-place, situated a little west of the site of the old brick church, and in the character of "Fort Hill" as it is called, located on the southeastern bank of the creek and opposite to the present village cemetery, that they did once exist, and that they were a numerous and powerful people. The ancient burying-grounds occupy an area of about four acres... Aaron Wright, Esq., in 1800, made a careful examination... and found... human bones blackened with time... Some of these bones were of unusual size, and evidently belonged to a race allied to giants. Skulls were taken from these mounds, the cavities of which were of sufficient capacity to admit the head of an ordinary man, and jaw-bones that might be fitted over the face with equal facility. The bones of the upper and lower extremities were of corresponding size.

On page 157 the writer relates how, on "the night of August 11, 1812," practically the entire population of Conneaut (then called New Salem) fled from a suspected invasion of British, Canadians, and their Indian allies, and "sought refuge on Fort Hill, where amidst its ancient ruins, then covered with a dense forest, they hoped to find a place of temporary security." How land owner Nehemiah King accomodated these unexpected guests, the historian does not relate; he only says that "Within the dilapidated walls of the old fort, hid among the bushes, they passed a most uncomfortable and tedious night, momentarily expecting to hear, the yells of the savages, or to witness from the hill the conflagration of their dwellings."

Finally, on page 159 the historian gives an account of New Salem resident Solomon Spalding and his being inspired to write a precursor to the Book of Mormon, in which he attempted "to show that the American Indians are the descendants of the Jews or lost tribes," and that "They buried their dead in large heaps, which caused the mounds so common in this country. Their arts, sciences, and civilization were brought into view in order to account for all the curious antiquities found in various parts of North America." Exactly how "the Book of Mormon has some connection with these mounds," (as reported by Dr. Peet on page 17) the 1878 history does not say. The account of Spalding on page 159 appears to have been largely taken from Henry Howe's 1847 history, and may have

GIANTS ON THE EARTH

been inserted into the later publication without any special input from Dr. Peet. Peet, it will be recalled, said that the topic of Spalding's writings "may have been suggested" by the Conneaut Creek earthworks and their strange contents, and that the "Rev. Mr. Spalding, lived in Conneaut, and the story [found in the Book of Mormon] is based on the common sentiment that the descendants of the lost tribes buried their dead in large heaps, which caused the mounds so common in this country."

Solomon Spalding Writes About The Giants of Conneaut

MARTHA D. SPALDING, the sister-in-law of the would-be novelist, Solomon Spalding, gave this interesting account in 1833: "I was at his house [Solomon Spalding's] a short time before he left Conneaut; he was then writing a historical novel founded upon the first settlers of America. He represented them as an enlightened and warlike people. He had for many years contended that the aborigines of America were the descendants of some of the lost tribes of Israel, and this idea he carried out in the book in question... disputes arose between the chiefs, which caused them to separate into different bands, one of which was called Lamanites and the other Nephites. Between these were recounted tremendous battles, which frequently covered the ground with slain; and their being buried in large heaps was the cause of the numerous mounds in the country. -- Some of these people he represented as being very large."

Although other old acquaintances of Solomon Spalding also gave their recollections of the man and his writings at about the same time that Martha gave hers, she is the only one among them who makes mention of the writer having "represented" a few of the ancient characters in his book "as being very large." For example, Solomon Spalding's widow, in 1839, confirmed much of what Martha had to say (speaking of "mounds and forts" in Ohio "of a race now extinct"), but the widow leaves out entirely any reference to "very large" characters in her husband's writings. Two questions naturally arise from a reading of Martha's statement: 1) how "large" was "very large;" did she mean "gigantic?" -- and, 2) how reliable is Martha's recollection; might she have introduced the "very large" notion mistakenly into an otherwise fairly accurate statement?

At least part of an answer may be found in the 1880 testimony of Solomon Spalding's adopted daughter, Matilda Spalding McKinstry. She says: "During the year of 1812, I was residing with my parents in a little town in Ohio called Conneaut... There were some round mounds of earth near our house which greatly interested him, and he said a tree on top of one of them was a thousand years old. He set some of his men to work digging into one of these mounds, and I vividly remember how excited he became when he heard that they had exhumed some human bones, portions of giant skeletons, and various relics. He talked with my mother of these discoveries in the mound, and was writing every day as the work progressed. Afterward he read the manuscript which I had seen him writing..."

While Spalding's adopted daughter does not exactly say that her father wrote about giant people in the novel he was then composing -- during the opening of the mound -- she clearly conveys the impression that what was found by his diggers in the "round mound of earth" influenced the content of the story he was writing. Josiah Spalding, a brother of Solomon's, is even more specific in this regard. Josiah had this to say in 1855:

I went to see my brother [in New Salem., Ohio, in 1812] and staid with him some time...

GIANTS ON THE EARTH

He began to compose his novel... In the town where he lived, which I expect is now called Salem, Ohio, there is the appearance of an ancient fort, and near by a large mound, which, when opened, was found to contain human bones. These things gave it the appearance of its being inhabited by a civilized people. These appearances furnished a topic of conversation among the people. My brother told me that a young man told him that he had a wonderful dream. He dreamed that he himself (if I recollect right) opened a great mound, where there were human bones. There he found a written history that would answer the inquiry respecting the civilized people that once inhabited that country until they were destroyed by the savages. This story suggested the idea of writing a novel merely for amusement. The title of his novel, I think, was 'Historical Novel,' or 'Manuscript Found.' This novel is the history contained in the manuscript found.

"He set some of his men to work digging into one of these mounds."

Spalding's Mound Builder Story

As luck would have it, one of Solomon Spalding's old stories has survived and may be consulted to see if he wrote anything about the "Conneaut Giants." This untitled manuscript (now on files in the archives of Oberlin College) contains either the same tale that his brother Josiah saw in 1812, or one based upon the same setting and scenario. Solomon begins his "Oberlin manuscript" with these words:

Near the west bank of the Coneaught River there are the remains of an ancient fort. As I was walking and forming various conjectures respecting the character, situation, & numbers of those people who far exceeded the present Indians in works of art and ingenuity, I hapned to tread on a flat stone. This was at a small distance from the fort, & it lay on the top of a small mound of Earth exactly horizontal. The face of it had a singular appearance. I discovered a number of characters which appeared to me to be letters..."

Here the writer sets the introduction to his story -- on the "west bank" of Conneaut Creek -- just above the spot where the creek makes a turn to the north and from there flows directly into Lake Erie. Consultation of a a map of the area in his time shows that his own dwelling was on the east bank of the creek and that directly opposite that, on the west bank, was an ancient mound. Beyond that, upstream a few hundred yards, is "Fort Hill," the ancient fortification which is situated on what was then the property of Nehemiah King. While Solomon may have had the prominent mound on the west bank of the creek in mind when he wrote his story, it appears that the tumulus his workers opened in about 1811 was a rather smaller artificial hill, located on his own property. As for the origin of the fictional narrator's discovery of "a flat stone" inscribed with "a number of characters" that seemed "to be letters," the reader need only recall the similar mysterious inscribed

GIANTS ON THE EARTH

stone discovered not far to the west, in about 1808, by the son of Peleg Sweet.

In giving a fictional description of the long extinct "mound-builders," Solomon says this, in his chapter 5: "As to their persons they were taller on an average than I had ever seen in any nation, their bones were large limbs strait & shoulders broad... As to their complexion it was bordering on an olive tho' of a lighter shade." So, it would seem, the novelist extended the "large" bones of a few ancient skeletons dug from the northern Ohio mounds and cemeteries to characterize an entire light-skinned nation, "taller on an average" than all others on the face of the earth. However, the author does not complete his imaginative description with these words. Later on in the story he introduces the character of Sambul King of Sciotia. This person Spalding pictures as a man of "gigantic grasp" and "gigantic body." Sambul is a "mighty" warrior with a "huge body" who fights with a "gigantic sword." Considering the fact that Spalding's fictional people were already taller than all others, Sambul must have been the Goliath of his day. Obviously the skeleton of such a man would correspond well with those of the "Conneaut Giants."

Solomon Spalding and Thomas Ashe

Solomon Spalding lived for several years at New Salem (Now Conneaut) in the far northeastern corner of Ohio, a region noted by its early settlers for a profusion of extant "Mound-Builder" earthworks and relics. Since Spalding conducted the opening of a small burial mound near his own residence on Conneaut Creek, one might think he had all the local information and experience necessary to write the opening pages of his Oberlin manuscript. At the beginning of his story Spalding provides a fictional account about his visiting a mound near the banks of Conneaut Creek, climbing to its summit, lifting a flagstone at the top, and descending down into an artificial vault where he discovers ancient relics and ancient writing. It appears, however, that Solomon Spalding preferred to copy from and paraphrase other writers rather than rely totally upon his own imagination to create fictional episodes in his own storytelling. There is good reason to believe that the would-be Ohio author copied a good deal of his fictional discovery account from the pages of an Irish traveler and writer, Thomas Ashe.

On pages 308-323 of his 1808 book, Travels in America, Thomas Ashe describes his inspection of one of several different ancient Indian mounds he visited in the then thinly settled Ohio valley. He gives an especially detailed account of how he and his helper visited a mound near the banks of the Muskingum river, climbed to its summit, lifted flagstones at the top, and descended into an artificial vault where Ashe reportedly discovered ancient relics and ancient writing. What is particularly interesting about Ashe's account is that he also speaks of "Mound-Builder" giants in his story of opening that particular mound. On pages 321-323 of his book, Thomas Ashe speculates that the pre-Columbian inhabitants of North America were inclined to select for their top leaders men of gigantic stature. Although Ashe's notion may not represent a universal truth, there are occasional documented instances of the leaders or "upper classes" in certain socially stratified Indian groups possessing an extraordinary stature. See, for example, "Tomb of Giants" on pp. 64-65 of the March 2001 issue of National Geographic for a depiction of "giants" in a Moche burial in Peru.

Moche Elite Compared to Average Indian
© 2001, National Geographic Society

GIANTS ON THE EARTH

This concept, of course, is exactly what Solomon Spalding followed in his unfinished mound-builder story, wherein he tells of the huge size and mighty feats of the ancient King Sambul of Sciota. It is evident that Solomon Spalding borrowed more than a few ideas from Thomas Ashe, even though most of those same ideas must have also been current among Spalding's own friends and neighbors in frontier Ohio. Probably Spalding chose to copy Ashe so closely because the Irishman's book was a popular one, with American reprints, and a proven sales record. Had Spalding's own prosaic fiction reached the level of Ashe's descriptive narrative, he too might have produced a salable book, years before James Fenimore Cooper and other native authors created romantic American fiction.

Solomon Spalding and Iroquois Legends

Throughout his unfinished Oberlin manuscript, Solomon Spalding attempts to provide believeable observations and explanations regarding both the less civilized and more civilized Indians of the distant past. To the modern reader it is obvious that Spalding picked up a great deal of his descriptive information from the published works of his day. It is also probable that the writer obtained source material from unpublished accounts, oral traditions, and common speculation. It is likely that the writer at some point came across some of the Iroquois legends purporting to give a history of the Indians long before the arrival of the Europeans. One such probable source for Solomon Spalding's ecclectic borrowing was David Cusick's Sketches of Ancient History... The problem in linking Spalding to this fantastic collection of stories is that Cusick did write his book until 1825 and did not publish it until 1827, more then ten years after Spalding's death. Even so, it sems probable that Spalding had some access to some of the same old legends which Cusick (a Tuscarora Indian) compiled from his peoples' past. A prominent character in Cusick's book is Tarenyawagua, -- the "Holder of the Heavens." This otherworldly personage appears to have been a god or demi-god who manifested himself among the ancient woodland Indians to teach and direct them in living a proper life. Tarenyawagua gives divine laws to the Iroquois. He also performs a number of miracles for their benefit. It seems that Cusick had also heard that Tarenyawagua once informed the Indians that a certain people "beyond the great water" had killed their Maker, but that the Maker rose again after suffering that death. Although this must be a direct reference to Jesus Christ, Cusick makes no claims that Tarenyawagua was a divinity of Christ's stature. He instead presents the "Holder of the Heavens" as a man who was capable of aging and death, but also of resurrection from the grave.

The promethian Tarenyawagua was just the sort of character from ancient American pre-history that the Mormons might make good use of in promoting the belief that the Christophany related in III Nephi was an actual event. For some unknown reason the LDS apologists seem to have chosen to keep silent on Cusick's "Holder of the Heavens" and on his Indian history as well. It seems reasonable to concede that Spalding had some general knowledge of the Iroquois stories about Tarenyawagua and that he used those stories as a basis for his character Lobaska -- a great teacher and founder of the fictional religion of the Mound-Builders in Spalding's "Oberlin story." Like Tarenyawagua, Spalding's Lobaska simply disappears from human view once his work among the lesser human beings is finished. It is an additional curiosity that the heroic Alma in the Book of

GIANTS ON THE EARTH

Mormon does the same at the end of his story. Of these two literary figures, however, Lobaska resembles Tarenyawagua much more than Alma the Elder does.

Perhaps some of the most interesting and entertaining portions of Cusick's writings have to do with ancient American giants. The writer presents stories of giants as individual Indians of great stature and also as a whole race of huge beings. His 1827 book is filled with stories of giant men and beasts and there is no reason to doubt that these have been the subjects of Iroquian legend for centuries. It is also interesting to see that Cusick couples one of his stories about giants with an account of an ancient people resembling the Mound-Builders. Probably some of the Iroquois legends are truly based upon those Indians' encounters with persons of huge size in the distant past.

Giants in the Book of Mormon?

As early as 1832 and 1833 certain persons were claiming that the Book of Mormon was based on an unpublished story written by Solomon Spalding during his 1809-12 residence in Ohio. Given the fact that his sister-in-law and adopted daughter both indicate that Spalding's writings were influenced by the idea of pre-Columbian giants, the reader might well expect to find at least some laconic references to such giants in the Mormon book -- that is, if Solomon Spalding had anything to do with the compilation of that book's story-line.

Joseph Smith, Jr., the purported translator of the "Nephite record" from which the Book of Mormon was said to have been derived, provided mentions of giants in two other of the latter day scriptures he gave to the world (in his additions to the biblical Genesis and the Mormons' unique Book of Abraham), but the "very large" characters of Spalding's known writings are largely absent from the Book of Mormon itself. What might be construed by some readers to answer for "giants" in the book are the men of "mighty stature" the text occasionally refers to. For example: "And it came to pass that his High Priest murdered him as he sat upon his throne... and his name was Lib; and Lib was a man of great stature, more than any other man among all the people" (Book of Ether) Two other examples: "And it came to pass that I, Nephi, being exceeding young, nevertheless being large in stature, and also having great desires to know of the mysteries of God, wherefore I did cry unto the Lord;" (1 Nephi); "And now I, Nephi, being a man large in stature, and also having received much strength of the Lord, therefore I did seize upon the servant of Laban" (1 Nephi).

Although the Book of Mormon's character King Lib might be conjectured to be just as much a "giant" as King Sambul in Spalding's Oberlin manuscript, he does not appear to have been a member of a race of giants; nor was Nephi, the man "large in stature," who accomplished such promethian exploits as building a sea-going ship from scratch in the Arabian desert a member of a race of giants. Nephi the son of Lehi may have been a mighty man indeed, but he was not one of the Hebrew nephilim, the biblical giants descended from fallen angels. What little is said of the "large and mighty men" of the Book of Mormon provides no direct evidence of their having any conceptual or literary ties to the "Conneaut Giants" discovered in Ohio during Spalding's day.

Mormon writer E. Cecil McGavin, in his 1948 book, Geography of the Book of Mormon, makes a modest effort to link the Book of Mormon Nephites with some near relatives of the "Conneaut Giants." On page 13 of his book he reprints the following old quote:

GIANTS ON THE EARTH

"Cayuga County [NY] yielded a rich harvest of giant skeletons among the ancient ruins, of which we read that 'entire skeletons have been found of people of giant proportions, the skulls and jawbones of which could cover the head and face of the most fleshy person of our day.' We are told of a tradition which asserts that a destructive war was waged 'in this very section of the country, and with such fury and determination on each side that practically all of the warriors were slaughtered. Erie County has yielded a vast store of ancient monuments, including many giant skeletons, spear points, war hatchets, and other weapons that seem too large for an average sized man to wield. Bones of 'giant size' have been uncovered. Similar discoveries have been made on Ontario County, 'skeletons of an early age, including many of unusual size have been found."

Although such references help to document the fact that "mound-builder" giants were not confined to the Ohio shores of Lake Erie, they do little to help support the Mormon cause, since the Book of Mormon itself says so little about its "large and mighty men." Anecdotal citations from the family of Joseph Smith, Sr. may indicate that certain Book of Mormon Nephites or Jaredites were huge men, sitting in great thrones, wearing gigantic breastplates, and peering at hieroglyphics through monster "interpreter" diamond spectacles, but the book itself is silent regarding such reported oddities. Elder Charles B. Thompson, one of the first Mormon writers to identify the "mound-builders" as Nephites, avoided making any claims for giants among "the people whose history is contained in the Book of Mormon."

On the other hand, Mormon writer Phyllis Carol Olive strongly advocates the idea that the Book of Mormon's scanty references to huge people are directly confirmed by evidence on the ground in the northeastern United States. Relying mostly on very old reports and out-dated speculation about an extinct white master race inhabiting the Americas of prehistoric times, Mrs. Olive has produced two books promoting the belief that most of the Book of Mormon story took place in the lands around the Great Lakes and that the mound-building Adena, Hopewell, and Mississippian cultures represent the civilized people whose story is related in the Mormon book.

On pages 30-34 of her 2001 volume, The Lost Tribes of the Book of Mormon, Mrs. Olive sets forth her evidence that the Book of Mormon people were not only the "Mound-Builders," but that they were also a "large and mighty nation living in the near vicinity of the Hill Cumorah and throughout the entire mound building region -- the giant, Mound Builders so long sought for; a people who bear remarkable similarities to those described in the Book of Mormon." While all of this imaginative conjecture must be exhilarating and vindicating to the faith of those already convinced of the literal truth of the Mormon book, it is not likely to make much of an impression upon the minds of those educated investigators whom Mrs. Olive dismisses as "the academics." Since the days when Martin Harris attempted to interest "academics" like Dr. Samuel L. Mitchell and Dr. Charles Anthon in the coming forth of the Book of Mormon, the LDS "true believers" have continually been disappointed and frustrated in trying to convince "the learned" that the Mormon book truly came forth "out of the earth" in fulfillment of biblical prophecy.

The one important fact in this matter (which has evidently escaped Olive's consideration entirely) is that the occasional "giant skeletons" found among the "Mound-Builder" ruins were reported and publicized well before the first copy of the Book of Mormon was ever sold to a credulous buyer. Author David Marks reports that he was drawn to inves-

GIANTS ON THE EARTH

tigate the newly published Book of Mormon in 1830, due to his "curiosity" while visiting in Ohio, "to know the origin of the numerous mounds and remains of ancient fortifications that abound in that section of the country..." and due to his "having been told that the 'Book of Mormon' gave a history of them." Rev. Marks might have just as well said that he had a curiosity to know the origins of the numerous huge skeletons dug form those same mounds. And, in that case, Phyllis Carol Olive would have a ready answer: that they are the same as "those described in the Book of Mormon." However, since the curiosity of such investigators as David Marks pre-dated the coming forth of the Book of Mormon, how can the Mormon apologist answer the question, "Could not the book have been written to explain (among other things) the mounds and giants which had already aroused peoples' curiosity?"

In the case of Solomon Spalding's productions, the answer to that question is "Yes, of course -- Spalding himself admits to that at the beginning of his story." If Solomon Spalding incorporated explanations of the prehistoric mounds, finds of huge skeletons, extinct American elephants, ancient seer-stones, and other such oddities in his 1812 book, in order to satisfy the curiosity of an inquiring public, could not have some writer compiled the Book of Mormon for much the same purpose? At the very least, the fact remains that people were inquisitive about the origin of the prehistoric giant skeletons long before either book was made available to their curious readers. The modern investigator is left to conclude that if Solomon Spalding did write a good deal of the Book of Mormon -- and if his supposedly purloined "Manuscript Found" story really said very much at all about ancient American giants -- that the text published in 1830 must have been significantly changed from whatever it was that Spalding wrote in Ohio two decades before.

The Allegewi, the Nephilim, and the Nephites

While most modern historians, anthropologists, and LDS apologists (other than Phyllis Carol Olive) shy away from saying much of anything about pre-Columbian giants, "fringe archaeology" periodicals like Ancient American welcome such revisionist claims with open arms. The 36th issue of that publication published an article by Steve Quayle, entitled "Giants and Ancient North American Warfare" which resurrects the Rev. John Heckewelder's antique reports about the so-called Allegewi. According to the Moravian missionary, Heckewelder (1743-1823): "Many wonderful things are told of this famous people. They are said to have been remarkably tall and stout, and there is a tradition that there were giants among them..." Exactly who these Allegewi were and how much credence may be put into Heckewelder's accounts of them, cannot at this late date be very well established. It may be significant, however, that Heckewelder was a Moravian and that the "Moravian Hospitality Tract" separated the lands sold by Solomon Spalding in Ohio from the lands he disposed of in adjacent Pennsylvania. Whether or not Spalding and Heckewelder ever met, Spalding may well have heard of the missionary's accounts of the ancient Allegewi. Up to this point Quayle's article provides some interesting possibilities. But, beyond this, the writer offers up his speculation about the Allegewi having been a "selected group" within the "late Adena" culture of "mound-builders," a sub-race produced by "selective breeding" for "the creation of a guardian or warrior class made up of physically superior men and women." Whatever the "Conneaut Giants" were, it is very doubtful that they were an "Adena" sub-race or that they came into existence through

GIANTS ON THE EARTH

"selective breeding" -- unless, of course, one takes into account the possibility that the ancient giants may have naturally preferred giantesses as their companions.

A series of on-line articles at the Great Serpent Mound website offer a slightly less revisionist theory than the one promulgated by Quayle. In "Holocaust of Giants: The Great Smithsonian Cover-up," the writer concludes that the prehistoric giants were a naturally occurring sub-group among certain populations of mound-building Indians -- that perhaps these were "tall, ruling chiefs and their wives." As previously mentioned by the current writer, no special evidence exists to indicate that these giant Indians belonged to any particular social group. If they did represent a "kingly" class, their physical stature might not have offered much of an advantage to them in woodland hunting and fighting. Southern Mississippian chiefs may have been carried around in fancy litters by their "stinkard" servants, but their northern contemporaries probably had to preserve their ruling privileges and positions by now and then demonstrating prowess in the hunt and on the field of battle. In their tribes, where maize cultivation had not become almost the predominent occupation of the people, a warrior's speed and agility in moving silently through the forest still counted for something. Human bodies over a certain size tend to become frail, less mobile, and subject to infirmities. The natural limits for robust hunters and warriors are probably to be found among some of the larger people of Polynesian ancestry. Even among those people, where bodily heaviness was sometimes associated with the ruling class, giantism in not recorded as offering any special advantages. The ancient American giants may just as well have been a priestly people or something like professional clowns and courtly fools. Something accounted for their continuation as a distinctive sub-group, but that "something" need not have been royal blood.

The one important fact in this matter (which has evidently escaped Olive's consideration entirely) is that the occasional "giant skeletons" found among the "Mound-Builder" ruins were reported and publicized well before the first copy of the Book of Mormon was ever sold to a credulous buyer. Author David Marks reports that he was drawn to investigate the newly published Book of Mormon in 1830, due to his "curiosity" while visiting in Ohio, "to know the origin of the numerous mounds and remains of ancient fortifications that abound in that section of the country..." and due to his "having been told that the 'Book of Mormon' gave a history of them." Rev. Marks might have just as well said that he had a curiosity to know the origins of the numerous huge skeletons dug form those same mounds. And, in that case, Phyllis Carol Olive would have a ready answer: that they are the same as "those described in the Book of Mormon." However, since the curiosity of such investigators as David Marks pre-dated the coming forth of the Book of Mormon, how can the Mormon apologist answer the question, "Could not the book have been written to explain (among other things) the mounds and giants which had already aroused peoples' curiosity?"

In the case of Solomon Spalding's productions, the answer to that question is "Yes, of course -- Spalding himself admits to that at the beginning of his story." If Solomon Spalding incorporated explanations of the prehistoric mounds, finds of huge skeletons, extinct American elephants, ancient seer-stones, and other such oddities in his 1812 book, in order to satisfy the curiosity of an inquiring public, could not have some writer compiled the Book of Mormon for much the same purpose? At the very least, the fact remains that people were inquisitive about the origin of the prehistoric giant skeletons long before

GIANTS ON THE EARTH

either book was made available to their curious readers. The modern investigator is left to conclude that if Solomon Spalding did write a good deal of the Book of Mormon -- and if his supposedly purloined "Manuscript Found" story really said very much at all about ancient American giants -- that the text published in 1830 must have been significantly changed from whatever it was that Spalding wrote in Ohio two decades before.

There were other sources than reports from Heckewelder and local "mound-builder" disinterments that may have reached Solomon Spalding and influenced his thinking about pre-Columbian giants. In 1705 the teeth and bones of a very large, unidentified animal were discovered near Albany, New York, inspiring the poet Edward Taylor to pen some lines about this "monster," in which he spoke of some Indian traditions concerning a prehistoric race of human giants. The connection having been made between the uncovered remains and ancient giants, the Rev. Cotton Mather (1663-1728) investigated the discovery and linked the teeth and bones to the biblical giants of "Mosaic history." Since Solomon Spalding came from New England (where the remains ended up) and since he lived for several years near Albany (where they were first uncovered) it is likely that he heard the old accounts of Rev. Mather identifying them as proof of the biblical nephilim. In fact, they turned out to be the remains of an extinct American elephant.

It was not until 1806 that Georges Cuvier gave the first formal description of prehistoric American elephants -- of mastodons and mammoths -- but the American scientists already knew of their existence in ages past and Thomas Jefferson speculated that the huge beasts still existed somewhere in the uncharted American hinterland. In his 1784 book, Notes on the State of Virginia, Jefferson spoke both of the "mound-builders" and of the extinct mammoths of Big Bone Lick on the Ohio. Solomon Spalding almost certainly read Jefferson's book and other contemporary speculation concerning mastodons and mammoths. Probably he also realized that the nephilim teeth that so excited Cotton Mather were actually elephant remains (see David Levin's "Giants in the Earth: Science and the Occult in Cotton Mather's Letters to the Royal Society" in William and Mary Quarterly, Vol. 45, Oct. 1988, p. 751-770). It is no coincidence that the eclectic Spalding mixed abnormally tall "mound-builders" and living mammoths together in the same story when he wrote his Oberlin manuscript. Whether or not he went a step beyond that and mixed Jaredite elephants, Ohio "mound-builders," and Nephite nephilim all into a subsequent piece of his writing remains unanswered -- and is probably forever unanswerable.

Epilogue: The "Whittlesey Culture" and the Conneaut Giants
Although the topic is barely mentioned in today's scientific literature, a quick browsing through various and sundry on-line offerings shows that the subject of the "mound-builder" giants remains a popular mystery, even today. Most of the web articles dealing with this topic make some mention of Heckewelder's Allegewi and Robert Silverburg's popular 1970 book, The Mound Builders. In that volume Silverburg has a little to say about the "search for a race of giant Mound Builders in the Ohio Valley" during the early 1800s (on pages 28-30) and a bit more to offer concerning "giant bones," the "evening conversations" of Joseph Smith, and "unpublished manuscripts of Mound Builder fables" (on pages 44-47). Silverburg's book does not advocate the ancient American giants claims but it has circulated that idea far and wide, when other, more scholarly writings have generally ignored the issue. But, beyond what any popular writer saying things about

GIANTS ON THE EARTH

the Indians has ever published, it has been the county and regional histories of northern Ohio, northwestern Pennsylvania, and western New York -- published mostly during the 1870s and 1880s -- which have added continual sustenance to the memory of the "Conneaut Giants" and their counterparts. The 1884 History of Erie Co., Pennsylvania adds these historical tidbits to the pile:

Many indications have been found in the county [Erie] proving conclusively that it was once peopled by a different race from the Indians who were found here when it was first visited by white men. When the link of the Erie & Pittsburgh Railroad from the Lake Shore road to the dock at Erie was in process of construction, the laborers dug into a great mass of bones at the crossing of the public road which runs by the rolling mill. From the promiscuous way in which they were thrown together, it is surmised that a terrible battle must have taken place in the vicinity at some day so far distant that not even a tradition of the event has been preserved... At a later date... another deposit of bones was dug up ... Among the skeletons was one of a giant, side by side with a smaller one, probably that of his wife. The arm and leg bones of this native American Goliath were about one-half longer than those of the tallest man among the laborers; the skull was immensely large, the lower jawbone easily slipped over the face and whiskers of a full-faced man, and the teeth were in a perfect state of preservation. Another skeleton was dug up in Conneaut Township some years ago which was quite remarkable in its dimensions. As in the other instance, a comparison was made with the largest man in the neighborhood, and the jawbone readily covered his face, while the lower bone of the leg was nearly a foot longer than the one with which it was measured, indicating that the man must have been eight to ten feet in height (pp. 167-169).

The township histories of this particular volume contribute even more details on the prehistoric "Whittlesey Culture" mounds and burial spots in Erie Co., some of these discoveies dating back to the days when Solomon Spalding was living a few miles away, across the state line in Ohio. In fact, some accounts say that Spalding actually did a good deal of his fictional writing in Erie Co., so the remarkable discoveries made there may have influenced his thoughts just as much as the ones made a bit closer to his home at New Salem.

The great heyday of publishing American county histories petered out with the turn of the century (except in the far west, where the initial settlement history was, in many cases, still being lived out) and those written after 1900 tend to say less and less about the discovery of gigantic human bones along the southern shores of the Great Lakes. Now and then the contemporary investigator can uncover an obscure newspaper or journal article that tells the story, however. The editor of the Jefferson Gazette of Ashtabula Co., Ohio offered his readers such an account in May of 1924, titled: "The Indians and Mound Builders of Ashtabula Co." In that piece the writer, a local antiquarian and "arrow head collector," has this to say:

The early settlers of Ashtabula have gone on record that where the east side cemetery is there were over 1000 graves when they came here, laid out with some evidence of mathematical skill. A few graves were opened and in some were found skulls and jaw bones of men whose size dwarfed the men who found the graves. The graves were not those of the Indian of the last or the previous century...

In the early days settlers in Conneaut found a number of mounds. On the west side

GIANTS ON THE EARTH

along the creek there was a great burial ground. It is said there were about 3000 graves there, laid out in some design and like the cemetery at Ashtabula the bones of the adults were exceptionally large... One of the most interesting stories arising from the old burial plot at Conneaut was the probable origin of the Book of Mormon... Rev. Spaulding, in about 1812... told that he found [a] manuscript in one of the old graves at Conneaut... A few years later it was uncovered by Sidney Rigdon, a preacher from Kirtland, Ohio, who had been prophesying that a great revelation was about to be made the chosen people at Kirtland. Rigdon conspired with Smith, father of Mormonism, to find the manuscript, which Smith did... from this scheme and the old Spaulding fraud may have come, and probably did come, the formation of the present great Mormon church of Utah.

New York: Land of Giants and Ancient Ruins
August 13, 2003

When the Whites arrived, Western New York was littered with the works of earlier people. Stone walls, graded roads, and fortifications were reported, though most commonly these markers were earthen mounds or enclosures. The Native Americans seldom had any tradition about the people who had put them in place. Most of us now believe that the influence of the Mississippian (Mound-Builder) culture was behind them. The settlement and the plow have been lethal to most of these fragile works, and even the old mound-fanatic E. G. Squier confessed ruefully in 1849 that the Western Door held little any more worth looking at. (read more)

As these works were destroyed in the last century a stablefull of curiosities seems to have come out.

T. Apoleon Cheney notes (in Illustrations of the Ancient Monuments of Western New York) that a twelve-foot high elliptical mound above Cattaraugus County's Conewango Valley held eight big skeletons. Most crumbled, but a thigh bone was found to be 28" long. Exquisite stone points, enamelwork, and jewelry (like that of Mexico or Peru) were also unearthed in the area. The mound looked like those of the Old World.

Cheney also mentions a skeleton seven-foot-five (with an unusually thick skull) from a Chautauqua County site near Cassadaga Creek. Inside a very old mound near Cassadaga Lake were some large skeletons that were examined by medical gentlemen." One measured nearly nine feet. (In 1938 Charles Hunnington of Randolph was so inspired by Doc Cheney's finds that he made two giant "wooden Indian" statues, probably still at the museum in Little Valley.)

The History of Cattaraugus County notes the town of Carrollton's "Fort Limestone," whose rough figure-eight enclosed five acres. In 1851 the removal of a stump turned up a mass of human bones. Some were enormous. Franklinville's Marvin Older virtually gamboled about the site with them: a skull fit over his size seven-and-a-half head; a rib curved all the way around him, a shinbone went from his ankle to above his knee, and a jaw - with bodacious molars - went over his own. Its first owner had probably stood eight feet tall.

Stafford Cleveland's History and Directory of Yates County refers to skeletons from a conical burial mound by Keuka Lake in the early 1800's. A Penn Yan doctor found that many were seven footers. (Tales of ghosts and buried treasure cling to this vicinity as well.)

GIANTS ON THE EARTH

Turner's History of the Holland Purchase reports an ancient three-acre earth fort in Orleans county (about one and a half miles west of Shelby Center) that covered seven- and eight-foot skeletons. Their skulls were well developed in front, broad between the ears, and flattened on top. Also, Turner notes that, upon digging a cellar on his town of Aurora farm, Charles P. Pierson found a giant of his own.

The 1879 History of Allegany County noted a circular mound between Philip's Creek and the Genesee in the village of Belmont. Several feet high and fifteen or so in diameter, it disgorged human bones, some very large, when the railroad was made in 1849 and 1850.

Giant human skeletons don't ring any bells with us. Some think the Scandinavians were in Western New York, and they were considered virtual giants in the ancient world (whose people were traditionally much shorter than those now). Many Vikings would seem tall even today, but they were not routinely seven-footers.

Not all the humanlike skeletons found about the Western Door were so surely human. Several old histories discuss the two very bizarre skulls taken in the early 1820's from a mound on Tonawanda Island near Buffalo. One early writer notes each "portentous, protruding lower jaw and canine forehead." Another adds that the burial customs were entirely unlike those of the region's natives.

Our County and Its People (Truman C. White, 1898) mentions skeletons that seem to have been "platycnemic" - flat-shinned. In the bluff at Fort Porter (Buffalo) one such skeleton was found near ancient implements. Burials of up to three such skeletons have been found high up on river or lake banks about the region. Their flat shins and "other skeletal peculiarities" were thought due to climbing and living in trees. These are odd stories to make up.

In nature's evident experiments toward Homo sapiens, some of the discontinued models were very large (Gigantopithecus comes to mind); none are thought to have set foot or dragged knuckle on any American soil. Jess Stearn (in Montezuma's Serpent) cites finds from the American southwest implying some giant, bestial hominid was here. Jim Brandon's Weird America lists two such accounts from just outside the Western Door.

An eight-footer turned up in an Ellisburg, PA mound (near Wellsville, NY) in 1886. The same year a team of professors and professionals found dozens of huge, oddly-skulled humans in a mound in Sayre, PA (near Elmira, NY). They averaged seven feet, though some were taller, and some had horny knobs on their foreheads. Several went to the American Investigating Museum in Philadelphia, into which they disappeared. Modern fans of Bigfoot (seen in almost all the states of the Union) might rejoice at historical testimony of monster bones; for the rest of us the matter is just... weird.

Hidden Proofs Of A Giant Race

As you read this series of extracts, try to visualize the proverbial series of contemporary evolution...something is amiss.

1. Large bones in stone graves in Williamson County and White County, Tennessee. Discovered in the early 1800s, the average stature of these giants was 7 feet tall.

2. Giant skeletons found in the mid-1800s in New York state near Rutland and Rodman.

3. In 1833, soldiers digging at Lompock Rancho, California, discovered a male skeleton 12 feet tall. The skeleton was surrounded by caved shells, stone axes, other arti-

GIANTS ON THE EARTH

facts. The skeleton had double rows of upper and lower teeth. Unfortunately, this body was secretly buried because the local Indians became upset about the remains.

4. A giant skull and vertebrae found in Wisconsin and Kansas City.

5. A giant found off the California Coast on Santa Rosa Island in the 1800s was distinguished by its double rows of teeth.

6. A 9-foot, 8-inch skeleton was excavated from a mount near Brewersville, Indiana, in 1879.

7. Skeletons of "enormous dimensions" were found in mounds near Zanesville, Ohio, and Warren, Minnesota, in the 1880s.

8. In Clearwater Minnesota, the skeletons of seven giants were found in mounds. These had receding foreheads and complete double dentition.

9. At LeCrescent, Minnesota, mounds were found to contain giant bones. Five miles north near Dresbach, the bones of people over 8 feet tall were found.

10. In 1888 seven skeletons ranging from seven to 8 feet tall were discovered.

11. Near Toledo, Ohio, 20 skeletons were discovered with jaws and teeth "twice as large as those of present day people." The account also noted that odd hieroglyphics were found with the bodies.

12. Miners in Lovelock Cave, California, discovered a very tall, red-haired mummy In 1911

13. This mummy eventually went to a fraternal lodge where it was used for "initiation purposes."

1. John Haywood, The Natural and Aboriginal History of Tennessee, McCowat-Mercer, Jackson, TN, 1958

2. Cyrus Gordon, Before Columbus, Crown Publishers, NY, 1971

3. David Hatcher Childress, Lost Cities of North America, Adventures Unlimited Press, Stelle, IL, 1992, p.509.

4. Cyrus Godron, Before Columbus, Crown Publishers, NY, 1971.

5. David Hatcher Childress, Lost Cities of North America-M, Adventures Unlimited Press, Stelle, IL, 1992, p.509.

6. Indianapolis, News News, November 10, 1975.

7. Cyrus Godron, Before Columbus, Crown Publishers, NY, 1971.

8. David Hatcher Childress, Lost Cities of North America, Adventures Unlimited Press, Stelle, IL, 1992, p.468.

9. Ibid.

10. St. Paul Pioneer Press, June 29, 1888.

11. Chicago Record, October 24, 1895.

12. Humboldt Star, May 13, 1928.

13. David Hatcher Childress, Lost Cities of North America, Adventures Unlimited Press, Stelle, IL, 1992, p 494.

14. In 1931, skeletons from 8 1-2 to 10 feet long were found in the Humbolt lake bed in California.

15. In 1932, Ellis Wright found human tracks in the gypsum rock at White Sands, New Mexico. His discovery was later backed up by Fred Arthur, Supervisor of the Lincoln National Park and others who reported that each footprint was 22 inches long and from 8 to 10 inches wide. They were certain the prints were human in origin due to the outline of

GIANTS ON THE EARTH

the perfect prints coupled with a readily apparent instep.

16. During World War II, author Ivan T. Sanderson tells of how his crew was bulldozing through sedimentary rock when it stumbled upon what appeared to be a graveyard. In it were crania that measured from 22 to 24 inches from base to crown nearly three times as large as an adult human skull. Had the creatures to whom these skulls belonged been properly proportioned, they undoubtedly would have been at least 12 feet tall or taller.

17. In 1947 a local newspaper reported the discovery of nine-foot-tall skeletons by amateur archeologists working in Death Valley.

18. The archeologists involved also claimed to have found what appeared to be the bones of tigers and dinosaurs with the human remains.

19. The Catalina Islands, off California, are the home of dwarf mammoth bones that were once roasted in ancient fire pits. These were roasted and eaten by human-like creatures who were giants with double rows of teeth.

20. One of the latest accounts of a race of giants that occupied Europe comes from the middle ages and involves a surprising figure: Saint Christopher. While modern stories of St. Christopher simply make him out as an ordinary man, or perhaps a somewhat homely man, those who actually saw him had a different story. According to his peers, he was a giant, belonging to a tribe of dog-headed, cannibalistic giants. Jacques de Voragine in The Golden Legend wrote of St. Christopher:"He was of gigantic stature, had a terrifying mien, was twelve coudees tall."

21. A coudee is an antique measurement equal to or larger than the English linear measurement of a foot. According to this ancient account, St. Christopher stood from 12 to 18 feet tall (a fact that has become hidden in or even erased from church history).

22. While Western icons don't picture St. Christopher as contemporary accounts described him, those of the Eastern churches do. Often the suggestion is seen in historic accounts that St. Christopher was the product of a tryst between a human being and an Anubis (a demon-like creature based on the Greek Anoubis, which came from the Egyptians jackal-headed god who was believed to lead the dead to judgment)

14. Ibid., p.496.
15. Ibid., p.497.
16. David Hatcher Childress, Lost Cities and Ancient M, Mysteries of South America, Adventures Unlimited Press, Stelle. IL, 1985, p.199.
17. The Hot Citizen, Expedition Reports Nine-Foot Skeletons," August 5, 1947.
18. Ibid.
19. David Hatcher Childress, Lost Cities North America, Adventures Unlimited Press, Stelle, IL, 1992, p.526.
20. Malcolm South, Mythical and Fabulous Creatures, Peter Berick Books, NY, NY, 1987, p.303.
21. Ibid.
22. Ibid.

1. In other words, according to the contemporary accounts of his day, St. Christopher was the product of a spiritual being who mated with a human woman. And once again the result of this union was a creature that matches the descriptions of the Nephilim.

GIANTS ON THE EARTH

GENESIS 6:4

There were GIANTS in the earth in those days; and also after that, when the SONS OF GOD (Fallen Angels) came in unto the daughters of men, and they bare children to them, the same became mighty men which were of old, men of renown.

1. One of the many races of giants.

...AND THEY BUILT STONEHENGE

There is ample reasons to believe that the monoliths in Salisbury, England, were not built by either the Druids or normal human beings. When one consider the megaliths proportions, tonnage, and lack of resources in terms of both nature and human; and the lack of technology, the possibility that I am suggesting is not so far-fetched as it may seem.

1. Not a lot is known about the people who would become known as the Celts. It is known that they migrated across Asia Minor, through northern Europe and into what have become the Celtic countries of Wales, Scotland and Ireland. Most accounts of them include references to the giants that were often found among them. The ancient Greek historian Pausanias called them "the world's tallest people."

2. "Modern historians now believe that, in fact, the giants among the Celts were a ruling class that held control over the indigenous population that formed the majority of the Celtic tribes.

3. As these 60-some tribes that comprised the Cimbri or Cimmerian peoples traveled across Europe, migrating and taking over areas and later being driven Eastward by other cultures, the name of the people changed. While they were in Asia Minor, they were known as the Gomarian Sacae; this was shortened and modified to become Celtae (meaning "potent and valiant men" similar to the "mighty men" on the Genesis 6 passage). The Greeks called them Galatai a corruption of Celtae; the Romans further changed this name to become Gauls.

4. Although the Romans 'would eventually devise methods of defeating these giant warriors, attacking long legs that couldn't be guarded by the massive shields these creatures carried, the blue-eyed, blond giants inspired terror among those facing them in battle for the first time.

The travels of the giants through the German region also most likely inspired the Teutonic legends of the Aryan race of superhumans (with the early name of "Cimmerian" having an obvious resemblance that is probably more than happenstance to Aryan). The Nazi ideal "superman" was a blue-eyed, blond giant; this is the exact historic description of the Celtae. DeLoach has also made a good argument that the giants ruling the Celtae may very well have been descendants of the Anakim, the giants the Israelites found in the Promised Land. His argument is based on the Roman poet Virgil's account of the Gauls which describes them:

"Golden is their hair and golden their garb. They are resplendent in their striped cloaks,and their milk-white necks are circled with gold."

5. These distinctive gold necklaces have also been discovered in numerous archeological finds, bolstering Virgil's observations.

1. Pausanias, 1.35.
2. Charles DeLoach, Giants. A Reference Guide From History, the Bible, and Recorded

GIANTS ON THE EARTH

Legend. Scarecrow Press, Meuchen, NJ, 1995, p.54.

3. Ibid.

4. Virgil, Aeneid, 8.658-660.

5. Charles DeLoach, Giants: A Reference Guide from History, the Bible, and Recorded Legend, Scarecrow Press, Meuchen, NJ, 1995, p.57.

6. This tight gold band around the necks of theCeltae is what ties them to the biblical accounts of the Nephilim. Remembering that the Anakim were one of the tribes that were listed as being giants in the Bible, the clue that links the Celtae to the Nephilim is the Hebrew word which is translated as "Anakim" in English: The actual word is Anaqiy, meaning "a descendent of Anak."

7. Now the word translated as "Anak" in the English version of the Bible is Anaq and was employed as another term for"Canaanite."

8. As noted earlier, this suggests that the culture that ruled much of the Promised Land when the Israelites invaded it was comprised of two classes with the Anakim acting as a ruling elite within a larger human population.

But there's more. Hebrew names are often based on common words, giving the names special meanings that relate it back to characteristics of the individual or thing being named. The word, Anaq, which was employed to name the Anak, used in other contexts means "a necklace so tight as to appear to be strangling." Use of this word suggests that the most noticeable feature of the descendants of Anak was a tight chain about the neck.

That same feature was the distinguishing characteristic that Virgil chose to remark on when describing the Gauls.

This leads to an important possibility. The Anakim, or giants that adopted their practices, were pushed out of Canaan by the Israelites, going northward and eventually traveling westward over Europe and, with the passage of several millennia, finally settled in the Celtic nations.

Their Religious Practices

9. If the Anakim and the giants among the Celtae were one and the same people, then it's possible to gain an insight into the religious practices of the Nephilim. While the Bible doesn't reveal much about the religious practices of the Anakim, it does hint at human and infant sacrifices and similar horrors. God ordered the Israelites to kill all the men,women and children in many of the cities taken during the invasion of the land by the Jews.

10.However, more Is known historically from non-Biblical sources about the religion that the Celtae practiced. Ancient historians had a variety of horrors to tell about the Celtae giants, including the fact that they were homosexuals (another crime which dictated the death penalty under Mosaic law). Athenaeus states that the giants were accustomed to sleeping with not one but two boys. The historian Diodorus also suggested that homosexuality was rampant among the giants when he wrote:

"Although their wives are comely, they have very little to do with them, but rage with lust in outlandish fashion for the embraces of males. And the most astonishing thing of all is that they feel no concern for their proper dignity but prostitute to others without a qualm the flower of their bodies; nor do they consider this a disgraceful thing to do, but rather when anyone of them is thus approached and refuses the favor offered him, this

GIANTS ON THE EARTH

they consider an act of dishonor."

These passages also provide important links that help prove the Celtae are Nephilim.

6. James Strong, Exhaustive Concordance of the Bible, Abingdon Press, NY, 1894/1970, 6062.

7. Ibid, 6061.

8. Ibid., 6060.

9. Deuteronomy 13:15, Deuteronomy 20:13, Joshua 6:21, Joshua 8:24, Joshua 10:28-39, Joshua 11:11, etc.

10. Diodorus, 5.32.

11. Not surprisingly, the religion that the Celtae practiced was also savage and brutal. This religion has come to be known best for the blood-thirsty priests who led its unspeakable acts, the "Druids." The actual practices of this religion have mercifully been lost to our modern age. This came about through the number of conquests of the areas ruled by the Celtae giants by the Romans and later the Norsemen, Normans and Saxons. The spread of Christianity through the region spelled the final death blow for the bloody practices of the Druids, leaving behind only altars designed for human sacrifices and the placement of "magic" stone monuments that have recently been discovered to have been carefully aligned with the stars, planets, sun and moon. The Druid religion is currently being revived by New Age and neo-pagan groups worldwide another horrifying fact that suggests another assault against the human race might be in place even as we speak.

Because Ireland was never successfully invaded by the Romans, it remained the last holdout of the human beings who practiced the religion of the Druids after the last of the Celtae giants had apparently died off. St. Patrick and St. Columcille are generally credited with bringing an end to the pagan practices. (St. Patrick was also credited with driving the snakes from Ireland; one might speculate that these "snakes" might have been serpents similar to the serpent in the Garden of Eden. If so, these might have been some sort of fallen angels in the form of reptiles.) There are a few horrific details that have filtered down to us about the Druids' practices, however. One is that these priests not only placed their blessings on human sacrifice, they often performed the rites themselves.

Julius Caesar wrote:

"The Gauls believe the power of the immortal gods can be appeased only if one human life is exchanged for another and they have sacrifices of this kind regularly established by the community. Some of them have enormous images made of wickerwork, the limbs of which they fill with living men; these are set on fire and the men perish, enveloped in the flames. They believe that the gods prefer it if the executed have been caught in the act of theft or armed robbery or some other crime. But when the supply of such victims runs out, they even go to the extent of sacrificing innocent men."

12. Diodorus had an even more horrifying story about how the Celtae giants attempted to read the future:

"They devote to death a human being and plunge a dagger into him in the region above the diaphragm, and when the stricken victim has fallen, they read the future from the manner of his fall and from the twitching of his limbs, as well as from the gushing of

GIANTS ON THE EARTH

the blood, having learned to place confidence in an ancient and long-continued practice of observing such matters."

The exact religious practices of the Anakim are unknown But suffice it to say that the little that has filtered down to us reflects the extreme wickedness and savagery of the Old Testament accounts of these creatures. That groups around the world are now in the process of reviving the Druid and Egyptian practices also speaks volumes about where many in our own times are headed, and what they are really trying to accomplish by reviving this depraved religion.... things are just not always what they appear to be.

11. Julius Caesar, Commentary, 6.16.
12. Diodorus, 5.31.

WHERE ARE THEY NOW?

"There were giantsin the earth in those days...."

[Revelation 9:1] And the fifth angel sounded, and I saw a star fall from heaven unto the earth: and to him was given the key of the bottomless pit.

[Revelation 9:2] And he opened the bottomless pit; ..."

1. The assertions starts with the burden of proof listed in, "GIANTS I", based on the following statement, and further proved beyond doubt that there were indeed a number of civilizations that were giants:

GENESIS 6:2
That the SONS OF GOD saw the daughters of men that they were fair; and they took them wives of all which they chose....

GENESIS 6:4
There were GIANTS in the earth in those days; and also after that, when the SONS OF GOD (Fallen Angels) came in unto the daughters of men, and they bare children to them, the same became mighty men which were of old, men of renown.

The standard contention is: is this biblical myth, or is this a historical reality of the past... and today?

The new challenging assertion set before you is this: where are they now, if they ever really did exist? The answer?...."the inner earth". And the entrances to this new homeland: one at the extreme northern axis of the earth, the other at the extreme southern axis.

Throughout history and various cultures, this new homeland has taken on various appellations:

The Ultimate Thule
Aggartha
Shamballa
Shangri-La
Elusian Fields
Asgard
Atlantis
Valhalla
Realm of Jason & the Argonauts, etc.

GIANTS ON THE EARTH

As fantastic as the assertion sounds, the burden of proof resides in this brief document- tation. But to save space, and not to try your patiences, I have only chosen select passages from each publications included therein. Nevertheless, let us start from the most ancient documentation, progressing to the more contemporary -

Your intellectual foundations are about to be challenged... For truth is sometimes much stranger than fiction

From the "SECRETS OF ENOCH"

2. "The men (literally, angels) took me on to the fifth heaven and placed me, and there I saw many and countless soldiers, called Grigori (rebellious angels), of human appearance, and their size was greater than that of great giants..."

3. "And I said to the Grigori: 'I saw your brethren and their works, and their great torments, and I prayed for them, but the Lord has condemned them to be under earth till heaven and earth shall end forever'. ...."

4. THE BOOK OF ENOCH (The Watchers)

5. "Then they (the angels) took wives, each choosing for himself, whom they began to approach, and with whom they cohabited; teaching them sorcery,

incantations, and the divining of roots and trees. And the women conceiving brought forth giants, whom stature was each three hundreth cubits. ....

6. "To Michael likewise the Lord said,... bind them for seventy generations underneaththe earth,..."

7. "From there I went on towards the extremities of the earth; where I saw large beasts different from each other, and birds various in countenances and forms,

as well as with notes of different sounds. ... "

8. "From there I advanced on towards the north, to the extremities of the earth. And there I saw a great and glorious wonder at the extremities of the whole earth.I saw there heavenly gates opening into heavens; three of them distinctly separated. The northern winds proceeded from them, blowing cold, hail, frost, snow, dew, and rain...."

THE BOOK OF JULBILEES

9. "...that the angels of God saw them (earthly women) on a certain year of this jubilee, that they were beautiful to look upon;

and they took themselves wives of all whom they chose, and they bare to them sons and they were giants. ..."

10."And against the angels whom He (God) had sent upon earth, He was exceedingly wroth, and He gave commandment to root them out of all their dominion,

and He bade us to bind them in the depths of the earth, and behold they bound in the midst of them..."

1.From, THE THE LOST BOOK OF... . Enoch was a distance grandson of Seth; Seth was the 3rd son of Adam. The book in it's entirety contains 45 rare manuscripts. First published in 1926 by Alpha House, Inc.; this reprint is by World Bible Publisher, Inc., and the compiler is Dr. Frank Crane.

2.Ch. XVIII: 1, pg. 87

3.Ch. XVIII: 5, pg 87

4.From, THE BOOKS OF ENOCH, THE WATCHERS, TGS Publishing, Yoakum, TX. 77995. Translated by, Richard Laurence, L.L.D.

GIANTS ON THE EARTH

The Watchers were angels whom were sent by God to instruct man.
Note also that this is an entirely separate publication.
5. Ch.7:10-12, pg. 3.
6. Ch.10:15, pg. 5.
7. Ch.32:1-2, pg. 13.
8. Ch.33:1-3, pg. 13.
9. Another separate publication from THE BOOK OF JUBILEES, pg. 23, Ch. 5:1-2, TGS Publishing, Yoakum, TX. 77995, Translated by R.H. Charles, 1913.
This is an ancient Pharisee text of about 153 BC.
10. Ch. 5:5-7, pg. 23.

ADMIRAL RICHARD B. BYRD'S DIARY (FEB - MAR.1947)
("The Inner Earth : My Secret Diary")
THE LAND BEYOND THE POLES - THE EXPLORATION FLIGHT OVER THE NORTH POLE.

I must write this diary in secrecy and obscurity. It concerns my Arctic flight of the nineteenth day of February in the year of Nineteen and Forty Seven.

There comes a time when the rationality of men must fade into insignificance and one must accept the inevitability of the Truth! am not at liberty to disclose the following documentation at this writing... perhaps it shall never see the light of public scrutiny, but I must do my duty and record here for all to read one day. In a world of greed and exploitation of certain of mankind, one can no longer suppress that which is truth.

1. FLIGHT LOG: BASE CAMP ARCTIC, 2119/1947

0600 HOURS - All preparations are complete for our flight north ward and we are airborne with full fuel tanks at 0610 Hours.....

0910 HOURS - Vast Ice and snow below, note coloration of yellowish nature, and dispersed in a linear pattern. Altering course for a better examination of this color pattern below, note reddish or purple color also. Circle this area two full turns and return to assigned compass heading. Position check made again to base camp, and relay information concerning colorations in the Ice and snow below.

0910 HOURS - Both Magnetic and Gyro compasses beginning to gyrate and wobble, we are unable to hold our heading by instrumentation. Take bearing with Sun compass, yet all seems well. The controls are seemingly slow to respond and have sluggish quality, but there is no indication of Icing!

0915 HOURS - In the distance is what appears to be mountains.

0949 HOURS - 29 minutes elapsed flight time from the first sighting of the mountains, it is no illusion. They are mountains and consisting of a small range that I have never seen before!

0955 HOURS - Altitude change to 2950 feet, encountering strong turbulence again.

2. 1000 HOURS - We are crossing over the small mountain range and still proceeding northward as best as can be ascertained. Beyond the mountain range is what appears to be a valley with a small river or stream running through the center portion. There should be no green valley below! Something is definitely wrong and abnormal here! We should be over Ice and Snow! To the portside are great forests growing on the mountain slopes.

1. To this point, Ch.7, pg. 80.
2. To this point, Ch.7, pg. 81.

GIANTS ON THE EARTH

1140 HOURS - Another radio message received. We begin the landing process now, and in moments the plane shudders slightly, and begins a descent as though caught in some great unseen elevator! The downward motion is negligible, and we touch down with only a slight jolt!

1.1145 HOURS - I am making a hasty last entry in the flight log. Several men are approaching on foot toward our aircraft. They are tall with blond hair.

2. In the distance is a large shimmering city pulsating with rainbow hues of color. I do not know what is going to happen now, but I see no signs of weapons on those approaching. I hear now a voice ordering me by name to open the cargo door. I comply.

END LOG

3. MARCH 11, 1947

I have just attended a staff meeting at the Pentagon. I have stated fully my discovery and the message from the Master. All is duly recorded. The President has been advised. I am now detained for several hours (six hours, thirty-nine minutes, to be exact.) I am interviewed intently by Top Security Forces and a medical team. It was an ordeal! I am placed under strict control via the national security provisions of this United States of America. I am ORDERED TO REMAIN SILENT IN REGARD TO ALL THAT I HAVE LEARNED, ON THE BEHALF OF HUMANITY! Incredible! I am reminded that I am a military man I must obey orders....

In further confirmation of Admiral Byrd's discovery are reports of individuals who claimed they had entered the north polar opening, as many Arctic explorers did without knowing they did, and penetrated far enough into it to reach the Subterranean World in the hollow interior of the Earth. Dr. Nephi Cottom of Los Angeles reported that one of his patients, a man of Nordic descent, told him the following story:

"I lived near the Arctic Circle in Norway. One summer my friend and I made up our minds to take a boat trip together, and go as far as we could into the north country. So we put one month's food provisions in a small fishing boat, and with sail and also a good engine in our boat, we set to sea.

4. At the end of one month we had travelled far into the north, beyond the Pole and into a strange new country. We were much astonished at the weather there. Warm, and at times at night it was almost too warm to sleep. Then we saw something so strange that we both were astonished. Ahead of the warm open sea we were on what looked like a great mountain. Into that mountain at a certain point the ocean seemed to be emptying. Mystified, we continued in that direction and found ourselves sailing into a vast canyon leading into the interior of the earth. We kept sailing and then we saw what surprised us - a sun shining inside the earth!"

5. Several of the inner earth inhabitants - huge giants - detected our boat on the river, and were quite amazed...

1. See "GIANTS 1", for more details on this description.
2. To this point, Ch.7, pg. 82.
3. Ch.7, pg. 85.
4. Ch.1, pg. 12-13.
5. Ch.1, pg. 13.
1. The presence of the open sea in the Northland is also explained. Olaf Jansen claims

GIANTS ON THE EARTH

that the northern aperture, intake or hole, so to speak, is about fourteen hundred miles across. In connection with this, let us read what Explorer Jansen 'writes, on page 288 of his book: "I have never had such a splendid sail. On to the north steadily north, with a good wind, as fast as stream and sail can take us, an open sea mile after mile, watch after watch, through these unknown regions, always clearer and clearer of ice, one might almost say: 'How long will it last?' The eye always turns to the northward as one paces the bridge. It is gazing into the future. But them is always the same dark sky ahead which means open sea." Again, the Norwood Review of England, in its issue of May 10, 1884, says: "We do not admit that there is ice up to the Pole - once inside the great ice barrier, a new world breaks upon the Explorer, the climate is mild like that of England, and, afterward, balmy as the Greek Isles."......

2. My name is Olaf Jansen. I am a Norwegian, although I was born in the little seafaring Russian town of Uleaborg, on the eastern coast of the Gulf of Bothnia, the northern arm of the Baltic Sea.

I was in my nineteenth year when we started on what proved to be our last trip as fishermen, and which resulted in the strange story that shall be given to the world, - but not until I have finished my earthly pilgrimage...

There was a tradition my father explained, that still farther northward was a land more beautiful than any that mortal man had ever known, and that it was inhabited by the Chosen.

3. My youthful imagination was fired by the ardor, zeal and religious fervor of my good father, and I exclaimed: 'why not sail to this goodly land? The sky is fair, the wind favorable and the sea open."....

The compass, which we had fastened back in its place, in fear of another storm, was still pointing due north, and moving on its pivot just as it had in Stockholm. The dipping of the needle had ceased. What could this mean? Then, too, our many days of sailing had certainly carried us far past the North Pole. And yet the needle continued to point north. We were sorely perplexed, for surely our direction was now south.....

4. Along the banks great forests miles in extent could be seen stretching away on the shoreline. The trees were of enormous size. We landed after anchoring near a sandy beach, and waded ashore, and were rewarded by finding a quantity of nuts that were very palatable and satisfying to hunger, and a welcome change from the monotony of our stock of provisions....

1. Excerpt from the author's Forward, pg. 5.
2. From this point on, all quotes are from Olaf Jansen, whom is dictating the story to W.G. Emerson. Pg. 7.
3. Ch.2, pg. 10.
4. Ch.3, pg. 15.

It was about the first of September, over five months we calculated, since our leave taking from Stockholm. Suddenly we were frightened almost out of our wits by hearing in the far distance the singing of people. Very soon thereafter we discovered a huge ship gliding down the river directly toward us. Those aboard were singing in one mighty chorus that, echoing from bank to bank, sounded like a thousand voices, filling the whole universe with quivering melody. The accompaniment was played on stringed instruments

GIANTS ON THE EARTH

not unlike our harps.

It was a larger ship than any we had ever seen, and was differently constructed....

The immense craft paused, and almost immediately a boat was lowered and six men of gigantic stature rowed to our little fishing-sloop. They spoke to us in a strange language. We knew from their manner, however, that they were not unfriendly. They talked a great deal among themselves, and one of them laughed immoderately, as though in finding us a queer discovery had been made. One of them spied our compass, and it seemed to interest them more than any other part of our sloop.....

1. "They seem to be kindly disposed," I replied, "although what terrible giants! They must be the select six of the kingdom's crack regiment. Just look at their great size...."

2. The surprise of my father and myself was indescribable when, amid the regal magnificence of a spacious hall, we were finally brought before the Great High Priest, ruler over all the land. He was richly robed, and much taller than those about him, and could not have been less than fourteen or fifteen feet in height. The immense room in which we were received seemed finished in solid slabs of gold thickly studded with jewels of amazing brilliancy....

3. I remember hearing my father remark that the giant race of people in the land of 'The Smoky God had almost as accurate an idea of the geography of the "outside" surface of the earth as had the average college professor in Stockholm.......

"That at the name of Jesus every knee should bow, of things in heaven, and things in earth, and things under the earth;" Phillipian 2:10

"And no man in heaven, nor in earth, neither under the earth, was able to open the book, neither to look thereon." Revelations 5:3

"Seven rivers I beheld upon earth, greater than all rivers, one of which takes its course from the west; it to a great sea its water flows. Two comes from the north to the sea, there waters flowing into the Erythraean sea, on the east. And with respect to the remaining four, they take their course in the cavity of the north" Book Of Enoch 76:6-7

1. Ch.3, pg. 16.
2. Ch.3, pg. 19.
3. Ch.4, pg. 21.

PROLOGUE:
IN THE FIRST PLACE PLEASE BEAR IN MIND THAT I do not expect you to believe this story. Nor could you wonder had you witnessed a recent experience of mine when, in the armor of blissful and stupendous ignorance, I gaily narrated the gist of it to a Fellow of the Royal Geological Society on the occasion of my last trip to London....

1. The erudite gentleman in whom I confided congealed before I was half through! It is all that saved him from exploding--and my dreams of an Honorary Fellowship, gold medals, and a niche in the Hall of Fame faded into the thin, cold air of his arctic atmosphere....

As I looked I began to appreciate the reason for the strangeness of the landscape that had haunted me from the first with an illusive suggestion of the bizarre and unnatural - THERE WAS NO HORIZON! As far as the eye could reach out the sea continued and upon its bosom floated tiny islands, those in the distance reduced to mere specks; but ever beyond them was the sea, until the impression became quite real that one was LOOKING

GIANTS ON THE EARTH

UP at the most distant point that the eyes could fathom -distance was lost in the distance. That was all - here was no clear-cut horizontal line marking the dip of the globe below the line of vision". A great light is commencing to break on me," continued Perry, taking out his watch. "I believe that I have partially solved the riddle It is now two o'clock. When we emerged from the prospector the sun was directly above us. Where is it now?"

2. I glanced up to find the great orb still motionless in the center of the heaven. And such a sun! I had scarcely noticed it before. Fully thrice the size of the sun I had known throughout my life, and apparently so near that the sight of it carried the conviction that one might almost reach up and touch it.....

When we had passed out of the amphitheater onto the great plain we saw a caravan of men and women - human beings like ourselves-and for the first time hope and relief filled my heart, until I could have cried out in the exuberance of my happiness. It is true that they were a half-naked, wild-appearing aggregation; but they at least were fashioned along the same lines as ourselves - there was nothing grotesque or horrible about them as about the other creatures in this strange, weird world.

3. But as we came closer, our hearts sank once more, for we discovered that the poor wretches were chained neck to neck in a long line,... With little ceremony Perry and I were chained at the end of the line, and without further ado the interrupted march was resumed....

4. On we stumbled beneath that hateful noonday sun. If we fell we were prodded with a sharp point. Our companions in chains did not stumble. They strode along proudly erect. Occasionally they would exchange words with one another in a monosyllabic language. They were a noble-appearing race with well-formed heads and perfect physiques. The men were heavily bearded, tall and muscular; the women, smaller and more gracefully molded, with great masses of raven hair caught into loose knots upon their heads. The features of both sexes were well proportioned..........

1 .As stated in the title, this is an excerpt from the author's Prologue, E.R. Burroughs; it ends here.

2. Ch.1, pg. 7. From this point forward, the quotes are quoted by David Innes to Burroughs.

3. Ch.3. pg. 13.

4. Ch.3. pg. 14.

MY EPILOGUE:

There are some additional notes I wish to point out before closing. According to the ancient manuscripts, the Watchers not only provoked God by going into earthly women but, they also provoked Him by going into different animals - bestiality. And they taught man these depraved acts as well. And the results of their offsprings, as you would probably surmise: terrible giants, unheard of abominations, horrible to look upon. Even the ancient historian Herodotus (circa 500 BC) made minute quotes of some of these attrocities (sic) of nature. But let us quote from another ancient manuscripts that was mentioned by the chroniclers of Joshua 10:13, and 2 Samuel 1:18 :

From THE BOOK OF JASHER

1."And their judges and rulers (which were the giants at this time) went to the daughters of men and took their wives by force from their husbands according to their choice,

GIANTS ON THE EARTH

and son of men of those days took from the cattle of the earth, the beasts of field, and fowls of the air, and taught the mixture of animals of one species with the other, in order therewith to provoke the Lord; and God saw that the whole earth and it was corrupt, for all flesh had corrupted its ways upon earth, all men and all animals."

From THE BOOK OF JUBULIEES

2."And lawlessness increased on the earth and all flesh corrupted its way, alike men and cattle and beasts and birds and everything that walks on the earth - all of them corrupted their ways and their orders, and they began to devour each other,..."

3. ...and the earth was filled with inquity (sic). And after this they sinned against the beasts and the birds, and all that moves and walks on the earth..."

I think it may be high time that we all had a little private conference with our teachers of Archaeology, Paleontology, Anthropology, Geology, and as well as Geography and Cartography.

"And the LORD said unto Satan, Whence comest thou? Then Satan answered the LORD, and said, From going to and fro in the earth, and from walking up and down in it." Job 1:7

"The devil is the evil spirit of the lower places..."
Secrets of Enoch 31:4

1. From, THE BOOK OF JASHER (The Upright Record), TGS Publishing, Yoakum, TX. 77995, Ch. 4:18, pg. 8.
2. THE BOOK OF JUBILEES, Ch. 5:2, pg. 23.
3. Ch. 7:24, pg. 28.

1. From, THE LOST BOOK OF... . Enoch was a distance grandson of Seth; Seth was the 3rd son of Adam. The book in it's entirety contains 45 rare manuscripts. First published in 1926 by Alpha House, Inc.; this reprint is by World Bible Publisher, Inc., and the compiler is Dr. Frank Crane.
2. Ch. XVIII:1, pg. 87
3. Ch. XVIII:5, pg 87
4. From, THE BOOKS OF ENOCH, THE WATCHERS, TGS Publishing, Yoakum, TX. 77995. Translated by, Richard Laurence, L.L.D. The Watchers were angels whom were sent by God to instruct man. Note also that this is an entirely separate publication.
5. Ch.7:10-12, pg. 3.
6. Ch.10:15, pg. 5.
7. Ch.32:1-2, pg. 13.
8. Ch.33:1-3, pg. 13.
9. Another separate publication from THE BOOK OF JUBILEES, pg. 23, Ch. 5:1-2, TGS Publishing, Yoakum, TX. 77995, Translated by R.H. Charles, 1913. This is an ancient Pharisee text of about 153 BC.
10. Ch. 5:5-7, pg. 23.

1.To this point, Ch.7, pg. 80.
2.To this point, Ch.7, pg. 81.

1.See "GIANTS I", for more details on this description.

GIANTS ON THE EARTH

2.To this point, Ch.7, pg. 82.
3.Ch.7, pg. 85.
4.Ch.1, pg. 12-13.
5.Ch.1, pg. 13.

1.Excerpt from the author's Forward, pg. 5.
2.From this point on, all quotes are from Olaf Jansen, whom is dictating the story to W.G. Emerson. pg. 7.
3.Ch.2, pg. 10.
4.Ch.3, pg. 15.

1.Ch.3, pg. 16.
2.Ch.3, pg. 19.
3.Ch.4, pg. 21.

----

1. As stated in the title, this is an excerpt from the author's Prologue, E.R. Burroughs; it ends here.
2. Ch.1, pg. 7. From this point forward, the quotes are quoted by David Innes to Burroughs.
3. Ch.3. pg. 13.
4. Ch.3. pg. 14.

----

1. From, THE BOOK OF JASHER (The Upright Record), TGS Publishing, Yoakum, TX. 77995, Ch. 4:18, pg. 8.
2. THE BOOK OF JUBILEES, Ch. 5:2, pg. 23.
3. Ch. 7:24, pg. 28.

GIANTS ON THE EARTH

Facts for the Times;
A Collection of Valuable Historical Extracts

Giants
In the first age of the world, man lived almost a thousand years; while now he rarely exceeds the allotted threescore and ten.

This is clearly shown, not only by the Bible and ancient history, but by the discoveries of antediluvian remains.

The Gospel Herald of Dayton, Ohio, gives the following account:

In the Scientific Department of one of our most popular weekly exchanges, we find an interesting account of a large human skeleton, recently discovered in Ain, France.

The frame is complete in all its parts, and is four yards in height. It was found in a soil of alluvium, the head buried in the earth, with the feet upward."

Day before yesterday, while the quarrymen employed by the Sauk Rapids Water Power Company (Minnesota) were engaged in quarrying rock for the dam which is being erected across the Mississippi at this place, they found embedded in the solid granite rock the remains of a human being of gigantic stature.

About seven feet below the surface of the ground, and about three and a half feet beneath the upper stratum of rock, the remains were found imbedded in the sand, which had evidently been placed in the quadrangular grave which had been dug out of the solid rock to receive the last remains of this antediluvian giant.

The grave was twelve feet in length, four feet wide, and about three feet in depth, and is today, at least two feet below the present level of the river.

The remains are completely petrified, and are of gigantic dimensions. The head is massive, measures thirty one and one half inches in circumference, but low in the os frontis, and very flat on the top.

The femur measures twenty six and a quarter inches, and the fibula twenty five and a half, while the body is equally long in proportion.

From the crown of the head to the sole of the foot, the length is ten feet nine and a half inches. The measure around the chest is fifty nine and a half inches. This giant must have

GIANTS ON THE EARTH

weighed at least nine hundred pounds, when covered with a reasonable amount of flesh.
Reprint: Facts for the Times; A Collection of Valuable Historical Extracts
pages 171-72; G.I. Butler. 1885

Ancient American
Issue #43, page17
Reprinted with permission
Giants and Ancient North American Warfare

Per the author's request, his following submission is presented unedited as received, without standard revision for grammar or clarity. As part of our open forum policy, writers may freely express themselves in their own words. Editor.

Long ago in central North America, there was a great civil war. It was a war owning many battles, and had an incredible loss of life. It wasn't the North versus the South, although it sponsored a confederacy against a union. It probably spanned the geography of a number of present day states commencing from the area that is the boundary line of the ancient Mississippi. There, the great tribes of the west encountered for the first time the great nation of the east, and the resultant history. Nor shall we say prehistory, ultimately shaped the pre-Columbian world far more than can ever be understood. Our archaeological record holds relatively limited data of this time period, much less this proposed event, and thus we are dependent to some extent on the invaluable resource of Native American transmission.

The ancient homeland of the Adena and Hopewell cultures enter the map of five states cover five present day states. Were the previous tenants of this region the Allegany People?

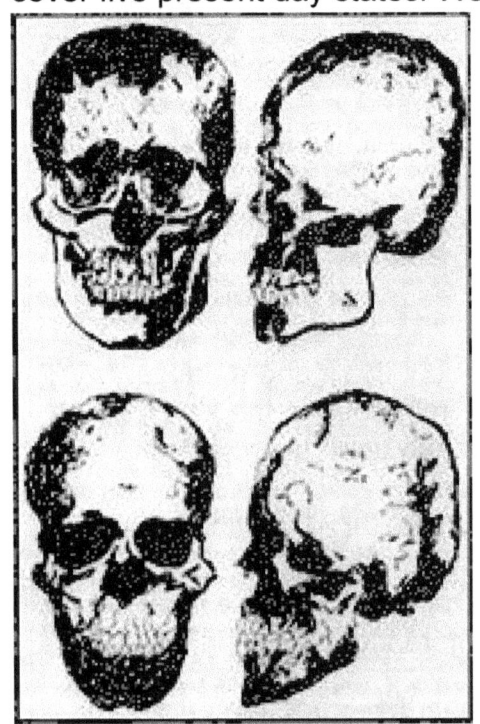

Adena male (top) and female skulls. Note the "bilateral protrusions" at the strong jaw hinge.

Our related science's present understanding of the pre-Adena (Archaic) inhabitants of the greater Ohio River valley is yet somewhat sketchy, what to say of the Adena themselves. However, many pieces to the puzzle are now thought to be in place. The timeline for the Adena begins around 1000 B.C.E. according to the carbon dating of Dragoo and others. The Archaic populous is not believed to have constructed mounds in the Ohio Valley region, although this is not known for certain due to several factors, including widespread destruction of the earthworks, without content cataloging, over the last 250 years. Most understanding is based upon the dating and trait-grouping of materials found in the diminished number of mounds and village sites yet existing after a formal discipline in archaeology and anthropology finally took over excavation and detailed record keeping.

There are Archaic era mounded structures, often intricate and complex, in the deep southern U.S., including Watson Brake, Poverty Point, Fig Island, and Sapelo. For this reason, theories have been put forth

GIANTS ON THE EARTH

that the moundbuilding tradition came into the Ohio Valley around the time of the Adena from the southern Mississippi, thereby tentatively associating the Adena people with older cultures from the south. In one way of looking at this idea, it supposes that moundbuilding was a phenomenon peculiar to only one geographical source, necessarily having been passed on. Unlike the Adena mounds however, the more ancient southern earthworks did not poignantly suggest a very specialized "cult of the dead."

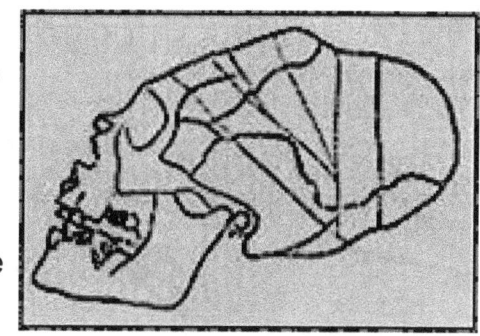

By their skeletal remains in the earlier studies, the pre-Adena people were known to have had slender or thin bodies, and been "long-headed," with "narrow" skulls (dolichocranic), i.e. having a breadth of skull small in proportion to length from front to back. The Adena people weren't physically akin to these Archaic people. Generally the Adena had more massive bone structure, according to these same studies. The pre-eminent theory of Adena origin at the time was that their ancestry had come from Mexico or even further south. However, the Adena body bone structure type was unusually difficult to trace with surety south of the Rio Grande where another distinguishing Adena-resonant trait was found practiced from earlier times. That practice was "cradleboard" head deformation.

The Adena were, as a group, more "short-headed" (brachycranic), i.e. the skull breadth was at least four-fifths its length from front to back. Shaping was an Non-Adena addition to this already distinguished skull type.

As shown in earlier studies, the pre-practice of skull deformation was part of the prehistoric "long-headed" type Peruvian, Middle American, and Mexican people's customs. Indian Knoll population practiced a form of skull-flattening. Thus this "art" was part of the local lore when the Adena made their first appearance. Their subsequent and perhaps more 'evolved' version of cradleboarding had the effect of giving the skull a more round dome, and is thought by some to have been strictly for class distinction in a hierarchical society. Their skull type has the highest cranial vault ever found anywhere in the world. In this, Adena folk are sometimes referred to as "round-headed," for they had the roundish skull to begin with, further shaping the vault to a dome.

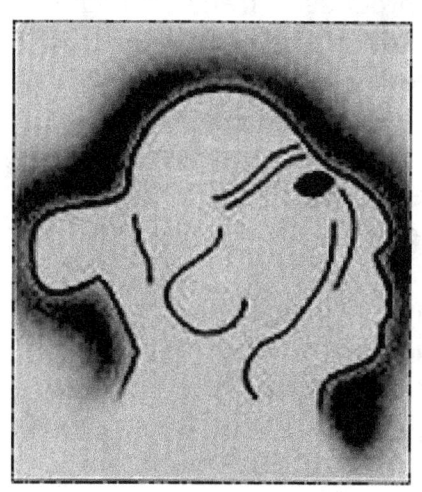

Outline of the head of a statue of a woman found in the bottom land of the Ohio River near Tolu, KY

Needless to say, these findings cast doubt on any exclusive Mexican head binding connection. That coupled with new studies suggesting the tough Adena skeletal type arriving not from Mexico, but from the southern margins of the Great Lakes, and the old pet theories were melting faster than the glaciers. New questions were being posed.

Since few or no other recognizable Mexican-type traits appeared among the Adena grave goods until the centuries-later Adena burials, why, after a many centuries lapse,

GIANTS ON THE EARTH

did the traits indicating Central and South American influence appear in the Ohio Valley?

It was beginning to seem that everything distinguishing the Adena, with the possible exception of mounds for the dead, was already in the region for a very long time. It was no longer solid ground to theorize the direct ancestors of the first Adena moving out of Mexico and, after a time, up the Mississippi watershed just because there was skull shaping in ancient Mexico, and earthworks in the deep south.

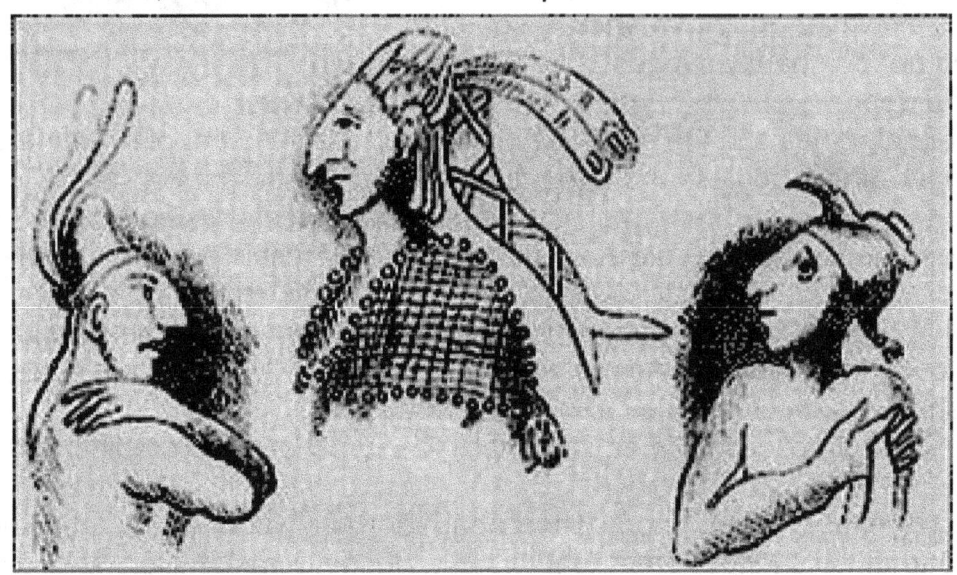

**Mexican emperor and attendants taken from Humboldt.
(Delafield, 1839)**

Like a real mystery, there were more questions than answers. Investigators began asking whether a fresh, new scenario should be considered to explain the origins of the Adena.

Popular Theories

In about 800 years, and after Adena villages and towns became established throughout what is now Ohio, Indiana, Kentucky, West Virginia, and Pennsylvania, a new stock or breed of people is, by inference, thought to have begun the process of transforming that culture very probably from within. So in a sense, after the Adena seemed to supplant an older culture in the Ohio Valley, another culture succeeded them in relatively linear fashion. Ultimately, this new culture redefined the older Adena. This proposed phenomenon of transformation and replacement characterized what is known as the "Hopewell" era, which term, like Adena and Indian, had been assigned by the inheriting whites. Anthropologists as archaeologists therefore ask these questions. How did the Adena begin, and why did they end, and in the same vein, how and why are they so intimately related to the Hopewell? Why did this supposedly "hybrid" Hopewell culture achieve such distinction and domination over their Adena predecessors, then, like small colonies of the Adena before them, seem to simply fade out from the Ohio valley?

The main theory holding interest for many years has been simply that after these round-headed people arrived in the Ohio Valley, they gradually (though not at first) interbred

GIANTS ON THE EARTH

with the existing long-headed people, and over a few centuries slowly generated what we call the Hopewell culture. The Hopewell are believed, though not fully proven, to have evolved agriculture and art further than the Adena, and some of the accomplishments in the latter category amaze us yet today. What has kept our science most intensely interested about the Adena however, is that they constructed mounds for honoring the dead, and were selective about how they went about it. Then, like some sort of magnificent catalyst, the Adena graciously seem to have wandered away, followed into lost history not long after by their believed progeny Hopewell.

It should be stated that until now, DNA testing has found no specific match between the Adena-Hopewell and any existing Native American group. Thus has the mystery deepened immeasurably, leaving our anthropological science with its logic, wits, and sometimes questionable carbon-14 analysis. Who were these people?

There may be alternative explanations, however conjectural, for the Adena origin and exit. Based first upon the physical analysis, speculations and summations of Webb, Snow, Dragoo, and their colleagues and predecessors, the thoughtful entering of Native American legend into the analysis provides some clear fuel for that soon to be mentioned lamp shedding light on what has too long remained a dim prehistory.

As inferred, it is believed that the traits related as Hopewell began to show up around 200 B.C.E. or so. No Hopewell traits have been found in Adena tombs, and thus it has been suggested that Adena chronologically preceded and were culturally anterior to Hopewell. It required some time before the archaeological analysis discerned the Adena as separable from the Hopewell who themselves finally left the region about the middle of the first millennium of the Common Era. It was determined that within just a few centuries after Hopewell began to appear. The purely Adena traits were virtually gone from the Ohio Valley.

The Hopewell thus had the valley to themselves for a few hundred years. During this time they yet practiced some limited cradleboard shaping, once almost universal among the Adena. Moundbuilding continued, but changed internally, emphasizing single individuals more. There was evidence of the Adena skeletal type, though in a diminished capacity. Yet artifact evidence of the Adena showed up in points to the south (the Copena Culture), and far to the east, such as the St. Lawrence and Delaware areas, before becoming extinct. The absence of Adena traits in the mounds of the later times ascribed to the Hopewell has prompted a few interesting theories, including a forced exclusion of the Adena by the Hopewell. But this may or may not tell the true story, if we are to rely at all upon the traditional history or legend of a certain elder tribe, who now are called the Lenni Lenape.

The Legend

From Henry Schoolcraft, noted scholar on the subject, we have this reference to a most antique and mysterious tribe or nation:

The oldest tribe of the United States, of which there is a distinct tradition, were the Alleghans. The term is perpetuated in the principal chain of mountains traversing the country. This tribe, at an antique period, had the seat of their power in the Ohio valley and its confluent streams, which were the sites of their numerous towns and villages. They appear originally to have borne the name of Alli, or Alleg, and hence the names of

GIANTS ON THE EARTH

Talligewi and Allegewi. By adding to the radical of this word the particle hany or ghany, meaning river, they described the principal scene of their residence namely, the Allegheny, or River of the Alleghans, now called Ohio. The word Ohio is of Iroquois origin, and of a far later period; having been bestowed by them after their conquest of the country, in alliance with the Lenapees, or ancient Delawares. (Phi. Trans.) The term was applied to the entire river, from its confluence with the Mississippi, to its origin in the broad spurs of the Alleghanies, in New York and Pennsylvania; and the designation, to its sources, is still continued in use by that people.

From the traditions of the Lenapees, given to the Moravian missionaries, while the lamp of their traditional history still threw out its flickering but enlivening flames, the Alleghans had been a strong and mighty people, capable of great exertions and doing wonders. Lenni Lenape

John Heckewelder

Schoolcraft, referring to the entire Appalachian chain as the Alleghenies, is believed to have secured his information specifically from the writings of John Heckewelder, assistant to the Moravian missionary David Zeisberger, himself from Moravia. Together Zeisberger and Heckewelder founded the town of Shoenbrun, near present day New Philadelphia, Ohio. They successfully converted as many as 400 Delaware to the Christian faith through peaceful persuasion, doubtless making many close allies during the work. Heckewelder's account may not be the only one concerning prehistoric America, but it is surely reliable for the conveyance of the tradition of the Delaware, who were derived, however indirectly, of the venerable Lenni Lenape. Heckewelder writes regarding the Allegewi:

Many wonderful things are told of this famous people. They are said to have been remarkably tall and stout, and there is a tradition that there were giants among them, people of a much larger size than the tallest of the Lenape.

Many centuries ago, the Lenni Lenape, for some undisclosed reason, moved en masse from the western half of the present day United States, toward the east. As the legend goes, these people found themselves at the shore of the Mississippi, the white man's enunciation of their Namesi Sipu, River of Fish. There they met up with the Mengwe, who had come from a bit further north and closer to the source of the Namesi Sipu, perhaps the present-day Missouri. It was a meeting of destiny, and was, at that time, a peaceful one. The Lenape sent out their scouts across the broad current.

James A. Jones, another writer of the time, relates of the occasion of the safe return of these "spies" for the Lenape, having reconnoitered the eastern side of the Mississippi:

They told, that they had found the further bank of the River of Fish inhabited by a very powerful people, who dwelt in great villages, surrounded by high walls. They were very tall, so tall that the head of the tallest Lenape could not reach their arms, and their women were of higher stature and heavier limbs than the loftiest and largest man in the confed-

GIANTS ON THE EARTH

erate nations. They were called the Allegewi, and were men delighting in red and black paint, and the shrill war-whoop, and the strife of the spear. Such was the relation and made by spies to their countrymen.

The legend moves very quickly then. In the words of Heckewelder:

...They sent a message to the Allegewi to request permission to settle themselves in their neighborhood. This was refused them, but they obtained leave to pass through the country and seek a settlement farther to the eastward. They accordingly began to cross the Namesi Sipu, when the Allegewi, seeing that their numbers were so great, and in fact they consisted of many thousands, made a furious attack on those that had crossed, threatening them all with destruction, if they dared persist in coming over to their side of the river. Fired at the treachery of these people, and the great loss of men they had sustained, and besides, not being prepared for a conflict, the Lenape consulted on what was to be done; whether to retreat in the best manner they could, or try their strength, and let the enemy see they were not cowards.

While one should always be aware that history as related by the victorious side may not be history as it actually occurred, never the less the resultant war is related as eventually becoming an overwhelming loss for the Alleghans. Whether the Lenape were considered deceitful in not disclosing their vast hoard is perhaps irrelevant. While one account says the Allegewi were extirpated, another relates of their escape down the Mississippi. The Lenni Lenape, having made an alliance with the Mengwe,

The settlements of the "Middle Adena" correspond precisely to Heckewelder's accounts of the prehistoric Lenni Lenape. took many years, and through a great loss of people, claim to have finally defeated the Alleghans through force of arms. As noted again later, these Mengwe followed after the Lenape in war, staying back to avoid injury as much as they might. Perhaps this was on account of their agreement, that upon the defeat of the Allegheny people, the Lenni Lenape would take for themselves the heartland of their adversaries, while the Mengwe would be awarded the lands to the north, nearer to the Great Lakes, and the latitude whence they came.

As the legend completes itself, the two triumphant tribes lived together in peace and cooperation for many centuries. But having done this, it is related that the lands to the east were found to be uninhabited by any enemies, and that they were rich and beautiful, the destiny of the Great Spirit for the people. On this account, they ultimately moved eastward, leaving again the Ohio country comparatively vacant.

Out of these ancient people of the Lenape (who are assumed to have bred with the Mengwe only to a lesser extent at the beginning), no less than 40 tribes are said thereafter to have arisen. In hindsight, not only would this have required a great number of generations, but also it may explain the difficulty in DNA pattern matching with an ancestral people living millennia before. As for the Mengwe, their destiny as the Iroquois is well known, being that of the Confederation of the Five Tribes, and then the Tuscorora [sic]. Later of course, the Lenni Lenape, as the Delaware, became bitter enemies with the Iroquois.

David Cusick, a Tuscorora [sic] by birth, writes in 1825 that among the legends of ancient stock, there was a powerful tribe called Ronnongwetowanca. They were giants, and had a "considerable habitation." He says that when the Great Spirit made the people, some of them became giants. The giants were said to have had a "silly" mode of attack,

GIANTS ON THE EARTH

waiting until their intended victim was not expecting anything. After a time, and having endured the outrages of these giants, it is said that the people ended together, and through the final force of about 800 warriors, successfully annihilated all of the abhorrent Ronnongwetowanca people. After that, it was said that there were no giants anywhere. This was supposed to have happened around 2,500 winters before Columbus discovered America, i.e. around 1000 B.C.E.-the time that the Adena seem to have arrive in the Ohio Valley.

There appears to be coincidental links, combining legend and archaeology, between the possible existence of a great nation having giants among their people, their struggle in war, and the beginning time of the Adena in the Ohio Valley.

The Mound Builders

It is no great stretch to reason the possibility that mound construction, especially mortuary, was not necessarily transferred to the Ohio region from the southeast region. In point of view, there may be logic in it. Heckewelder writes:

Having thus united their forces, the Lenape and Mengwe declared war against the Allegewi. And great battles were fought, in which many warriors fell on both sides... An engagement took place in which hundreds fell who were afterwards buried in holes or laid together in heaps and covered over with earth.

Such an after-battle chore would be the warriors' choice. Mound building of this type is as ancient a practice as can be imagined. It was not only clean, but was practical, and probably respectable as well.

Then from where the Mengwe are thought to have come before they joined the Lenni Lenape, i.e. from the region of the Mississippi's source confluence at the Dakota Missouri, we have this, originally entitled "A Prehistoric Cemetery:"

Two miles from Mandan, on the bluffs near the junction of the Hart and Missouri Rivers, says the local newspaper, the Pioneer, is an old cemetery of fully 100 acres in extent filled with bones of a giant race. This vast city of the dead lies just east of the Fort Lincoln road. The ground has the appearance of having been filled with trenches piled full of dead bodies, both man and beast, and covered with several feet of earth. In many places mounds from 8 to 10 feet high, and some of them 100 feet or more in length, have been thrown up and are filled with bones, broken pottery, vases of various bright colored flint, and agates. The pottery is of a dark material beautifully decorated, delicate in finish, and as light as wood, showing the work of a people skilled in the arts and possessed of a high state of civilization. This has evidently been a grand battlefield, where thousands of men ... have fallen. Nothing like a systematic or intelligent exploration has been made as only little holes two or three feet in depth have been dug in some of the mounds, but many parts of the anatomy of man and beast, and beautiful specimens of broken pottery and other curiosities, have been found in these feeble efforts at excavation. Five miles above Mandan, on the opposite side of the Missouri, is another vast cemetery as yet unexplored. We asked an aged Indian what his people knew of these ancient graveyards. He answered: "Me know nothing about them. They were here before the redman."

Mounds wherein the dead were placed and covered with earth to avoid open decay and the diseases associated with it are as easy to accept as yesterday's news. This is a possible explanation for the origin of mounds for the honored dead-the slain heroes and

GIANTS ON THE EARTH

men sacrificed in discharging the dreadful arts of war. Through the eyes of the participant warriors, such a battlefield practice may have served as a fitting memorial, reminding them of their struggles. Later, it could have been reenacted in quieter surroundings by the Adena. Such mounds or cemeteries as quoted above, holding the remains of people of above average stature, even giants, possibly pushes the practice of moundbuilding back into an undisclosed period of prehistory.

The inclusion of broken pottery in the above mound is similar to the Adena practice of placing broken pottery in the fill of their mounds (Dragoo. Mounds For the Dead, 1963, p.246). Could this be symbolic of the soul's "vessel" being broken? Because Webb and Snow (Adena People, 1981 p.314-15) are emphatic that the Adena showed no signs of being engaged in any warfare practice at all, one might assume that the practice was pre-Adena, re-enacted to become as tradition by them.

From History of Huron and Erie Counties (Ohio), we also have this excerpt recorded by W.W. Williams in 1879:

In the township of Milan there were three clearly-defined [sic] as first seen by him when the first settlers came into the country, and they are still not entirely leveled by the plowshare. All three were upon the highbanks of the Huron ...F. W. Fowler, one of the pioneers of Milan, describes these earth-works [sic], as first seen by him, to have been from two to four feet above the surface of the ground. Large trees were growing upon some of these embankments. Near these forts were mounds or hillocks, which were found to contain human bones, promiscuously thrown together as if a large number of bodies had been buried at one time. The skull bones, when found entire, were shown by measurement to be larger, upon the average, and all exhibited marks that would indicate that life had been taken in deadly combat. Scattered among the skulls and vertebrae, and arm and leg bones, were stone pipes and fragments of burnt clay.

Could these earthworks and remains have been slightly pre-Adena? The accounts of the Allegheny say that they built strong fortifications. Although the above notices offer some beginning evidence for earlier mounds, according to the 20th century archaeological investigations, the Adena seem to have started the practice of moundbuilding for the dead. Curiously, the Adena had "tall members" among their people, extraordinarily tall, in fact, and massive in skeletal structure, exactly the way the Allegewi were first described. This however does not mean that the Allegewi were the Adena, for there is no sign that the Adena were makers or recipients or war. This may be important to remember.

Unlike the Allegewi, and in accord with the statistics of Webb and Snow, in the majority of Adena skeletons cataloged, the average height of a man was considerably less than six feet (168.0 cm or about 5'6"), and the women were proportionally smaller (158.8 cm or about 5'3"). But there were also numbers of burials catering to a special class of individuals, wherein the skeletal length-of six feet was not uncommon. So while on one hand relatively fewer tall skeletons were discovered by academic archaeological efforts in the last century, on the other enough were found to give rise to special theories concerning these people. Most Adena folk were apparently cremated.

Don Dragoo, in discussing these "honored dead" and referring to this taller Adena stature, says in his Mounds For the Dead:

Two outstanding traits have been noted repeatedly for this group. One is the protrud-

GIANTS ON THE EARTH

ing and massive chin often with prominent bilateral protrusions (Webb and Snow, 1959, p. 37). The second trait is the large size of many of the males and some of the females. A male of six feet was common and some individuals approaching seven feet in height have been found ... Not only were these Adena people tall, but also the massiveness of the bones indicates powerfully built individuals. The head was generally big with a large cranial capacity.

"Massive in skeletal structure" perhaps reflects the term "stout" used by Heckewelder. These observances were in the late Adena tombs, and although the earlier Adena graves yielded far fewer measurable remains, large skulls were also discovered among those graves. Webb and Snow suggested the possibility of "sexual and social selection" being factors in the development of the large-chinned Adena type. Thus it is of course generally interpreted that these people possibly bred selectively. Dragoo agrees, adding:

If only certain inbreeding individuals of the total population were members of the "selected group" genetic factors would also have played an important part in the establishment of the unique Adena physical type found in the late Adena tombs. Any changes (mutations) in the gene pool either dominant or recessive would soon be distributed among all the members of the group. Dragoo, Mounds For the Dead

It would make sense that such selective breeding would be assiduously practiced, and for several good reasons. The main purpose could have been the creation of a guardian or warrior class made up of physically superior men and women. With any luck, these people would also have an above average intellectual capacity as well. But did the genetic traits for larger, more powerful human beings commence with the Adena? The grave evidence does not suggest it. As anyone who does breeding, albeit on the animal level knows, it's far easier to start with an established type that to start from scratch. It would be most difficult to attempt such a selective process if all you had to start with were a handful of unfortunate people owning the conditions of acromegaly and giantism.

Thus it would seem that these Adena folk already had among their race a very rare ancestral lineage and line descent. They had, in other words, people of pedigree. Studies have also indicated, as in the case of the Adena, when a people settle down and have a good nutritional food supply, they grow larger and stronger.

Robert Silverberg, in his well accepted The Mound Builders, after referencing similarly the appropriate authorities, writes:

This band of people of great size forced its way into the Ohio Valley about 1000 B.C., it seems.

Yes, it seems that way. Shortly after, he adds this interesting note:

Perhaps there was a small elite of round-headed giants dominating and ruling an existing long-headed Ohio Valley population.

It is not difficult to share Mr. Silverberg's wisdom in the speculation of an elite group of very tall people, perhaps a ruling class, being with the Adena. It might be reiterated as well that such a genetic trait could, in the light of practicality, be pre-Adena.

How ancient were the Allegewi? Did the practice of funerary moundbuilding stem from the post war necessity of quick physical interment? Were the "honored dead" buried in the tradition of the warrior class, in the non-cremation style, after the practice of mass mound-graves following great battles? Were the taller, perhaps more accomplished

GIANTS ON THE EARTH

members of the Adena given special rank and privilege? Why did these giants show up with greater distinction in the later Adena burials? How long would it have taken the Adena to build a new tradition from Allegewi stock?

A Tradition of Giants

In Silverberg's words, Heckewelder's reference to the Allegewi as giants "touched off a search for a race of giant mound builders in the Ohio Valley."

Indeed, the pioneering whites and their descendants enthusiastically performed their own examination of the uncounted mound-tombs, leaving relatively few for the archaeologists some years later. Stretching in large part from Pennsylvania to Indiana, the sheer number of raised earthen and stone works boggled the imagination. Upon life's end, some Adena would be interred fight into the floor of their home, the whole covered with earth, making little clusters of mounds at intervals throughout the countryside, preserving the sites of their former hamlets. As it turned out, there were many extra-large skeletons reported in the various records of townships and counties, all independent of one another. Whether Heckewelder and others touched off this search may be irrelevant, because it was virtually irresistible for these early settlers to look inside these ancient earthworks, located in their "back 40" as it were.

Being mostly of Euro-Celtic decent, these pioneering-types enjoyed comparing the giant jawbones of the skulls they found with their own. Says Dragoo:

One of the peculiar features present in at least one-half of the observed examples is the great width of the bony chin formed by bilateral eminences rarely found among the skulls of the much earlier Shell Heap People or among the later Hopewell People. Mounds For the Dead

From the Ironton Register, a small Ohio River town newspaper, dated May 5th, 1892, we found this:

Where Proctorville now stands was one day part of a well paved city, but I think the greater part of it is now in the Ohio river [sic]. Only a few mounds, there; one of which was near the C. Wilgus mansion and contained a skeleton of a very large person, all double teeth, and sound in a jaw bone that would go over the jaw with the flesh on, of a large man; the common burying ground was well filled with skeletons at a depth of about 6 feet. Part of the pavement was of boulder stone and part of well preserved brick.

Then we found this account from Historical Collections of Ohio in Two Volumes. p. 350-351. Noble County. Ohio:

In Seneca township was opened, in 1872, one of the numerous Indian mounds that abound in the neighborhood. This particular one was locally known as the "Bates" mound. Upon being dug into it was found to contain a few broken pieces of earthenware, a lot of flint-heads and one or two stone implements and the remains of three skeletons, whose size would indicate they measured in life at least eight feet in height. The remarkable feature of these remains was they had double teeth in front as well as in back of mouth and in both upper and lower jaws. Upon exposure to the atmosphere the skeletons crumbled back to mother earth.

And finally this taken from A History of Ashtabula County, (Ohio, 1878), in two separate entries:

In cultivating the soil in the vicinity implements have been found and in excavating

GIANTS ON THE EARTH

the ground for graves it is said that bones have been exhumed which seemed to have belonged to a race of giants. This land at one time belonged to a Mr. Peleg Sweet, who was a man of large size and full features; and it is narrated that at one time he, in digging, came upon a skull and jaw which were of such size that the skull would cover his head and the jaw could be easily slipped over his face, as though the head of a giant were enveloping his ...

This second entry may be of some interest, for it describes non-mound burials, perhaps characterizing the typical trench burial of the Archaic period, i.e., pre-Adena.

The graves were, distinguished by slight depressions in the surface of the earth, disposed in straight rows, which, with intervening spaces or valleys, covered the entire area. The number of these graves has been estimated to be between two and three thousand. Aaron Wright, Esq., in 1800, made a careful examination of these depressions, and found them invariably to contain human bones blackened with time, which upon exposure to the air soon crumbled to dust. Some of these bones were of unusual size, and evidently belonged to a race allied to giants. Skulls were taken from these mounds, the cavities of which were of sufficient capacity to admit the head of an ordinary man, and jaw-bones [sic] that might be fitted over the face with equal facility. The bones of the upper and lower extremities were of corresponding size.

Certainly there was more curiosity than hysteria among the early settlers however, leading to the conclusion of there being less of a competitive spirit to prove the existence of a lost and superior race. Besides, a fortunate number of mounds were left untouched, possibly because they seemed less interesting, but perhaps through wise foresight. The accounts all seem quite honest and matter-of-fact, some writers not bothering to report the exact lengths of skeletal remains (were it possible). Convinced perhaps that the giant race was a well-established aspect of prehistory for the region, the postRevolutionary War people took it for granted that the larger stature was commonplace enough to take the bones in stride. Only a few scholarly measures were taken toward the preservation of sites and contents, reflecting such an attitude.

Consequently, and because of the rigorous standards of the later academics, the 19th century accounts and diaries have never been considered part of the professional criterion. In any event, the larger and more interesting shaped mound structures were the first to be excavated, leaving the rest for the analysis of the professionals.

In Muskingum County's Brush Creek Township, in a document dated March 3, 1880, a mound located on the farm of J.M. Baughman was measured 64 feet in width, 90 feet in length and 11feet, 3 inches in height. It was flat on top, an unusual condition for a mound. The mound achieved its odd shape possibly because of the stone altar, owning similar dimensions, found within. The structure was located on the summit of a hill, 152 feet above the Brush Creek. In it were discovered the bones of men and women, buried in couples-the length of their skeletons exceeding eight and even nine feet. The excavation was started in early December, 1870. There was another "dig" included as well. This reflected an attitude toward the then-existing archaeologists, whom these people apparently held in low regard.

The above report contains nothing but facts briefly told, and knowing that the public has been humbugged and imposed upon by archaeologists, we wish to fortify our own statements by giving the following testimonial...

GIANTS ON THE EARTH

At the bottom of the three-page account, the signature of six citizens was affixed in an affidavit verifying the truth, correctness, and non-deviation from the facts. It is quite possible that these people reported on something a bit rarer than ever expected. The mounded structure was possibly Archaic Allegheny. If a tradition of giants existed among these ancient people, surely a firm genetic base in people of more than seven feet in height would occasionally produce even taller members.

Needless to say, it is for reasons as the described indifference between the property owners and the archaeologists that discoveries of the remains of giant human beings in North America are questionable to seated academics. This may be especially true currently among those who have never engaged in a more thoughtful reading of the exponents of Adena analysis, especially the summations of Dragoo. The scientific community today has its own tradition fraught with skepticism, academic disapproval, and outright dismissal of the old citizenry's accounts. A part of the problem may be wrapped up in the politics and policies of the anthropological and archaeological communities. Credibility is always a point of vital interest. Few who bear degrees and use their letters as levers in their theories will step off the beaten path into "alternative" areas of research.

Nevertheless, gigantic stature among men and women has been known since the beginnings of recorded history, the Bible's Genesis itself relating of giants. They're referred to as "sons of God," and "men of renown." This seems to echo the words of Schoolcraft referring to the Allegewi as "a strong and mighty people, capable of great exertions and doing wonders." The Greeks have extensive mythological accounts of such people owning a grand stature as well. They were often held as a reclusive race, perhaps for self-preservation whose lineage went back to a time of great antiquity, perhaps prior to the last Ice Age.

The odd thing about large men, however, is that in ancient times of warfare, they were the ones selected first-often the "champions" of kings. This practice of taking the big men first is believed to have systematically depleted the gene pool among the older European, Asian, and Middle Eastern stocks, reducing the average height of modern man to something less than it could possibly have been. David slew Goliath, and it was part of a pattern. Could this have been the fate of the Allegewi big men in defense of their homeland against the Lenape-Mengwe?

Heckewelder indeed said that there was a tradition that there were giants among the Allegewi. Tradition is consciously passed down from time to time, generation to generation. Is it coincidence that there was an apparent tradition of giants among the Adena? If one were to conspire to weave legend with archaeology, there are a number of coincidences possibly equating the early Adena with the ancient Allegewi, indirectly at least. The Lenni Lenape seem to be intimately involved, for it is from them that we have the story.

Weaving Legend and Science

Did the Adena simply wander into the Ohio Valley or were they already here, genetically at least, in the form of a race with very dominant genetic traits? Did a severely compromised Archaic Lenape interbreed with the remaining Allegheny inhabitants of the region, in effect continuing the strong characteristic breed of the former Allegewi race, giving rise to the Adena? Were some of the disinterred giant humans representa-

GIANTS ON THE EARTH

tive of actual Allegewi?

It is tempting, in other words, to demonstrate a philosophical matching between transmitted history and hard facts, creating a sort of weave to hold them together. Like the making of a belt of wampum, such a weave may have a practical as well as ornamental purpose.

To start, here are a few additional accounts of giant skeletons found in the 19th century, both in and out of the state of Ohio. This first refers the general character of the human remains found in Logan County, Illinois:

It is sometimes difficult to distinguish the places of sepulture raised by the Mound Builders from the more modern graves of the Indians. The tombs of the former were in general larger than those of the latter, and were used as receptacles for a greater number of bodies, and contained relics of art, evincing a higher degree of civilization than that attained by the Indians. The ancient earth-works of the Mound Builders have occasionally been appropriated as burial places by the Indians, but the skeletons of the latter may be distinguished from the osteological remains of the former by their greater stature. History of Logan County Illinois, 1886

Similarly this next one from Vermillion Township, Erie County, Ohio:

There are quite a number of mounds, in the township, where the bones, and sometimes the whole skeleton of the human race have been found. The bones and skeletons found are very large, and some of the inhabitants think they must have belonged to a race of beings much larger in size than the Indians found here by the first settlers. Firelands Pioneer, 1858

In 1829, when the hotel was built in Chesterville, a mound near by was made to furnish the material for the brick. In digging it away, a large human skeleton was found, but no measurements were made. It is related that the jaw-bone was found to fit easily over that of a citizen of the village, who was remarkable for his large jaw. The local physicians examined the cranium and found it proportionately large, with more teeth than the white race of today: The skeleton was taken to Mansfield, and has been lost sight of entirely. History of Morrow County and Ohio, 1880

In digging the cellar of the house, nine human skeletons were found, and, like such specimens from other ancient mounds of the country, they showed that the Mound Builders were men of large stature. The skeletons were not found lying in such a manner as would indicate any arrangement of the bodies on the part of the entombers. In describing the tomb, Mr. Albert Harris said: "It looked as if the bodies had been dumped into a ditch. Some of them were buried deeper than others, the lower one being about seven feet below the surface. When the skeletons were found , Mr. Harris was twenty years of age yet he states that he could put one of the skulls over his head, and let it rest upon his shoulders, while wearing a fur cap at the same time. The large size of all the bones was remarked, and the teeth were described as "double all the way round." The History of Medina County, 1881

On the Wappatomaka have been found numerous Indian relics among which was highly a finished pipe, representing a snake coiled around the bowl. There was also discovered the under jaw-bone of a human being (says Kercheval) of great size, which contained eight jaw-teeth in each side, of enormous size; and, what is more remarkable the teeth stood transversely in the jaw-bone. It would pass over any man's face with entire

GIANTS ON THE EARTH

ease. Historical Collections of Virginia, 1845

There are many more such-like accounts, and all will be published in a book with a title similar to this article.

The now lost Brush Creek Tablet was found among skeletons measuring over 8 and 9 feet in length in Brush Creek Township, Muskigum County, Ohio, in the early 1880's

Could the ancient ancestors of the Lenni Lenape have taken over the lands of the Allegewi, then intermarried with the former subjects of the Allegewi hierarchy, producing the Adena, but with an added twist? That twist would ask whether some of the select Allegewi women were spared of the supposed genocide becoming participants, willing or not, for the procreation of what was to become the "tall members" of the Adena? Were any alliances made in the course of the long war that allowed a taller Allegewi male to live on? Were the Adena people themselves the result of a "fusion" or commingling of two or even three separate and distinct cultures? Heckewelder writes:

The war that was carried on with this nation, lasted many years, during which the Lenape lost a great number of their warriors, while the Mengwe would always hang back in the rear, leaving them to face the enemy.

The loss of that many men may very well have inhibited their ability to reestablish a new and thriving generation quickly, and so perhaps the surviving members of the Allegewi, taking the Lenape as their new masters, shared not only their lands, but themselves as well. This might help to explain the strong physical type of those later Adena found preserved in mounds, if the Adena also developed a ceremonial system of selective breeding, even as the Alleghans were supposed to have done. In this, the stronger, more dominant Allegewi gene type may have survived the annihilation of the Allegewi themselves, becoming the children of their conquerors.

The romantic James A. Jones relates how, on the eve of the first armed encounter with the Allegewi, the strong love of a man of the Lenni Lenape for a beautiful maiden of the Allegewi was born:

It was night; the bands of the confederate nations were sleeping in their cabins, dreaming dreams of victory and glory, when Wangewaha, or the Hard Heart, sleeping in his tent, was aroused by the tread of a light foot on the earth at his side, and a voice sweeter than that of the linnet or the thrush. Looking up he saw, by the beams of the moon, a tall and beautiful woman, straight as a hickory, and graceful as a young antelope. She wore over her shoulders a cloak made of the tender bark of the mulberry, interlaced with the white feathers of the swan, and the gay plumage of the snake bird and the painted vulture. Wangewaha started from his sleep, for he knew her to be the beautiful maiden whom he had seen in his dream, ere he quitted the land of his father's bones-the shape tall and erect, the eye black and sparkling, the foot small and swift, the teeth white and

GIANTS ON THE EARTH

even, the glossy dark hair, and the small plump hand.

The warrior (whose callus name, infers Jones, could have been changed at the sight of the tall beauty), listened to her story of how she was being made to marry one she could never love. Wengewaha, after consoling the young woman, bade her to spend the remainder of the night with his sister, who was nearby.

But the passion of love arose in the warrior's heart, and he determined that, if the Great Spirit should give him victory in the approaching contest, the beautiful maiden should become his wife.

Thus is related the story of the Lenape commingling romantically with the Lenape Cusick carries out this understanding of the mixing of giants with folk of [lesser stature only reversing the sexes. He relates the story of a giant abducting the daughter of a noble chieftain. Her brothers search for her, and are taken unaware when they find she has fallen in love with the giant, becoming uninterested in returning to her family. Interestingly, there is biblical reference to such relations between giants and people of smaller physical type:

And it came to pass, when men began to multiply on the face of the earth, and daughters were born unto them, That the sons of God saw the daughters of men that they were fair; and they took them wives of all which they chose. Genesis 6:1-2

The possibility of the Allegewi having passed on their "tradition" of giants may not be far fetched at all, especially in the understanding that the Lenape folk, in crossing over the Mississippi, likely did so with their woman and children, not suspecting an attack. In the course of the Great War, would it not have been feasible that the Allegewi, as likewise the Lenape, took to themselves, at any given opportunity, the desirable womenfolk of their adversaries? Hence would come an explanation for the selected taller members of the Adena, especially among the later Adena, when enough time had passed to refine the mating ritual of the elite stock. For these children, after all, would have been in the direct lineage of they that had so bravely risked their lives in the defeat the Allegheny warriors.

Adena Fate, Hopewell Destiny Heckewelder writes:

In the end, the conquerors divided the country between themselves, the Mengwe made choice of the lands in the vicinity of the great lakes, and on their tributary streams, and the Lenape took possession of the country to the south.

So the Mengwe (later Iroquois) took the lands north, and, as we may assume from the account, the Lenape took for their own the Ohio Valley with all its tributaries and streams. In this might we not assume the new masters of the Ohio Valley inherited not only the possessions of the Allegewi, but their lore of the region's natural resources as well? Being prompted and educated by the extant inhabitants, would they not have quickly developed the supposedly unique arts and crafts of the "Adena?" Unfortunately we cannot discern a possible Allegewi trinket from an Adena one, for if the ancient post war scenario resembled anything like what the white settlers enacted, that would explain less evidence for any perceivable Allegheny legacy.

Heckewelder also notes that many of the Lenape people stayed back on the western shores of the Namesi Sipu, being frightened by the fierce reception of the Allegewi. This might explain the presence of only the stronger and more necessarily hierarchical "Mexican" traditions being applied at the onset of the Adena culture, if they came along at all.

GIANTS ON THE EARTH

That, combined with the possibility of a diminished number of men, and the probable nonadmittance of the northern Mengwe in their new local politics, could have manifested itself in the difficult-to-explain origins of the Adena with their skeletal type. But then, as the peace extended itself, and more of the formally diffident Lenape cultural messengers arrived and took root in the region from west of the Mississippi, the effect could have been more of the "missing" Mexican traits appearing in the later tombs. At the same time, and as the old Lenape tradition asserted itself more and more, the stronger diagnostic traits of the early Adena, rich in the possible spoils of the great war, would have exited, leaving evolved and improved versions to be associated with the emerging Hopewell.

But what became of the Adena? Were they indeed forced out by the Hopewell? In this, Heckewelder recounts this interesting bit of information:

For a long period of time, some say hundreds of years, the two nations resided peaceably in this country, and increased very fast; some of their more enterprising huntsmen and warriors crossed the great swamps, and falling on streams running to the eastward, followed them down to the great Bay River thence into the Bay itself which we call Chesapeake [sic]. As they pursued their travels, partly by land and partly by water, sometimes near and at other times on the great Saltwater Lake, as they call the Sea they discovered the great river, which we call the Delaware; and thence exploring still eastward the Scheyiekba country, now named New Jersey, they arrived at another great stream, that which we call the Hudson or North River.

The "great swamps" are said to be the old wetlands along the west base of the Appalachians. The account then returns some of these men after their long absence to the main body of people, and they tell of the natural resources and the gifts that lay to the east. Heckewelder continues:

Satisfied with what they had seen, they (or some of them) after a long absence, returned to their nation and reported the discoveries they had made; they described the country they had discovered as abounding in game and various kinds of fruits, and the rivers and bays with fish, tortoises, &c, together with abundance of water-fowl, and no enemy to be dreaded. They considered the event as a fortunate one for them, and concluding this to be the country destined for them by the Great Spirit they began to emigrate thither, yet in small bodies, so as not to be straitened for want of provisions by the way, some even laying by for a whole year; at last they settled on the four great rivers (which we call Delaware, Hudson Susquehanna, and Potomack) [sic], making the Delaware ... the center of their possessions.

Our best Adena scholars have studiously submitted that the Adena, having lived in the Ohio Valley for a number of centuries, showed evidence of outlying settlements, by the appearance of their known traits, in places far to the east. Says Dragoo:

Ritchie's extensive archaeological studies in the Northeast indicate Adena influence also spread into that region (Ritchie and Dragoo, 1960 p.26-62). Although some Adena traits may have filtered into New York state [sic] from the upper Ohio Valley earlier in Adena the majority of traits appear similar to those of the late Maryland and Delaware Adena sites. The distribution of Adena materials along the east coast and in the Northeast also indicates that there may have been a migration route from Chesapeake Bay to Delaware Bay then northward via the Delaware River into New Jersey and beyond. Some

GIANTS ON THE EARTH

Adena peoples also may have moved from the Chesapeake Bay area up the Susquehanna River into New York.

He then adds that in his and his colleague's opinion, it is more than coincidental that the extensions of these ancient folk occurred about the same time in the middle Adena period. He goes on to say that the presence of artifacts in these outlying areas cannot be considered the result of "the wandering of traders in search of new markets or raw materials." He then asks the question of why groups of Adena people would find it a necessity to leave their homeland in the Ohio Valley.

Was the later Hopewell, after the loss of the Adena type to migration, dominantly composed of the northern Mengwe ancestral stock? In the words of Dragoo in his summations of Webb and Snow:

The traits shared by Adena and Hopewell were those already present in late Adena and donated by Adena to the new Hopewell culture which formed after the contact of Adena peoples with a long-headed population which had lived north of the area of Adena occupation.

Since Heckewelder's accounts preceded even the broader knowledge of the Ohio Valley mounds, we may have a series of clues to begin to help answer our better investigators' questions concerning these mysteries of the Adena. The time of a supposed entry in the Ohio Valley, followed by a few centuries of settlement (middle Adena) and the subsequent movement eastward-virtually identical to Heckewelder's descriptions-may be valuable considerations in the now centuries long inquiry embodying the mystery of the Adena. A possible movement southward by the Mengwe only reinforces the understanding that the Adena, having recognized themselves as physically and ancestrally different from the Mengwe, chose to move on eastward, maintaining their stock for awhile.

Author's Note

The notion of whether the Cherokee were in the region of the Ohio Valley in relatively recent times (approximately 1000 C.E. upward) is quite possible, they having inherited the name of "Talligewi" in loose legend. It may well be that history in a sense repeated itself in that the Delaware and (or) the Iroquois still held claim to the Ohio territory, and drove these people out, even as they were squatters claiming the vacated premises, considered still as hunting grounds to the former occupants. Besides that, the Cherokee have never claimed to have constructed mounds, though it is said they built atop existing mounds. In addition, there have never, at any time, been giants among the Cherokee, such as related by the antique legends.

Selected Bibliography

Dragoo, Don W., Mounds For The Dead. Pittsburgh, PA: Carnegie Museum, 1963.

Heckewelder, John, History, Manners, and Customs of the Indian Nations, The Historical Society of Pennsylvania, 1876 (originally published in 1819).

Jones, James Athearn, Traditions of the North American Indians, London: Colburn and gently, 1830.

Silverberg, Robert, The Mound Builders, Athens, Ohio: Ohio University Press, 1986.

Webb, William S. and Charles E. Snow, The Adena People, Lexington, KY: University of Kentucky, 1945.

GIANTS ON THE EARTH

Accounts of Giants in North America
Alvarez and the Giants
Arizona Giant
Barranc de Cobre Giants
Bates, Captain Martin Van Buren
California Giants
Colorado River Giants
Copafi
Coronado's Giant Discoveries
De Soto's Encounters with Giants
De Vaca and the Giants
Florida Giants
Freeman, Charles
Horned Giants
Indiana Giants
Karankawas
Lompock Rancho Giant
Melius, Angelina

Page Two
Alvarez and the Giants (See Mississippi and Texas Giants)
Arizona Giant
In 1891, at Crittenden, Arizona, some workers digging the foundation for a new building struck at a depth of eight feet a huge stone sarcophagus. When they were able to open the lid, they saw inside the remains of a nine-foot giant which time had reduced mostly to a pile of dust.1

(See California Giants; Cocopa Giants; Copafi; Coronado's Giant Discoveries; De Soto's Encounters with Giants; Florida Giants; Graveyards of the Giants; Horned Giants; Indi-

GIANTS ON THE EARTH

ana Giants; Mississippi and Texas Giants; Montana's Giants; Ocala; Ohio Giants; San Francisco Giants; Seri Giants; Tuscaloosa; Yuman Giants; also see Barranc de Cobre Giants; Mexico's Giants; Quiname; Tlaxcala's Giants)

Barranc de Cobre Giants

While searching a cave near the great canyon of Barranc de Cobre in northern Mexico in the early 1930s, explorer Paxton Hayes came across thirty-four mummified men and women. All had blond hair. All once rose to heights between seven and eight feet.2

(See Mexico's Giants; Quiname; Tlaxcala's Giants; also see Arizona Giant; California Giants; Cocopa Giants; Copafi; Coronado's Giant Discoveries; De Soto's Encounters with Giants; Florida Giants; Graveyards of the Giants; Horned Giants; Indiana Giants; Mississippi and Texas Giants; Montana's Giants; Ocala; Ohio Giants; San Francisco Giants; Sen Giants; Tuscaloosa; Yuman Giants)

Bates, Captain Martin Van Buren

When the War Between the States broke out, Martin Van Buren Bates left Emma Henry College in Virginia to enlist as a private in the Fifth Kentucky Infantry. Although only sixteen at the time, he already stood a little above six-feet tall. Apparently the youngster conducted himself well on the battlefield, for over the next couple years he received several promotions, the last as a captain in the Seventh Confederate Cavalry.

CAPTAIN MARTIN BATES and ANNA SWAN, the world's tallest couple of record, posed for this picture with friend Lei McFarland.

(Courtesy Medina County Historical Society)4But all through the war, and for several years afterward, Captain Bates kept growing. By his own account, he finally stopped in his twenty-eighth year, after having reached a height of seven feet and eight inches and a weight of four hundred and seventy pounds.3

After the war, the Whitesburg, Kentucky, giant earned his living by exhibiting himself in the United States and Canada. In 1870, Judge H. P. Ingalls, a well-known promoter, asked him to come to Elizabeth, New Jersey, and join a company he was organizing to tour Europe. There his eyes beheld Anna Haining Swan, a seven-foot, eleven-inch Scottish lass from Nova Scotia, and a courtship began.

In April, 1871, Judge Ingalls' company sailed for England. The two enormous sweethearts became an instant hit with the British public, and on June 2, Queen Victoria commanded their appearance at Buckingham Palace. Two weeks later, on June 17, the former Confederate captain and his fiancee, attired in her white satin gown with orange blossoms, spoke their vows before a large crowd in London's historic St.-Martin-in-the-Fields church. Wedding presents from Queen Victoria included a cluster diamond ring for the bride and a watch and chain for the groom. The wedding made world headlines and put the Bates in the record books as history's tallest known married couple.5

After a brief honeymoon, the couple returned to London where they gave a private reception for the Prince of Wales, who invited them to be his guests at Marlborough House. They appeared a second time before the Queen, at Windsor, then set out on a tour of the provincial towns in England and Scotland.

Upon their return to the States, the Bates decided to take a vacation tour of the West and Midwest, then buy a farm and settle down. While in Ohio, they passed through Seville. That country appealed to them, so Captain Bates purchased one hundred and thirty acres of good farm land near the town and drew plans for a house big enough to accommodate

GIANTS ON THE EARTH

giants. "The house he built on that farm... astounded visitors of ordinary size for 70 years," writes Lee Cavin. "It had 14-foot ceilings in the principal wing. The doors were 8 feet high. The furniture was built to order. Captain Bates delighted in seeing normal-size people dwarfed in his house, saying, 'Seeing our guests make use of it recalls most forcibly the good Dean Swift's traveler in the land of Brobdingnag.6

"In 1878,1879, and 1880," continues Cavin, "the giant couple returned to the road as members of the W. W. Cole Circus. This circus, founded in 1871, was noted because it was the first to play many western towns. Its special train was close on the heels of railroad construction throughout the area. The reasons for the return to the road of the couple should be familiar ones to anyone who has built a new home. According to Seville contemporaries, the cost of the giant house exceeded expectations."

Mrs. Bates bore the Captain two children. During the second year of their British tour, an eighteen-pound daughter died at birth. In the winter of 1879, after a difficult delivery, she gave birth to a twenty-three pound boy that measured thirty inches in length. However, the child died the next day. In 1888, after years of declining health, Anna Swan Bates also died. The Seville Times devoted three columns to her obituary.

About a dozen years later, Captain Bates married Lavonne Weatherby, a daughter of the pastor of the Seville Baptist Church, which he and his first wife had long attended. The new Mrs. Bates stood just over five feet tall.

Seville's most famous resident lived seventy-four years, but in January, 1919, he finally yielded to a lingering illness. (Also see Swan, Anna Raining)

California Giants

In 1833, some soldiers digging a pit at Lompock Rancho, California, unearthed a twelve-foot giant with a double row of teeth, both uppers and lowers.7 The Lompock giant's teeth, while unusual, were not unique. For another ancient skeleton later found on Santa Rosa Island off the California coast showed the same dental peculiarity. Also, in 1888, in a burial mound near Clearwater, Minnesota, seven skeletons, with skulls containing double rows of teeth, were dug up, but they were not giants.

(See Arizona Giant; Cocopa Giants; Copafi; Coronado's Giant Discoveries; De Soto's Encounters with Giants; Florida Giants; Graveyards of the Giants; Horned Giants; Indiana Giants; Mississippi and Texas Giants; Montana's Giants; Ocala; Ohio Giants; San Francisco Giants; Seri Giants; Tuscaloosa; Yuman Giants; also see Barranc de Cobre Giants; Mexico's Giants; Quiname; Tlaxcala's Giants)

Colorado River Giants (See Coronado's Giant Discoveries)

Copafi

When Hernando De Soto reached the territory of the Apalachee around Tallahassee, Copafi, that tribe's cacique, insolently refused to meet with him. To avoid playing a subservient role, the chief, described as "a man of monstrous proportions," fled into the woods. De Soto and some of his men pursued and captured the giant and brought him in.

(See Arizona Giants; California Giants; Cocopa Giants; Coronado's Giant Discoveries; De Soto's Encounters with Giants; Florida Giants; Graveyards of the Giants; Horned Giants; Indiana Giants; Mississippi and Texas Giants; Montana's Giants; Ocala; Ohio Giants; San Francisco Giants; Serf Giants; Tuscaloosa; Yuman Giants; also see Barranc de Cobre Giants; Mexico's Giants; Quiname; Tlaxcala's Giants)

Coronado's Giant Discoveries

GIANTS ON THE EARTH

Across the continent, at the same time that De Soto was blazing his famous trail, an expedition led by Coronado searched for the fabulously rich "Seven Cities of Cibola." Near Mexico's present-day border with California and Arizona they ran into several tribes of Indian giants. Starting out from Mexico City with some three hundred Spaniards and eight hundred native Indians, the Coronado expedition marched west to the Pacific Ocean. Then turning north-ward, they ascended the coast through regions that later became known as Sinaloa and Sonora. While this march was underway, Hemando de Alarcon set sail with two ships up the coast, transporting the baggage and supplies for the soldiers. The original plan called for Alarcon and the army to keep in frequent touch and to rendezvous at suitable harbors along the coast. So when the army reached the province of Senora, a force under Don Rodrigo Maldonado set out to find the harbor and scan the horizon for Alarcon's ships. Maldonado sighted no ships, but he did return with an Indian who stood so tall as to astonish the Spaniards. Pedro de Castaneda, who accompanied Coronado and later wrote the most complete and factual history of the expedition, records this unusual event as follows: "Don Rodrigo Maldonado, who was captain of those who went in search of the ships, did not find them, but he brought back with him an Indian so large and tall that the best man in the army reached only to his chest. It was said that other Indians were even taller on the coast."8 This giant evidently belonged to the Seri. This great Indian tribe occupied the island of Tiburon and the adjacent Sonora coast on the Gulf of California. Historians testify to their tall stature.

Soon after this, while still trying to establish contact with Alarcon, Captain Melchior Diaz came across another tribe of giants. Taking twenty-five of his "most efficient men" and some guides, Diaz struck out toward the north and west in search of the seacoast and the ships. "After going about 150 leagues," reports Castaneda, "they came to a province of exceedingly tall and strong men--like giants " Evidently, these were the Cocopa, a Yuman tribe. According to Castaneda, these huge Indians went about mostly naked. "They . . . live," he adds, "in large straw cabins built underground like smoke houses, with only the straw roof above ground. They enter these at one end and come out at the other. More than a hundred persons, old and young, sleep in one cabin. When they carry anything, they can take a load of more than three or four hundredweight on their heads. Once when our men wished to fetch a log for the fire, and six men were unable to carry it, one of these Indians is reported to have come and raised it in his arms, put it on his head alone, and carried it very easily."

(For a similar feat, see San Francisco Giants)

While among these Cocopas, the captain learned that ships had been seen at a point three days down toward the sea. But when Diaz' finally reached this place, he saw no sign of a sail, even to the distant horizon. On a tree near the shore, however, his party found this written message: "Alarcon reached this place; there are letters at the foot of this tree." Diaz dug up the letters and learned from them how long Alarcon had waited for news of the army and that he had gone back with the ships to New Spain, i.e., Mexico.9

But on his way back Alarcon changed his mind--and thus became the discoverer of the Colorado River giants. Sailing into the port of Culiacan, he came unexpectedly upon the San Gabriel, loaded with provisions for Coronado. This chance meeting with the San Gabriel probably figured in Alarc6n's decision to resume efforts to locate the explorer's party. At any rate, he added this third ship to his fleet and continued up the coast. They

GIANTS ON THE EARTH

sailed the Gulf of California until they entered the shallows near the head of the gulf. After hazarding the murky shoals there and almost losing all three ships, he and his crew reached the mouth of the Colorado River. Dropping anchor here, Alarcon and his exploratory party launched two boats against the river's furious current. "Thus began," writes historian Herbert Eugene Bolton, "the historic first voyage by Europeans up the Colorado River among the tall Yuman peoples who lived along its banks on either side."10

A piece up the river Alarcon and his men came upon their first settlement. About two hundred and fifty giant Cocopa warriors stood on the banks, ready to attack them. But the captain, by making signs of peace and offering gifts, won them over. Further upstream more than a thousand giant Indians appeared with bows and arrows, but Alarcon knew they intended them no harm because their women and children accompanied them. These Cocopas he described as "large and well formed, without being corpulent. Some have their noses pierced, and from them hang pendants, while others wear shells. . . . All of them, big and little, wear a multi-colored sash about the waist; and tied in the middle, a round bundle of feathers hanging down like a tail.... Their bodies are branded by fire; their hair is banged in front, but in the back it hangs to the waist." The women, meanwhile, "go about naked, except that, tied in front and behind, they wear large bunches of feathers."11

(See Arizona Giants; California Giants; Cocopa Giants; Copafi; De Soto's Encounters with Giants; Florida Giants; Graveyards of the Giants; Horned Giants; Indiana Giants; Mississippi and Texas Giants; Montana's Giants; Ocala; Ohio Giants; Seri Giants; Tuscaloosa; Yuman Giants; also see Barranc de Cobre Giants; Mexico's Giants; Quiname; Tlaxcala's Giants)

De Soto's Encounters with Giants

In 1539, probably while the survivors of Narvaez' crew were making their way across the country, another Spanish explorer, Hernando De Soto, sailed nine ships into Tampa Bay. There he put ashore six hundred lancers, targeteers, cross-bowmen, and harquebusiers, along with two hundred and thirteen horses. As they ventured inland, the first Indians they encountered were friendly Timucuans. While some of their leaders were giants, most of these people stood, on average, only a foot taller than the explorers. Their vast territory extended from Tampa Bay north to the present Jacksonville area and west to the Aucilla River, which runs along the eastern border of modern Jefferson County and empties into the gulf.

As De Soto marched through the various Indian provinces, he met with their caciques. It was his custom after these conferences to courteously "detain" the cacique and some of his nobles--as a precaution against attack. He also required them to furnish him with porters. The Indians' reaction to this policy varied. After some reluctance, the cacique of Ocala, "an Indian of enormous size and amazing strength,"12 finally agreed to become De Soto's "guest." Vitacucho, the cacique in the neighboring province of Caliquin (present-day Alachua County), consented only after his daughter chanced to fell into De Soto's hands. But even while being detained, Vitacucho and his tall warriors secretly managed two serious uprisings. Copafi, the cacique of the Apalachee around Tallahassee, described as "a man of monstrous proportions,"13 refused even to meet with De Soto, but a party led by the governor himself finally captured the giant and brought him in.

After wintering at Ambaica Apalachee, the Spanish explorers crossed over into Geor-

GIANTS ON THE EARTH

gia. But there they received a kindly reception, with the nation of the Creeks greeting them everywhere in a warm, friendly manner. The several other caciques who guided them through the Carolinas and into Tennessee were, for the most part, also friendly, and even those who may have been offended by the governor's invitation to accompany him offered no serious objection. So all went well--until De Soto's company reached the borders of the giant cacique Tuscaloosa. As suzerain over many caciques, he ruled a wide territory that included most of modern Alabama and Mississippi. Though proud and haughty, Tuscaloosa sent an embassy headed by his huge son to greet and welcome De Soto and his men.

Tuscaloosa's heir apparent, who, at eighteen years, already stood as tall as his father, came to De Soto while he stayed at Tallise, a large Indian town located on the bank of a great river. The young giant delivered to the governor the following communication from Tuscaloosa: "The grand cacique of Tuscaloosa, my master, sends me to salute you. He bids me say, that he is told how all, not without reason, are led captive by your perfection and power; that wheresoever lies your path you receive gifts and obedience, which he knows are all your due; and that he longs to see you as much as he could desire for the continuance of life. Thus, he sends me to offer you his person, his lands, his subjects; to say, that wheresoever it shall please you to go through his territories, you will find service and obedience, friendship and peace. In requital of this wish to serve you, he asks that you so far favor him as to say when you will come; for that the sooner you do so, the greater will be the obligation, and to him the earlier pleasure."[14]

Dismissing the cacique of Coca, who had accompanied him to Tuscaloosa's borders, De Soto set out to meet with Tuscaloosa. Early on the morning of the third day, the governor, his master of the camp, and fifteen cavalrymen entered the village where he was quartered. Having heard daily reports from his scouts on De Soto's progress, the Indian chieftain was prepared to receive them in state. As they rode in, they saw Tuscaloosa stationed on a high place, seated on a mat. Around him stood one hundred of his noblemen, all dressed in richly colored mantles and plumes. Tuscaloosa appeared to be about forty years old. His physical measurements, writes Garcilaso de la Vega, who accompanied De Soto, "were like those of his son, for both were more than a half-yard taller than all the others. He appeared to be a giant, or rather was one, and his limbs and face were in proportion to the height of his body. His countenance was handsome, and he wore a look of severity, yet a look which well revealed his ferocity and grandeur of spirit. His shoulders conformed to his height, and his waistline measured just a little more than two-thirds of a yard. His arms and legs were straight and well formed and were in proper proportion to the rest of his body. In sum he was the tallest and most handsomely shaped Indian that the Castilians saw during all their travels."[15]

As the cavaliers and officers of the camp who preceded De Soto rode forward and arranged themselves in his presence, Tuscaloosa took not the slightest notice of them, even as they made their horses curvet and caracole as they passed. Determined to excite his at ten-ti on, some spurred their horses up to his very feet, to which "he, with great gravity, and seemingly with indifference, now and then would raise his eyes, and look on as in contempt."[16] He made no move to rise even when De Soto approached. So the governor took him by the hand, and they walked together to the piazza. There they sat on a bench and talked for several minutes.

GIANTS ON THE EARTH

Two days later De Soto decided to resume his journey toward Mobile.17 He also decided to take Tuscaloosa with him. On these marches the cacique in custody always rode alongside the governor. So De Soto ordered a horse for Tuscaloosa. But owing to the cacique's huge size and great weight, not even the largest horse they brought forward was able to bear him. At last, a pack horse accustomed to heavy burdens proved strong enough to carry the chief. But when he mounted Tuscaloosa's feet almost touched the ground. This description accords with Garcilaso de la Vega's statement that the chief stood a half-yard taller than the tallest men around him. Though no one recorded Tuscaloosa's actual size, these two measurements give us some idea of his height. If these descriptions are accurate, then we cannot err too much in estimating his stature at about eight feet.

Even while they were on the trail to Mobile, De Soto's party encountered an ominous sign of what awaited them. Two soldiers turned up missing. The Spaniards suspected that the Indians caught the two men some distance from camp and killed them. When De Soto questioned Tuscaloosa about their whereabouts, the cacique testily replied that the Indians were not the white men's keepers. Vigilance was now increased, and the governor dispatched two of his best men to Mobile under the pretext of making arrangements for provisions. Four days later, as the Spaniards approached the town, the scouts rode out to De Soto and reported that many Indians had gathered inside and that some preparations had been made. They then suggested the army camp in the woods nearby. Unfortunately, the doughty De Soto refused to heed his scouts' advice.

While the army waited, the governor with his small party approached the town and its high walls. Just then a welcoming committee of painted warriors, clad in robes of skins and head-pieces with many feathers of very brilliant colors, came out to greet them. A group of young Indian maidens followed, dancing and singing to music played on rude instruments. The governor entered the town with Tuscaloosa, his son, and the cacique's entourage. Seven or eight men of his own guard plus four cavalrymen also accompanied him. They seated themselves in a piazza. From here, De Soto saw that there were only about eighty houses, but several of them large enough to hold one thousand to fifteen hundred people. Unknown to him, more than two thousand Indian warriors now stood in concealment behind these walls, waiting.

After some of the chief men from the town joined him, Tuscaloosa withdrew a short distance from De Soto. With a severe look, he warned the governor and his party to leave at once. In attempting to regain custody of the chief, a tussle between a Spaniard and an Indian ignited an all-out war. Under a hail of arrows, De Soto and most of his men retreated from the village. The governor then ordered the town besieged. After a time, the Spaniards gained entry, set fire to the buildings, and conducted a massacre. According to Alvaro Fernandez, about two thousand five hundred Indians died that day, while only eighteen Spaniards fell. Among the Indian dead was Tuscaloosa's giant son and heir apparent. Tuscaloosa himself escaped. At the start of the battle, some of his chiefs, wanting to protect his life for the good of their nation, persuaded him to flee Mobile. Tuscaloosa reluctantly agreed, departing with twenty brave bodyguards soon after the battle began.

(See Arizona Giants; California Giants; Cocopa Giants; Copafi; Coronado's Giant Discoveries; Florida Giants; Graveyards of the Giants; Horned Giants; Indiana Giants; Mis-

GIANTS ON THE EARTH

sissippi and Texas Giants; Montana's Giants; Ocala; Ohio Giants; San Francisco Giants; Seri Giants; Tuscaloosa; Yuman Giants; also see Barranc de Cobre Giants; Mexico's Giants; Quiname; Tlaxcala's Giants)

De Vaca and the Giants (See Florida Giants)

Florida Giants

In 1528, or almost ten years after Alonzo Alvarez de Pineda's discovery of giants on the Mississippi River, the ill-fated explorer Panfilo de Narvaez put three hundred men ashore at Tampa Bay. His mission was to search the Florida mainland for its riches, while his five ships sailed just off the coast. Only Alvar Nunez Cabeza de Vaca and three companions survived this expedition. Afterward they crossed the North American continent from shore to shore, becoming the first white men to do so. In his history, Cabeza de Vaca mentions some giant Florida Indians who attacked the Narvaez party. "When we came in view of Apalachen," he writes, "the Governor ordered that I should take nine cavalry with fifty infantry and enter the town.18 Accordingly the assessor and I assailed it; and having got in, we found only women and boys there, the men being absent; however these returned to its support, after a little time, while we were walking about, and began discharging arrows at us. They killed the horse of the assessor, and at last taking to flight, they left us.... The town consisted of forty small houses, made low, and set up in sheltered places because of the frequent storms. The material was thatch. They were surrounded by very dense woods, large groves and many bodies of fresh water. . . Two hours after our arrival at Apalachen, the Indians who had fled from there came in peace to us, asking for their women and children, whom we released; but the detention of a cacique [the Indians' chief] by the Governor produced great excitement, in consequence of which they returned for battle early the next day, and attacked us with such promptness and alacrity that they succeeded in setting fire to the houses in which we were."19

After twenty-five days, Narvaez' army departed Apalachen. But a short while later, as they attempted to cross a large lake, they came under heavy attack from many giant Indians concealed behind trees. "Some of our men were wounded in this conflict, for whom the good armor they wore did not avail," continues Cabeza de Vaca. 'There were those this day who swore that they had seen two red oaks, each the thickness of the lower part of the leg, pierced through from side to side by arrows; and this is not so much to be wondered at, considering the power and skill with which the Indians are able to project them. I myself saw an arrow that had entered the butt of an elm to the depth of a span.... The Indians we had so far seen in Florida are all archers. They go naked, are large of body, and appear at a distance like giants. They are of admirable proportions, very spare and of great activity and strength. The bows they use are as thick as the arm, of eleven or twelve palms in length, which will discharge at two hundred paces with so great precision that they miss nothing."20

Harassments by these Indian giants continued. So Narvaez decided to head south for the gulf coast and escape by the sea. Arriving there after much hardship, he and his men constructed five crude boats, in order to search along the coast for a Spanish settlement. Unfortunately, a sudden, fierce storm caught them some distance from land. The high winds drove all the boats, with all their men aboard, far out to sea. All were subsequently lost except Cabeza de Vaca and three companions who managed to reach the shore. They walked across Texas and northern Mexico, finally reaching the Pacific coast where

GIANTS ON THE EARTH

they linked up with Francisco Vazquez de Coronado in 1541.

(See Arizona Giants; California Giants; Cocopa Giants; Copafi; Coronado's Giant Discoveries; De Soto's Encounters with Giants; Graveyards of the Giants; Horned Giants; Indiana Giants; Mississippi and Texas Giants; Montana's Giants; Ocala; Ohio Giants; San Francisco Giants; Serf Giants; Tuscaloosa; Yuman Giants; also see Barranc de Cobre Giants; Mexico's Giants; Quiname; Tlaxcala's Giants)

Freeman, Charles

Michigan-born Charles Freeman could lift fifteen hundred-weight, and "could throw an astounding number of somersaults in succession and run and jump like a deer."[21] But he knew almost nothing about professional boxing. After gazing upon his seven-foot, six-inch frame and witnessing his feats of great strength and agility, one-time British prizefighter champion Ben Caunt decided that did not matter. He envisioned great things for Freeman in the ring and persuaded the young man to return with him to London.

Before leaving, Caunt tipped the New York press. The writers, of course, pounced on the story. They built Freeman up, giving him a fictitious record, while the editors caught their readers' attention with headlines proclaiming that the huge American was crossing the Atlantic to lay claim to the "Championship of the World."

On December 14, 1842, near Sawbridgeworth, Freeman fought seventy rounds with William Perry, known as "The Tipton Slasher," but the bout "was adjourned due to darkness falling." Six days later they resumed the match, "but Perry fell before receiving a blow and was disqualified."[22]

Freeman gave up boxing for the stage. In early 1843, he appeared at the Olympia Theatre in The Son of the Desert and Demon Changeling, a piece written expressly for him. He also did a stint with the circus. "His great circus performance," according to a Hunterian Museum report, "was to ride two horses at a time, galloping around the arena, with his arms above his head balancing a man."[23] Perhaps to make ends meet, he later became a barman at the Lion and Ball tavern in Red Lion Street, Holborn.

The giant barman excited the Lion and Ball's regular crowd and attracted many new patrons, who got to see him for only the price of a whiskey. Either Freeman or one of his promoters penned the following poetic invitation to the British public to visit him:

You need not unto Hyde Park go,
For without imposition,
Smith's Bar Man is, and no mistake,
The true Great Exhibition.
The proudest noble in the land,
Despite caprice and whim,
Though looking down on all the world,
Must fain look up to him.
His rest can never be disturbed
By chanticleer in song,
For though he early goes to bed,
He sleeps so very long.
Though you may boast a many friends,
Look in and stand a pot;

GIANTS ON THE EARTH

You'll make a new acquaintanceship,
The longest you have got.
Then come and see the Giant Youth,
Give Edward Smith a call,
Remember in Red Lion-street,
The Lion and the Ball.
Liquors of a Giant's Strength.24 (See Toller, James)

Horned Giants

Pursuit, in its July, 1973, issue, reported that in the 1880s, while digging in a mound at Sayre in Bradford County, Pennsylvania, a reputable group of antiquarians found skeletons of humans measuring not only above seven feet tall but having skulls with horns.25 The diggers, which included two professors and Pennsylvania's state historian, turned what they found over to the American Investigating Museum in Philadelphia, but the bones were afterward misplaced, stolen, or lost. A story about the horned skulls appeared in a Reader's Digest book, Mysteries of the Unexplained.

(See Ariels; Origin of the Giants--Biblical Account; also see Arizona Giants; Barranc de Cobre Giants; California Giants; Cocopa Giants; Copafi; Coronado's Giant Discoveries; De Soto's Encounters with Giants; Florida Giants; Graveyards of the Giants; Indiana Giants; Mexico's Giants; Mississippi and Texas Giants; Montana's Giants; Ocala; Ohio Giants; Quiname; San Francisco Giants; Seri Giants; Tlaxcala's Giants; Tuscaloosa; Yuman Giants)

Indiana Giants

1879, some Indiana archaeologists dug into an ancient burial mound at Brewersville, Indiana, and unearthed a human skeleton that measured nine feet eight inches in length. A mica necklace still hung around the giant's neck. The bones, which were stored in a grain mill, were swept away in the 1937 flood.26

In 1925, several amateurs digging in an Indian mound at Walkerton, Indiana, uncovered the skeletons of eight very ancient humans measuring in height from eight to almost nine feet. All eight giants had been buried in "substantial copper armor."

(See Arizona Giants; California Giants; Cocopa Giants; Copafi; Coronado's Giant Discoveries; De Soto's Encounters with Giants; Florida Giants; Graveyards of the Giants; Horned Giants; Mississippi and Texas Giants; Montana's Giants; Ocala; Ohio Giants; San Francisco Giants; Seri Giants; Tuscaloosa; Yuman Giants; also see Barranc de Cobre Giants; Mexico's Giants; Quiname; Tlaxcala's Giants)

Karankawas (See Mississippi and Texas Giants)

Lompock Rancho Giant (See Graveyards of the Giants)

Melius, Angelina

Angelina Melius, a good-looking American giantess almost seven feet tall, arrived in England about 1821. On her exhibition tour there she was accompanied by her two-foot-two-inch page, Senor Don Santiago de los Santos of Manilla.27

(See Chang Woo Gow; Giants and Dwarfs)

GIANTS ON THE EARTH

Mexico's Giants

About 1542, within months of De Soto's and Coronado's expeditions, five-year-old Fray Diego Duran moved with his family to Mexico. He thus grew up among the central Mexican Indians and later served as a missionary to them. While living here, he several times came in contact with giant Indians. Of these encounters, he later wrote: "It cannot be denied that there have been giants in this country. I can affirm this as an eyewitness, for I have met men of monstrous stature here. I believe that there are many in Mexico who will remember, as I do, a giant Indian who appeared in a procession of the feast of Corpus Christi. He appeared dressed in yellow silk and a halberd at his shoulder and a helmet on his head. And he was all of three feet taller than the others."[28]

Spending his childhood in Texcoco gave Duran a unique opportunity to learn firsthand a great deal about the Aztecs and to become acquainted with early Mexican culture. Fortunately for us, he made the most of it. Because of his long and close association with these Indians, he became a recognized authority on their language, customs, and preColumbian history. For that reason, most scholars regard Duran's work as of "extraordinary importance." In his seventy-eight chapters, he details the history of Mexico from its origins down to the conquest and complete subjection of the country by the Spaniards. In gathering his information, Duran used a great number of pre-Hispanic, picture-writing manuscripts, which had to be explained to him by Indians well-trained in interpreting native hieroglyphics. During his thirty-two years among the Aztecs, he also interviewed many old Indians knowledgeable in the ancient ways and traditions of their people. From all these sources he learned about the giants. Bernardino de Sahagun and Joseph de Acosta, two other notable historians of about the same period, also knew about a tribe of giants who once occupied central Mexico, but Duran's book offers us the best and most complete account.

Duran writes that, according to the Aztecs, the giants and a bestial people of average size once had this land all to themselves. Then, in A.D. 902, six tribes of people from Teocolhuacan (also called Aztlan, i.e., "Land of Herons"), which "is found toward the north and near the region of La Florida," began arriving in Mexico. They soon took possession of the country. These six kindred tribes included the Xochimilca, the Chalca, the Tecpanec, the Colhua, the Tlalhuica, and the Tlaxcalans. A seventh tribe, the Aztecs, were brothers to these people, but they "came to live here three hundred and one years after the arrival of the others."

When these six tribes had settled, Duran continues, "they recorded in their painted books the type of land and kind of people they found here. These books show two types of people, one from the west of the snow-covered mountains toward Mexico, and the other on the east, where Puebla and Cholula are found. Those from the first region were Chichimecs and the people from Puebla and Cholula were 'The Giants,' the Quiname, which means 'men of great stature.'

"The few Chichimecs on the side of Mexico were brutal, savage men, and they were called Chichimecs because they were hunters. They lived among the peaks and in the harshest places of the mountain where they led a bestial existence. They had no human organization but hunted food like the beasts of the same mountain, and went stark naked without any covering on their private parts....

"When the new nations came, these savage people showed no resistance or anger, but

GIANTS ON THE EARTH

rather awe. They fled towards the hills, hiding themselves there.... The newly arrived people seeing, then, that the land was left unoccupied, chose at will the best places to live in.

"The other people who were found in Tlaxcala and Cholula and Huexotzinco are said to have been 'Giants.' These were enraged at the coming of the invaders and tried to defend their land. I do not have a very true account of this, and therefore will not attempt to tell the story that the natives told me even though it was long and worth hearing, of the battles that the Cholultecs fought with the Giants until they killed them or drove them from the country.

"These Giants lived no less bestially than the Chichimecs, as they had abominable customs and ate raw meat from the hunt. In certain places of that region enormous bones of the Giants have been found, which I myself have seen dug up at the foot of cliffs many times. These Giants flung themselves from precipices while fleeing from the Cholultecs and were killed. The Cholultecs had been extremely cruel to the Giants, harassing them, pursuing them from hill to hill, from valley to valley, until they were destroyed.

"Even if we detain the reader a little, I should like to tell the manner in which the people of Cholula and Tlaxcala annihilated that evil nation. This was done by treason and deceit. They pretended to want peace with the Giants, and after having assured them of their good will they invited them to a great banquet. An ambush was then prepared. Some men slyly robbed the guests of their shields, clubs, and swords. The Cholultecs then appeared and attacked. The Giants tried to defend themselves, and, as they could not find their weapons, it is said that they tore branches from the trees with the same ease as one cuts a turnip, and in this way defended themselves valiantly. But finally all were killed."29

Bernardino de Sahagun, who arrived in the Americas in 1523 and became the foremost authority in his time on the pre-conquest Aztec culture, mentions in his twelve-volume history on central Mexico that the "giants" of Quinametin were Toltecs and that they built both Teotihuacan and Cholula.30

In his History of the Indies, Joseph de Acosta tells a story of the giants very similar to Duran's, but he also adds this eyewitness account: "When I was in Mexico, in the year of our Lord one thousand five hundred eighty six, they found one of those giants buried in one of our farms, which we call Jesus del Monte, of whom they brought a tooth to be seen, which (without augmenting) was as big as the fist of a man; and, according to this, all the rest was proportionable, which I saw and admired at his deformed greatness."31

(See Barranc de Cobre Giants; Quiname; Tlaxcala's Giants; also see Arizona Giants; California Giants; Cocopa Giants; Copafi; Coronado's Giant Discoveries; De Soto's Encounters with Giants; Florida Giants; Graveyards of the Giants; Horned Giants; Indiana Giants; Mississippi and Texas Giants; Montana's Giants; Ocala; Ohio Giants; San Francisco Giants; Seri Giants; Tuscaloosa; Yuman Giants)

Mississippi and Texas Giants

In 1519, a year before Magellan discovered the Patagonians, Alonzo Alvarez de Pineda encountered some giants on the banks of the Mississippi River, not far from where it empties into the Gulf of Mexico. Sent to search for a strait across Florida, Pineda came first upon the northern gulf coast, reconnoitered it, then sailed south, coasting the west-

GIANTS ON THE EARTH

ern shore of Florida until he reached its southern tip. Finding the peninsula offered no strait, he then retraced his course. Landing at strategic places along the coasts of Florida, Alabama, Mississippi, Louisiana, Texas, and even down to Tampico in Mexico, Pineda made maps and notes of the rivers and bays, established landmarks, and took possession of all these lands in his king's name. That done, he sailed back to the mouth of the Mississippi River. There he "found a large town, and on both sides of its banks, for a distance of six leagues up its course, some forty native villages." These Indians proved friendly, so he remained here forty days while his crew careened their four ships and made necessary repairs. In his report on the country, Pineda noted that it provided the natives with an abundance of food, that many of its rivers contained so much gold that they commonly wore it as ornaments in their ears and noses, around their necks, and over other parts of the body, and that there lived on the banks of this river "a race of giants from ten to eleven palms in height."32

On his return from Tampico to the Mississippi, Pineda also, unknowingly, sailed right past a tribe of equally huge Texas Indians. For historian Woodbury Lowery, along with several others, places "the giant Karankawas" nation around Matagorda Bay at that time.33

In a report on the Karankawas, John R. Swanton, of the Bureau of American Ethnology, describes the men as being "very tall and well formed.... Their hair was unusually coarse, and worn so long by many of the men that it reached to the waist. Agriculture was not practised by these Indians, their food supply being obtained from the waters, the chase, and wild plants, and, to a limited extent, human flesh; for, like most of the tribes of the Texas coast, they were cannibals. Travel among them was almost wholly by the canoe, or dugout, for they seldom left the coast. Head-flattening and tattooing were practised to a considerable extent. Little is known in regard to their tribal government, further than that they had civil and war chiefs, the former being hereditary in the male line."34

The first positive notice of them, adds Swanton, is found in the accounts of La Salle's disastrous visit to this area.35 They also later engaged in a fierce battle with Lafitte and his band of pirates, who had abducted one of their women. But the Karankawas proved no match for the buccaneers, who, having superior arms and firepower, inflicted heavy casualties upon them and forced them to retreat. When Stephen Austin built his settlement on the Brazos in 1823, the tribe began to decline. "Conflicts between the settlers and the Indians were frequent," says the ethnologist, "and finally a battle was fought in which about half the tribe were slain, the other portion fleeing for refuge to La Bahia." By 1840, the Karankawas had been reduced to about one hundred souls living on Lavaca Bay.36

(See Arizona Giants; California Giants; Cocopa Giants; Copafi; Corona-do's Giant Discoveries; De Soto's Encounters with Giants; Florida Giants; Graveyards of the Giants; Horned Giants; Indiana Giants; Montana's Giants; Ocala; Ohio Giants; San Francisco Giants; Seri Giants; Tuscaloosa; Yuman Giants; also see Barranc de Cobre Giants; Mexico's Giants; Quiname; Tlaxcala's Giants)

Montana's Giants

In 1903, on an archaeological outing at Fish Creek, Montana, Professor S. Farr and his group of Princeton University students came across several burial mounds. Choosing one to dig in, they unearthed the skeleton of a man about nine feet long. Next to him lay

GIANTS ON THE EARTH

the bones of a woman, who had been almost as tall.37

(See Arizona Giants; California Giants; Cocopa Giants; Copafi; Coronado's Giant Discoveries; De Soto's Encounters with Giants; Florida Giants; Graveyards of the Giants; Horned Giants; Indiana Giants; Mississippi and Texas Giants; Ocala; Ohio Giants; San Francisco Giants; Seri Giants; Tuscaloosa; Yuman Giants; also see Barranc de Cobre Giants; Mexico's Giants; Quiname; Tlaxcala's Giants)

Narvaez and the Giants (See Florida Giants)

Ohio Giants

Nature, in its December 17, 1891, issue, reported that at a depth of fourteen feet in a large Ohio burial mound excavators found the skeleton of a massive man in copper armor. He wore a copper cap, while copper moldings encased his jaws. Copper armor also protected his arms, chest, and stomach. A necklace made of bear's teeth and inlaid with pearls decorated his neck. At his side lay the skeleton of a woman, probably his wife.38

In the 1860s, some excavators digging in a hill in Marion, Ohio, uncovered thirty skeletons who also ranged in height from seven to eight feet.39

(See Arizona Giants; California Giants; Cocopa Giants; Copafi; Coronado's Giant Discoveries; De Soto's Encounters with Giants; Florida Giants; Graveyards of the Giants; Horned Giants; Indiana Giants; Mississippi and Texas Giants; Montana's Giants; Ocala; San Francisco Giants; Seri Giants; Tuscaloosa; Yuman Giants; also see Barranc de Cobre Giants; Mexico's Giants; Quiname; Tlaxcala's Giants)

San Francisco Giants

When Sir Francis Drake dropped anchor in a small bay just north of modern San Francisco, the Indian natives, who had never seen a white man before, took the Englishmen to be gods. Francis Fletcher, Drake's chronicler of the voyage, says the king, "a man of large body and good aspect," even set his own crown--a headdress of feathers--on Drake's head and pleaded with him to exercise dominion over the land. He also describes these Indians as a tall people with herculean strength. "Yet are the men commonly so strong of body," he writes, "that that which two or three of our men could hardly bear, one of them would take upon his back, and without grudging carry it easily away, up hill and down hill an English mile together."40

(See Arizona Giants; California Giants; Cocopa Giants; Copafi; Coronado's Giant Discoveries; De Soto's Encounters with Giants; Florida Giants; Graveyards of the Giants; Horned Giants; Indiana Giants; Mississippi and Texas Giants; Montana's Giants; Ocala; Ohio Giants; Sen Giants; Tuscaloosa; Yuman Giants; also see Barranc de Cobre Giants; Mexico's Giants; Patagonia's "Big-feet" Giants; Quiname; Tlaxcala's Giants)

When Sir Francis Drake dropped anchor in a small bay just north of modern San Francisco, the Indian natives, who had never seen a white man before, took the Englishmen to be gods. Francis Fletcher, Drake's chronicler of the voyage, says the king, "a man of large body and good aspect," even set his own crown--a headdress of feathers--on Drake's head and pleaded with him to exercise dominion over the land. He also describes these Indians as a tall people with herculean strength. "Yet are the men commonly so strong of

GIANTS ON THE EARTH

body," he writes, "that that which two or three of our men could hardly bear, one of them would take upon his back, and without grudging carry it easily away, up hill and down hill an English mile together."41

(See Arizona Giants; California Giants; Cocopa Giants; Copafi; Coronado's Giant Discoveries; De Soto's Encounters with Giants; Florida Giants; Graveyards of the Giants; Horned Giants; Indiana Giants; Mississippi and Texas Giants; Montana's Giants; Ocala; Ohio Giants; Sen Giants; Tuscaloosa; Yuman Giants; also see Barranc de Cobre Giants; Mexico's Giants; Patagonia's "Big-feet" Giants; Quiname; Tlaxcala's Giants)

Seri Giants

When his army reached the province of Senora, Coronado dispatched some men to the coast to search for the supply ships. The party sighted no ships, but they did return with a friendly Indian who stood so tall as to astonish the Spaniards. In his history, Pedro de Castaneda, a member of the expedition, mentions this event in these words: "Don Rodrigo Maldonado, who was captain of those who went in search of the ships, did not find them, but he brought back with him an Indian so large and tall that the best man in the army reached only to his chest. It was said that other Indians were even taller on the coast."42 This giant evidently belonged to the Seri, a great tribe of Indians who occupied the island of Tiburon and the adjacent Sonora coast on the Gulf of California.

(See Arizona Giants; California Giants; Cocopa Giants; Copafi; Coronado's Giant Discoveries; De Soto's Encounters with Giants; Florida Giants; Graveyards of the Giants; Horned Giants; Indiana Giants; Mississippi and Texas Giants; Montana's Giants; Ocala; Ohio Giants; San Francisco Giants; Tuscaloosa; Yuman Giants; also see Barranc de Cobre Giants; Mexico's Giants; Quiname; Tlaxcala's Giants)

South Carolina Giantess

The after-classes moonlighting of a young South Carolina giantess attending an English boarding school caught the attention of the British press. In the September 5, 1826, issue of the Public Ledger, a reporter gave this account of her: "We yesterday visited the tall young lady, who is now exhibiting as a giantess, at Bourke's dancing rooms, Change-alley, Cornhill. She stands about seven feet high without her shoes; but with the aid of them, and a most lofty plume of feathers, her visitors would imagine her to be at least eight feet high. She is not only pleasing in her countenance, but extremely well made and proportioned. She is only 18 years of age; and, having all the advantages of a fine person, would be no bad match for the celebrated Monsieur Louis, the French giant.... Her manners are extremely pleasing, and indeed her whole demeanour, instead of embarrassing, commands respect in the spectator. She is a native of South Carolina, and has been for the last four years at a boarding-school in England. From the number of black servants that are continually running about her, persons passing through King's Arms-passage imagine her to be a native of India. She is, indeed, well worth being seen."43 (See Frenz, Louis)

GIANTS ON THE EARTH

Swan, Anna Haining

Born at Mill Brook, Nova Scotia, in 1846, Anna Haining Swan joined P. T. Barnum's gallery of wonders in the early 1860s and became the best known giantess of her day. Barnum proclaimed that his four male giants stood above eight feet and advertised Miss Swan's height as seven feet eleven inches. However, according to Dr. A. P. Beach, her physician when she lived at Seville, she only measured seven feet nine inches.

One of thirteen children born to Scottish immigrants Alexander and Ann Swan, Anna grew so rapidly that at age six she already stood as tall as her mother. By age sixteen she towered seven feet high and had many curious people following her through the streets.

Barnum, in his autobiography, recounts that he "first heard of her through a Quaker who came into my office one day and told me of a wonderful girl, 17 years of age, who resided near him at Pictou, Nova Scotia, and who was probably the tallest girl in the world.

"I asked him to obtain her exact height. He did and sent it to me, and I at once sent an agent who in due time came back with Anna Swan.

"She was an intelligent and by no means ill-looking girl, and during the long period she was in my employe she was visited by thousands of persons."44

In February, 1864, Barnum took his American Museum to New York where crowds flocked to see the curiosities. But on July 13, 1865, fire broke out in the museum and spread so quickly that the giantess barely escaped. Rescuers found Miss Swan at the top of the stairway "in a swooning condition from the smoke." Because of her great size, it took eighteen men using a block and tackle to remove her from the burning building. The blaze reportedly cost her every-thing she owned except the clothes on her back. Her trunk, which the fire destroyed, contained $1,200 in gold plus a sizable amount of "greenbacks."

Anna Swan towers over her sister Maggie, who visited the Bates at their farm near Medina, Ohio (Courtesy Medina County Historical Society)

In 1870, Miss Swan met Captain Martin Van Buren Bates from Letcher County, Kentucky, when the two giants joined Judge H. P. Ingalls' company for a tour of Europe. The next year, following their presentation to Queen Victoria, they were married in London's historic St-Martin-in-the-Fields church. After a grand tour of England and Scotland, the couple returned to the States and bought a farm near Seville, Ohio. The giantess gave birth to two "abnormally large" children, but both soon died. In 1888, tuberculosis claimed her own life.

In its obituary, the Seville Times described Anna Swan as a learned woman who "at an early age developed an inquiring mind" and a thirst for knowledge. "Even when independent of the resources of her native home," the newspaper added, "she continued her habits of study; she had thus acquired a breadth of information and a facility of expression which made her very interesting as a companion and conversationalist.... Her knowledge of the world was wide and varied, a fact which in no small degree added to her

GIANTS ON THE EARTH

ability to entertain and instruct."

(See Bates, Captain Martin Van Buren; also see McAskill, Angus, another famous giant from Nova Scotia)

Tennessee Giants (See Graveyards of the Giants)

Texas Giants

The long-haired "giant Karankawas," who occupied a large territory around Matagorda Bay on the Texas gulf coast, engraved their bodies with many tattoos and occasionally ate human flesh. The tribe thrived until Stephen Austin built his settlement on the Brazos in 1823. Conflicts between the settlers and the Indians then became frequent, writes John R. Swanton, "and finally a battle was fought in which about half the tribe were slain, the other portion fleeing for refuge to La Bahia."[45]

(See Arizona Giants; California Giants; Cocopa Giants; Copafi; Coronado's Giant Discoveries; De Soto's Encounters with Giants; Florida Giants; Graveyards of the Giants; Horned Giants; Indiana Giants; Mississippi and Texas Giants; Montana's Giants; Ocala; Ohio Giants; San Francisco Giants; Seri Giants; Tuscaloosa; Yuman Giants; also see Barranc de Cobre Giants; Mexico's Giants; Quiname; Tlaxcala's Giants)

Tlaxcala's Giants

Bernal Diaz del Castillo, who served in the army of Hernan Cortes during his conquest of Mexico and later wrote an "exceptionally accurate and reliable" narrative of that brilliant campaign, recounts that in 1519, after the Spaniards defeated the Mexican city-state of Tlaxcala, the Tlaxcatecs became Cortes' most faithfulally. While relating to the Latins something about their history, the Tlaxcatecs mentioned that a race of enormous size had once inhabited their land. "They said their ancestors had told them that very tall men and women with huge bones had once dwelt among them," continues Diaz, "but because they were a very bad people with wicked customs they had fought against them and killed them, and those of them who remained had died off. And to show us how big these giants had been they brought us the leg-bone of one, which was very thick and the height of an ordinary-sized man, and that was a leg-bone from the hip to the knee. I measured myself against it, and it was as tall as I am, though I am of a reasonable height. They brought other pieces of bone of the same kind, but they were all rotten and eaten away by the soil. We were all astonished by the sight of these bones and felt certain there must have been giants in that land."[46]

(See Barranc de Cobre Giants; Mexico's Giants; Quiname; also see Arizona Giants; California Giants; Cocopa Giants; Copafi; Coronado's Giant Discoveries; De Soto's Encounters with Giants; Florida Giants; Graveyards of the Giants; Horned Giants; Indiana Giants; Mississippi and Texas Giants; Montana's Giants; Ocala; Ohio Giants; San Francisco Giants; Serf Giants; Tuscaloosa; Yuman Giants)

Tuscaloosa

On his march through Alabama, De Soto courteously detained the giant cacique

GIANTS ON THE EARTH

Tuscaloosa--as a precaution against attack. As suzerain over many caciques, Tuscaloosa ruled a wide territory that included most of modern Alabama and Mississippi. According to Garcilaso de la Vega, who accompanied De Soto, the chief stood a half-yard taller than his tallest men. Accompanied by the haughty chief and his equally gigantic eighteen-year-old son, as hostages, De Soto's party crossed the state with the loss of only two men. But at Mobile the Castilians were surprised by a well-planned ambush--which ended in disaster for Tuscaloosa's braves.

(See Arizona Giant; California Giants; Cocopa Giants; Copafi; De Soto's Encounters with Giants; Florida Giants; Graveyards of the Giants; Horned Giants; Indiana Giants; Mississippi and Texas Giants; Montana's Giants; Ocala; Ohio Giants; San Francisco Giants; Seri Giants; Yuman Giants; also see Barranc de Cobre Giants; Mexico's Giants; Quiname; Tlaxcala's Giants)

West Giantess

In 1833, a seven-foot giantess from North America appeared in Crockett's show at London's Bartholomew Fair under the name of Miss West.47

Yuman Giants

Upon reaching the mouth of the Colorado River, Hernando de Alarcon's three ships dropped anchor, while his exploratory party launched two boats against the river's furious current. On this historic first voyage up the Colorado River the Europeans came across the giant-like Yuman peoples who lived along its banks. Pedro de Castaneda, who accompanied Coronado on this expedition and wrote the most complete and factual history of it, described them as "large and well formed, without being corpulent. Some have their noses pierced, and from them hang pendants, while others wear shells. . . . All of them, big and little, wear a multi-colored sash about the waist; and tied in the middle, a round bundle of feathers hanging down like a tail.... Their bodies are branded by fire; their hair is banged in front, but in the back it hangs to the waist."48

(See Arizona Giants; California Giants; Cocopa Giants; Copafi; Coronado's Giant Discoveries; De Soto's Encounters with Giants; Florida Giants; Horned Giants; Indiana Giants; Mississippi and Texas Giants; Montana's Giants; Ocala; Ohio Giants; San Francisco Giants; Seri Giants; Tuscaloosa; also see Barranc de Cobre Giants; Mexico's Giants; Quiname; Tlaxcala's Giants)

References

1 Roy Norvill, Giants: The Vanished Race of Mighty Men (Welling-borough, Northamptonshire: The Aquarian Press, 1979), p. 82.
2 Norvill, Giants: The Vanished Race, p. 84.
3 Captain Bates' actual height is uncertain. Some claim that for show purposes he added a couple of inches.
4 Guinness Book of World Records (New York: Sterling Publishing Co., 1990), p. 344
5 Lanier, A Book of Giants, p. 307.

GIANTS ON THE EARTH

6 Lee Cavin, There Were Giants on the Earth (Seville, OH: Seville Chronicle, publisher, 1959), p. 11.

7 Frank Edwards, Stranger Than Science (New York: Lyle Stuart, 1959), p. 129.

8 Castaneda, "Expedition of Coronado," p. 301.

9 Ibid.

10 Herbert Eugene Bolton, Coronado, Knight of Pueblos and Plains (New York and Albuquerque: McGraw-Hill Co., and The University of New Mexico Press, 1949), p. 157.

11 No reference given.

12 Miguel Albornoz, Hernando De Soto: Knight of the Americas (New York: Franklin Watts, 1986), p. 289.

13 Ibid., p. 295.

14 Alvaro Fernandez, "Expedition of Hernando De Soto," in Spanish Explorers, ed. Hodge and Lewis (New York: Barnes & Noble, 1959), p. 186. Though Fernandez does not say so, Tuscaloosa's son evidently made this eloquent speech before De Soto in Indian sign language

15 Garcilaso de la Vega, The Florida of the Inca, ed. John and Jeanette Varner (Austin: University of Texas Press, 1951), p. 349.

16 Fernandez, "Expedition of Hernando De Soto," p. 188.

17 Modern Mobile is not located exactly on the same site.

18 Some historians believe the territory referred to here comprised the northern part of Leon and Jefferson counties, a land of many lakes. They think Apalachen was located on Lake Miccosukee.

19 Alvar Nunez Cabeza de Vaca, "Narrative of Cabeza de Vaca," Spanish Explorers in the Southern United States (New York: Barnes & Noble, 1959), pp. 28-29.

20 Ibid., pp. 31-32.

21 Information Sheet No. 3, Hunterian Museum, London.

22 Ibid.

23 Ibid.

24 Wood, Giants and Dwarfs, pp. 222-223.

25 These were located about two inches above the eyebrows.

26 Mysteries of the Unexplained (Pleasantville, NY: The Reader's Digest Association, 1983), p. 40.

27 Wood, Giants and Dwarfs, p. 209.

28 Fray Diego Duran, The Aztecs (New York: Orion Press, 1964), pp. 5-6. The manuscript lay for nearly three centuries in the National Library of Madrid. The first of three volumes from it was first published in 1867, under the title History of New Spain.

Mexico's Giants

29 Ibid., pp. 9-12.

30 Ibid., note, p. 332. Also see "Mexico and Central America" in the Nar-rative and Critical History of America, Vol. I, Justin Winsor, editor (New York: Houghton, Mifflin and Co., 1889), p. 39, note, p. 141.

31 Joseph de Acosta, History of the Indies, Vol. II, translated by Edward Grimston (New York: Burt Franklin, publisher, 1970), pp. 453-454.

32 Woodbury Lowery, The Spanish Settlements (New York: Russell & Russell, Inc., 1959), pp. 149-150. Webster's Dictionary defines a palm used as a unit of measurement to

range from seven to ten inches.

33 Ibid., p. 64. Matagorda Bay is located about one hundred miles below modern-day Galveston.

34 Handbook of American Indians North of Mexico, Part 1, edited by Frederick Webb Hodge (New York: Rowan & Littlefield, publishers, 1971), pp. 657-658.

35 The Clamcoets, who massacred all but five of the people LaSalle left at the fort he built on Matagorda Bay, are identified with the Karankawa. The massacre took place in 1687.

36 Handbook of American Indians North of Mexico, Part 1, p. 657.

37 Norvill, Giants: The Vanished Race, pp. 82-83.

38 Mysteries of the Unexplained (Pleasantville, NY: The Reader's Digest Association, 1983), p. 40.

39 Wood, Giants and Dwarfs, p. 230.

40 Francis Fletcher, The World Encompassed by Sir Francis Drake (Ann Arbor, MI: University Microfilms, 1966), p. 72.

41 Ibid.

42 Castaneda, "Expedition of Coronado," p. 301.

43 Ibid., pp. 215-216.

44 Cavin, Giants on the Earth, p. 6.

45 Handbook of American Indians North of Mexico, Part 1, pp. 657-658.

46 Wood, Giants and Dwarfs, p. 220.

47 Bernal Diaz, The Conquest of New Spain, translated by J. M. Cohen (New York: Penguin Books, 1963), p. 181.

48 Bolton, Coronado, Knight of Pueblos and Plains, pp. 158-159.

GIANTS ON THE EARTH

"Gigantic" Newcomers to the Prehistoric St. Lawrence River Valley

A strange people intruded into the St. Lawrence Valley around 2,000 BC, huge, rugged, very tall, with massive skulls, very round-broad heads. They were physically different the long-narrow headed native "Archaic" peoples. The big, roundheaded newcomers brought D-shaped 11-inch celts [sic]. There appears to have been a link between their society and the isolated Meadowood Culture of 800 to 500 BC on the border of the lower St. Lawrence river at Quebec-New York-Ontario. They also formed a nexus with the Adena culture of huge round-heads. Prufer and Dragoo always insisted that Adena came from eastern Lake Ontario, via upper New York to West Virginia and the Ohio River.

Now the Canadian Museum of Civilization (a citadel of conservative isolationism and liberal political-correctness) admits that in the Terminal phase (2,000 to 1,000 BC of the "Middle Great Lakes-St. Lawrence Culture" (previously called "Laurentian Late Archaic") a tall people (women 170 cm and men 180.7 cm) with "hyperdontia, or extra teeth... a genetic trait... biological...", dwelt in the St. Lawrence-Ottawa Valley (J.V. Wright, History Native Peoples of Canada: 10,000 to 1000 BC). Strangely, the skeletal remains of children were very rare. Plenty of cremations, though, in glaring contrast to the Red Paint People, whether Maritime or Laurentian Archaic, who had elaborate burials for kids.

On December 6, 1960, the skeletal remains of a man who lived in the area about 700 BC were discovered by Douglas Yaxley of Peterborough, Canada. Buried with the man were twenty-nine artifacts attributed to the Point Peninsula Culture, which occupied the Trent River system before the Christian era.

Right: Adena skull from the Ohio State Archaeological Museum, Columbus, Ohio.

Irish tradition recounts that the brutal, warlike Fomorians were "giants" who invaded in ships from Africa, and demanded chil-

GIANTS ON THE EARTH

dren at Halloween time. Pict tradition held the same. They were finally driven north to the Hebrides Isles off northwest Scotland and to Tory Island off northwest Ireland in the deep Atlantic. From there, they preyed on the people of Ulster. The Formorian giants were supposedly endowed with double-rows of teeth. Interestingly, Anglo-American settlers in the upper Ohio were told Native traditions of "giants," and early settlers claimed they were digging up (from Lake Erie-to the Ohio River) the skeletons of "giants" with massive skulls and double rows of teeth.

The skeletal remains of pygmies (often of Australoid type), especially in the Tennessee Valley have been excavated, confirming Native traditions. The Mandarins of the Canadian Museum of Civilization (Hull/Ottawa) also at long last admit: "Historically documented native beliefs in Canada appear to have been quite similar to those of the preChristian Celtic, Germanic and old Scandinavian peoples of northwestern Europe" ... (Old Scandinavian means Lapps and Finns).

Reprinted with permission
Ancient American by G. Iudhael Jewell
Volume 6, Number 42. Page 23

Idaho's Flood-Giants Remembered

The Great Basin is an area of inland drainage located in western United States. On its northern edge is a wondrous region known as the Owyhee country. Everywhere is evidence of early human struggles for existence.

Conventional theories positing wandering peoples out of Siberia dates these struggles to the last 12,000 years. Surface evidence clearly indicates the presence of huntergatherers to ten or more millennia ago. But something more materially significant may have prospered in Owyhee Country even earlier.

While Establishment scholars refuse to consider any possibilities for existence of so any a society on our continent, some Native Americans preserve oral traditions which speak of a time, very long ago, when their ancestors came into conflict with "giants" that roamed the region, interfered with activities.

These tribal accounts show some resemblance to biblical stories of a pre-flood world likewise inhabited by giants. For example, Genesis tells of the Nephilim, supposedly of great size and strength. The Judaic tradition affirms that these giants sprang from the union of fallen angels with the daughters of Cain.

They were heavenly "watchers" heaven assigned to pray for mankind, but were instead seduced to father a race of giants. These were fallen angels, sons of God, the Wnai Elohim (Job 38.7). Stories and legends of giants are not confined to the Old Testament or Native American traditions, however. Although varied from region to region, their fundamental similarities present a haunting commonality.

The giants were generally portrayed with an insatiable thirst for blood, and, because of this savage lust, were violently swept away by a great deluge. Most of them perished, but a few survivors supposedly made their way to various parts of the world.

Scientists dealing with hard data naturally dismiss such stories as mere fables. They explain widespread belief in giants found among cultures around the planet as the result of a "collective unconscious," or universal fear of overwhelming forces beyond their control.

GIANTS ON THE EARTH

These same conventional archaeologists likewise deny the occurrence of any natural catastrophe, such as a deluge, powerful enough to obliterate a previous worldorder. [sic] Geologists, however, continue to uncover more evidence establishing that truly cataclysmic flooding did indeed take place with the close of the last Ice Age, about 12,000 years ago, when areas inhabited by early human population centers in Europe and North America were overwhelmed by major pluvial events.

The violence of these catastrophes and the ten or more millennia that separate their time from ours have obscured almost all physical evidence of that pre-delluvian era. But more imperishable than material artifacts are the tribal memories of peoples who ancestors actually survived. Something of those memories may have survived in the Owyhee Country. There a river, reputed to be one of the deepest on the North American continent, is surrounded by walls so steep that sunlight never penetrates to the banks far below.

The Bruneau River was named after a French fur-trader in the mid-17th Century. Near its headwaters stretches the legendary land of the giants who terrorized Shoshone forefathers, frightening them from their ancestral hunting grounds.

These were found in the Pine Nut Mountains, along the Jarbridge River. Here, the the [sic] huge Tsawhawbitts, evil spirits in superhuman form, ravaged the Indians. Their old stories tell that these giants possessed an appetite for human flesh, and could cross creeks with a single step, or scale mountains in few strides. They chased and captured people, putting hapless victims in huge baskets, which they carried to the mountaintop for cannibal feasts.

Some Tsawhawbitts gazed from a single eye, and hopped around on one leg. They were sometimes observed high on the rocky peaks digging for unknown objects. People learned to stay far from these lofty crests, because the giants, in addition to their prodigious size, were known to exercise supernatural powers. They could paralyze their prey with a glance from their large red glowing eyes, then harpooning their quarry with razor sharp hooks.

The natives so feared such peaks, that present-day natives still refer to central Idaho's Sawtooth Mountains as the Coapiccan Kahni or Giants House. A Shoshone version describes Tso'apittse, a rocky giant with pitchy hands that fed upon human flesh.

Tribal elders repeatedly warned their young to be careful around the pools of water at the springs, as these were dangerous areas inhabited by evil-spirited giants. Staring into the water, allowing one's image to be reflected, would conjure the giants to the surface. Was this a mythic recollection of the titans supposedly overwhelmed in antiquity by the Great Flood?

The Shoshone legend adds that the giants could be killed by fire or ice, but using these, weapons too enormous courage and cunning. If a Tso'apittse was found in its deep mountain cave, a large fire was built at the entrance, and allowed to eventually burn inward until the giant was consumed.

Other stories tell of the use of ice. One night, a Tso'apittse kidnapped a little girl and promptly ate her. In its greed, the giant returned for her parents and add to its bag. [sic] The Tso'apittse soon found the father, chased and captured him, then put him in the basket. But on the way back to the mountain peak, the man escaped, and ran ahead to the cave.

GIANTS ON THE EARTH

A freezing blizzard began outside, while he filled the cave's entrance with trees and branches. When Tso'apittse returned, he tried to free the obstructing materials, but they were lodged in too tightly. During the night, the father could hear the giant whining. By morning, the sounds had ceased. The Tso'apittse was frozen to death.

Tales such as these have been told and retold for unguessed generations in tribal communities. Folkish memories of events surrounding the evil giants lived on through these narratives, which are still considered factual by many Native Americans. Like all myths, they undoubtedly have at least a seed of truth buried deep within the age-old accounts.

In any case, oral tradition eventually materialized into numerous rock petroglyphs throughout the Sawtooth Mountain area. Their interpretation continues to elude academic scholars, who sometimes describe the petroglyphs as the meaningless scratching of bored Indians. Several anthropologists have used terms such as idle scrawls and doodles to characterized native rock art.

But for a preliterate people, such images still resonate with tribal memories of a time in the very deep past, when giants and monsters were purged from the Earth by a Great Flood. These petroglyphs are their only memorials, preserved in the otherwise incomprehensible marks of ancient rock art, and the minds of those who maintain the old ways.

by Thomas E. Farner, Ph.D.

Ancient American, Volume 6, Issue 41, page 9, Reprinted with permission

Niagara's Ancient Cemetery of Giants

I respected the spelling used in the text. Fredenburg is first used and later it is spelled "Fredinburg." The site was about 40 miles west of Niagara Falls, according to recent maps; Dunnville is at the mouth of the Grand River which flows into Lake Erie. A "Six Nations First Nation Territory" is along the Grand River today, but I cannot say if the site was in it, or out of it. More information is needed to flesh out any veracity to this story, which 21st Century readers may take with a grain of salt.

Headlines: "A REMARKABLE SIGHT-- Two hundred skeletons of ANAKIN [sic] in Cayuga Township; A singular discovery by a Torontonian and others -- A vast Golgotha opened to view -- Some remains of the 'Giants that were in those days.' From our own correspondents."

Cayuga, August 21-- "On Wednesday last, Rev. Nathaniel Wardell, Messers. Orin Wardell (of Toronto), and Daniel Fredenburg, were digging on the farm of the latter gentleman, which is on the banks of the Grand River, in the township of Cayuga. When they got to five or six feet below the surface, a strange sight met them. Piled in layers, one upon top of the other, some two hundred skeletons of human beings nearly perfect -- around the neck of each one being a string of beads.

"There were also deposited in this pit a number of axes and skimmers made of stone. In the jaws of several of the skeletons were large stone pipes -- one of which Mr. O. Wardell took with him to Toronto a day or two after this Golgotha was unearthed.

"These skeletons are those of men of gigantic stature, some of them measuring nine feet, very few of them being less than seven feet. Some of the thigh bones were found to be at least a foot longer than those at present known, and one of the skulls being examined completely covered the head of an ordinary person. These skeletons are supposed

GIANTS ON THE EARTH

to belong to those of a race of people anterior to the Indians.

"Some three years ago, the bones of a mastodon were found embedded in the earth about six miles from this spot. The pit and its ghastly occupants are now open to the view of any who may wish to make a visit there."

Later: Dunnville, August 22, "There is not the slightest doubt that the remains of a lost city are on this farm. At various times within the past years, the remains of mud houses with their chimneys had been found: and there are dozens of pits of a similar kind to that just unearthed, though much smaller, in the place which has been discovered before, though the fact has not been made public hitherto. The remains of a blacksmith's shop, containing two tons of charcoal and various implements, were turned up a few months ago.

"The farm, which consists of 150 acres, has been cultivated for nearly a century, and was covered with a thick growth of pine, so that it must have been ages ago since the remains were deposited there. The skulls of the skeletons are of an enormous size and all manner of shapes, about half as large again as are now to be seen. The teeth in most of them are still in almost perfect state of preservation, though they soon fall out when exposed to the air.

"It is supposed that there is gold or silver in large quantities to be found in the premises, as mineral rods have invariably, when tested, pointed to a certain spot and a few yards from where the last batch of skeletons was found directly under the apple tree. Some large shells, supposed to have been used for holding water, which were also found in the pit, were almost petrified. There is no doubt that were a scheme of exploration carried on thoroughly the result would be highly interesting. A good deal of excitement exists in the neighborhood, and many visitors call at the farm daily.

"The skulls and bones of the giants are fast disappearing, being taken away by curiosity hunters. It is the intention of Mr. Fredinburg to cover the pit up very soon. The pit is ghastly in the extreme. The farm is skirted on the north by the Grand River. The pit is close to the banks, but marks are there to show where the gold or silver treasure is supposed to be under. From the appearance of the skulls, it would seem that their possessors died a violent death, as many of them were broken and dented.

"The axes are shaped like tomahawks, small, but keen, instruments. The beads are all of stone and of all sizes and shapes. The pipes are not unlike in shape the cutty pipe, and several of them are engraved with dogs' heads. They have not lost their virtue for smoking. Some people profess to believe that the locality of Fredinburg farm was formally an Indian burial place, but the enormous stature of the skeletons and the fact that pine trees of centuries growth covered the spot goes far to disprove this idea."

Ancient American Volume 6, Issue 41, p. 9

Researched and submitted by Benoit Crevier

Originally published in The Daily Telegraph (Toronto, Ontario), Wednesday, August 23, 1871, page 1

Reprinted with permission

Giants in our Midst?
Tall Skeletons Reported Found in Marion County, WV
One of the many archaeological mysteries from this area was the reported finding of

GIANTS ON THE EARTH

giant prehistoric human skeletons.

"On the earth there once were giants." Greek poet Homer wrote in 400 B.C.

Of the many archaeological mysteries, one of the most enigmatic has been discoveries of giant prehistoric human skeletons.

Marion County was home to part of the ancient civilization which historical accounts and artifacts indicate existed in this region - a culture with many clues and questions concerning its existence. What mysterious people constructed earthen forts, burial mounds, macadamized roadways? Who left pictographs, inscribed stones and giant skeletons lo be discovered?

In the 1850s while excavating a root cellar in Palatine (East Fairmont), workers uncovered two very large human skeletons. Measuring the bones, people were amazed to find the entombed humans had been more than 7 feet tall.

Many curious onlookers observed the skeletons which mysteriously disappeared overnight, apparently stolen for greedy purpose. A lucrative market in "Indian relics" existed in the early l9th century. Artifacts from all over Marion County were sold to travelers and purchasing agents representing Eastern museums.

It was reported that hundreds of ancient pieces of pottery, flint weapons, stone carvings and skeletons were peddled at the Valley Falls railroad station. Some of the finest specimens were purchased by visiting German royalty and taken to Europe as curios.

In 1875 workmen were constructing a bridge near the mouth of Paw Paw Creek at Rivesville. While digging through heavy clay soil they were astonished to uncover three giant skeletons strands of reddish hair clinging to the skulls. A local doctor was called to examine the remains.

Exposure to air deteriorated the bones rapidly but the doctor was able ascertain after careful measurement, the skeletons had supported people approximately 8 feet tall.

In September 1882 amateur archaeologist F.M. Fetty and his wife were exploring along White Day Creek. As Mr. Fetty crawled back into the recesses of an over-hanging cliff shelter he noticed an unusual pattern in the rock formation.

Upon close examination a false wall was discovered in the back of the shallow cave. Removing several large stones the Fettys were startled by what they found. The remains of a giant human in a sitting position with artifacts of stone and flint surrounding the prehistoric cadaver.

In the summer of 1883 James A. Faulkner unearthed an unusually large human skeleton in the same area. Dr. Samuel Kramer of Smithtown measured this skeleton and found it to be 7 feet 4 inches long. Dr. Kramer deduced the living person must have been almost 8 feet tall.

There have been historical references to a mystic race of giant red-haired humans inhabiting this continent in the distant past. Respected Biblical scholars think a lost tribe from Israel once lived in North America. Evidence exists of 5th-century Irish monks exploring West Virginia. Many questions remain to be answered.

Everyone loves a mystery and these giant skeletons reported by reputable people would make Sherlock Holmes scratch his head. This is another intriguing story of Marion County's past that will forever be unexplained.

GIANTS ON THE EARTH

Giants of the Royal Incas

Per the request of the author, the following submission is presented as received, without editorial revision. As part of Ancient American's open forum policy, readers may freely express themselves in their own words. Editor.

Nine-and-a-half feet tall is large for a human mummy, especially when it is found among today's diminutive Peruvians, whose average stature is just five feet. Understandably, professional anthropologists find tales of ancient giants amusing, but nothing more. Physical evidence may nonetheless exist to demonstrate that an oversized race of men did indeed dominate parts of prehistoric South America.

Oral stories of giant kings among the native Indians (principly [sic] the Aymara) looking for gold in Peru go back as far as the great Irish King Ophir mentioned in the Old Testament (I Chronicles 29: 3-9, Job 22: 24 Job 28: 16 Isa 12: 13).

That was a time when one could pick the gold nuggets out of the streams with your hands. The petroglyphs and legends of King Ophir still exist in Peru. As I said they [sic] are oral legends and no university has ever catalogued them. They are found like the petroglyphs along the Mississippi that pertain to the Burrows Cave. Mark Twain wrote about them and several others, but largely they have been ignored.

The same is true in Peru. There are petroglyphs along mountain paths and at the sites of ruins such as Tiahuanacu, but there are also petroglyphs right downtown Lima associated with the adobe pyramids. Nobody has chronicled these structures. There are several of them right in the middle of one of the major cities of the world. Now that may not satisfy you, but I can't help that. One would have thought that someone from the Discovery Channel would have produced a show on these structures. However, they haven't! It almost never rains in Lima and these adobe pyramid structures were built somewhere between 400 AD and 1000 AD. I enclosed a photo of one from a distance. Even now anthropologists refuse to make any connection between the old and new worlds before the arrival of Columbus.

The once famous King Ophir who lived before 600 BC and probably at the time of David the King, as mentioned in the Bible (because his craft was used in the temple) learned how to work in gold and overlay the walls and pillars, as is evident from the Biblical passages, from his travels in the ancient Americas. The three pictures included in this article are golden overlays that covered the interior walls of Inca Temples. These were not just designs stamped into the surface of the gold, but brilliant woven patterns made to appear like wallpaper tapestries. One can only imagine that this was the very same workmanship on the walls of the temple built under the direction of King David by the hands of the craftsmen of Ophir.

However, the craftsmanship of gold up-Nile was primitive and clumsy and not the craftsmanship necessary for the fine temple golden-woven wall paper used in the temple of Solomon. Lastly, there are impurities in the mining of all metals. These are the signatures for the source of the metal. One of the newest archeological techniques is to search for the source of metal at a dig sight based on the impurities of the metal. The Discovery Channel Program Curse of the Cocaine Mummy suggesting the drug link between Peru and ancient Egypt also suggested a signature metal connection between the two countries.

What should be painfully obvious to us today is that the secret of the ancient world of

GIANTS ON THE EARTH

Palestine was not where one could mine gold in the desert, but that one could find gold by sailing on boats and how to navigate the oceans. There were no gold mines in the ancient deserts and all the gold that was used in the merchant traffic before Christ came from somewhere outside the Holy Land. That secret became almost a religion of its own by the time of the birth of Christ and was institutionalized by the time of Diocletian the Roman Emperor after Constantine, the editor of the Bible.

The secret at the time of Christ was that you could travel forty times farther in a day by ship than you could travel by camel . That concept by the time of Diocletian was refined to suggest that 1200 pounds of goods would double in price if taken three hundred miles overland. However, the same goods could be shipped almost anywhere in the known world for a third that cost.

The fraternal order of the Phoenician Pirates keep the secrets of where and how they had navigated the oceans. Their fingerprints exist around the world. These fraternal orders were secret orders with passwords, handshakes and signs and tokens. They had initiation rights etc. All of this secret banter centered over the secrets of how to navigate the oceans and where in the world was the treasure. It was not accident that Columbus looked to the West for gold. Others had been there before him and brought home wealth.

Giant mummified head of an Inca King. Notice shadow of individual on the right of the glass case for perspective. Photos were frowned upon and had to be acquired discretely.

The mummy in the photo was clearly a giant man. There were two different mummies of Inca Kings in this private museum located at Jose's home. That is important because it down-plays the idea that maybe one of the kings was a mutation of some sort. Both men, would exceed the height of anyone we know in our world today.

Rumors of giant men walking the earth are not new at all. Genesis 6: 4 speaks specifically about them. Philo was very well aware of the classic traditions of the giants. Philo was a Jew who lived in Alexandria from 20 BC to the beginning of the Jewish wars in 66 AD. It is amazing to understand that he wrote his extensive works during the lifetime of Jesus and not very far away.

Those scholars who have naively suggested that there was no one else writing about Jesus during his lifetime except Josephus are lazy people indeed. Philo was one of the sources for the movie "The Ten Commandments". Director Cecil B. Demille did something very unusual in order to gain credibility for his movie. He opened the epic by appearing on a curtain-clad stage and told the world his historical sources for his version of the tale of Moses. One the of three principle sources was Philo.

Philo lived among thousands Jews in Alexandria during the lifetime of Christ. Alexandria was at the mouth of the Nile River and was the seat of learning for the world. It was a major merchant port...all issues making it larger than Rome by several times. Perhaps there were almost as many Jews in Egypt at the time of Christ as there was in Palestine.

At that time the Greeks dominated Egyptian culture and religion. The immediate proceeding ten pharaohs prior to the time of Philo couldn't even speak the Egyptian language with the exception of Cleopatra. After the conquest of Egypt by Alexander the Great Egypt and especially Alexandria the populace wrote slept and ate Greek culture and lore.

It should be no surprise that Philo was well aware of the legends and histories of the Giants. Philo was emphatic on this point when he said, "He utters no fable whatsoever

GIANTS ON THE EARTH

respecting the giants; but he (God) wishes to set this fact before your eyes, that some men are born of the earth, and some are born of heaven, and some are born of God: those are born of the earth who are hunters after the pleasures of the body." The most critical point of this entire discussion of Philo and the Giants is that Philo mentions King Ophir in his specific notes relating to the giants in the ancient world. Either Philo thought King Ophir was one of the giants himself, which is unlikely, or Philo knew of the connection between the Peruvian traveler Ophir and the giants in the Americas. If the latter is true then the mummified kings depicted in this article take on even greater significance. Clearly there were giant kings in Peru. Who knew about these giant kings still remains speculative. However, it is amazing to suggest that Philo himself may have made that connection by the time of Christ.

I had no dating for the Peruvian Kings themselves. This was a private gold museum and not likely to allow me, or anyone else for that matter, to do any testing that might threaten the ownership of this golden treasure.

Part of me wants to think of these particular kings as living long after the time of Ophir somewhere around a thousand AD. Of course that would ruin the tale of the connection between King Ophir of the Bible and these mummies. The state of the mummy coincide with the tales of the Incas in one thousand AD. However, I have found after this discovery many mummified remains in Peruvian museums and many of the oldest dating from long before 600 AD were in exactly the same state of decomposition. I was relieved that the story of Ophir and these mummies remains intact.

The actual mummified head of the crowned king in the photograph is almost twice as large as my own and I wear the largest hat of anyone in my acquaintance. When we were invited to the private gold museum to begin with I was expected to be dazzled by gold. However, it dawned on me the minute I walked through the door that the size of the head, and indeed his whole body, was the unique feature of this king. The gold was impressive, but the size of the man was something more impressive than gold.

The golden tunic that hung on the wall was made of spun gold. This was the first time in my life I had seen gold woven into a fabric for clothing. The tunic was over eight feet tall and tailored in such a way as to suggest that it was not intended to drag on the floor behind a king, but rather to hang straight down to the floor and no further. That made the tunic itself a measuring device for the original height of the giant king. It was shocking to imagine a man who could first wear this tunic without looking like a small child playing with his mother's clothing and secondly it was shocking to imagine the shear weight of the garment. The golden necklace at the foot of the tunic would have hung to the floor around the neck of anyone I know. The golden shoulder shield in the photograph was almost twice the size of shoulder pads used by professional football players.

There was also a set of golden gloves whose hands and fingers extended from the wrist to the tip of the middle finger about twelve to fourteen inches. I couldn't tell exactly because they were kept behind security glass.

Second mumified [sic] head of a giant man richly decorated in gold headgear and body covering. Right: Interior view of the private museum revealing an arrary [sic] of golden artifacts. Photos © Glenn Kimball.

It is important to note that this gold museum is private and not open to the public. Perhaps this is the only way precious golden relics like this could ever have been pre-

GIANTS ON THE EARTH

served. The governments of South America have often plundered the wealth of their own history. Many times the leaders of governments would plunder artifacts because these would be the treasures least missed by the people. It is horrifying to imagine how many precious things have been melted down into bars and sold for spot prices on the world market just to line the pockets of the greedy who should have been the ones to protect the artifacts to begin with. One can only imagine how many artifacts were melted by Cortez when he pillaged the great temple artifacts and writings of Montezuma in Mexico in the fifteen hundreds. The rumors in Spain were that Cortez could have built a bridge home to Spain from the Gold of Montezuma. Of course that is not literal, but figurative. Most of the world's best estimates of how much gold there is in world circulation suggest that one could fit all the gold in a two car garage! That makes the gold in this museum even more amazing.

Someone should have asked the question long ago, why did Cortez expect to find gold in the Americas in the first place? Why did the crew on the boats of Columbus expect to find gold? Why did the marauding Spaniards kill eight million native American Indians looking for gold. The truth is that the royal families of England and Spain had spoken as far back as King Arthur in 530 AD that their "treasure house" was located in the "Mericas" (Source for this statement needed Landaff Charters from the sixth century).

The German who suggested that we named the Americas after Amerigo Vespucci recanted his story when he found the tales of the "Mericas" stars which lead the way to the "promised land".

Regardless of the date the actual discovery or age of golden-clad giant kings in Peru the story still suggests something well beyond our common anthropological tales. Where were the anthropologists when I was traveling Lima in the sixties? Why haven't they caught up to this find in the last thirty years? I wonder if I am that good an archaeologist or that they are that bad. Sadly, I think the latter to be the case.

by Glenn Kimball, Ph.D
Ancient American, Volume 5, Issue #34, pages 36-38
Reprinted with permission

Assam Giant
A human skeleton measuring eleven feet was found some years ago at Tura in Assam, near the border of East Pakistan, reports Peter Kolosimo.1

CHANG WOO GOW, who became a sensation in Britain, was accompanied on his tours by his wife King-Foo and the dwarf Chung, his constant companion.

Chang Woo Gow
The Chinese giant Chang Woo Gow showed himself in England in 1865/1866 at the old Egyptian Hall in Piccadilly. A courtly gentleman and able scholar, he was invited to visit the Prince and Princess of Wales. He stood eight feet two inches. He was not the tallest in his family, however, for one sister measured eight feet four inches. On his British tour, the nineteen-year-old Chang was accompanied by his bride, King-Foo ("The Fair Lily") and by a three-foot dwarf named Chung, who always stood at his side during the giant's public appearances.2 (See Chinese Colossus; Chinese Giants, Other; Giants and Dwarfs; Melius, Angelina)

GIANTS ON THE EARTH

Chinese Colossus

Purchaas, in his Pilgrimes, 1625, says that while he was in China he saw a man who "was cloathed with a tyger's skin, the hayre outward, his armes, head, and legges bare, with a rude pole in his hand; well-shaped, seeming ten palmes or spans long, his hayre hanging on his shoulders."3 (See Chang Woo Gow; Chinese Giants, Other)

Chinese Giants, Other

The Chinese, in whose land archaeologists have found some of the earliest skeletal remains of giants, insist they once had among them some men as much as fifteen feet tall. We could dismiss this as just another tall tale, except that Melchior Nunnez, in his letters from India, vouches for the fact that China grew some giants to that tremendous size. He "speaks of porters who guarded the gates of Peking who were of that immense height; and in a letter dated in 1555, he avers that the emperor of that country entertained and fed five hundred of such men for archers of his guard."4 They were still there to be seen seventy years later, for George Hakewill, in his Apologie, 1627, issues a similar report.5 (See Chang Woo Gow; Chinese Colossus)

Monstrous Tartar (See Tartar Giants)

Tartar Giants

In 1575, when the Tartars invaded Poland, Jacobus Niezabilo-vius slew a warrior of enormous size who fought in their ranks. After the battle, Polish soldiers marveled that as he lay dead on the ground "his body was of so prodigious a bulk that... his carcass reached to the navel of any ordinary person standing by the side of it."6 (See Graveyards of the Giants)

And James Paris du Plessis, in his Short History of Human Prodigies, Dwarfs, etc., reports that a Hungarian, known as the "Monstrous Tartar," was exhibited at "Ye Globe in the ould Baily in February 1664. He was taken prisoner by Count Serini and was a creature of extraordinary strength and valour, who, having spent all his arrows in fight against the Christians, was taken alive and so continues being carefully kept in those parts."7

References
1 Peter Kolosimo, Timeless Earth (New York: University Books, 1968), p. 32.
2 Thompson, Mystery and Lore of Monsters, pp. 181-182.
3 Ibid., p. 231.
4 No reference given.
5 No reference given.
6 Ibid.,pp. 95-96.
7 Thompson, Mystery and Lore of Monsters, p. 149

GIANTS ON THE EARTH

MIDDLE EAST GIANTS

Abishai, Giant Killer

Abishai, the brother of Joab, struck down the giant Ishbi-benob as he was about to deliver the death blow to a fallen King David in one of Israel's wars with the Philistines. (See David vs Goliath)

Abraham and the Giants

Biblical and historical records, along with credible archaeological evidence, show that when Abraham pulled up his tent stakes at Ur of the Chaldeans and moved his family and flocks to Canaan, many giants already occupied Transjordan. The scriptures also say that when this first Hebrew patriarch later established his headquarters at Hebron, he lived for some years among the Anakim giants who founded that city.

Although the Anakim in later times became the most numerous--and the most feared--of Canaan's giants, the Avvim and Hurrians (or Horites, as they are called in Genesis) apparently were the first tall people to occupy that land. Archaeological experts admit to having no direct proof of this. But, according to H. R. Hall, "recent excavations of the Palestine Exploration Fund at Gezer and various other researches have shewn that Palestine was originally inhabited by a stone-age population that lived in caves, and was probably related to the troglodytic people of the desert between the Nile and the Red Sea, who are mentioned by Strabo.1 We may identify them with the preCanaanite Horites or Avvim of Biblical tradition. They developed into or were succeeded by the Anakim or Rephaim, the 'Giants' of tradition, who built the megalithic monuments, the dolmens and menhirs, of Moab and eastern Palestine.2 To them may be due the earliest stone walls of the Canaanite cities."3

Elmer W. K. Mould also affirms that the earliest race to occupy Canaan was non-Semitic and of gigantic stature. The "authentic names of aboriginal settlers," he declares, "are really preserved in the legendary Anakim, Avvim, Rephaim, Emim, and Zamzummim, which are referred to several times. These legendary peoples pre-ceded the Amorites in Palestine, but afterward, through a blur of tradition, they came to be mistakenly regarded as Amorite subdivisions. So far as can be learned from the records, the Emim ('dreadful ones') lived in the area of Moab; the Zamzummim ('murmurers' or 'stammerers,' i.e., speakers of a barbarous tongue), or Uzim,4 in the area of Ammon, east of Jordan. There were Horites in the Mount Seir region before the Edomites displaced them. In southern and southwestern Palestine were the Anakim, centering around Hebron, and the Avvim, near Gaza. 'Rephaim' ('giants') was perhaps a collective name for all these aborigines.... Such names as 'Nephilim,' 'Rephaim,' and 'Anakim,' whatever they may mean, point to the existence in Palestine of tall men who were non-Semitic. East of the Jordan, in Bashan, Og, king of Bashan, and his people constituted a remnant of the Rephaim. Somewhere in central Canaan, west of Jordan, there was a land of the Rephaim. Near Jerusalem there was a Valley of the Rephaim."5

Such then were some of the enormous inhabitants who lived in and about Canaan at the time Abraham and his nephew Lot moved their families, servants, and flocks to Canaan. These aborigine half-breeds apparently gave Abraham no trouble--or at least none is recorded. But the giants of Transjordan and Mount Seir later figured in a war the

GIANTS ON THE EARTH

Hebrew patriarch became involved in.

In Canaan both Abraham and Lot prospered. Eventually their herds and flocks increased to such numbers that "the land could not sustain them while dwelling together."6 Competition for pastureland and disputes over water rights sometimes led to strife between the herdsmen of both men. Determined to stave off any chance of trouble developing between themselves, Abraham one day suggested to Lot that they separate. "Is not the whole land before you?" He asked his nephew. "If you take the left hand, then I will go to the right; or if you take the right hand, then I will go to the left."7

This fateful day the two men stood on the highest ridge between Bethel and Ai. As Abraham waited, Lot pondered which way to go. Looking northward and southward, he could see the gently sloping hills and vales with patches of wheat and barley waving in the refreshing mountain breeze. Also within his sight were the famous vineyards and groves of olives, pomegranates, figs, apricots, and almonds. But turning eastward he saw "the whole plain of the Jordan was well watered, like the garden of the Lord, like the land of Egypt, toward Zoar." Following the course of the Jordan River through a valley green with a perennial verdure, his gaze finally came to rest on the Salt Sea, shimmering now under the sun's bright light. At the sea's southern end, Sodom and Gomorrah beckoned. These largest of the five rich cities of the plains basked now, as they did the year round, in a delightful climate that produced a lush tropical vegetation on the surrounding land. All things considered, it seemed to Lot that the Jordan valley, with its tropical luxuriance, offered him the best opportunity. Plus, it also afforded him an easy accessibility to city life.

After separating from Lot, Abraham drove his flocks south and established his headquarters under the oak of Mamre, about twenty miles below Bethlehem. At this time many Anakim giants and some Hittites of normal size lived in that area. Practically next door to Abraham's camp stood Kiriath Arba, later called Hebron. This place the Anakim had named after their famous forefather, Arba.8 At the time of the Exodus so many giants occupied Kiriath Arba that a Hebrew army of over six hundred thousand men rebelled against Moses rather than go up and attack it. But when Abraham lived there Kiriath Arba probably was no more than a large rural community.

After he left Abraham on the mountain, Lot at first only pitched his tent near Sodom. Moses tells us, however, that he soon afterward moved his family inside that depraved city. He thus willingly established his home among a people apparently defiled to some extent by Nephilim blood (see Origin of the Giants--Biblical Account). This we learn from Jude, who mentions that the people of Sodom and Gomorrah "indulged in gross immorality and went after strange flesh."9 Merrill F. linger also interprets this passage to mean that cohabitation between "beings of a different nature" probably took place.10 And exactly that happened. For no creatures of a strange flesh ever lived on this earth except the evolved Nephilim and their mongrel Gibborim offspring. Both Ecclesiasticus (16:8-9) and the Book of Jubilees (20:5), incidentally, confirm that giants lived in Sodom and Gomorrah. And according to G. Ch. Aalders, Birsha, king of Gomorrah, probably was a giant. "On the basis of the Arabic language," he says, "the name . . . Birsha, king of Gomorrah," can be interpreted "as 'large man'."11 Also in Abraham's day so many giants occupied nearby Bashan that it became widely known as "the land of Rephaim."12 The Rephaim giants exerted control over Gilead, too, and all the land of Edom fell under

GIANTS ON THE EARTH

their sway.

Now Moses, in his chronicles, relates that two years before Abraham left Haran for Canaan,13 King Chedorlaomer invaded the Valley of Siddim, attacked Sodom, Gomorrah, Admah, Zeboiim, and Bela and brought them under his rule. With these victories, Chedorlaomer not only gained access to the cities' highly prized resources of bitumen, copper, and salt, but he also established control over the caravan routes from Arabia into Canaan and Egypt and the surrounding countries. Little else is known about this first campaign, except that Amraphel king of Shinnar, Arioch king of Ellasar, and Tidal king of Goiim accompanied Chedorlaomer and helped him conquer the five cities.

For twelve years following their overthrow, the kings of Sodom and Gomorrah and the three small neighboring cities served Chedorlaomer and paid him an annual tribute. Later events suggest, however, that soon after their surrender the vassals resolved to throw off Chedorlaomer's yoke and began making long-range plans to regain their independence. They not only shored up their defenses and strengthened their military capabilities, but they also apparently made a league with several communities of giants in the Jordan Valley and with the immense Horim people in Edom and the Negev.

Emboldened by their preparations, and no doubt, too, by the great distance that separated them from Chedorlaomer and his army,14 the kings of the five city-states grew more and more defiant of Elam's rule. Finally, in their thirteenth year, they rebelled.

Though commentators agree that the vassals' refusal to send any more shipments of asphalt, copper, or salt played some part in Chedorlaomer's subsequent action, some think two far greater considerations motivated him. First of all, they explain, as "a conqueror, aiming at extensive empire," Elam's mighty sovereign obviously could not allow the rebellion of such petty kings to succeed--because of the bad example it would set for the other provinces under his lordship. Secondly, he also would have been reluctant to relinquish control over the lucrative trade route that meandered from the Euphrates, via Damascus, through the Jordan Valley, down to the Red Sea and Egypt.

"The importance of keeping open the valley of the Jordan," comments Marcus Dods, "is obvious to every one who has interest enough in the subject to look at a map. That valley was the main route for trading caravans and for military expeditions between the Euphrates and Egypt. Whoever held that valley might prove a most formidable annoyance and indeed an absolute interruption to commercial or political relations between Egypt and Elam, or the Eastern powers.... A rebellion therefore of these chiefs occupying the vale of Siddim was sufficiently important to bring the king of Elam from his distant capital."15

So, in the fourteenth year, Chedorlaomer and the three kings allied with him gathered their armies and set out for the plain of the Jordan--a distance of nearly one thousand miles in a straight line. But, because of Arabia's intervening desert terrain, the armies with Chedorlaomer could not cross in a straight line. They most likely took the customary route, fording the lower Tigris and then following the east bank of the Euphrates all the way into Northern Assyria. At Carchemish they would have crossed over the river, then turned south toward the Jordan Valley and the rebellious city-states.

Somehow, perhaps from spies, Chedorlaomer learned of the military alliance that the five cities had made with the giants who occupied Bashan, Gilead, and Edom. He thus chose not to strike the first blow at Sodom, Gomorrah, Adman, Zeboiim, or Bela, but

GIANTS ON THE EARTH

moved instead to cut off help from their Rephaim neighbors. This decision may not have been so daring a move as we may think. In those days giants in great numbers walked the earth (see Giants Who Became Gods; Gomarian Giants). So Chedorlaomer no doubt had recruited some of these oversized warriors into his own ranks. Interestingly, Arioch, one of the Babylonian kings that accompanied Chedorlaomer on this campaign, was himself a giant, his name being derived from arik, which means "tall among the giants."[16]

Of course, no ancient records exist that tell us how many giants served under Chedorlaomer. He may have had only Arioch, or that towering king plus a few others, or he may have had many such men in his service. In any event, the results of their opening battle with the Jordanian giants clearly show that he commanded a far superior force. Sweeping down the valley, his army quickly laid siege to Ashteroth Karnaim. This chief city of the Rephaim lay in the district of Bashan, about six miles northwest of Edrei. These giants worshipped Astarte, the goddess of the crested moon.[17] They were greatly decimated. Continuing along what the ancients called the King's Highway, a trade route that ran the entire length of the Trans-jordanian plateau to the Gulf of Aqabah,[18] Chedorlaomer and his confederate kings next fell upon the enormous Zamzummim people at Ham. Some archaeologists identify this city with modern Ham, which is located in eastern Gilead, about four miles south of Irbid. After this, the kings from Elam and Mesopotamia attacked and cut off the terrible Emim giants at nearby Shaveh Kiriathaim.[19] These people, described as "great and many and tall," occupied the land that the Moabites later took.

Sodom and Gomorrah, at the southern tip of the Salt Sea, stood next in line. They quickly got ready to defend themselves, expecting the worst. But to their amazement the invaders passed them by. Pressing on southward into the rough mountain range of Seir, Chedorlaomer waged war instead against the giant Horites.[20] He also conquered the Negev to eliminate any threat from that quarter. Having thus neutralized all the country round, he finally turned his attention upon the rebellious Sodom and Gomorrah and their neighbors.

Giving up whatever security their fortified walls afforded them, "the king of Sodom and the king of Gomorrah and the king of Admah and the king of Zeboiim and the king of Bela (that is, Zoar) came out," notes Moses; "and they arrayed for battle against them in the valley of Siddim, against Chedorlaomer king of Elam and Tidal king of Goiim and Amraphel king of Shinar and Arioch king of Ellasar--four kings against five."[21]

This bold strategy to meet the invaders in the open field was decided by the surrounding treacherous terrain. Many slime pits, dug to obtain pitch or mortar for building, transversed the area.[22] While most English translations simply describe the Valley of Siddim as being "full of slime pits," the force of the original Hebrew language, according to Speiser, conveys to the reader a picture of "one bitumen pit after another." The locals were most familiar with the locations of these pits. The invaders were not. They were also accustomed to the foul-smelling, boiling waters on whose surface floated lumps of asphalt or bitumen the size of bulls. The enemy, they hoped, would be at least a little disconcerted by the unfamiliar terrain and terrible odor and afraid of falling into the boiling waters.

But the pits failed to deter the invaders. Indeed, they soon turned them to their own advantage. In the resulting warfare, many in the defenders' ranks saw death. Alarmed by the way the battle was progressing against them, the five local kings and their armies

GIANTS ON THE EARTH

panicked and attempted to flee the field. The slime pits, however, made retreat difficult. In the confusion, two of the fleeing kings--and presumedly many men with them--fell into the tar pits. Those who escaped fled into the mountains.

For a time some scholars disbelieved this Genesis story, labeling it a fiction. But evidence dug up by archaeologists in recent years verifies that in Abraham's time a great destruction came upon the very places mentioned in Chedorlaomer's invasion. Dr. Nelson Glueck, whose work in this area extended from 1932 until 1947, when it was halted by the Israeli-Arab disturbances, reports that the highly developed civilization which flourished here during the Middle Bronze I period (c. 2100-1900 B.C.) came to an abrupt and savage end. This well-known archaeologist found that not only the cities mentioned in Genesis but also many villages--beginning with Ashtaroth-Karnaim and proceeding south through Transjordan and the Negev to Kadesh Barnea in the Sinai--were systematically gutted. "From southern Syria to central Sinai, their fury raged," he writes. "A punitive expedition developed into an orgy of annihilation. I found that every village in their path had been plundered and left in ruins, and the countryside laid waste. The population had been wiped out or led away into captivity. For hundreds of years thereafter, the entire area was like an abandoned cemetery, hideously unkept, with all its monuments shattered and strewn in pieces on the ground."23

Following their victory in the field, Chedorlaomer's warriors plundered Sodom and Gomorrah and the other cities and took some of their principal inhabitants away captive. Among these were Lot and his family. To the king of Elam's great misfortune, however, one who had managed to escape from Sodom came and reported this news to Abraham. Lot's uncle at this time still lived in tents pitched near the great trees of Mamre the Amorite. Mamre was a brother of Eshcol and Aner. All three were Abraham's allies. When Abraham heard that his relative had been taken captive, he called out the three hundred and eighteen "trained men born in his household," and, being joined by the forces of Mamre, Eshcol, and Aner, he pursued the enemy as far as Dan.24 When the right opportunity presented itself, Abraham and his men came upon Chedorlaomer's camp in the dead of night, took the confused, frightened foe by surprise, put them to a rout, rescued Lot and his fellow captives, and recovered all Chedorlaomer's plundered goods. (See Argob's Sixty Cities of the Giants; also see Giants Who Became Gods; Gomarian Giants)

Acmon, Early Giant Ruler

According to the most ancient historians, a prince named Acmon, the son of Maneus, headed the nation of Gomarian Sacae giants that seized Cappadocia and Pontus. Not many years after these conquests he passed over the river Halis and made incursions into Greater Phrygia.

Following his land grabs in Asia Minor, Acmon and his tall subjects built at least two cities, Themicyra, on the southern shores of the Black Sea, and Acmonia, near the river Thermodon.

The first historians also declare that the Gomarian giants who followed Acmon into Asia Minor worshipped him as the "Most High" god, and in both Cappadocia and Phrygia they consecrated woods and groves to him. (See Giants Who Became Gods; Gomarian Giants.)

GIANTS ON THE EARTH

Ahiman

Ahiman was one of three giant brothers whose great stature so terrified ten of the men Moses sent to spy out Canaan that they later persuaded the Hebrews not to attack. The three brothers apparently ruled the Anakim nation from Hebron, which was later captured by Caleb. Of the three, ancient rabbinical tradition holds that Ahiman was the most feared. (See Canaan's Anakim; Israel's Wars with the Giants)

Amorites

The Amorites, probably the most numerous people in Canaan at the time of Israel's invasion, were near giants in both stature and strength. Their hugeness is confirmed by these words that the prophet Amos later wrote: "Thus says the Lord, '... It was I who destroyed the Amorite before them, though his height was like the height of cedars and he was strong as the oaks.'"25 (See Israel's Wars with the Giants; Sihon's and Og's Overthrow)

Anab's Giants

After Debir fell to them, Joshua's legions attacked and completely destroyed nearby Anab, which the giant Anakim occupied.

The city's name still survives today as Khirbet Anab, which is located about thirteen miles southwest of Hebron. (See Israel's Wars with the Giants)

Argob's Sixty Cities of the Giants

Deuteronomy 3:4 states that the Argob, which Jair seized from the giant King Og, contained sixty cities built by the huge Rephaim. To those who never saw it, it seemed incredible that an oval-shaped district only twenty-two miles long and fourteen wide could accommodate that many cities. But archaeologists and other travelers to that region can still vouch for it. For the ruins, even after all these centuries, not only remain, but, in fact, still stand in a great state of preservation. "The streets," observes Cyril Graham, "are perfect, the walls perfect, and, what seems more astonishing, the stone doors are still hanging on their hinges. . . . Some of these gates are large enough to admit of a camel passing through them, and the doors are of proportionate dimensions, some of the stones of which they are formed being eighteen inches in thickness. The roofs also are formed of huge stone slabs resting on the massive walls. All betoken the workmanship of a race endowed with powers far exceeding those of ordinary men; and [all] give credibility to the supposition that we have in them the dwellings of the giant race that occupied that district before it was invaded by the Israelites. We could not help being impressed with the belief that had we never known anything of the early portion of Scripture history before visiting this country, we should have been forced to the conclusion that its original inhabitants, the people who had constructed those cities, were not only a powerful and mighty nation, but individuals of greater strength than ourselves."

Continues Graham: "When we find one after another, great stone cities, walled and unwalled, with stone gates, and so crowded together that it becomes almost a matter of wonder how all the people could have lived in so small a place; when we see houses built of such huge and massive stones that no force which can be brought against them in that country could ever batter them down; when we find rooms in these houses so large

GIANTS ON THE EARTH

and lofty that many of them would be considered fine rooms in a palace in Europe; and, lastly, when we find some of these towns bearing the very names which cities in that very country bore before the Israelites came out of Egypt, I think we cannot help feeling the strongest conviction that we have before us the cities of the Rephaim of which we read in the Book of Deuteronomy."26

Another traveler to this area, professor J. L. Porter, agrees with Graham that giants built these cities. "Moses," he writes, "makes special mention of the strong cities of Bashan, and speaks of their high walls and gates. He tells us, too, in the same connection, that Bashan was called the land of the giants (or Rephaim, Deut. iii. 13), leaving us to conclude that the cities were built by giants. Now the houses of Kerioth and other towns in Bashan appear to be just such dwellings as a race of giants would build. The walls, the roofs, but especially the ponderous gates, doors, and bars, are in every way characteristic of a period when architecture was in its infancy, when giants were masons, and when strength and security were the grand requisites. I measured a door in Kerioth: it was nine feet high, four and a half feet wide, and ten inches thick,--one solid slab of stone. I saw the folding gates of another town in the mountains still larger and heavier. Time produces little effect on such buildings as these. The heavy stone slabs of the roofs resting on the massive walls make the structure as firm as if built of solid masonry; and the black basalt used is almost as hard as iron. There can scarcely be a doubt, therefore, that these are the very cities erected and inhabited by the Rephaim, the aboriginal occupants of Bashan."27 (See Beit Jibrim; Rephaim Giants; Sihon's and Og's Overthrow)

Ariels

Benaiah, one of David's mighty men, reportedly killed two Ariels from Moab. Ariels, according to the King James Version, were "lion-like men," that is, their human features still retained some resemblance to the lion. (See David vs Goliath; Horned Giants; Origin of the Giants)

Arioch, the Giant King

According to the Targum of Palestine on Genesis 14:9, Arioch, one of the Babylonian kings who joined Chedorlaomer in his punishing war against Sodom and Gomorrah and their three neighboring cities was a giant. Because of his great height he was called Arioch, which is derived from arik and means "tall among the giants."

Ashdod's Giants

Joshua lists Ashdod, one of the five Philistine cities on Canaan's southwest coast, as a place where the Anakim survived following Israel's campaign against the giants. The giant population here must have been especially large, for the Egyptian Execration Texts often refer to Ashdod as a "city of the giants." (See Beth-Paleth's Giants; Oath's Giants; Gaza's Giants)

Ashteroth Karnaim's Giants

Located about six miles northwest of Edrei, Ashteroth Karnaim served as the Rephaim's chief city in Bashan. These giants worshipped Astarte, the goddess of the crested moon. They came under attack by Chedorlaomer in the nineteenth century B.C., and though

GIANTS ON THE EARTH

Moses described them as "great and many and tall," they were nonetheless greatly decimated. (See Abraham and the Giants)

Avvim

Experts believe the Avvim and Hurrians were the first giants to occupy Canaan. According to Moses, the Avvim lived on the plains around Gaza, but they were almost annihilated by the Caphtorim who came in ships from Caphtor. Those who escaped the Caphtorim afterward founded a city in the territory that later fell by lot to the tribe of Benjamin. To perpetuate their name, they called it Avvim. (See Israel's Wars with the Giants)

Bashan's Giants (See Argob's Sixty Cities of the Giants; also see Abraham and the Giants; Sihon's and Og's Overthrow)

Beit Jibrim

Beit Jibrim means the "House of the Gibborim," i.e., of "the Giants." The town, which still exists even to this day, commands the entrance to the Valley of Zephathah on the road from Jerusalem to Gaza. Because of its enormous caverns, it has been called "one of the most amazing cave-cities in the world." Some of the caves measure up to four hundred feet long, while their ceilings reach to heights of eighty feet. (See Argob's Sixty Cities of the Giants; Giants, Valley of the; Israel's Wars with the Giants; Rephaim, Land of the)

Beth-Paleth's Giants

Although the Hebrews were successful in their campaign to rid the promised land of all the giants, Joshua writes that some Anakim still survived in Gaza, Gath, and Ashdod. He apparently meant to say that they occupied a sizable territory around these chief cities of the Philistines. For when Sir Flinders Petrie, a British archaeologist, dug up Beth-Paleth some eighteen miles south of Gaza, he found artifacts indicating that it, too, had been inhabited by giants.28 (See Ashdod's Giants; Gath's Giants; Gaza's Giants)

Birsha

Gomorrah's King Birsha, against whom Elam's King Chedorlaomer made war, apparently was a giant. "On the basis of the Arabic language," declares G. Ch. Aalders, "the name. . . Birsha, king of Gomorrah," can be interpreted "as 'large man'."29 (See Abraham and the Giants)

Canaan's Anakim

Even while they served Pharaoh, all Israel knew about the giant people who occupied Canaan. In patriarchal times these huge Nephilim half-breeds grew so numerous and became so famous for their feats of strength and daring that Abraham, Isaac, and Jacob no doubt told their children stories about them. In turn, these accounts were repeated, probably with some embellishments, to all later generations of Hebrews. So, even while they toiled at making bricks in Egypt, tales about the terrible giants became a part of Hebrew lore.

GIANTS ON THE EARTH

When the Hebrews fled Egypt some four centuries after Abraham's time, these monstrous creatures still occupied Canaan, as did many Canaanites of about the Hebrews' own size. From the outset, therefore, these former slaves realized that they could never possess the promised land unless they killed or expelled them. As they sat in the warming glow of their campfires, they must have discussed this problem. Unfortunately, these conversations only reinforced their dread of the giants. So after their first year in the Sinai, when Moses ordered that all the men twenty years old and older be numbered for war, their apprehension about fighting the giants surely increased. And their fears, in whatever measure, must have mounted even higher when the great Hebrew prophet, led by the cloud,30 set out across the Desert of Paran toward Canaan's southern border.

This trek across that fearful desert of hot sand took a couple of months. But suddenly, out of the barren and desolate expanse of burning desert-waste, the weary Israelites came upon Kadesh Barnea,31 an oasis created by the brief course of a stream arising at the foot of a limestone cliff. Located in the southeastern corner of the Negeb, Kadesh Barnea was a well-known stopping place for the ancient donkey caravans en route between Egypt and Canaan. It also watered flocks and herds from the high and dry grazing grounds, both near and far. Here Moses ordered a halt, and for some distance around this elongated stretch of verdure and great beauty the Israelites pitched their tents.

Since leaving Egypt, the twelve wandering tribes, by the round-about route they followed, had walked over four hundred miles. Now, at last, less than fifty miles separated them from the good land the Lord God had long ago deeded to them. All they needed now to do, Moses told them, was to cross over the Negeb and wrest it from the fierce, warlike inhabitants. But gazing north across the parched badlands to the cool mountain strongholds of the giants, they wavered. Moses, not unaware of their doubts and fears and wild imaginations, urged all the men numbered for war not to be afraid nor discouraged, but to go up at once and claim their inheritance. Some tribal leaders, however, suggested: "Let us send men ahead to spy out the land for us and bring back a report about the route we are to take and the towns we will come to."32

Such use of spies being a common practice in the ancient Near East, Moses consented to their request. For this dangerous mission, each tribe chose one of its chief men. The twelve selected included Joshua of Ephraim and Caleb of Judah. Besides determining the best route for attack, Moses instructed the scouts to find out the number and character of the inhabitants, the strength of their towns and fortresses, and something about the fertility of the land.

In his journal, Moses noted that the spies set out across the hot southern steppe at the ripening of the first grapes. This almost certainly establishes early August as the time, for it was usually then to the first clusters were gathered in Canaan. The second ripening W grapes occurred in September, and the third followed in October. According to ancient rabbinical tradition, Moses had the spies pose as traders while they made their way through the northern settlements in the Negeb.33 This dry land, being suited only for pasturage, Comprised the poorest part of Palestine. Nevertheless it was inhabited by enough Amalekites and Canaanites to people twenty-nine cities, besides villages. Moses instructed the men to begin, as traders ordinarily do, by showing their ordinary wares first. Then, as they worked their way north, to offer their more valuable things.34 In such banner, the spies traversed all Canaan. In fact, as Moses was later to report, some walked

GIANTS ON THE EARTH

all the way to Hamath, a city situated on the Orontes River about one hundred and twenty miles north of Damascus. We should not think that all twelve traveled together, lest they be suspected. They probably went in pairs, or threes, or fours, and rendezvoused at certain places along the way.

The country the spies saw perhaps may be best visualized as Comprising three parallel strips of land running north and south. The first, called the Maritime Plain, extends inward from the Mediterranean coast to a distance of from four to fifteen miles. This fertile strip includes the famous Plain of Sharon and the Lowlands of the Philistines. Behind this flat country rises the hills. These, in turn, give way to the mountains that form the backbone of the Holy Land. In eastern Palestine, the mountains and hills fall precipitously down to the fertile Jordan River Valley and the bitter waters of the Salt Sea. East of the Jordan lie the highlands of Gilead, Ammon, and Moab--lands then ruled by Rephaim giants.

At this time many Rephaim and some Horim, Avvim, and Anakim giants occupied the hill country of northern Canaan, while the Anakim completely dominated the south. The spies must therefore have seen these frightening fellows every place they went. But in their later report to Moses they mentioned only the Anakim giants--apparently because they struck more terror in them than all the rest. For ferociousness and daring, the Anakim set the standard. Against them, in fact, all the other giants were measured. Moses himself confirmed their superiority when he wrote in his book this famous proverbial saying: "Who can stand before the sons of Anak?"[35]

The names of places that Moses recorded suggest the route the spies took followed "along the course of the Jordan in their advance, and their return was by the western border, through the territories of the Sidonians and Philistines."[36] Thus it appears that, leaving the Maritime Plain, they entered the southern foothills and began a three-thousand-foot climb toward Kiriath Arba (later called Hebron), which the giants had built on the Judaean ridge's highest elevation.

Close by Kiriath Arba lay the cave of Machpelah where the revered Abraham, his wife Sarah, and some other Hebrew patriarchs were buried. So the twelve no doubt looked forward to this part of their journey. But some of them also experienced little alarms. They now trod deep in Anakim country. Every step brought them closer to this chief city and ancestral home of the giants. Here lived the feared giants Sheshai, Ahiman, and Talmai. They ruled the three tribes of the Anak, who were called by their names.[37] From Sheshai's name we get some idea of their height. For Sheshai, declares Bochart, "refers to his stature, which measured six cubits," i.e., nine feet.[38] The Anakim also occupied nearby Debir and Anab,[39] and many others could be found living throughout the hill country of Judah. A significant number of these part-animal, part-man creatures had also established communities in Gaza, Gath, and Ashdod on the Mediterranean coast.[40]

In the plural, Anakim means "people of the necklace" or "neck-piece," and so it is explained by the ancient rabbis. The name comes from anaq, the Hebrew word for "necklace."[41] Moses, in Numbers 13:33, affirms that they descended from the Nephilim. Their uncommon height was, of course, enough to arouse in people of normal size some uneasiness. But the Anakim were also a fierce, half-wild people, given to deeds of great daring. Consequently, they loved war and regarded it as a normal way of life. So ingrained was their inclination to fight that when no common enemy could be found against

GIANTS ON THE EARTH

whom they could exercise their natural belligerency, they fought among themselves.42 Such a hostile attitude, combined with their extraordinary stature, caused shivers in most people who came in contact with them.

We have, incidentally, other records besides the Bible that bear witness to the Anakim. The Execration Texts of the Twelfth Dynasty (c. 1900 B.C.), for instance, clearly reveal that the Egyptians regarded the huge Anakim as their enemy. Written on pottery vases and clay figurines, these official documents contained the names of actual and potential enemies of the state. They also enumerated Pharaoh's curses upon them. Prepared by the priest-sorcerers, these execrations supposedly gave Pharaoh great power over his foes. The Egyptians believed that when he ordered these vases or figurines smashed, the written curses immediately fell upon those named thereon. Professor Alan F. Johnson says one recovered text, now on display at the Berlin Museum, contains "an incantation directed towards certain enemy cities and territories among which are Palestinian areas and which names specific rulers of an area called 'Iy-'aneq'." These, he adds, "could well be the Anakim of biblical materials).... In Numbers 13:33, RSV, they are mentioned as descendants of the 'Nephilim'."43

Josephus offers another historical verification of the Anakim. Jews who lived at Hebron as late as his day, he remarks, occasionally dug up human bones of a gigantic size.44 A design from the interior of the great temple of Abu Simbel furnishes yet another proof. Presented at a meeting of the Syro-Egyptian Society in May, 1856, it depicted "the king contending with two men of large stature, light complexion, scanty beard, and having a remarkable load of hair pendant from the side of the head." Other representations of the same tall people were seen at the royal tombs of Biban-el-Moluk, at Medina Tabu, at Karnak, and at the tomb of Oimenepthah I, which Belzoni opened. On a wall of the latter tomb Belzoni found a picture representing a son of the Anak. He is depicted as tall and light-complexioned. In the hieroglyphic inscription Belzoni read his name as Tanmahu, "or, by elision, Talmia,' the name given to one of the tribes of the children of Anak."45

The above-mentioned inscriptions give us some idea of what the Anakim looked like: blond giants, without much beard, and with their hair done up in such a way as to seem somehow suspended--a fashion similar to the Pan-like hairstyles of the fair-skinned, fair-headed, necklace-wearing Celtic giants who later dominated much of Europe. Such then was the physical appearance of the giants that the spies saw as they entered Hebron. As they trudged the streets hawking their wares, it soon became evident to them that the three clans of Anakim giants ruled by Ahiman, Sheshai, and Talmai made up most of that city's population. Of course, with over two million former slaves to Pharaoh bivouacked near Canaan's southern border, the spies came under the giants' suspicion and close scrutiny. Some of them may even have been questioned. At least something happened on this visit that made a lasting impression on ten of the Hebrew scouts--something that gave them the idea that the much larger Anakim regarded them in the lowest esteem, as inconsequential as grasshoppers.

It probably was on this occasion that Ahiman spoke the words the ancient rabbis attribute to him. These doctors of Jewish tradition report that, of the three Anakim rulers, Ahiman was the most feared. They further claim that he enjoyed frightening passersby with this sporting invitation: "Whose brother will fight with me?"46 In any event, as they gazed up at these creatures, the hearts of ten spies melted within them. Only Caleb and

GIANTS ON THE EARTH

Joshua kept their courage; no matter their size, they remained convinced that the Israelites could fight against them and drive them off God's land.

Upon taking their leave of Hebron, the spies remembered Moses' instructions to "bring back some of the fruit of the land"--to prove to all the congregation its extraordinary fertility. Gathering the samples presented no problem. It being now about mid-September, the surrounding country abounded with excellent produce. So the spies stopped in the valley of Eshcol that opened upon the city to pluck some pomegranates and figs and to cut off a branch bearing an enormous cluster of grapes. From ancient times, the Hebron region has been especially celebrated for its vineyards. Even today clusters from twelve to almost twenty pounds, with the grapes themselves being as large as small plums, can be found there. The spies tied the branch of grapes to a pole, along with the pomegranates and figs they had picked.47 Two men took turns carrying it.

The scanty vines the Israelites grew in Egypt had produced only small grapes. So when the reconnoitering party returned to Kadesh Barnea and showed their specimens of the land's fruitfulness, the enormous cluster of grapes quickly became the talk of the camp. As many Hebrews gathered around to hear their report on Canaan, the spies acknowledged that the land did indeed "flow with milk and honey," just as the Lord had said,48 and to prove it they exhibited to all the crowd the large, succulent grapes, the figs, and the pomegranates.

But ten of the spies then solemnly warned their fellow Hebrews: "We can't attack those people. The people who live there are powerful, and the cities are fortified and very large.... They are stronger than we are. The land we explored devours those living in it. All the people we saw there are of great size. We saw the Nephilim there, the descendants of Anak come from the Nephilim. We seemed like grasshoppers in our own eyes, and we looked the same to them."49

The ten spies said nothing that was not true. They had, for a fact, seen many giant Anakim in Canaan. The cities there were well-fortified. And the Canaanites bore weapons that were far superior to their poorly armed divisions. These things neither Caleb nor Joshua disputed. But both men dissented from the "evil report" by their ten frightened fellows. They instead urged the people: "We should go up and take possession of the land, for we can certainly do it."50

Moses also pleaded with the alarmed multitude: "Do not be terrified; do not be afraid of them. The Lord your God, who is going before you, will fight for you, as he did for you in Egypt, before your very eyes, and in the desert. There you saw how the Lord your God carried you, as a father carries his son, all the way you went until you reached this place."51

From his study of the archaeological diggings, Werner Keller came to sympathize with the disheartened Hebrews for the dilemma they faced at Paran. "The reports that the spies brought back telling of the strongly fortified cities of Canaan, 'great and walled up to heaven' (Deut. 1:28), and of their superbly armed inhabitants were not exaggerated," he says. "Turreted fortresses were to the children of Israel an unaccustomed and menacing sight. In the land of Goshen, which for many generations had been their home, there was only one fortified town, Raamses. In Canaan the fortresses were practically cheek by jowl. The country was plastered with them. Numerous strong points stared down from hilltops and mountain peaks, which made them look even more powerful and

GIANTS ON THE EARTH

terrifying. Little wonder that the report of the scouts was shattering in its effect.

"Israel was quite unskilled in the use and manufacture of implements of war. They had at their disposal only the most primitive weapons--bows, javelins, swords, knives--but certainly no horse-drawn chariots which the Canaanites possessed in vast numbers. Israel was still spoiled by the 'fleshpots of Egypt,' for which the older people among them were continually sighing and bemoaning their present lot. Despite their new faith and the experiences of the Exodus which they had shared together, they were not yet welded into a community which would be prepared to risk a clash with superior forces."52

The congregation knew the ten alarmed spies as honorable men, trustworthy, "the bravest among their tribes." So what they said about Canaan and the giants carried a lot of weight. On the other hand, they did not trust Caleb and Joshua, because those two were too closely associated with Moses and too much under his influence. Supposing, then, from what they had heard from the others, that it was impossible to get possession of the promised land, all the Hebrew men numbered for war--a total of 603,550 above the age of twenty--flatly refused to go up. Caleb and Joshua tried to change their minds. But the more they sought to persuade the people the more agitated they became. As ill feelings against the two heightened, some in the crowd threatened to stone them. They also rebuffed Moses, shouting him down. They even began murmuring against God for bringing them into the wilderness to die.

"And when the congregation was dissolved," relates Josephus, "they, their wives and children, continued their lamentation. They also blamed Moses, and made a clamour against him and his brother Aaron, the high priest. Accordingly they passed that night very ill, and with contumelious language against them; but in the morning they ran to a congregation, intending to stone Moses and Aaron, and so to return back into Egypt."53

The 603,550 who refused to go up to battle because they feared the giant Anakim fell under immediate divine judgment. As punishment for their rebellion, Moses told them they must wander forty years in the wilderness--one year for each day they explored the land. He also advised them that only two men of the 603,550 previously numbered for war would live to enter the land. The carcasses of all the rest, he said, would fall in the desert. The two men who were to survive he identified as Caleb and Joshua. Moses also wrote in his journal that Caleb, as a reward for his faithfulness, would inherit the Anakim stronghold of Hebron and the surrounding territory forever.54

To pay for their insubordination, the Israelites wandered in the wilderness exactly forty years, according to Moses' word. The final days of that wandering brought them at last to the plains of Moab on the eastern side of the Salt Sea. Here, while making preparations for the Hebrews' opening attack upon Canaan, Moses ordered a second census taken. This numbering revealed an entirely new population of 601,730 men who were twenty and above and fit for war. According to the chronicler, not one man remained of those first numbered by Moses ... except Caleb and Joshua.55 All the rest of those formerly numbered in the Sinai wilderness, who had refused to enter Canaan on account of the giants, now lay buried in the desert. (See Abraham and the Giants; David vs Goliath; Israel's Wars with the Giants; Jericho's Giants; Sihon's and Og's Overthrow)

GIANTS ON THE EARTH

Christopher, Saint

When Offerus, a giant Arabian warrior, converted to Christianity, the Christian hermit Babhlas baptized him and gave him the Christian name of Christopher. Having decided to devote his life to helping others, Christopher built himself a shack on the nearby river, which at times became impassable because of its high raging waters. On such occasions, he used his great size to ford the river and bodily carry stranded travelers across.

He also talked to the wayfarers about Jesus and converted many to the faith. He became so successful at this that King Dagnus of Samos demanded that he stop. When he refused, Dagnus cast him into a prison and ordered that he be severely tortured; in A.D. 250, unable to get the giant to renounce his faith, the king had him put to death.

Following his martyrdom, the church granted Christopher saint-hood, making him the patron of travelers. Storytellers of course made him the hero of many later legends.56

Corinthian Giants (See Phlegra's Giants)

David vs Goliath

Although the giants after Joshua's time never again posed a real danger to the children of Israel, as a nation, battles with some revengeful descendants of those who escaped to Philistia continued long afterward. Of these, the most memorable were young David's fight with Goliath and his later, losing encounter with the giant Ishbi-benob, who hailed from Goliath's hometown.

According to the chronicler of 1 Samuel, David and Goliath came face to face after the Philistines, with some giants in their ranks, invaded Israel with the intent to once more make themselves masters of God's land. To check this hostile incursion, King Saul called the nation to arms. Of Jesse's eight sons, three of the oldest left to join Saul's army, while David, the youngest, remained behind to tend the sheep.

When reports reached him that the Philistines had advanced as far as Socoh in Judah, Saul marched his army down from Benjamin to the Valley of Elah. There he took up a position on the rocky northern height opposite the one the Philistines were beginning to occupy on the other side of the small valley. These opposing slopes, now being covered by the two rival armies, rose to a height of about five hundred feet. Between them lay the rich alluvial valley, perhaps little more than a quarter-mile wide and "cut in two by the red banks fringing the white shingly bed of the torrent." Because such a move would have placed them in the open and at some disadvantage, neither Saul nor the Philistines seemed willing to strike first across the small valley floor. So, from the first day, the confrontation settled into an uneasy standoff. A war of nerves ensued.

Unfortunately, Israel soon found itself losing this psychological war and losing it decisively. The reason for their growing dismay appeared twice daily before them--in the form of a terrifying nine-foot-nine giant.57 Each morning and evening this famous Goliath of Gath would descend with his shield-bearer into the valley between the low, rocky, bush-covered hills occupied by the two encampments. From here, with his terribly loud voice, this champion warrior of the whole Philistine army hurled vile insults at the whole Israelite army. On these occasions he would dare them to produce from their miserable ranks a champion who might in single combat with him decide this issue between the two nations.

GIANTS ON THE EARTH

Goliath's intimidations and his challenge to a one-on-one duel only followed the custom of those times. Such a hero warrior, be-cause he stood halfway between the opposing armies to make his challenge, became known as "the man of the midst." The practice involved a religious belief, prevalent in those days, that the gods of the various nations accompanied their armies on the battlefield. The army whose god proved the strongest naturally won. So, finding out which god that day was the strongest by single combat was seen as a way to settle differences with little bloodshed. The chief gods of the Philistines were Dagon, Baal, and Beelzebub. These pagan deities Goliath flaunted before the Israelites, while casting aspersions upon the God of Israel. Also on this occasion, according to the Chaldee Targum, the giant warrior loudly boasted to Saul's men that it was he who slew Hophni and Phinehas at Aphek and captured Israel's sacred Ark of the Covenant.58

From atop their hill, those in Saul's army stared down upon this slayer of countless men. His abusive and threatening words both galled and shamed them. But no man among them, not even those who had proven their valor on many fields of battle, dared to step out and fight him. Just the sight of this Gibborim mongrel standing down there, waiting, instilled in the hearts of even the bravest Hebrews on the northern hill an awful dread. The weight of his armor and the size of his weapons both awed and unnerved them. On his massive head he wore a bronze helmet. The rest of his large body he protected with bronze greaves or leggings and a coat of mail. Around his thick waist hung a great sword, and across his broad back was slung an oversized javelin. The spear he carried in his hand bore a blade weighing twenty pounds.

For forty days now the Hebrews had endured Goliath's arrogance and abuse. Seeing the morale of his men sink lower and lower with the giant's every appearance, King Saul despaired. Hoping to find in his ranks a man willing to fight the Philistine, he offered a reward, plus his daughter in marriage, and a lifetime tax exemption for the family of the Hebrew champion.

This settled gloom David encountered the moment he walked into the Hebrew encampment. Just minutes after the young shepherd arrived with provisions sent by his father to his older brothers, Goliath again stepped out from the Philistines' lines and descended to the valley floor. There he took up his usual menacing stance before Saul's army and shouted out to them his usual loud invectives and insolent defiance of Israel and its God. As he stood now gazing down at the giant, listening to him taunt the Israelites with boasts and insults and pleading with them to send out to him their most feared warrior, David could hardly believe his ears. Nor his eyes--for no man among all Saul's legions stirred to take up Goliath's challenge.

A youth now in or near his twentieth year, David lacked formal training for armed combat, but, to protect his sheep, he had on occasion fought and killed "both the lion and the bear."59 This question he put to some men near him was not therefore without genuine contempt for the boastful giant: "Who is this uncircumcised Philistine that he should defy the armies of the living God?"60

In a stratagem to make King Saul aware of his desire to answer Goliath's challenge, David moved about the camp, making the same statements to others. As he had hoped, Saul soon sent for him. Declining the king's offer of his personal tunic, coat of armor, and sword, he took only his shepherd's staff and goat's-hair sling and walked out of the He-

GIANTS ON THE EARTH

brew encampment. As he stepped down an incline toward the still-blustering manslayer, the entire Hebrew army gathered on the front of their hill and on the slopes to watch and cheer their young champion on. Upon reaching the red banks of the torrent that still separated them, David stepped into the stream and chose five smooth stones. Putting these in his pouch, he resumed his walk toward the oncoming Goliath and his shield-bearer. David had already settled on his strategy. During his years as a shepherd, he had become an expert slinger--so that he usually hit anything he aimed at.61 He now intended to stun the Philistine giant with a rock hurled full force at his forehead and then kill him before he could recover.

When Goliath drew near enough to see that not much more than a boy had come out against him and one armed only with a staff and a sling at that, he became enraged. Seething at the insult, he apparently declined the use of his shield. "Am I a dog, that you come at me with sticks?" He bellowed. "Come here and I'll give your flesh to the birds of the air!" The giant then cursed David by his gods Dagon, Baal, and Beelzebub and devoted the young Israelite as a sacrifice to them.62

Setting a stone in his sling, David calmly answered the nearly ten-foot-tall warrior: "You come against me with sword and spear and javelin, but I come against you in the name of the Lord Almighty, the God of the armies of Israel, whom you have defied. This day the Lord will hand you over to me, and I'll strike you down and cut off your head."63

Even without his shield, Goliath's other armor protected him all over his body, except his arms and face. Now, as he came on, in fury, David--not hampered by the heavy weight of armor--ran quickly toward him. Feinting to the right and left, he suddenly

GIANTS ON THE EARTH

stopped, whirled the sling around his head, and let the stone fly. The smooth white projectile flew straight toward the giant's one vulnerable spot. The rock struck Goliath on his forehead with such force that it penetrated the bone. As he fell forward, like an axed tree, a great cheer went up from the Hebrews' hill. David ran to him, unsheathed his heavy sword, and cut off his head.64

The Philistine army, having seen its great champion go down, stood a few moments motionless, in stunned disbelief. Then a sudden stirring in Saul's camp, accompanied by war whoops, awakened them. To the Philistines, Goliath's defeat meant that Israel's God had, at least on this occasion, overcome their gods. Accepting that fact as an ill omen for their side, they fled in panic. Saul's now enthusiastic army, spurred on by the conviction that the Almighty God of Israel now watched over them, pursued the Philistines even to the gates of Gath and Ekron, wreaking upon them a great slaughter. Josephus, in recounting this mostly downhill, twenty-five-mile chase, says that thirty thousand Philistines were slain that day, with twice that number being wounded."65

Not surprisingly, Goliath's slaying placed David's name on the tongues of all his countrymen. Overnight he became the national hero. Made a man of war, he afterward led Saul's army as they came in and went out, winning victory after stunning victory. Saul, upon seeing David's fame eclipse his own, eventually grew jealous. Viewing the young man now as a threat to his throne, the king more than once attempted to kill him. These attempts on his life eventually drove David and a small band of his loyal followers into a life of outlawry. These perilous times he also survived. Then upon Saul's death on the battlefield at Mount Gilboa, in yet another battle with the Philistines, the one-time shepherd boy, by popular mandate, ascended the throne and began his rule over the covenant nation.

But neither Israel nor David had seen the last of the giants. In Goliath's hometown of Gath there lived others, at least four of whom were also warriors. They were the sons of Rapha. The scriptures identify one of these as Goliath's brother, and some scholars think all were his brothers. Their names, as we have them, were Lahmi, his brother, who was equally huge and bore a spear just as massive; Ishbi-benob, whose armor vied in weight with Goliath's; Sippai, whose enormous height and size were the wonder of all; and besides these, one, unnamed, who had six fingers and six toes on each hand and foot. These giants probably descended from either the Anakim or Rephaim who fled to the five Philistine cities in Joshua's day. No doubt they heard the news of David's crowning with keen interest. All of them understandably would be out to avenge him for Goliath's death.

After David was anointed king, he reigned the next seven years at Hebron. It was probably during these years, or soon after he transferred his capital to Jerusalem, that Benaiah, one of his thirty mighty men, did the exploits that won him renown. These included Benaiah's killing of two mighty Ariels, or, as the King James Version describes them, "two lion-like men" from Moab;66 his going down into a pit on a snowy day to fight a lion; and his delivering the deathblow to an Egyptian giant. The big Egyptian that Benaiah fought wielded a spear as large as a weaver's beam, while Benaiah was armed only with a club. But, in the sparring, Benaiah snatched from the giant his own spear and dispatched him with it.67

David had his second encounter with a giant on the battlefield some while after this-- in Israel's continuing wars with the Philistines. When this battle went decisively against

GIANTS ON THE EARTH

the pagans and they turned and fled the field, the king alone stayed in hot pursuit of them. And when he had tired himself out, writes Josephus, he was seen by Ishbi-benob. "He had a spear, the handle of which weighed three hundred shekels, and a breastplate of chainwork and a sword. He turned back, and ran violently to slay David... for he was quite tired out with labor; but Abishai, Joab's brother, appeared on the sudden, and protected the king with his shield, as he lay down, and slew the enemy. Now the multitude were very uneasy at these dangers of the king, and that he was very near to be slain; and the rulers made him swear that he would no more go out with them to battle lest he should come to some great misfortune by his courage and boldness, and thereby deprive the people of the benefits they now enjoyed by his means, and of those that they might hereafter enjoy by his living a long time among them."68

Later on, having heard the Philistines had gathered around the city of Gob, near Gezer, David sent an army against them. In the ensuing battle, Sibbecai the Hushathite slew the giant Sippai. According to Josephus, Sibbecai that day slew several others who "bragged they were the posterity of the giants, and vaunted them-selves highly on that account."69 In another skirmish with these people at Gob, Elhanan felled Lahmi in single combat and put the rest to flight. Lastly, in an Israelite attack on Gath, the boastful giant with six fingers on each hand and six toes on each foot came out and taunted Israel. Jonathan, son of Shimeah, David's nephew, accepted his challenge to single combat and killed him. After this, the Philistines no more made war against Israel.70 (For other one-on-one fights with giants, see Colbrand the Giant vs Sir Guy of Warwick; from Retenu)

Debir's Giants

Debir, one of the Anakim giants' principal strongholds, stood as a frontier town between the hill country and the Negeb. Located about eleven miles southwest of Hebron, it rivalled Jericho in size. In earlier times, it was known both as Kiriath Sepher ("City of Books") and Kiriath Sanna ("City of the Scribes"), so scholars think it once served as a cultural center for Canaan. It is identified with modern Dhaheriyeh.

Archaeologist John Garstang says that Debir's ruins yielded evidence of an overthrow like Jericho's, including "a terrific conflagration." After the fortress-city fell to them, the Hebrews slew its king and all the giants who did not escape. But while Israel was occupied in the northern campaign the giants who managed to escape reoccupied the city. After that campaign ended, however, Caleb and his men returned and retook Debir. (See Israel's Wars with the Giants; also see Anab's Giants; Hebron's Giants)

Eleazar the Giant

According to Josephus, a Jew named Eleazar the Giant, who stood over ten feet high, was among the hostages that the king of Persia sent to Rome to insure a peace. Vitellius no doubt referred to this same incident, for he declared that when "Darius, son of Artabanes, was sent as a hostage to Rome, he took with him, with divers presents, a man 7 cubits high, a Jew named Eleazar, who was called a giant by reason of his greatness."71 (See Josephus on the Giants)

GIANTS ON THE EARTH

Elhanan

Elhanan, the son of Jair, killed Lahmi, the brother of Goliath, in one of Israel's battles with the Philistines at Gob. (See David vs Goliath; Ishbi-benob; Sippai; Six-fingered, Six-toed Giant)

Emim

The huge Emim ("dreadful ones") lived in that area later taken over by the descendants of Moab, before Israel's invasion of Canaan. (See Abraham and the Giants; Sihon's and Og's Overthrow)

Execration Texts

The so-called Egyptian Execration Texts, composed between 1900 and 1700 B.C., substantiates the biblical account of a gigantic people called the Anakim. These texts, written on Pharaoh's orders, put curses on some Anakim chieftains who lived in Canaan.

For example, one of the Execration Texts of the Twelfth Dynasty (c. 1900 B.C.), now on display at the Berlin Museum, contains "an incantation directed towards certain enemy cities and territories among which are Palestinian areas and which names specific rulers of an area called 'Iy-'aneq'," which most scholars read as Anak. The texts also often refer to Ashdod as a "city of the giants." (See Canaan's Anakim; Ras Shamra Texts)

Gabbaras, the Arabian Giant

Pliny mentions that in the reign of Claudius (A.D. 41-54), a nine-foot-nine-inch giant named Gabbaras was brought to Rome from Arabia. Claudius placed him at the head of the famed Adiutrix legions. The giant so awed his troops that some worshipped him as a god. (See Giants Who Became Gods; Graveyards of the Giants)

Gath's Giants

Many giants apparently made Gath, one of the five great Philistine cities, their home. Their prominence in the city is borne out by Joshua's statement that at the end of his campaign "there were no Anakim left in the land of the sons of Israel; only in Gaza, in Gath, and in Ashdod some remained." Goliath, whom young David killed in later times, lived here. Rapha, believed by some scholars to have been Goliath's father, also lived here, as did four other of his giant sons.72 (See Ashdod's Giants; Beth-Paleth's Giants; Gaza's Giants)

Gaza's Giants

According to Joshua 11:22, Gaza remained a well-known abode of the Anakim giants after Israel conquered most of Canaan. As one of the five principal Philistine cities, it occupied an important position on the trade routes from Egypt to West Asia. Before the Anakim came, this very ancient city was inhabited by the Avvim giants, who were driven out by the Caphtorim, afterward called the Philistines. (See Ashdod's Giants; Beth-Paleth's Giants; Oath's Giants)

Giants, Valley of the

From the earliest times, a three-mile-long vale that begins at the top of the valley of

GIANTS ON THE EARTH

Hinnom and stretches south along the road to Bethlehem was known as the "Valley of the Rephaim," or "Valley of the Giants." Today it is called the Baqa'. (See Israel's Wars with the Giants)

Gibborim, House of (See Israel's Wars with the Giants)

Gibeonites

The Gibeonites, who tricked Israel into signing a treaty with them at the time of the conquest (Joshua 9:3-27), are classified mainly as Amorites and Hivites, but, according to the Septuagint, they are identified also with the giant Horim, who had formerly lived in Edom. (See Israel's Wars with the Giants)

Goliath (See David vs Goliath)

Gomarian Giants

When the great rainstorms finally ceased and the heaped-up waters began to recede, Noah's ark came to rest on the mountains of Ararat. Strange as it may seem, Noah's unusual three-storied vessel may still lie on this Armenian mountaintop, preserved in ice. At least, while flying over Ararat in 1917, a Russian aviator named Wladimir Roskovitsky spotted what looked like the skeleton of a huge ship whose prow jutted out from the ice pack. And in 1955, the French explorer Fernand Navarra reported finding near the summit of this mountain the remains of what he believed was Noah's ark. He returned with a five-foot piece of the ancient timber impregnated with bituminous pitch.[73] The Institute Forestal at Madrid, Spain, the Centre Technique de Bois at Paris, France, and the Institut de Prehistoire de l'Université at Bordeaux, France, after testing a sample by the "degree of lignite formation, gain in density, cell modification, and the degree of fossilization," described the timber as of "great antiquity."[74]

These two news stories created much excitement--and some controversy. But the sightings of a ship high up on Ararat amounted to nothing new. Such a vessel has been seen on this mountain since ancient times. The historian Berosus, for example, recorded that in his day, circa 475 B.C., the people still climbed Mount Ararat to see the ark and to scrape off bits of bitumen for talismans or souvenirs. The Jewish historian Josephus also writes that the Armenians of his time (A.D. 37-95) showed tourists the ark at its final resting place. Even that famous traveler Marco Polo, who lived thirteen centuries later, mentioned the ark while describing Mount Ararat. Navarra's discovery has led to some lively arguments among the experts as to what his find really represents. Some claim the ice-encased structure is Noah's ark. Others say not. Whatever the truth of this debate, there remains one indisputable fact: at the foot of Mount Ararat sits the ancient city of Naxuana, or Nakhichevan. It claims the tomb of Noah. And its name, translated, means: "Here Noah settled."[75]

So, after the great flood, Noah and his three sons, Shem, Ham, and Japheth, apparently settled in this area. No longer having the antediluvian giants to worry about, they began making for them-selves a new life and repeopling the earth. Eventually their families grew into three separate and distinct races. Noah himself predicted this would happen. One day, in a prophetic mood, he said to the three: "Blessed be the Lord, the God of

GIANTS ON THE EARTH

Shem! May God extend the territory of Japheth; may Japheth live in the tents of Shem, and may Canaan be his slave."76 All these things came true. From the loins of Shem came the Hebrews, through whom the promised Messiah would one day be born. Shem's male issue included Elam, Asshur, Arphaxad, Lud, and Aram. As for Japheth, he greatly enlarged himself. His descendants soon possessed half of Asia, practically all of Europe, a portion of Africa, and in more modern times most of America. Born to Japheth were Gomer, the eldest, who fathered the Gomarian giants, then Magog, Madai, Javan, Tubal, Meshech, and Tiras. And just as Noah said, the descendants of Canaan, Ham's youngest son, eventually became servants to those of his brothers. The other sons of Ham included Cush, Mizraim, and Put.

For perhaps a century after the cleansing flood, Noah's fast-growing family remained free of the Nephilim's destructive influences and the giants' tyranny. Humans, nevertheless, were again enticed into ways that were not good. For instance, they got deeply involved in astrology. They also began worshipping idols. Needing a place to gather for these degenerate activities, the people decided to build in Babel a tall tower, called a ziggurat. This stepped temple contained two sanctuaries--one at ground level and one at the summit, where worshippers believed their pagan god sometimes appeared. Moses relates, however, that one night God overthrew this tower, confused the people's language, and scattered them abroad.77

Remarkably, an ancient tablet recovered in recent years from the ruins of a tower located in the center of old Babylon seems to con-firm the biblical account. Found by G. Smith, it contained this fateful report: "The building of this illustrious tower offended the gods. In a night they threw down what they had built. They scattered them abroad, and made strange their speech."78

Commenting on this find, Henry H. Halley writes: "This seems like a tradition of Babel." The site, he adds, "is now an immense hole 330 feet square, which has been used as a quarry from which to take bricks. When standing it consisted of a number of successive platforms one on the top of another, each smaller than the one below, a sanctuary to Marduk on the top." Halley also explains the Bible's description of a tower with its top in heaven as "an expression of the vast pride of the first builders of 'ziggurats,' the artificial temple hills of Sumeria and Babylonia . . . Ziggurats still exist in ruin at Ur and Erech (modern Warka) and their construction illustrates Genesis 11:3, 4. Their whole purpose whenever found was idolatrous worship and herein lay the sin of the Babel builders."79

Following the tower's overthrow, the people of Babel found themselves no longer able to understand one another, so they began scattering toward all points on the compass. But still blessed with robust health and long life, these clans flourished. When their numbers became too great, many pushed out into other lands. Unfortunately, during these migrations, they once more encountered the evolved Nephilim people. And when these fallen, earthbound sons of God saw that the daughters of Noah were more beautiful than their own, they took them for wives. So the Gibborim, the huge, hellish children born of such marriages, once more appeared on earth.

Though these movements occurred in dim antiquity, the ancient historians have been able to track many of them. Gomer's clans, for instance, settled in "Higher Asia," in lands not too distant from one another. Here they came in contact with some Nephilim flood survivors and apparently entered a close association with them, for, after being defiled

GIANTS ON THE EARTH

by genes from this "strange flesh," they eventually evolved into a race of giants. From them, affirms the Celtic scholar Paul Pezron, sprang the enormous blond Sacae that overran parts of Asia and Asia Minor and some Fertile Crescent countries, possibly including Canaan. In later times, having changed their derisive name Sacae to Celtae, they conquered most of Europe.

Documentation for this genealogy appears in Pezron's book, The Antiquities of Nations. First translated into English in 1706, this remarkable volume leads us through a shadowy past even back to the overthrow of the tower of Babel. To prove that Gomer was the father of the Celts, Pezron uses a wide range of early historical sources, ancient poems, and postdiluvian monuments, along with his knowledge of several tongues, including the Celtic, and his ability to trace Celtic migrations through the names they gave their people, towns, mountains, plains, rivers, and bays. Along the way, he also shows that the Titans of Roman and Greek mythology were far from mythical. In truth, these giants at one time possessed many provinces in Asia Minor, and all those in Greece and the neighboring countries.80 And though first called Titans, they were in reality just another tribe of greatly oversized Celtic warriors who, by their legendary exploits, made a great name for themselves in ancient times.

Pezron's first clue to the origin of the Titans and their blond Gallic descendants came, incidentally, from reading Josephus' histories. Concerning this discovery, he reports:

"Josephus in his first book of the antiquity of the Jews, makes a kind of a comment upon the tenth chapter of Genesis, where Moses sets down the fathers and heads of each nation; and when he comes to speak of Gomer, who was the eldest son of Japhet, he says directly, and without any hesitation, that he was the founder, condi-dit, of those people anciently called Gomarians, to whom the Greeks now give the name of Gauls.81 It's very plain from the words of this learned Jewish historian, that Gomer was the father and founder of the Gomarians or Gomerites, and that these ancient people were no other than what the Greeks afterwards called Galatians, which was the same as Gauls, so that there is no need of contesting this matter any farther.

"Now," he continues, "it's proper, to inquire where those people were, named Gomarians, of whom Josephus speaks; Are they to be found in any part of Europe? No: Where then could they be, but in Asia? Let us but cast our eyes a little upon the books and maps of Ptolemy,82 the famous geographer, and survey but for a moment the provinces of Higher Asia, I mean those between Media, Bactriana and the Caspian Sea, there we shall easily find the Chomarians or Comarians, who are no other than the Gomarians of Josephus. ... The Gomarians therefore, according to Josephus, were the Galatians or Gauls: but how could he know a thing which at this day appears to us so obscure and dark? It's not at all strange for him to say, that Gomer was the founder of the Gomarians; the likeness of names makes that easily out. But who could inform him that the Gauls came from the Gomarians, but either the truth of ancient history, or the tradition of his fathers, the Hebrews?"83

While pursuing his studies, Pezron soon discovered that Josephus was not the only early writer to make Gomer the father of the Gauls. Eustathius of Antioch, author of the Commentary upon the Hexameron, also held this opinion. He relates that Gamer (the Greek Septuagint's spelling for Gomer) was the founder of the Gamarians, "whom we now call Galatians or Gauls." Jerome, one of the most learned men of his time and the one

GIANTS ON THE EARTH

who gave us the Vulgate or Latin version of the Bible, agrees with Eustathius' statement and declares with him mat the Galatians, or Gauls, descended according to Hebrew traditions from Gomer. The kinship between the Galatians and the Gauls, says Pezron, was also confirmed by St. Isidore, bishop of Seville. In his famous book, Origines, which endured for many centuries as one of the most important of all reference books, Isidore wrote: "We find that Japhet had seven sons, which Gomer the eldest was the father of the Galatians, that is to say, the Gauls." Yet another witness, the Chronicle of Alexandria, said that it was Gomer "from whom the Celtae had their origin."

If anyone requires still more testimony, Pezron cites an early Jewish historian named Joseph Goronidis, "who has said somewhat concerning the origin of nations many ages ago: The sons of Gomer are the Franks, that dwell towards the Seine in France. These are the words of that Jew, and 'tis very manifest that by the sons of Gomer he means the Gauls, whom he calls Franks, or French dwelling near the Seine, in order to distinguish them from the Franks in Germany. In short, my design in producing all these evidences of truth, has no other tendency than to show that Josephus, the Jewish historian, had reason on his side in making the Gauls to be the descendants of Gomer."[84]

By consulting the most famous ancient geographers, such as Ptolemy, Pliny, Pomponius Mela, and Dionysius of Alexandria,[85] Pezron also learned that after the fall of the tower of Babel Comer's people settled in Bactnana and Margiana, lands to the southeast of the Caspian Sea. Ptolemy, he notes, divided the Gomarians into two clans. Those called Chomarians he placed in Bactnana, "pretty near the Oxus." Some old maps of Bactriana that Pezron looked at confirmed this, for on them he found a city called Chomara, which he took to be "the capital of these people." As for their cousins, called Comarians, Ptolemy located them "towards the most eastern boundaries of Sogdiana, not far from the sources of the Jaxartes, and in the country of the Sacae." Mela, the earliest Latin geographer, also separated these kindred peoples, but on his map he settled the Comarians toward Sogdiana and Bactriana, while locating the Chomarians a little above the Caspian Sea and toward the Massagetae. Pezron sees no contradiction in this. "'Tis clear enough from hence," he says, "that both these people came from the same stock; that at first they were founded by Gomer towards the countries of Margiana and Bactriana, and that in process of time they separated from one another; that one continued in Bactriana, their ancient habitation, and that the other moved towards those countries that lay to the east, beyond the Jaxartes, between the spring of that river and Mount Imaus."[86]

In these lands, watered by large rivers and described by Strabo as the most agreeable and fruitful parts of all Asia, Gomer's descendants apparently came in contact with the surviving Nephilim and began intermarrying with them. For certain, it was here that the exceptionally tall Gomarians developed into a fierce warlike people and even fought among themselves over the land. Although these civil wars occurred in the most obscure times, ancient historians have been able to piece together some of what happened. Pezron summarizes what they found, in these words:

'This people in process of time increasing to a vast multitude could not always live in repose and tranquility; the seeds of dissensions and jealousies began to spring up amongst themselves: Amid these factions and difficult commotions, those who proved the weakest either in number or strength, were expelled by the other, and forced to seek for a retreat in the neighboring countries; so that passing over those vast moun-

GIANTS ON THE EARTH

tains, which are to the south of Margiana, they entered into a country then in possession of the Medes, who were known by the name of Arii. Those fugitives fixed themselves either by force or consent in this country they had made their way to, which was surrounded by high mountains: And as they were a people that had been driven out of their native country, they were called Parthians; the same signifying as much as persons separated from others, exiles or banished people; and it was from this name, which is very ancient, and sticks to them to this day, that that province was called Parthia, where these fugitives fixed their habitation. This is the true origin of the Parthians, which is ancienter than that of the Persians, who came from them. Trogus Pompeius has given an ample account of them in his 41st book, of which we have but a small abridgment: We find what he says confirmed by Arrian in his Parthicis, by Stephen of Byzantium, and some others."87 Even though the ancient historians knew about the Parthians' separation from the Gomarians, they could not pinpoint when. But Pezron says it certainly took place before the days of Ninus and the founding of the Assyrian empire, and so even long before Abraham's time.

As for the name Parthians, which the Gomarians gave to those they drove away from among them, it comes, Pezron tells us, from the word Parthu, "which to this very day in the Celtic signifies to divide or separate." These exiled Parthians, out of spite, also stuck a derisive name on their victorious Gomarian cousins. Seeing that they could not otherwise take revenge on them except by abusive language, they called those giants who drove them off their own land the Sacae. In the Celtic, Sacae denotes a thief, robber, or the like.88 He also points out that after the Gomarian exiles assimilated with the Persians, a great number of Celtic or Gallic words found their way into the Persian language--a thing that still baffles many modern Celtic experts who are not aware of this ancient connection between the Celtics and those Gomarians who became the Parthians.89

Moreover, adds Pezron, "it will be proper [here] to observe, that those, who at first had the opprobrious name of Sacae given them, were Gomarian Scythians, who dwelt, as aforesaid, in Margiana.... Here I pray you take notice that these Margians or Amyrgians wore breeches according to Herodotus, and it was from them that the Celts, who afterwards came into the west brought them into Gaul, insomuch, that some part of their people there were called Galli Braccati;90 to which we may add the arms of these Amyrgians, set forth by the same historian, which were like unto those born by the ancient Gauls: Wherefore we may upon the whole find in the Gomarians of Margina, the language, arms, habit, with the restless and warlike nature of our ancient Celtae."91

While tracing their origins for his geography, Ptolemy found that some Sacae also continued to refer to themselves as Gomarians.92 Those who settled near the Jaxartes in the vast plains that lie between that river and Mount Imaus he identified as the Nomadan Sacae. "These people," Pezron learned, "always led a vagrant and savage life, and that was the reason why they were called Nomadan Sacae. . . It is very likely the Cimbrians, Cimmerians, or Celtick people, came from them, of whom we shall speak hereafter."93

When the provinces of Margiana, Hyrcania, and Bactriana became too small for their growing numbers, the Gomarian Sacae also began spilling over into other lands in Asia Minor and the Fertile Crescent. These expansions usually took the form of invasions. One of the first countries they overran, according to the ancient authors, was Armenia, a province of great beauty and fertility. But not content with having seized the best part of

GIANTS ON THE EARTH

Armenia, they soon after crossed over into Syria and probably made inroads as far as Arabia. They also became neighbors to the Chaldeans. "Having gone thus far," concludes Pezron, "we have no cause to wonder that the Celtick tongue, even at this day, is full of Syriack, Chaldee and Arabick words."[94] Pezron could find no evidence to prove that the Sacae also invaded nearby Canaan, but he firmly believes they did. "I am strangely mistaken," he remarks, "if they were not these Giants . . . meant by the Hebrew word Rephaim"[95] who took over many parts of God's land long before Abraham came to sojourn there.

But even these conquests failed to satiate the giants' ravenous appetite for new lands to conquer and places to plunder. Delightful Cappadocia on Armenia's western border fell next under their covetous gaze. The Cappadocians no doubt opposed, as best they could, the ensuing influx of Gomer's mighty hordes, and they probably retained some land the choosey invaders did not want. But they proved no match for the huge Sacae, who afterward settled in the most desirable parts, particularly those areas bordering upon the Black Sea.[96] To this country they gave their name, calling it Sacastena.[97] "Sacastena," explains Pezron, "properly signifies the country of the Sacae: For start and tan in the Celtick tongue implies a region. This word we find in that of Brittania, for so it should be writ, as should Aquitania, Lusitania, and many more after the same manner. . . The Persians and Parthians, who make use of stan instead of tan, as you may see in the words Chusistan, Indostan, and the like, have had it as well as many others, from the Asiatick Sacae: Which still is a pregnant proof that the language of the Sacae or Gomarians was the Celtick tongue."[98]

Graveyards of the Giants

Following their successful campaign in Cappadocia, the Gomarian giants passed over into Pontus and Upper Phrygia and also brought those lands under their dominion. With these conquests, they now exercised complete control over a large area of Asia Minor, including all the southern shores of the Black Sea. Now only the narrow Strait of Bosporus separated them from the early Greeks' eastern coast. And now beyond that strait lay all the spoils of Europe, waiting for them to take. (See Abraham and the Giants; Giants and the Flood; Giants Who Became Gods; Origin of the Giants--Biblical Account)

Ham's Giants

In his campaign against Sodom and Gomorrah, Elam's King Chedorlaomer attacked and practically annihilated the huge Zamzummim people at Ham. Some archaeologists identify this ancient city of the giants with modern Ham, located in eastern Gilead, about four miles south of Irbid. (See Abraham and the Giants)

Hebron's Giants

Called Kiriath Arba until Caleb took it, Hebron served as the capital city of the numerous Anakim giants who lived in Canaan, particularly in the southern part, at the time of Israel's invasion. The Anakim giants divided into three clans. They were ruled from Hebron by Ahiman, Sheshai, and Talmai, descendants of Arba. (See Canaan's Anakim; Israel's Wars with the Giants)

GIANTS ON THE EARTH

Horim, or Horites
In the nineteenth century B.C., just before he attacked Sodom and Gomorrah, Elam's Chedorlaomer waged war against the giant Horim who occupied the rough mountain range of Seir. They never fully recovered from that blow, and the Edomites, the descendants of Esau, later displaced those that remained. Some scholars also identify the Jebusites at Jerusalem and the Perizzites of the forested hill country that Ephraim later occupied with the Horim. (See Abraham and the Giants)

Ifrikish ibn Kais
Of those that the Hebrews came across when they overran Jericho, none were spared, say the scriptures, except the harlot Rahab and her family. But, according to The Jewish Encyclopedia, some of Jericho's giants somehow managed to escape. "Those who survived," it states, "were led by a certain Ifrikish ibn Kais to Africa, and, having killed the king of that country, settled there. The Berbers are their descendants." (See Jericho's Giants; also see Chad's Giants; Curigueres; Sudan's Giants; Watusi Giants; Zanzibar's Giant's)

Ishbi-benob
Ishbi-benob, an Atlas-sized Philistine warrior from Gath, whose armor vied in weight with Goliath's, was at the point of delivering the deathblow to a weary, fallen David, when Abishai, one of his mighty men, rushed to the king's aid, shielded him against the blows of Ishbi-benob's large "new sword," then killed the giant. (See David vs Goliath; Lahmi; Sippai; Six-fingered, Six-toed Giant)

Israel's Wars with the Giants
After razing Jericho, Israel's brave sons next eyed the hills and mountains of Canaan. They knew from Joshua and Caleb--Moses' two surviving spies--what to expect up there. All across the land many strong fortresses manned by numerous giants and warriors their own size awaited them. The south country, which Joshua planned to attack first, belonged almost entirely to the giant Anakim. In Hebron, Debir, and Anab, and their environs, they lived in great numbers. They also inhabited "all the hill country of Judah" to the Negeb.99 Some Anakim found the Maritime Plain to their liking, and an unusually large population of them lived at Gaza, Ashkelon, and Ashdod.100 Indeed, the Egyptian Execration Texts frequently refer to Ashdod as the "city of the giants."101

At this time many Rephaim giants evidently occupied a fertile valley just southwest of Jerusalem. Now called the Baqa´, this three-mile-long vale begins at the top of the valley of Hinnom and stretches south along the road to Bethlehem. But from the earliest times it was known as the "Valley of the Rephaim," or "Valley of the Giants."102 Because of its name, most scholars accept that this place once had "some connection with the giant race to which the term Rephaim was applied."103

Meanwhile, just north of Jerusalem lived the big Avvim. They originally inhabited the great western lowlands. Then came the Caphtorim, or the Philistines, as they are now commonly called.

These invaders from the sea wiped out most of the Avvim giants and took over their entire territory. The Avvim who survived fled to the mountains. There they settled on the

GIANTS ON THE EARTH

land that later fell by lot to Benjamin. There they also built themselves a town, which--to perpetuate their name--they called Avvim.

Beit Jibrim, another ancient town connected by name with the giants, exists even to this day. Commanding the entrance to the Valley of Zephathah on the road from Jerusalem to Gaza, this "House of the Gibborim" (for that is what Beit Jibrim means) contains "one of the most amazing cave-cities in the world."104 Here you can see "labyrinths of caves of varying size and complexity" that once housed a large tribe of giants. Historian A. T. Olmstead describes one of Beit Jibrim's enormous caves as measuring four hundred feet long, with a ceiling reaching to a height of eighty feet. He also saw another that contained as many as sixty chambers. Pick marks found on the walls of the huge rock chambers testify to the excavation work that their enormous inhabitants did on them. "We can understand why the name [Beit Jibrim] has persisted," says Olmstead, "when we enter the huge cave tombs . . . with their cisterns and oil presses. From the marks of metal implements on their walls we know that they cannot be earlier than Chalcolithic times."105

Many Rephaim giants also inhabited the north country. A historical source separate from Joshua's chronicles, but written about the same time, verifies that they ranged at least as far north as Ras Shamra (ancient Ugarit) on the Syrian coast. Discovered in 1928, these writings, which came to be called the Ras Shamra Texts, reveal not only the history, economy, and religion of Ugarit but also discusses in some detail the Canaanite religion and culture. Linguists who deciphered the cuneiform texts found in them frequent mention of the Rephaim.

Clearly, then, at the time of Israel's invasion, the Anakim, Awim, and Rephaim occupied all parts of God's land. And closely allied with them were their near-giant cousins, the Amorites.106 So it appears that in their many combats for possession of the land the Hebrews encountered many warriors of much greater height and bulk. Besides these, they also had to fight the militant Hivites, Hittites, Girgashites, Jebusites, Perizzites, and Canaanites. Because of interbreeding, the latter peoples no doubt included some giants in their ranks. But for the most part they stood about the size of the Israelites.

Even the brutal Amorites appear to have once been a people of normal stature. After they settled in Canaan early in the third millennium B.C., however, they evidently interbred with the Rephaim and Anakim, for Amos later described them as reaching the "height of cedars."107 Following its study of the social contacts between these two early Canaanite peoples, The Universal Jewish Encyclopedia suggested such a link. "The real Anakim," it declares, "may perhaps be identified with the Amorites, by whom they may have been ab-sorbed."108

While watching the billows of black smoke pile into the air from Jericho's burning, the Amorites who occupied the first mountainous strongholds and their Anakim neighbors who lived higher up no doubt wondered what the intruders would do next. They did not have to wonder long. For while the ruins of Jericho yet smoldered, Israel marched on Ai. It lay about ten miles west of Jericho, as the crow flies. But due to the winding mountain trails, the attacking force had to walk twice that far on foot. After overcoming Ai, the Hebrews slaughtered its twelve thousand inhabitants and also put that city to the torch. Up till now, the plan of attack mapped out by Moses and now being executed by Joshua had worked to precision. East of the Jordan the kingdoms of the giants Sihon and Og had

GIANTS ON THE EARTH

been subdued. On these lands the tribes of Reuben and Gad and part of Manasseh had settled. Those conquests, plus the razing of Jericho, removed the threat of hostile forces attacking the Hebrews in their rear. They next struck through Canaan's central highlands. This move effectively sliced the country in two, thus preventing the northern and southern tribes from forming a united front. The capture of Ai and the subsequent fall of Bethel also gave the poorly armed Israelites another tactical advantage. For, with the overthrow of these two fortified cities, they gained command of the main high-way that ran north and south through the promised land. In later campaigns, control of this road would enable them to strike quickly to the south or march into the fertile northern districts unopposed.109

The destructions of Jericho, Ai, and Bethel, followed by an astounding defeat of Adonizedek's confederated armies at Gibeon, shocked Central Palestine's population. As the Hebrews continued their advance, fear so seized some of the Amorites and Hittites, that, according to a later statement by Isaiah, they forsook their cities and fled before Israel.110 Those who chose to stay and fight soon felt the sharp cutting edges of the Hebrews' swords, or crumpled under a barrage of rocks hurled from deadly accurate slings, or perished when well-aimed arrows pierced their flesh.

With the Canaanite forces thus reeling, Joshua quickly took Makkedah, then Libnah, then Lachish; then, after demolishing the army of Horam, king of Gezer, on the battlefield, he moved on to Eglon and done to it as he had done to all the other places in the Hebrews' train. Just how many giants the Hebrews fought at Gezer and in these other earlier battles we are not told.111 But now, with Eglon and Gezer having fallen, the sons of those Hebrews who at the first had refused to cross over into Canaan for fear of the giants boldly gathered before the gates of Hebron--the Anakim's chief city and major stronghold.

Before the Israelites renamed it Hebron, the Anakim called it Kiriath Arba, or City of Arba, in honor of their forefather, Arba. He was a great hero of the Anakim.112 In time, Arba's overgrown children grew so numerous that they were able to possess much of southern Canaan. These giants divided into three clans. They were ruled from Hebron by Ahiman, Sheshai, and Talmai, descendants of Arba,113 but Hebron also had its own king (Joshua 10:37).

Standing 3,040 feet above sea level, this fortified city overlooked a shallow, fertile valley surrounded by rising hills. Through it ran the main highway connecting Jerusalem and parts farther north with Egypt, the Negeb, and the coastland. Joshua therefore viewed Hebron's capture as having both a strategic and a morale-breaking importance; strategic because it was the most southerly road-crossing center of the highland system; and morale-breaking because, as the principal mountain stronghold of the Anakim, its downfall would further demoralize the natives. At Joshua's command, the Israelites stormed Hebron, drove out Ahiman, Sheshai, and Talmai, slew its king, and put all its huge occupants who could not escape to the sword.

Following the battle at Hebron, the invaders struck out across the Negeb toward Debir (modern Dhaheriyeh). It stood as a frontier town between the hill country and the Negeb, some eleven miles southwest of Hebron. Excavators say it rivalled Jericho in size. And in earlier times it apparently had been a seat of an old Canaanite culture, for it was known both as Kiriath Sepher ("City of Books") and Kiriath Sanna ("City of the Scribes"). In Joshua's

GIANTS ON THE EARTH

day, however, many Anakim giants occupied the city. Here no trees grew, so Debir, being located on a higher elevation than the surrounding bald hills, became visible to Israel's marching legions from a long way off.

John Garstang says the protecting walls that confronted the Hebrews here "were for the most part about ten feet thick, but attained in places to as much as thirteen feet, and these were further strengthened on the outside, in characteristic fashion, by a sloping revetment of stonework. In detail of construction this masonry was less massive than the contemporary work of Shechem or Hattin, but is comparable with much of that of Jericho."114 In his excavations, the archaeologist also found clear evidence of a time when Debir thrived as a center for culture and learning--until its overthrow by the Hyksos from Egypt about 1550 B.C. But when the city was rebuilt, he writes, it "showed indications of relative poverty: the houses were poorly built and departed by open spaces containing grain pits. In this period the derelict fortifications of the earlier period were restored, and the east gate was entirely rebuilt, on the same general plan."115

When this fortress-city of the giants fell to them, the Hebrews slew its king and all who were unable to escape. Garstang mentions mat the ruins at Debir yielded evidence of an overthrow like what he saw at Jericho. "The destruction of the city (at Level C)," he adds, "was accompanied by a terrific conflagration, and by the complete demolition of the fortifications." 116

After this great slaughter, the Hebrews marched on Anab. In earlier times, another people occupied this city. But the Anakim giants assailed it, wiped out its inhabitants, and made it their possession. Anab, the name of which still survives today as Khirbet Anab, stood amid the Judean hills, only a short distance from Debir. After breaching its walls, Israel's legions totally demolished the city and put to death all its giants. After this, the Hebrews likely cleared a number of giants out of the "Valley of the Rephaim" southwest of Jerusalem.117 Also about this time they probably slaughtered the remnant of the monstrous Awim, who lived at nearby Avvim. Then they captured Jerusalem, or at least that part of it that was known as the "lower city." Despite their greatest efforts, however, they were unable to dislodge the Jebusites from the "upper city." These few but determined people occupied the narrow plateau of Mt. Ophel, just southeast of Jerusalem. Bounded by the Kidron, Tyropoeon, and Zedek Valleys, Jebus encompassed no more than eleven or twelve acres. But because of its bold rock escarpments, the small city stood as an impregnable bastion, and "not to be taken without great difficulty, through the strength of its walls, and the nature of the place."118 And, indeed, it was not taken until some four centuries later, in the time of David. When Joshua attacked it, some Horim giants supposedly lived among the Jebusites.119

Except for several pockets of resistance, like this one at Jebus, much of southern Canaan now belonged to the Hebrews.120 So Joshua ordered his legions to invade the north country. We have no way of knowing how many giants the Hebrews fought in these latter campaigns, for Joshua, who kept careful records of his battles against the Anakim in the south, now devoted much less time to the chores of journal-keeping. Concerning the northern giants, he penned the briefest summary, noting only that the Anakim occupied "all the hill country of Israel,"121 meaning all the territory later allotted to the ten northern tribes. He also barely mentions the Rephaim--and then only in connection with a complaint by Ephraim and the half-tribe of Manasseh. That complaint came after the

GIANTS ON THE EARTH

tribes had received their land allotments. Feeling that they had not gotten a fair shake, the sons of Joseph grumbled that their allotment was not sufficient for their great numbers. So Joshua told them: "If you are so numerous, and if the hill country of Ephraim is too small for you, go up into the forest and clear land for yourself there in the land of the Perizzites and of Rephaites."122 The Perizzites, whom some scholars also identify with the giant Horim,123 lived in the vicinity of Shechem. A large clan of the Rephaim occupied a territory just north of them, with their settlements extending perhaps as far as the Valley of Jezreel. The children of Joseph apparently took Moses' advice and destroyed or drove out all these giants, for afterward they occupied that land.

Against the northern cities Joshua waged war a long time. But while they were thus occupied with the conquest of upper Canaan, and bent upon cleansing it of the giants, the Anakim who had escaped the Israelites' swords during their earlier sieges in the south later returned and reoccupied Hebron and Debir, cities that were assigned to Caleb. Consequently, after the land was divided by lot among Israel's twelve tribes, some men of Judah, with Caleb at their head, returned to the south country and again came against these places.

An account of Caleb's renewed campaign against the giants who reoccupied Hebron appears in Josephus histories. After telling what great difficulty the people of Judah faced in their long siege against Jebus, or upper Jerusalem, he relates that they removed their camp to Hebron to assist Caleb against the Gibborim there. "And when they had taken it," he adds, "they slew all the inhabitants. There were till then left a race of giants, who had bodies so large, and countenances so entirely different from other men, that they were surprising to the sight, and terrible to the hearing. The bones of these men are still shown to this very day, unlike to any credible relations of other men."124

After retaking Hebron, Caleb proceeded southward to the re-occupied Debir (i.e., Kiriath Sepher). Upon reaching that place, he said to his chief men: "I will give my daughter Acsah in marriage to the man who attacks and captures Kiriath Sepher."125 Quick to volunteer, Othniel, a son of Caleb's younger brother, advanced with his men into the city, slew all its defiant giants, and retook it. So Caleb gave his daughter Acsah to him in marriage.

With Caleb's recapture of Hebron and Debir, Israel's seven-year campaign against the giants and Canaan's other inhabitants came to an end. Their many victories put the Hebrews in control of much of the country and broke the once awesome military power of its people.126 But the legions of Israel failed to exterminate or drive all the other pagan trespassers off God's land, as they had been commanded. Even a few cities remained untaken.127 Had they done as well in dispossessing all the other Canaanites as they had the giants, later Hebrew history may have followed a much different and less tragic course. But after seven long years of intense fighting and much gore, the Hebrews grew weary of war. So, assenting to their plea, Joshua gave them rest from war.

Even though these few places of resistance remained throughout the country, Israel's men of war had at least accomplished their major objective--to cleanse God's land of the Gibborim. That this cleansing was complete we learn from our chronicler. In his final summary of the campaign, he wrote: "Then Joshua came at that time and cut off the Anakim from the hill country, from Hebron, from Debir, from Anab and from all the hill country of Judah and from all the hill country of Israel. Joshua utterly destroyed them with their

GIANTS ON THE EARTH

cities. There were no Anakim left in the land of the sons of Israel; only in Gaza, in Gath, and in Ashdod some remained."[128] But these giants who survived Joshua's campaigns and fled to the Philistines on the coast, or to Africa and other countries, were so few that they never again posed a serious threat to the children of Israel. (See Abraham and the Giants; Canaan's Anakim; David vs Goliath Jericho's Giants; Sihon's and Og's Overthrow)

Jericho's Giants

From the most ancient times Jericho was known as the world's oldest city. Modern excavators confirm its great antiquity. They say Jericho's ruins show it to be the earliest instance of urban civilization known to man. In olden days it also became widely known as the "city of the giants"[129]--because so many Gibborim once lived within its walls.

Today, however, most people remember Jericho for its unique place in the annals of warfare. For here, in Joshua's day, occurred perhaps the strangest battle of all time. According to the biblical records, which have now been verified by modern archaeological work, Jericho's high, fortified walls collapsed before the Hebrews' onslaught, as if literally knocked down by the hand of God. This took place after the Hebrews, at Joshua's command, marched around the city for seven days. The sudden buckling of the walls at the end of the seventh-day's march, at the sound of the last trumpet, followed by the besiegers' mighty shout, was foretold by Joshua.

In his journal, Joshua also mentions Jericho's giants. This brief reference, recorded in Joshua 6:2, quotes the Lord as saying to him: "See! I have given Jericho into your hand, its king, and the mighty men of valor." The mighty men here denotes the Gibborim, this phrasing being derived from the same Hebrew word that Moses used in Genesis 6:4 to signify the giants. Thus, Joshua indicates that when Jericho's walls fell outward and the Israelites charged over the dusty pile of rubble into the city some of the combatants they met and slew were the Gibborim. An ancient tradition, incidentally, confirms this scripture, for it relates that some of Jericho's giants escaped the doomed city and fled to Africa.[130]

Before its destruction, Jericho occupied a large, lush oasis, surrounded by a sunbaked wasteland where temperatures in summer-time sometimes reached 120 degrees. Crowded within its double walls were the royal residence of the king and several solidly built stone structures and public buildings that archaeologists say exhibited "excellent architectural technique." It contained both large and small dwelling places, but space was at such a premium that some houses were built across the top of the walls.[131] Watered year round by a copious, bubbling spring (now called 'Bin es-Sultan), the broad extremely fertile plain round about the city yielded plentiful crops and provided groves of date palms, balsams, sycamores, and henna, for which Jericho became famous. Because of its strategic location, the city also thrived as a center for trade. Besides its various woods and agricultural crops, its merchants trafficked in salt, sulphur, copper, and bitumen, all being found in great abundance in the region around the Salt Sea. Jericho also abounded in silver and gold, and articles of bronze and iron.[132] From its widespread trade, its merchants grew wealthy, and its citizens lived in comfort and safety behind its well-fortified walls.

Having been built to a considerable height and breadth, these walls "were of a type which made direct assault practically impossible," writes Leon Wood. "An approaching

GIANTS ON THE EARTH

enemy first encountered a stone abutment, eleven feet high, back and up from which sloped a thirty-five degree plastered scarp reaching to the main wall some thirty-five vertical feet above. The steep smooth slope prohibited battering the wall by any effective device or building fires to break it. An army trying to storm the wall found difficulty in climbing the slope, and ladders to scale it could find no satisfactory footing. The normal tactic used by an enemy to take a city so protected was siege, but Israel did not have time for this, if she was to occupy all the land in any reasonable number of months."133

While they still stood, Jericho's high walls enclosed about seven acres and made it the strongest fortress in Canaan. So when the vast Hebrew army crossed over the Jordan, the "thick population round-about" hurriedly left their homes to enter the city and join in preparations for its defense. Meanwhile, on the plain of Gilgal just opposite Jericho, the Israelites pitched their camp. The Jordan Valley at this juncture widens to almost fourteen miles, becoming the broadest expanse in its entire length. At the time of Israel's invasion, a forest of noble palms nearly three miles broad and eight miles long stood between their camp and the city.134 But from Gilgal's elevated ground the Hebrews could see over this grove to the stout walls of Jericho some two miles in the distance. Beyond the city they viewed the hills of the western highlands rising abruptly from the plains. Just behind the hills, a mountain cliff, called Jebel Kuruntul, rose so high that in the early afternoon its cooling shadow enfolded the town. High up there stood the Amorites' first strong-holds. These the Israelites also had to demolish before making assaults on the several independent kingdoms located farther inland.

From the time they spied out the land, Joshua knew that the only trails offering access to the Holy Land began in these foothills.135 But Jericho stood in the way. Serving as an outpost for the three passes, it prevented hostile invasions of Canaan from the east. So the capture and annihilation of the rich, depraved city became imperative. To accomplish this objective, Joshua announced to all the armed men and the priests a most unusual plan of attack.136

Waiting behind their stout walls, the inhabitants of Jericho fully expected the Hebrews' hundreds of thousands of warriors to begin a head-on assault. Much to their surprise, no attempt was made to scale the walls or force the gates. Instead, reports the historian Henry Hart Milman, "they saw what might seem a peaceful procession going regularly round the walls of the city. The army marched first, in total silence. In the rear came the Ark, escorted by seven priests, blowing seven trumpets, made of ram's horns. For six successive days this mysterious circuit took place; no voice was heard from the vast and breathless army--nothing but the shrill wailing of the trumpet. On the seventh day this extraordinary ceremony was repeated seven times. At the close of the last round, the whole army on a sudden set up a tremendous shout, the walls of the city fell, and the defenseless people found the triumphant enemy rushing along their streets."137 The men of Jericho, Josephus adds, were so astounded and "affrighted at the surprising overthrow of the walls that their courage became useless, and they were not able to defend themselves."138

A German-Austrian team led by John Garstang came upon the ruins of the collapsed walls while digging in the Tell es-Sultan mound in the 1930s. What his team found was the remains of two high walls, running parallel and spaced about ten feet apart. The outer wall, the city's first line of defense, measured only six feet across. The higher inner wall,

GIANTS ON THE EARTH

however, was twelve feet broad. Its massive thickness ordinarily would have presented any potential enemy with a real problem. But as the three continued digging they saw how the walls were destroyed, and what they saw astounded them. With great excitement, Garstang, Pere Vincent, also an archaeologist, and Clarence Fisher, a pottery and architectural expert, detailed their extraordinary findings in a statement that all three signed. In part, they reported: "... The outer wall suffered most, its remains falling down the slope. The inner wall is preserved only where it abuts upon the citadel, or tower, to a height of eighteen feet; elsewhere it is found largely to have fallen, together, with the remains of buildings upon it, into the space between the walls which was filled with ruins and debris. Traces of intense fire are plain to see, including reddened masses of brick, cracked stones, charred timbers and ashes. Houses alongside the wall are found burned to the ground, their roofs fallen upon the domestic pottery within." Then the three men added this particularly interesting statement: "As to the main fact, then, there remains no doubt; the walls fell outwards so completely that the attackers would be able to clamber up and over their ruins into the city."139

News of their discovery eventually brought other famous archaeologists to the excavations at Jericho. One of these, Sir Charles Marston, after carefully examining the ruins of the walls, filed this report: "Study of the geological strata, in addition to archaeological work on the walls themselves, now has revealed undoubted evidence that the wall was raised by an earthquake."140

Evidence of an earthquake, continues Marston, "does not destroy belief in a miracle. Surely it was a miracle that the earthquake could take place at the particular time when the city was besieged by the Israelites."141

Obeying Joshua's instructions to devote Jericho as a holocaust, the Hebrews set fire to the whole city. They also burned the country round about it. What structures escaped the fire, they tore down. Garstang reports that while sifting through the ruins of the royal residence, and many other homes and storerooms, he found a thick layer of ash, sometimes knee-deep. He also saw a lot of wheat, bar-ley, dates, lentils, and other foods, all of which had been turned into charcoal by intense heat. In the kitchen of one home, the archaeologist uncovered "a family provision of dates, barley, olives, a piece of bread, and a quantity of unbaked dough, all charred but unmistakable. It was sad evidence of a people cut off in full activity."142

The scriptures relate that the Hebrews left none they found inside alive, save the harlot Rahab and her family. But by some means at least some of Jericho's giants managed to escape. "Those who survived," says The Jewish Encyclopedia, "were led by a certain Ifrikish ibn Kais to Africa, and, having killed the king of that country, settled there. The Berbers are their descendants."143

Other records also reveal that some Canaanites fled for their lives to Africa. According to Procopius, some of these dispossessed peoples settled in Libya and then overspread Africa as far as the Pillars of Hercules.144 He further declares that in the sixth century A.D., "two marble pillars were to be seen in the Numidian town Tigisis, with a Phoenician inscription, in these terms: 'We are those who fled from the face of Jesus (Joshua) the robber, the son of Nun.' Suidas states this also; giving the words as, 'We are Canaanites, whom Jesus the robber drove out,' and the Talmud reveals that the Girgasites driven out by Joshua wandered to Africa."145 (See Canaan's Anakim; Israel's Wars with

GIANTS ON THE EARTH

the Giants; Sihon's and Og's Overthrow; also see Chad's Giants; Curigueres; Sudan's Giants; Watusi Giants; Zanzibar's Giants)

Jonathan
In an Israelite attack on Gath, a boastful giant with six fingers on each hand and six toes on each foot, came out and dared any Israelite to fight him. Jonathan, David's nephew, accepted his challenge to single combat and dispatched him. (See David vs Goliath)

Josephus on the Giants
After telling in his histories what great difficulty the people of Judah faced in their long siege against Jebus, Josephus next reports that they left there to assist Caleb against the giants at Hebron. "And when they had taken it," he adds, "they slew all the inhabitants. There were till then left a race of giants, who had bodies so large, and countenances so entirely different from other men, that they were surprising to the sight, and terrible to the hearing. The bones of these men are still shown to this very day, unlike to any credible relations of other men."146

Josephus also writes that Jews who lived at Hebron as late as his day occasionally dug up human bones of a gigantic size that apparently belonged to the Anakim who once dominated that region.147 He further declares that the king of Persia sent a Jew called Eleazar the Giant, who stood seven cubits, or over ten feet tall, to Rome along with some other hostages as part of a peace agreement.148 (See Eleazar the Giant; Israel's Wars with the Giants)

Kiriath Arba
Kiriath Arba was the chief city and ancestral home of the Anakim, who named the place after their famous forefather, Arba. The twelve spies that Moses sent out visited here, and ten felt great terror when they looked upon the Anakim's astounding stature. Following the Hebrews' conquest of Canaan, this "highest town in Palestine" became the possession of Caleb, who renamed it Hebron. (See Abraham and the Giants; Canaan's Anakim; Israel's Wars with the Giants)

Lahmi
Lahmi, who was as huge as Goliath and bore a spear just as massive, was slain by Elhanan, the son of Jair, on the battlefield at Gob. (See David vs Goliath; Ishbi-benob; Sippai; Six-fingered, Six-toed Giant)

Mercury, the Giant (See Giants Who Became Gods)

Nephilim
According to Moses, the Nephilim (i.e., the fallen ones) came in to the beautiful daughters of men and fathered the giants. They are described by Jude as a people of "strange flesh" because they evolved out of the animal kingdom. (See Origin of the Giants--Biblical Account)

GIANTS ON THE EARTH

Offerus (See Christopher, Saint)

Origin of the Giants—Biblical Account

Calculations by Bible chronologist James Ussher indicate that God created Adam and Eve about 4004 B.C.149 But they were not the earth's first people. That distinction, as Moses himself tells us, belonged to an evolved people called the Nephilim (i.e., the fallen ones). So, even on the day the first man and woman established their home in the Garden of Eden, this already ancient race lived outside God's divinely protected estate in great numbers.

Because the actual world to which Adam and Eve were later banished stands in so sharp a contrast to the popular notion, we perhaps need to review what archaeologists say it looked like. From the evidence they have dug up, we learn that after God drove the disobedient man and woman off His estate about the year 4000, they stepped not out into a virgin world, as most think, but into an already thriving society. Evidently they soon conformed to the ways of their Nephilim neighbors, for Cain and Abel, the firstborn of Adam and Eve, grew up and entered the same occupations--keeping flocks and farming--that provided most families of this advanced society with their livelihoods.150

From her study of the diggings, the eminent British archaeologist and historian Jacquetta Hawkes concluded that even three thousand years before Adam these evolved people were already living "relatively settled" lives in agricultural villages.151 Their building styles, she reports, "varied with local conditions, but in general houses were built to last and were equipped with fixed corngrinders, ovens and good provision for storing grain. In the southern Levant, with its strong Natufian tradition, the earliest houses were round. But after 7000 B.C. rectangular plans were adopted there and elsewhere; they were presumably found to be far better suited to compact buildings for villages and towns.

"Layouts," she adds, "differed from region to region, some houses had no more than a living room and storage area while others had several rooms, a courtyard, and even a second storey. Very often amenity and pride of possession was shown in highly polished plaster floors with rush matting, and decorated walls of coloured dadoes and simple painted patterns.

"One great craft invention was fired pottery. The earliest certainly known example (c. 7000 B.C.) is from the Zagros region.... Spinning and weaving, usually of wool, was another important invention of the seventh millennium. Weighted spindles were used but nothing is yet known of looms."152

About this time, some craftsmen began to engage in distant trade. As might be expected, this greatly speeded up cultural and commercial development. Traders now not only exchanged commodities but brought back to their communities reports on the advancements they saw in their travels. Obsidian, found in the volcanic regions of central Anatolia and around Lake Van, seems to have been the most popular article for trade. But their expanding commerce also involved items of luxury, the best of flints, and attractive things for adornment, such as turquoise and other semiprecious stones.

Meanwhile, the Nephilim population reached such proportions in some areas that a few cities of some size sprang up. Archaeologists say that the world's oldest was probably ancient Jericho. It sat on a fat oasis in the Jordan Valley nearly one thousand feet

GIANTS ON THE EARTH

below sea level. Those who dug up the town estimate that it supported at least two thousand inhabitants as far back as 8000 B.C. An unfailing spring, which they used to irrigate their corn fields and vegetable crops, no doubt attracted Jericho's first settlers. But this perennial source of water evidently caught the envious eyes of aggressive outsiders. For the town's citizens, in an effort to fend off raiders and potential land-grabbers, erected a twenty-six-foot stone tower and surrounded their settlement with a massive stone-faced wall that stood at least thirteen feet high.

Jarmo, another preadamic town, sprang into existence about 6500 B.C. Located above the valley of the Touq Chae in the Kurdish uplands of northeastern Iraq, this settlement covered four or five acres. An estimated one hundred and fifty people lived here in multi-roomed, rectangular houses of compacted clay or pise set on stone foundations and outfitted with reed floors. To cook their meals, they used built-in baking ovens and lit fires in clay-lined basins sunk into their floors. Excavators say that the earliest inhabit-ants of Jarmo apparently knew nothing about pottery. Instead they cut their bowls and dishes from soft limestone, then polished them to a smooth, pleasing surface.

Only a couple of centuries later, on the Konya plain of southern Anatolia, the Nephilim built Catal Hüyük. The pottery and other relics this city yielded to the archaeologists' shovels date it back to about 6250 B.C.--or more than two thousand years before Adam. These Anatolians enjoyed great prosperity. For a living, they farmed, raised cattle, manufactured things, and engaged in considerable trade. Artifacts unearthed here also reveal that Catal Hüyük produced beads and other trinkets from copper and imported Syrian flint to make its finest implements. This industrious town became widely known for its highly skilled wood workers, textile and basket weavers, stone polishers, and potters.[153]

In Egypt, some eight hundred miles southwest of Catal Hüyük, archaeologists discovered the Fayum and Tasian settlements. They flourished as early as the sixth millennium B.C. These inventive delta people adopted the world's first known calendar. Like our modern calendar, it consisted of twelve months, but with each containing thirty days and five holy days added at year's end. This calendar yields the first fixed date in history-- 4241 B.C.[154] So even a calendar was being used more than two centuries before the coming of our "first" parents.

In addition to being correct timekeepers, the Tasians and Fayumis were evidently a stylish people. We know they used cosmetics, for modern diggers have found some stone palettes that still showed traces of red pigment or malachite green, with which these early Nephilim people probably highlighted their eyes. They also decked themselves with perforated shells from the Mediterranean and Red Seas and ornamented their persons with ivory beads and bangles. The Nephilim males here wore their hair long but kept their faces clean-shaven. The females wove their hair into braids and used ivory combs with carved animal heads for adornment. Archaeologists say the preadamic Tasians worked in flour mills, at looms, made rough pottery, and tended crops. The Fayumis raised domestic animals and grew emmer wheat and barley. Traces of linen found in the ruins prove that they also cultivated flax and practiced weaving. Both peoples fished with hooks made of shell and horn. They hunted with bows and arrows. The Fayumis, the digs showed, even stalked the hippopotami.

Some other cities that definitely preexisted Adam and Eve include Lepenski Vir on

GIANTS ON THE EARTH

the Danube River, Byblos in Lebanon, Megiddo on the fertile Esdraelon Plain in Israel, Nippur in Iraq, Uruk (the Erech of Genesis) on the Plain of Shinar, Eridu and Ur in Babylonia, Abydos in Egypt, and Beycesultan in Turkey.

Besides the cities, several small villages were built on the fertile banks of the Tigris and Euphrates. As early as 7000 B.C., some of these evolved beings--now equipped with well-developed farming skills--began settling on the fertile alluvial soil of the Mesopotamian plains. Archaeologists who dug into the tells of Samarra, Halaf, and Hassuna determined that these early Mesopotamians hunted wild game, herded sheep and goats, raised pigs, and grazed a few cattle. They lived in round or rectangle pise houses, they almost certainly knew how to spin linen from flax, they developed painted pottery, they made figurines, and they painted dancing girls on vases.155 As in most other Neolithic settlements, all three groups revered the Mother Goddess and practiced fertility rites associated with her cult.

These ancient Nephilim people Moses mentions only briefly, but his few words reveal a lot about them. For instance, even though they lived in obvious, blatant opposition to God, he says they, like Adam, were called "sons of God." Moses also indicates, in Genesis 6:1-4, that after the disobedient man and woman were expelled from the garden, they established their new home among these fallen ones. Next he explains that the Nephilim in the neighborhood, smitten by the good looks of Adam's daughters, took them for wives. Then he reports that from this unholy mating of ungodly evolved beings with God's created people sprang a race of terrible giants.

Some think that in composing the Genesis 6:1-4 verses, Moses drew upon a traditional account, popular in his day, that explained the origin of the giants. Those holding this view say he then reduced the story to its briefest possible form, writing it down as follows: "When men began to increase in number on the earth and daughters were born to them, the sons of God [i.e., the Nephilim] saw that the daughters of men were beautiful, and they married any of them they chose.... The Nephilim were on the earth in those days--and also afterward--when the sons of God went to the daughters of men and had children by them. They were the heroes of old, men of renown."156

Early Jewish tradition interpreted this passage as a reference to the fallen angels. The Greek Septuagint, the earliest extant trans la-ti on of the Hebrew Old Testament, for example, renders bene Elohim as "angels of God."157 And so the words were understood by many prominent ancient writers. The Jewish historian Josephus so translated them, and the Jewish philosopher Philo also gave them this meaning.158 Moreover, many Early Church Fathers, such as Justin Martyr, Tatian, Athenagoras, Clement of Alexandria, Tertullian, Cyprian, and Lactantius, adopted this reading. And the apocryphal Book of Enoch contains a passage similar to Genesis 6:1-4. It tells in the plainest language that those who lusted after the "beautiful and comely daughters" of men were none other than the fallen angels.159

Most modern commentators agree. Merrill F. linger, for instance, maintains that the thought of Genesis 6:1-4 "is of spirit beings (fallen angels, demonic powers) cohabiting with women of the human race [and] producing what later became known in pagan mythologies as demigods, partly human and partly superhuman. This is not mythology but the truth of the intermixture of the human race with the angelic creation from which later mythology developed 'the Titans' (giants, partly superhuman). Greek mythology (Hesiod,

GIANTS ON THE EARTH

Pseudo-Apollodorus) recalls such beings. Zeus,160 one of the great gods, had to battle with a group of giants known as Titans. Phoenician lore (earlier than the Greek) also echoes a similar tradition. Hittite texts containing Human myths have been discovered that carry the idea back even earlier to the source of all of this sprang either from the love of a god for a mortal woman, or of a mortal man for a goddess." Quoted by Marcus Dods, The Book of Genesis (Edinburgh: T. & T. Clark, n.d.), p. 32. in the revealed facts given in 6:1-4. Gilgamesh, the hero of the Babylonian flood story, was himself a demigod, partly human, partly divine."161

But since angels are spiritual beings without sexual and reproductive powers, Moses' words perplex many scholars. For this reason, the noted German commentator C. F. Keil, among others, found himself unable to reconcile what the great Hebrew lawgiver said. The Genesis 6:1-4 passage, he admits, "may be very well interpreted, as they were by the earlier Christian theologians, as relating to the fall of Satan and his angels." But if we give it this interpretation, he argues, then we must be prepared to attribute to these fallen spiritual beings bodies of flesh that would enable them to copulate with the fleshly daughters of men and get them pregnant with children. Otherwise, he concludes, the idea that these sons of God refer "to the angels must be given up."162

But even while they admit being baffled by the problem, Keil and those of like minds readily identify the sons of God mentioned in Genesis 6:1-4 with the disobedient angels castigated by Jude (v. 6). The Apostle treats this subject with even fewer words than Moses, but his one bit of information helps complete the primeval jigsaw puzzle. For he reveals that the 6:1-4 angels, who had joined themselves to the rebellious archangel Lucifer in some former age, did not afterward "keep their own domain, but abandoned their proper abode." Many scholars correctly interpret this to mean that the defiant angels, after abandoning heaven, descended upon earth and made it their new home. But then they stumble over the trouble-some question that Keil and some others always ask: How could angelic spirits become flesh, with sexual powers that would enable them to get the daughters of men pregnant with children?

To clear up this scriptural difficulty, let us suppose that in their war against heaven the fallen angels schemed to create a people on earth first. The immediate objection to this, of course, is that, according to the Bible, only Almighty God has powers to create. That granted, how can it be explained that noncreative angels still managed to originate such a race? Jude 6, combined with Genesis 6:1-4, provides a possible answer. For these verses show that the rebels resolved the problem by simply clothing themselves with flesh that already existed. That which already existed included the fish of the sea, the fowl of the air, the beasts of the field. Of course, they found that the beasts best suited their purpose. But how did they eventually evolve out of them a people bearing their image? In this fashion: when they abandoned their natural abode, Lucifer and the many angels loyal to him made their way into this material world and started playing around in the animals. As spirits, they entered the beasts at will. And as beings of a higher order, they quickly gained complete control over them. Their play with the animals no doubt took many forms, but they probably derived their greatest fun and pleasure in matings. Naturally, the more these spirits played around the more they got themselves entangled in the flesh and its lusts. In time, the world of the flesh began to exert such an irresistible pull upon them that they became permanent incarnations in the beasts. From these in-

GIANTS ON THE EARTH

carnations sprang the Nephilim who--millenniums later--fathered the giants.

Of course, even while they lived in Nephilim bodies these fallen angels still bore God's image.163 So it happened that after a long period of evolution the outward appearances of the animals, particularly the two-footed ones, began to undergo changes that brought their facial and bodily features into a closer resemblance to the images of the rebellious spirits within them. Thus, by the year 4004 B.C., they looked strikingly similar to Adam. Studies of their fossilized skeletal remains show that they stood tall and were well built.

Origin of the Giants—Other Theories

Anthropological forensic reconstruction of their skulls reveals strong faces, with full smooth foreheads, narrow noses, and prominent chins. Their long craniums also gave them a brain capacity far above today's average. Except that some probably retained animal appendages, they resembled humans in every way.

So close was this resemblance, writes Moses, that the Nephilim began marrying the beautiful daughters descended from Adam, thus corrupting humanity with animal flesh. The genes of these two different races, being mixed, gave birth to creatures who were partly animal and partly human. Because of their endocrine abnormalities, many of these half-breeds grew to adulthood with colossal statures. But the name given the male giants characterizes their superhuman strength, not their great height. The ancients called them the Gibborim, a word meaning mighty men. Their daring, complemented by their great height, bulk, and bodily power, gained for them a widespread fame. Moses implies that they were fierce and warlike. For centuries they struck terror in the hearts of antediluvians of normal size. This fear they inspired no doubt enabled them to lord it overall Mesopotamia.164 And their many oppressions, Moses' 6:1-4 passage declares, continued right down to the first days of the great rain. (See Giants and the Flood; Giants Who Became Gods; Gomarian Giants; also see Ariels; Horned Giants; Origin of the Giants--Other Theories; Shamhazai)

Perizzites

When Israel invaded northern Canaan, the Perizzites occupied the "forest country" near Shechem. Some scholars identify them with the giant Horim. Just to the north of the Perizzites lay a sizable territory belonging to the Rephaim giants. Toward the end of the northern campaign, the tribes of Ephraim and Manassah fought these giants and took their lands. (See Israel's Wars with the Giants)

Phlegra's Giants

Besides his other accounts about the giants, Strabo informs us that on a narrow isthmus to the peninsula of Pallene stood "a city founded by the Corinthians, which in earlier times was called Potidaea, although later on it was called Cassandreia, after the same King Cassander, who restored it after it had been destroyed.... And further, writers say that in earlier times the giants lived here and that the country was named Phlegra."164

Rapha

Some scholars identify Rapha, a giant of Gath, as the father of Goliath and four other giants who are mentioned in the scriptures as feared Philistine warriors. (See David vs

GIANTS ON THE EARTH

Goliath; Ishbi-benob; Lahmi; Sippai; Six-fingered, Six-toed Giant)

Ras Shamra Texts

Written records recovered from a mound that marks the site of the ancient city of Ugarit, located on the Syrian coast opposite Cyprus, provide a separate verification of the biblical giants.

Found in 1928, these Ras Shamra Texts frequently mention the Rephaim, whose communities apparently ranged that far north. Linguists who deciphered the cuneiform texts say they were written about Joshua's time. Ras Shamra is the modern name given to an ancient mound located on the Syrian coast opposite Cyprus. (See Execration Texts; Israel's Wars with the Giant)

Rephaim Giants

According to H. R. Hall, the Rephaim built the megalithic monuments, the dolmens, and the menhirs of Moab and eastern Palestine. Fields of dolmens still may be seen in many parts of northern Jordan. The most notable ones are found in the foothills of the Jordan valley to the east of Damiah bridge, in the foothills east of Talailat Ghassul, around Irbid, and in the hill country near Hasban. (See Argob's Sixty Cities of the Giants; Beit Jibrim)

Rephaim, Land of the

In the widest sense, the "land of the Rephaim" once comprised all Transjordan and Canaan, because the giants occupied those regions in great numbers. At the time of Israel's invasion, they remained a people to be reckoned with, but their population had dwindled to the extent that the Anakim--their cousin--now dominated the land. Yet, in one place, they retained sufficient numbers and power to be still called the "land of the Rephaim." That territory lay in central Canaan, just north of the Perizzites. Scholars say their large settlement extended from there to perhaps as far as the Valley of Jezreel. (See Abraham and the Giants; Argob's Sixty Cities of the Giants; Beit Jibrim; Israel's Wars with the Giants; Giants, Valley of the)

Rephaim, Valley of the

This abode of the giants was located southwest of Jerusalem, beginning at the valley of Hinnom and stretching three miles along the road to Bethlehem. The valley got its name from some early giant inhabitants called the Rephaim. (See Israel's Wars with the Giants)

Sacae Giants (See Gomarian Giants)

Shamhazai

The ancient rabbis say that the Rephaim giants Sihon, king of the Amorites, and Og, king of Bashan, were grandsons of Sham-hazai, a fallen angel.165 Of course, such a genealogy supposes that Shamhazai was one of the Nephilim. (See Sihon's and Og's Overthrow; Origin of the Giants--Biblical Account)

GIANTS ON THE EARTH

Shaveh Kiriathaim's Giants

The terrible Emim giants at Shaveh Kiriathaim were overthrown by Elam's King Chedorlaomer in the nineteenth century B.C. Some scholars identify that ancient city with modern Kureyat, located ten miles north of Arnon and ten miles east of the Dead Sea. The Emim, described as "great and many and tall" before Chedorlaomer's invasion, never fully recovered. Their land was later taken over by the Moabites. (See Abraham and the Giants)

Sheshai

Moses identified Sheshai as one of the three giant brothers who ruled a clan of the Canaanite Anakim from Hebron when the He-brews were encamped at Kadesh Barnea. The terrifying sight of Sheshai, Ahiman, and Talmai inspired ten of Moses' spies to return with a recommendation to forget an invasion of the promised land. Their "evil report" so frightened the Hebrew congregation that they rebelled against Moses. Sheshai apparently took his name from his great height, for, declares Bochart, it "refers to his stature, which measured six cubits," i.e., nine feet.166 He was later driven out of Hebron by Caleb's men. (See Canaan's Anakim; Israel's Wars with the Giants)

Sibecai

Sibecai the Hushathite, one of David's mighty men, delivered a fatal blow to the giant Sippai during a battle at Gob. (See David vs Goliath)

Sihon's and Og's Overthrow

Late winter of their fortieth year in the wilderness found the Israelites encamped at Eziongeber, a small port town on the Gulf of Elath (modern Aqaba). As the time to invade Canaan approached, over two million men, women, and children began a two-hundred-mile trek north toward ancient Jericho. For all the hardship it brought, that earlier mission of the twelve spies to search out Canaan had served one good purpose. As a result of his later debriefings of the twelve, Moses now had a far better idea of the land's physical features, the strength of its occupants, and the logistical problems and other obstacles that the invading Hebrews would encounter. From their intelligence reports, he learned, too, that many giants occupied the south country, but that not many now lived in the lands east of the Jordan River. So central Canaan seemed to him the most vulnerable place to attack. He therefore decided that the Hebrew legions should strike first from across the Jordan, near Jericho.

Their long march toward this well-known city of the giants took the Hebrew multitude through Edom, Moab, Gilead, and Bashan. Some four hundred years earlier, many Rephaim, Horim, Emim, and Zamzummim giants had possessed these lands. Then came Chedorlaomer and his Babylonian cohorts. On their punitive raids throughout Transjordan and Edom they slew many giants and wasted their cities. An unknown number managed to escape Chedorlaomer's sword, but their once-firm hold on those countries was forever broken. The "land of the Rephaim," so-called because the giants had so completely dominated it, was no more. In later times, the Rephaim that still lived in Transjordan and Edom were defeated by the numerous descendants of Lot and Esau. This interesting bit of history appears only in Moses' journal. In his account of the He-brews' wearying march

GIANTS ON THE EARTH

toward Canaan's eastern border, the great lawgiver included several entries--written parenthetically--that tell us how the Gibborim mongrels that survived Chedorlaomer's onslaught were finally dispossessed.

After leaving Elath, the Israelites first passed beyond the sons of Esau, who lived in Seir. This country, Moses wrote, was formerly occupied by the tall Horites, but the "sons of Esau dispossessed them and destroyed them from before them and settled in their place." Writing of their passage through the wilderness of Moab, he also noted: "The Emim lived there formerly, a people as great, numerous, and tall as the Anakim. Like the Anakim, they are also regarded as Rephaim, but the Moabites call them Emim." When they came opposite the land of Ammon's descendants, Moses gave orders that they not be provoked, explaining that the Lord God had given that country to the sons of Lot for a possession. "It is also regarded as the land of the Rephaim," he added, "for Rephaim formerly lived in it, but the Ammonites call them Zamzummim, a people as great, numerous, and tall as the Anakim, but the Lord destroyed them before them. And they dispossessed them and settled in their place, just as He did for the sons of Esau, who live in Seir. . . . And the Avvim, who lived in villages as far as Gaza, the Caphtorim who came from Caphtor destroyed them and lived in their place."167

Thus, in Transjordan, only a remnant of the Rephaim survived. But the Israelites still faced a considerable threat there. For many Amorites now inhabited that same vast territory. They stood not quite as tall as the Rephaim, Horim, Emim, and Zamzummim. But biblical records and ancient monuments still represent them as a people of great size and strength. The prophet Amos, in a later reference to this campaign, describes them in these words: "Thus says the Lord,'... It was I who destroyed the Amorite before them, though his height was like the height of cedars and he was strong as the oaks.'"168 The cedar, of course, denotes the Amorites' exceptional tallness. The oak symbolizes their great might. Some monuments discovered by archaeologists bear out Amos' description. On these, says historian Philip Hitti, the "Amorite stature appear tall and martial. Their size and culture must have so impressed the primitive and short troglodytic inhabitants of southern Syria that legends grew that a giant race came and intermarried the daughters of men-- legends which were passed on to the Israelites."169

Over these Transjordanian Amorites reigned two giant kings, Sihon and Og. Moses refers to them as remnants of the Rephaim. Og later became the most famous of the two, because of his great bedstead. But from what records we have, Sihon appears to have been the most powerful and probably posed the greatest threat to the advancing Hebrews' plan of attack. Having completed their long, hard march across Edom and Moab, Moses' legions now waded the Arnon, which formed the border between Moab and Sihon's kingdom. That night they pitched camp on the Bamoth plateau in the mountains of Abarim, not far from the famed peaks of Pisgah and Nebo. From this plateau the Israelites got their first view of the land promised to them. Only Sihon now stood between them and their resolve to enter and possess it. War with the giant king and his tall warriors thus seemed unavoidable. As a courtesy, Moses sent messengers of peace to Sihon, saying: "Let me pass through your land. We will not turn off into field or vineyard; we will not drink water from wells. We will go by the king's highway until we have passed through your border."170

In their day, Sihon and Og commanded wide respect as great and mighty monarchs.171

GIANTS ON THE EARTH

Although Sihon is not described in scripture as a giant, as Og was, other sources definitely place him among the Rephaim. Rabbinical literature, for instance, identifies him as Og's brother. The ancient rabbis likewise list both kings as grandsons of Shamhazai, a fallen angel (Niddah 61a), who evidently was of the Nephilim. Sihon, they further write, resembled Og in stature and bravery (Midrash Agadah, Hukkat, ed. Buber, p. 130a). These old writings also identify him with Arad the Canaanite (Numbers 21:1), who was called Sihon because he resembled the foals in the desert for swiftness.172 Accordingly, the rabbis sometimes referred to him as "the Canaanite," claiming that he was overlord of that land and had over there many vassal kings who paid him tribute. The five Midianite kings later slain by the Israelites (Numbers 31:8; Joshua 13:21) came under his suzerainty. Sihon, himself, when the Israelites asked permission to pass through his territory to enter Canaan, advised them that he was in that land only to resist their attack upon his Canaanite kings (Tan., Hukkat, 52, ed. Buber, p. 65a).173

That he came primarily to defend his Canaanite territories, and not his Transjordan kingdom, sounds reasonable. For Sihon could not have viewed the Hebrews as much of a threat to his eastern domain. Experts who have visited this area say that if the king had retained his troops in the various cities of his Transjordan realm, the Israelites would have been able to take them only with the greatest difficulty. But as suzerain over several kingdoms west of the Jordan, Sihon apparently felt some obligation to protect them. Most likely he was also moved by arrogance. These small-statured desert nomads, he believed, could not possibly stand before his much taller, better-armed Amorites. He therefore denied Moses' request for passage. Then, mustering a great army, he marched out to check Israel's advance toward Canaan. At Jahaz, a small town on the plains of Moab, he led a charge against the Hebrews. What he thought would be an easy battle for his mighty Amorites against the puny Israelites suddenly turned into a rout of the Amorites. On that day at Jahaz the giant king and all his sons fell, mortally wounded.174

Giving a fuller account of this important battle, Josephus writes: "As soon as the Hebrews saw them giving ground, they immediately pursued them close; and when they had broken their ranks, they greatly terrified them, and some of them broke off from the rest, and ran away to the cities. Now the Hebrews pursued them briskly, and obstinately persevered in the labors they had already undergone; and being very skilful in slinging, and very dexterous in throwing of darts, or anything else of that kind, and also having nothing but light armor, which made them quick in the pursuit, they overtook their enemies; and for those that were most remote, and could not be overtaken, they reached them by their slings and their bows, so that many were slain."175 Even many who had earlier managed to escape, according to Josephus, were later slaughtered as they crowded, in an agony of thirst, into the bed of a cool mountain stream.

Following up their stunning victory over Sihon at Jahaz, the Hebrews seized Heshbon, his capital. It lay about twenty miles east of the Jordan River, on parallel with the northern end of the Salt Sea. After wandering forty years in the wilderness, these former slaves and sons of slaves now owned, by right of conquest, a piece of land. On that day they must have looked with exhilaration beyond the smoldering ruins of Heshbon to the surrounding countryside. Westward from where they stood on the crown of this low rocky hill, the Hebrews had the land of Canaan before them. Turning northward, they saw an elevated land crossed by well-wooded mountain ridges with broad fertile valleys inter-

GIANTS ON THE EARTH

vening. Eastward they beheld a wide expanse of fruitful, rolling plains that extended unbroken to the desert. Beyond that distant wasteland rose a range of purple-fringed mountains. Greatly encouraged by their successes on the battlefield, they next besieged and captured the walled cities of Nophah, Medeba, and Dibon, putting all their lofty inhabitants to death. The rest of Sihon's towns and villages, being without protecting walls, soon afterward fell. The whole rich country situated between the Arnon to the south, the upper Jabbok to the north, and the Jordan to the west, along with its cities, crops, and cattle, thus came into the Hebrews' immediate possession.

"The wanderers were now masters of a wide region of splendid upland pastures, intersected by numerous fertile valleys, and abounding in streams," relates historian Cunningham Geikie. "The crossing of the Arnon and the digging of the first well had already kindled the poetry of the camp;176 but such a conquest as this was still a more worthy theme for their inspiration. The vast tent city of the host, therefore, soon resounded with songs in praise of the conquerors, now returning to camp in triumph. Taunts and derision of their foe mingled in these strains, of which one has happily come down to us."177 Around their campfires that night, the ballad singers, as if calling to the vanquished Amorites, sang:

Come back (will ye not) to Heshbon!
Build again and restore the city of Sihon!
For there went forth fire from Heshbon,
A flame from the stronghold of Sihon;
It has consumed the city of Moab;
And the lords of the heights of Arnon!... The balladeers, telling of the final victory of Israel, then jubilantly proclaimed:
We have hurled them down! Heshbon has perished even to Dibon!
We have laid them waste even to Nophah
(We have laid them waste) with fire, to Medeba.178

Through Heshbon ran the main north-south highway that connected Edom and Moab to Bashan. From here the road westward ribboned rapidly down into the Jordan Valley, past Abu Shittim and the Meadow of die Acacias, to the fords opposite Jericho. This way to the promised land now lay open to them. But the Hebrew legions looked north. That way lived the giant King Og and his cedar-tall Amorite warriors. They remained a threat.

When Gilead's King Sihon marched out against Israel, Bashan's King Og, for some reason, made no move to join forces with him. He, like Sihon, probably viewed Israel as not much of a threat. He perhaps thought Sihon could, with his own forces and without much trouble, check the Hebrew invasion. Time and distance also could have been factors. Bashan was situated some sixty miles up the Jordan River from the point where Israel planned to cross over into Canaan. So Og may not have had enough time to prepare for such a distant campaign. Or, he may have been at odds with his brother. At any rate, for whatever reason, he remained at home. Being that far away, he now stood in no position to stop Israel's invasion. But Moses still regarded the enormous Amorite ruler as a most dangerous foe, and unwilling to have such a powerful enemy at Israel's back, he placed Jair and Nobah, chief men of the tribe of Manasseh, at the head of two divisions

GIANTS ON THE EARTH

and ordered them to carry out strikes against the north country of Gilead and all Bashan.179 While Nobah and his men marched toward Kenath in Gilead, Jair's army made haste toward Og's capital of Edrei, a strange city cut out of rock in the upper Yarmuk River valley.

An exceptional giant, Og ruled a country with sixty strongly fortified cities (see Argob's Sixty Cities of the Giants). His kingdom, extending from the Jabbok River to Mount Hermon, enjoyed a good, year-round climate. Bashan was also blessed with an exceedingly rich soil that yielded abundant crops, and its lush pasturelands produced many choice cattle. Consequently, in ancient times it became a byword for fruitfulness. The lord of this ideal land, according to Josephus, stretched to a colossal height and possessed great strength. "Now Og had very few equals, either in largeness of his body or handsomeness of his appearance," he writes. "He was also a man of great activity in the use of his hands, so that his actions were not unequal to the vast largeness and handsome appearance of his body; and men could easily guess at his strength and magnitude when they took his bed at Rabbath, the royal city of the Ammonites; its structure was of iron, its breadth four cubits, and its length a cubit more than double thereto."180

Og lived not at Edrei but at Ashtaroth, his principal capital. So, when he heard the stunning news of Israel's crushing defeat of his brother Sihon, and that Jair and his army were marching on Edrei, a few miles southeast of Ashtaroth, he rushed to that city's defense. As Jair approached from the south, Og marshaled his forces on the plain outside Edrei to oppose him. This move has long baffled military experts, for Edrei "was in ordinary circumstances almost unassailable, since it was, strange to say, built in a hollow artificially scooped out of the side of a hill, which the deep gorge of the Hiero-max or Yarmuk isolates from the country round."181

In other words, had he stayed put inside his subterranean city, which lay about seventy feet below the surface of the hill, "it would have been impossible, humanly speaking, for the Israelites to have conquered him," declares Cyril Graham. "The only hope they would have had of taking the place would be by a long siege, and that would hardly have been possible to maintain, because they could not, without great difficulty, invest the city. The western side, next to the plain, they might watch, and cut off all supplies from that quarter--the most fruitful, indeed, in that part of Bashan; but to reach the eastern side of Edrei they must have penetrated some distance among the rocks; and not only would this have been too dangerous a work to attempt, but, even were they able to watch ever so well on that side, the people of Argob, knowing all the winding ways within the rocks, could always have managed to bring provisions to the city without being seen. The only real hope of taking the city was by drawing the Rephaim out into the plain. Whether some ruse was employed to entice the people from their stronghold, or whether Og, in full confidence of his great strength and invulnerability, planned a sudden attack, or, as we should now say, a sortie, on the Israelites as they lay before the city, we are not told. Either would be difficult. It would require no small amount of skill to entice these people from behind walls; and it is more improbable that such a people should of their own free will risk a battle in the open plain."182

Of course, Og's full confidence in his great strength and invulnerability, could have moved him to his fatal, colossal blunder. But Graham prefers to believe that "some almost miraculous interference in favour of the Israelites" occurred.183 He believes this

GIANTS ON THE EARTH

interference was huge swarms of hornets that providentially drove Og and his Amorites out of their underground stronghold. For his evidence the historian points to Joshua 24:11-13. In this little noticed passage, Joshua reveals that these highly combative insects with their powerful stings played an important role in this and many of the Israelites' later campaigns.184

Thus discomforted and driven out of their unusual city by an army of angry hornets, Og and his Amorites divisions confronted Jair and his smaller men on the plains. In the ensuing battle, the Hebrews slew the giant king and his sons, slaughtered most of his army, and took possession of Edrei. In subsequent battles in the Argob, Jair captured some sixty cities that were fortified with high walls, gates, and bars, "besides a great many unwalled towns."185

The battle deaths of Sihon and Og wrote a finis to the story of the Transjordan giants. We know little else about them except that they were warlike, even amongst themselves; that they possessed phenomenal strength; that some of them were men of good intelligence and ability, like Sihon and Og. Just how tall they were we do not know. But we may get some idea from Og's bed. The Ammonites, following behind the Hebrew army as scavengers, found the iron bed in Og's sleeping quarters at either Edrei or Ashtaroth. They took it to Rabbath, the royal city of the Ammonites. There it became a famous "museum piece." It drew curious crowds for many centuries, probably even down to the time of the Babylonian captivity (c. 586 B.C.). This great bed, reports the chronicler of Deuteronomy, measured "nine cubits long and four wide, according to the common cubit," i.e., thirteen-and-a-half feet by six feet.186

"Allowing the bedstead to have been one cubit longer than Og, which is certainly sufficient, and allowing the cubit to be about eighteen inches long, for this is perhaps the average of the cubit of a man, then Og was twelve feet high," says Adam Clarke. "This may be deemed extraordinary, and perhaps almost incredible, and therefore many commentators have, according to their fancy, lengthened the bedstead and shortened the man, making the former one-third longer than the person who lay on it, that they might reduce Og to six cubits; but even in this way they make him at least nine feet high."187

Sinuhe vs the Giant from Retenu

The conquests of Og's Bashan by Jair and Gilead by Nobah, with the earlier capture of Sihon's territory, gave Israel possession of all Transjordan. They now claimed all the land from the Arnon River in the south, which formed Moab's northern boundary, to the snow-capped Mount Hermon in the north, a distance of one hundred and thirty miles. These early victories were, of course, crucial. They were also remarkable achievements and were celebrated long afterward.188 Unquestionably, they boosted the courage and confidence of the much shorter invading Hebrews. At the same time they must have dismayed and demoralized, at least to some extent, the giant warlike Anakim, Avvim, Rephaim, and their big Amorite cousins beyond the Jordan. (See Canaan's Anakim; David vs Goliath; Israel's Wars with the Giants; Jericho's Giants)

In ancient times people thrilled to Sinuhe's account of his duel with a mighty giant chieftain from Retenu.189 Sinuhe lived during the reign of Amenemhat I, of Egypt's Twelfth Dynasty (c. 2000 B.C.). A "prince and count" under Amenemhat, he fled to Syria when that great king was assassinated. In this new land, Sinuhe eventually rose to a position of

GIANTS ON THE EARTH

power and wealth. Among his many adventures in exile, he relates the following:

"Once on a time there came a strong man from Retenu and challenged me in my tent. He was a combatant without a rival, and he had it [the land Retenu] completely subdued. He said he wished to fight with me; he meant, he intended to rob me. He proposed to make booty of my herds, on the advice of his tribe.... During the night I stretched my bow and put my arrow in place; I sharpened my dagger and polished my weapons. When it became light... the land of Retenu drew up [in battle array]; its tribes had assembled, and its neighboring peoples had joined with them. When they thought of this fight, each heart burned for me. Women and men cried out, and every one was anxious about me. They said: 'Is there indeed any strong one who can fight with him?' Then he took his shield and dagger, and held an armful of spears.... He made for me, and I shot him, so that my arrow stuck fast in his neck. He cried out and fell on his face, and I pinned him down with his dagger. I raised my cry of victory on his back, and all the Asiatics [in his army] cried out. I praised the god Montu [Egyptian war-god], but his people sorrowed for him.... Then I took over his possessions and his flocks--what he had thought to do to me, that did I to him... "190 (See Colbrand the Giant vs Sir Guy of Warwick; David vs Goliath)

Sippai
The giant Sippai, of Gath, who some scholars suppose was one of Goliath's four brothers, stood to such an enormous height and size that all wondered at him. But in Israel's battle against the Philistines at Gob, Sibecai the Hushathite, one of David's mighty men, struck him down. (See David vs Goliath; Ishbi-benob; Lahmi; Six-fingered, Six-toed Giant)

Six-fingered, Six-toed Giant (See Jonathan; David vs Goliath)

Sodom's and Gomorrah's Giants
Both Ecclesiasticus (xvi.8-9) and the Book of Jubilees (xx.5) relate that in the time of Abraham giants lived in Sodom and Gomorrah. (See Abraham and the Giants)

Talmai
From Hebron, the giant Talmai and his huge brothers, Sheshai and Ahiman, ruled the three tribes of the Anakim who were called by their names. A generation after they came out of Egypt the Hebrews defeated them and took possession of all their lands. On a wall of the tomb of Oimenepthah I appears a drawing representing a son of the Anak. He is depicted as tall and light-complexioned. Belzoni, who opened the tomb, read the hieroglyphic inscription as Tanmahu, "or, by elision, 'Talmia,' the name given to one of the tribes of the children of Anak." (See Canaan's Anakim; Israel's Wars with the Giants)

Uzim (See Zamzummim)

Zamzummin
The huge Zamzummmim191 ("murmurers" or "stammerers," i.e., speakers of a barbarous tongue), lived east of the river Jordan, in the area later conquered by the descen-

GIANTS ON THE EARTH

dants of Ammon. Moses described these giants as "a people as great, numerous, and tall as the Anakim." (See Sihon's and Og's Overthrow)

Zuzim (See Zamzummim)

References
1 See The Geography of Strabo, 17.786.
2 Fields of dolmens still may be seen in many parts of northern Jordan. The most notable ones are in the foothills of the Jordan valley to the east of Damiah bridge, in the foothills east of Talailat Ghassul, around Irbid, and in the hill country near Hasban.
3 H. R. Hall, The Ancient History of the Near East (London: Methuen & Co., 1963), pp. 183-184.
4 Also called the Zuzim.
5 Elmer W. K. Mould, Essentials of Bible History (New York: The Ronald Press, 1966), pp. 29-30.
6 Genesis 13:6.
7 Genesis 13:9.
8 Following the Hebrews' conquest of Canaan, Caleb renamed it Hebron.
9 Jude 7 New American Standard Bible.
10 Merrill F. Unger, Biblical Demonology (Wheaton, IL: Van Kampen Press, 1952), p. 50.
11 G. Ch. Aalders, Bible Student's Commentary, Vol. I, Genesis (Grand Rapids, MI: Zondervan, 1981), p. 283.
12 Deuteronomy 3:13.
13 The time of this first invasion is established from certain scriptures. When Isaac was born, Abraham was one hundred years old and Ishmael thirteen. So Ishmael was born when Abraham was eighty-seven. Chedor-laomer's second raid occurred before Ishmael was even conceived by Hagar, Sarah's maidservant. Genesis 14:5 says his second raid took place fourteen years after the first raid. Thus when Chedorlaomer first con-quered the five cities, Abraham was no more than seventy-three (87-14=73), and still lived in Assyria. When he left for Canaan, he was seventy-five (12:4).
14 Elam lay east of the Tigris and Euphrates Rivers on Babylonia's southeastern border. The scriptures identify it with Persia, but, remarks Robert Candlish, "it may here denote that part of Persia which was known in ancient history by the name of Elymais." Studies in Genesis (Grand Rapids, MI: Kregal Publications, 1982), p. 210.
15 Marcus Dods, The Expositor's Bible, Vol. I (Grand Rapids, MI: William B. Eerdm^ns, 1940), p. 35.
16 See Targum of Palestine on Genesis 14.
17 "The worship of this Syrian goddess was, though under a variety of forms, almost universal in patriarchal times, and her statue in the sanctuaries of all the Rephaite people was that of a cow-headed female, bearing on her head a globe between two horns, as is still seen on Phoenician coins and antique gems. It may be added that the Rephaim wore helmets surmounted by a metallic globe between horns, in honour of their national deity." Robert Jamieson, A. R. Fausset and David Brown, A Commentary on the Old and New Testaments, Vol. I (Chicago: Moody Press, 1945), p. 137.

GIANTS ON THE EARTH

18 "The best indications which the limited archaeology of this considerable region has been able to provide do confirm, indeed, that from Ashtaroth to Edom the King's Highway passed through a region that was throughout densely settled during this period with which we are presumably concerned, Middle Bronze Age I, or perhaps the earlier part of Middle Bronze E" Bruce Vawter, On Genesis (New York: Doubleday, 1977), pp. 191-192.

19 Probably modern Kureyat, located ten miles north of Arnon and ten miles east of the Dead Sea.

20 In this campaign, Chedorlaomer journeyed as far south as El-paran, which most scholars identify with the modern archaeological site Ezion Geber, on the Gulf of Aqabah.

21 Genesis 14:8-9 NASB.

22 Because masses of bituminous matter could often be seen floating on it, the Salt Sea in ancient times was also called Asphaltic Lake.

23 Nelson Glueck, Rivers in the Desert (New York: Farrar, Straus, and Cudahy, 1959), pp. 11, 72-73.

24 That Mamre, Eshcol, and Aner accompanied Abraham on this mission can be proved from the Genesis record. For when the grateful king of Sodom urged Abraham to keep the goods he had recovered from Chedorlaomer for himself, as a reward for returning his people, the patriarch replied: "I will accept nothing but what my men have eaten and the share that belongs to the men who went with me--to Aner, Eshcol and Mamre. Let them have their share" (Genesis 14:24).

25 Amos 2:1,9 NASB.

26 Cyril Graham, "The Ancient Bashan and the Cities of Og," Cambridge Essays, 1858. Quoted by J. L. Porter in The Giant Cities of Bashan (New York: Thomas Nelson & Sons, 1873), pp. 85-86.

27 No reference given.

28 Lee, Giant: The Pictorial History, p. 41.

29 Aalders, Bible Student's Commentary, Vol. I, p. 283.

30 Numbers 10:11-12.

31 But known today as Ain Kadis, i.e., "Holy Spring."

32 Deuteronomy 1:20-22 New International Version.

33 Tan. Shelah, 12.

34 Ibid.

35 Deuteronomy 9:1-2.

36 Jamieson, Fausset and Brown, A Commentary on the Old and New Testaments, Vol. I (Chicago: Moody Press, 1945), p. 546.

37 Numbers 13:22.

38 Samuel Bochart, Geographia Sacra, 1692, p. 362.

39 Joshua 11:21.

40 Joshua 11:22.

41 See Wycliffe Bible Encyclopedia, Vol. 1 (Chicago: Moody Press, 1975), p. 64, and The Jewish Encyclopedia, Vol. 1 (New York: KTAV Publishing House, 1901), p. 552. Also see Proverbs 1:9 and Song of Solomon 4:9.

42 Such is the interpretation put on Numbers 13:32 by Alfred Edersheim, in Bible History (Wilmington, DE: Associated Publishers and Authors, n.d.), P-153.

GIANTS ON THE EARTH

43 Wycliffe Bible Encyclopedia, Vol. 1, p. 64.

44 Flavius Josephus, The Antiquities of the Jews, translated by William Whitson (Peabody, MA: Hendrickson Publishers, 1987), 5.2.3.

45 Jamieson, Fausset and Brown, Commentary on the Old and New Testaments, Vol. I, p. 547.

46 Num. R. xvi. and Tan., Shelah, 7, ed. Buber, 11.

47 George M. Lamsa, translator of the Arabic Peshitta into English, ex-plains that in the Middle East, "branches of vine are often cut down with grapes on them and carried from place to place. The branch with its fresh leaves helps to preserve the grapes in the hot climate." Old Testament Light (Philadelphia: A. J. Holman Co., 1967), p. 198.

48 Numbers 13:27 NIV.

49 Numbers 13:28, 31-33 NIV.

50 Numbers 13:30 NIV.

51 Deuteronomy 1:29-31 NIV.

52 Werner Keller, The Bible As History (New York: William Morrow and Co., 1956), p. 135.

53 Josephus, Antiquities, 3.14.3.

54 Numbers 14:21-34.

55 Numbers 26:64-65.

56 Lee, Giant: The Pictorial History, pp. 53-54.

57 Goliath's height is given as six cubits and a span. The common cubit is eighteen inches and a span half that amount. According to Unger's Bible Dictionary, "Skeletons recovered in Palestine attest the fact that men as tall as Goliath once lived in that general region" (p. 419).

58 Targum on 1 Samuel 4:11.

59 Romantics like to portray David as a young boy, but this is disproved by the fact that soon after he slew Goliath, Saul made him a commander of his army. Israelites did not enter military service until the age of twenty. See Numbers 1:2-3.

60 1 Samuel 17:26 NIV.

61 "Slings are still in use among shepherds in Palestine, not only to drive off wild animals but to guide their flocks. A stone cast on this side or that, before or behind, drives the sheep or goats as the shepherd wishes. It was the familiar weapon of hunters, and also of light-armed fighting men, especially among the Benjamites, whose skill was famous. A good slinger could hit at 600 paces, and hence at a short distance the force of the blow given must have been very great." Cunningham Geikie, The Holy Land and the Bible, Vol. I (New York: James Pott & Co., 1899), p. 106.

62 1 Samuel 17:43 NIV.

63 1 Samuel 17:45-46 NIV.

64 That David's victory had a religious aspect is borne out by his placing Goliath's sword in the sanctuary at Nob.

65 Josephus, Antiquities, 6.9.5.

66 The word ariels thus seems to designate men who had Nephilim blood in their veins and whose human features still retained some resemblance to the lion.

67 2 Samuel 23:20-23.

68 Josephus, Antiquities, 7.12.1.

GIANTS ON THE EARTH

69 Ibid., 7.12.2.

70 Accounts of these last fights with the giants appear in 2 Samuel 21:15-22 and 1 Chronicles 20:4-8.

71 Thompson, Mystery and Lore of Monsters, p. 132. The cubit equals eighteen inches.

72 See 2 Samuel 21:22.

73 See Genesis 6:14.

74 From a March, 1970, news release by Search Foundation, Inc., Washington, D.C. "The Madrid laboratory," the report added, "estimates the age of the sample at approximately 5,000 years. The Centre Technique de Bois gave 4,484 years."

75 Henry H. Halley, Halley's Bible Handbook (Grand Rapids, MI: Zondervan Publishing House, 1965), p. 74.

76 Genesis 9:26-27 NIV.

77 Genesis 11:1-9. That place afterward was called Babel, says Moses, "because there the Lord confused the language of the whole world."

78 Halley's Bible Handbook, p. 84. The traditional Tower of Babel is located at Borsippa, ten miles southwest of the center of Babylon, but archaeologists commonly believe the actual site was the center of Babylon, in the tower ruins in which Smith found the ancient tablet.

79 No reference given.

80 Pezron, Antiquities of Nations, preface vi.

81 See Josephus, Antiquities, 6.1, where he makes this statement: "For Gomer founded those whom the Greeks now call Galatians, but were then called Gomerites."

82 See Ptolemy, Geography, 6.11 and 13.

83 Pezron, Antiquities of Nations, pp. 13-14.

84 Ibid., pp. 13-16.

85 Pezron gives the following as his sources: Ptolemy, Geography, 6.11, &c. 13; Pliny, 6.16; Mela, 1.2.; Dionysius, Per., 5. 700.

86 Ibid., pp. 17-18.

87 Ibid., pp. 24-25.

88 Ibid., pp. 25, 27.

89 Ibid., p. 26.

90 That is, loosely translated, people of the breeches. See Herodotus, 1.

91 Pezron, Antiquities of Nations, p. 29.

92 Ptolemy, 6.13.

93 Pezron, Antiquities of Nations, pp. 28-30.

94 Ibid., p. 35.

95 Ibid., p. 54.

96 Formerly known as the Euxine Sea.

97 So the name appears in the Parthian Stathmas of Isidore of Charax, who interprets it to mean the conquering Sacae nation. Strabo gives a slightly different spelling, referring to the country as Sacacena.

98 No reference given.

99 Joshua 11:21.

100 Joshua 11:22. Centuries later several giants from this area fought against Israel. The most famous of these was, of course, the champion Philistine warrior Goliath, of Gatli,

GIANTS ON THE EARTH

whom a young David slew with his sling.

101 The Glory of the Old Testament (New York: Villard Books, 1984), p. 108.

102 Because of its exceedingly rich soil, the valley's broad plain became proverbial for its choice "ears of grain." See Isaiah 17:5.

103 The Imperial Standard Bible Encyclopedia, Vol. VI, Patrick Fairbairn, editor (Grand Rapids, MI: Zondervan, 1957), p. 5.

104 Harry Emerson Fosdick, A Pilgrimage to Palestine (New York: Macmillan Publishing Co., 1949), p. 33.

105 A. T. Olmstead, History of Palestine and Syria (Grand Rapids, MI: Baker Book House, 1931), p. 23.

106 "The Amorites," writes Roland DeVaux, "were regarded as the successors or the descendants of the legendary giants of prehistory--the Rephaim of Bashan and of Gilead." The Early History of Israel (Philadelphia: The Westminster Press, 1978), p. 133. The Amorites descended from the fourth son of Canaan. See Genesis 10:16 and 1 Chronicles 1:14.

107 Amos 2:9. The Midrash uses the identical phrase--"tall as cedars"--to describe the giant Anakim and Rephaim. Incidentally, Amorite blood may have run through the veins of the Rephaim giants Sihon and Og, for the scriptures refer to them as descendants of both these peoples.

108 The Universal Jewish Encyclopedia, Vol. 1 (New York: KTAV Publishing House, 1969), p. 293.

109 Alfred Edersheim, Bible History (Wilmington, DE: Associated Publishers and Authors, n.d.), p. 193.

110 Isaiah 17:9. The Septuagint gives the best, most explicit rendering.

111 Archaeological excavations at Gezer and other sites in that area "bear out the unusually tall stature of individuals in ancient Palestine." The Wycliffe Bible Encyclopedia, Vol. 1 (Chicago: Moody Press, 1972), p. 709.

112 See Joshua 14:15, 21:11.

113 Numbers 13:22.

114 John Garstang, The Foundations of Bible History (London: Constable &Co., 1931), p. 212.

115 Ibid., pp. 212-213.

116 Ibid., p. 213.

117 Joshua left no definite record of such a battle, but see Joshua 11:21-23, which indicates that one took place.

118 Josephus, Antiquities, 5.2.2.

119 For the Jebusites' identification with the Horim, see the Wycliffe Bible Encyclopedia, p. 61.

120 Excepting, of course, the land of the Philistines on the coast.

121 Joshua 11:21.

122 Joshua 17:14-18 NIV.

123 Harper's Bible Dictionary (San Francisco: Harper & Row, 1985), p. 772.

124 Josephus, Antiquities, 5.2.3.

125 Judges 1: UNIV.

126 In campaigns west of the Jordan River, Israel killed thirty-one Canaanite kings.

GIANTS ON THE EARTH

The names of their cities are given in Joshua 12:7-24.

127 See Joshua 13:16; 17:16.

128 Joshua 11:21-23 NASB.

129 The Jewish Encyclopedia, Vol. 5 (New York: KTAV Publishing House, 1901), p. 659.

130 According to Joshua 6:21, the Hebrews destroyed every living thing in Jericho--men and women, young and old, cattle, sheep, and donkeys. But this statement does not say that none escaped, though some read it so.

131 During his excavation work, Dr. John Garstang discovered the ruins of several houses that had been built across the top of the two walls. When the outer wall fell outward, it dragged the inner wall and the houses with it down the hillside. Also see Joshua 2:15.

132 Joshua 6:24.

133 Leon Wood, A Survey of Israel's History (Grand Rapids, MI: Zondervan Publishing House, 1970), p. 174.

134 Because of this large grove, Jericho also became known as the "City of Palms." The dates it harvested from the grove were eagerly sought by peoples in the surrounding nations.

135 Midrash, Tan., Beha'aloteka, ed. Vienna, p. 206b.

136 See Joshua 6:2-5.

137 Henry Hart Milman, The History of the Jews, Vol. I (New York: A. C. Armstrong, 1886), p. 265.

138 Josephus, Antiquities, 5.1.6,7.

139 Joseph P. Free, Archaeology and Bible History (Wheaton, IL: Van Kampen Press, 1950), p. 130.

140 L. Sale-Harrison, Palestine: God's Monument of Prophecy (Chicago: Van Kampen Press, 1933), pp. 76-77.

141 Ibid., 77.

142 The Biblical World, Charles F. Pfeiffer, editor (Grand Rapids, MI: Baker Book House, 1966), p. 308.

143 Vol. 5, p. 659.

144 William Garden Blaikie, The Expositor's Bible (London: A. C. Armstrong & Son, 1905), p. 246.

145 Cunningham Geikie, Hours with the Bible, Vol. 2 (New York: James Pott & Co., 1903), p. 463.

146 Josephus, Antiquities, 5.2.3.

147 Ibid., 5.2.3.

148 Thompson, Mystery and Lore of Monsters, p. 132.

149 Most Bible chronologies differ only a few hundred years on the creation, but scholars accept Ussher's as the most accurate.

150 Cain's brief biography, by the way, contains two references to the Nephilim. The first occurs in Genesis 4:13, just after he murdered his brother Abel. Judged by God and sentenced to wander all his days in the lands to the east, a crestfallen Cain moaned: "My punishment is more than I can bear. Today you are driving me from the land, and I will be hidden from your presence; I will be a restless wanderer on the earth, and whoever finds me will kill me" [emphasis mine]. "Not so;" the Lord reassured him, "if anyone kills

GIANTS ON THE EARTH

Cain, he will suffer vengeance seven times over." Then the Almighty put a mark on Cain so that no one he encountered in his wanderings would dare kill him. The second reference occurs in the next statement: "After this he went out from the Lord's presence and lived in the land of Nod east of Eden. There he built a city." A city? For whom?

151 Ms. Hawkes, of course, viewed these people as manifestations of early humanity.

152 Jacquetta Hawkes, The Atlas of Early Man (New York: St. Martin's Press, 1976), p. 40.

153 Ibid., p. 41.

154 Carl Whiting Bishop, Man from the Farthest Past, Vol. 7 (Washington, DC: The Smithsonian Series, 1949), p. 298.

155 Hawkes, Atlas of Early Man, pp. 43-44.

156 In his Cratylus, Plato (c. 400 B.C.) mentioned a similar tradition. "Do you not know that the heroes are demigods?" he wrote. "... All of them

157 See Alexandrine Text.

158 Josephus, Antiquities of the Jews, 1.3.1; Philo, The Giants, 2.6.

159 1 Enoch 6:1-8; 7:1-6. Also see the Zohar (I:58a)

160 Zeus, the god of the heavens and supreme deity of the ancient Greeks, was called Jupiter by the Romans. In his earthly life, Jupiter was a mighty giant. (See Giants Who Became Gods)

161 Unger's Commentary on the Old Testament, Vol. I (Chicago: Moody Press, 1981), p. 37.

162 C. F. Keil and F. Delitzsch, Commentary on the Old Testament, Vol. I (Grand Rapids, MI: William B. Eerdmans Publishing Co., n.d.), pp. 131-138.

163 Humans were later created in this same image. In Genesis 1:27, as He was about to create Adam, the Almighty Angel of the Lord said to the angelic host: "Let us make man in our image, after our likeness," i.e., in the likeness of angels.

164 The Geography of Strabo, 7.25.

165 See Niddah 61a.

166 Bochart, Geog. Sac., p. 362.

167 Deuteronomy 2: 8-12, 19-23 NASB.

168 Amos 2:9 NASB.

169 Philip Hitti, History of Syria (New York: Macmillan, 1951), p. 195.

170 Numbers 21:21-22 NASB. Until Sihon came and took it from them, this land east of the Jordan was possessed by the Moabites.

171 See Psalm 136:17-22, where they are spoken of in the same breath with Pharaoh.

172 To get some idea of how fast giants could run, see Maximinus.

173 See The Jewish Encyclopedia, Vol. 11 (New York: KTAV Publishing House, 1901), p. 335.

174 Deuteronomy 2:33.

175 Josephus, Antiquities, 4.5.2.

176 See Numbers 21:16-18, for an account of the first well the Hebrews dug and the song they sang.

177 Geikie, Hours with the Bible, Vol. 2, pp. 400-401.

178 Ibid., adapted from Numbers 21:27-30.

179 See Numbers 32:41-42; Deuteronomy 3:14.

GIANTS ON THE EARTH

180 Josephus, Antiquities, 4.5.3.

181 Geikie, Hours with the Bible, Vol. 2, p. 402.

182 Cyril Graham, "The Ancient Bashan and the Cities of Og," Cambridge Essays (1858). Quoted by Jamieson, Fausset and Brown, Commentary on the Old and New Testaments, Vol. I, p. 628.

183 Ibid.

184 After their conquest of Canaan, Joshua reminded the tribes of the help they had received from the hornets. To the people gathered before him, he said: "This is what the Lord, the God of Israel, says: '... The citizens of Jericho fought against you, as did also the Amorites, Perizzites, Canaanites, Hittites, Girgashites, Hivites and Jebusites, but I gave them into your hands. I sent the hornet ahead of you, which drove them out before you-- also the two Amorite kings. You did not do it with your own sword and bow. So I gave you a land on which you did not toil and cities you did not build; and you live in them and eat from vineyards and olive groves that you did not plant.'"

185 Deuteronomy 3:4-5, 14.

186 Deuteronomy 3:11.

187 Adam Clarke, Clarke's Commentary, Vol. I (Nashville, TN: Abingdon Press, 1977), a reprint of the 1851 edition, pp. 744-745.

188 The Israelites ranked these conquests with their deliverance from Egypt and their passage through the Red Sea. Thus, in Psalms 135 and 136, the overthrow of Sihon and Og are given equal space with the downfall of Pharaoh.

189 Some scholars identify "the land of Retenu" with Canaan.

land of Retenu" with Canaan.

190 Ira M. Price, The Monuments and the Old Testament (Philadelphia: Judson Press, 1925), p. 250.

191 Also called the Uzim or Zuzim.

GIANTS ON THE EARTH

Point of View:
We have a Biblical viewpoint on the world. Ooparts are evidence, we think, that the Flood actually happened. News items or magazine articles that report them may not have the same perspective that Christians do. When we read for instance, a scientific article that puzzles over our lack of genetic variability, we think of the Flood of Noah. We would include that article here, without editing, because we expect Christians to use their filters on such an article. That does not mean that we agree with the evolutionary timeframe given in said article.

We think it's more interesting when general newspaper articles or science articles observe data that they might see one way, but that Christians might see another way given our own knowledge about God, creation and the flood. It"s more interesting to quote Stephen Jay Gould saying that "the lack of transitional fossils is the trade secret of paleontology", than it might be to hear another Christian say it.

So, no we don"t believe the universe is millions or billions of years old. We don"t know how old it is"we just know who created it and how long it took Him. We do not believe in pre-Adamic races, though we do believe that there were "civiilizations" prior to the Flood. We don"t believe in space aliens or cooties. We expect you to use your own knowledge filter on this site.

INTRO
Do unexplained technologies of the ancients provide possible proofs of Pre-flood civilizations? If you believe that the flood of Noah actually happened, what was the state of the technology of pre-flooders? Could they have left physical evidence of their existence?

Much of what we think we know about the past is wrong. Columbus discovered America? That's wrong for so many reasons--and must have come as some surprise to the people who were living here at the time. First manned flight by the Wright brothers at Kitty Hawk? No! Marconi invented the radio? Not at all!

Why is the oldest pyramid, the Great Pyramid, the one built with the highest technology; bigger blocks with closer fit? "Newer" pyramids are crumbling because they were

GIANTS ON THE EARTH

Photo 1

built with less skill. Some are suggesting that the Great Pyramid of Giza is much, older (relatively) than previously thought. (For more on the incredible, Great Pyramid, see further in this section.)

It's also been said that the Great Pyramid is the largest and most accurately designed single building in the world even by today's standards.

On these pages, we want to look at history through another lens.

Photo 1, is a section of a relief on an Egyptian temple wall at Abydos; (photo by Dr. Ruth Hover). Photo 2, the Saqqara Bird. Both items are dated at a minimum of 2000 years. Note the other interesting bas relief objects in Photo 1.

Photo 2

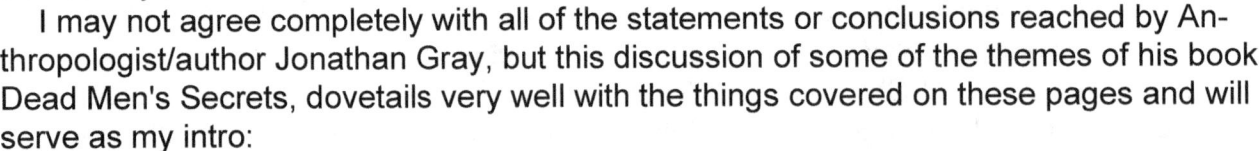

The Saqqara Bird is a "cargo plane" and the helicopters and chase planes are also electronically snipped items from the wall at Abydos in Photo 1. More about these and other such items later.

I may not agree completely with all of the statements or conclusions reached by Anthropologist/author Jonathan Gray, but this discussion of some of the themes of his book Dead Men's Secrets, dovetails very well with the things covered on these pages and will serve as my intro:

"..On November 17, 3398 B.C., two billion people, with their astonishing technology, vanished from the face of the earth. This lost super race beat us to the moon(?), to computers, and to nuclear war. A cosmic disaster occurred which wiped out a super civilization and generated 6,000 foot tidal waves, the disaster known to early civilizations worldwide as the great flood (the deluge mentioned in the book of Genesis in the Bible, for which Noah constructed the Ark to save a remnant of mankind).

...The descendants of this super race branched out from Ararat (Armenia) to create civilizations less advanced technologically, but still with some knowledge of their original civilization. The theory of evolution, which believes in the gradual progression of man, cannot stand up to the evidence governed by the laws of thermo-dynamics. The evidence of fully developed cities and an advanced technology of a superior man, whose society deteriorated over time is irrefutable.

...Early "cave men" wore clothes like ours? (more later & see Those Sophisticated Cave Men) That man knew the secret of flight before the twentieth century? That early civilizations performed open-heart surgery and fluoroscopy? That there were once shining cities illuminated by a means of electricity unknown to us today. The list is endless and fascinating, pointing to a super civilization, evidences of which can no longer be ignored.

..Archaeological and anthropological evidence that something very big happened on this planet in the past..something so big it wiped traces of just about everything from the face of the earth. From around the world, "impossible" ancient inventions have been surfacing of late, and some of them from a technology as advanced as our own.

Nearly all the writings of ancient people worldwide tell the same story, that of decline from an original "Golden Age." That a cataclysmic disaster wiped out the advanced world. Today's diggings worldwide show that these traditions tally with the facts.

Enormous stone masses or metal fragments are there; they cannot be argued away.

GIANTS ON THE EARTH

(Photo shows ancient stone hewn from single block and weighs at least 2.4 million pounds. No modern crane could move it. More later.) I believe that this original advanced world, gave impetus to all succeeding civilizations, and is well within the framework of scientific thinking.

PHYSICAL REMAINS ALSO

There are recently discovered artifacts that cannot be dismissed, namely, objects of metal sitting in museums, unquestionably made in the ancient world, that would have required very advanced technology to produce. A technology not to be repeated until our day.

The entire world is really a "dead man's tomb," a treasure hunter's paradise. As we pry open the coffin, suspense builds. Slowly we're lifting the lid on a lost technology which almost smacks of science fiction?

THE DELUGE

The global flood catastrophe is one of the key facts of all history. Not only is there a mass of geological evidence, it has left an indelible impression on the memory of the entire human race. An analysis of some 600 individual flood traditions reveals a widespread concurrence on essential points: the prior corruption of mankind, a flood warning unheeded by the masses, a survival vessel, the preservation of up to eight people with representative animal life, the sending forth of a bird to determine the suitability of reemerging land, significance in the rainbow, descent from a mountain, and the re-population of the whole earth from a single group of survivors.

(Photo: under water monument off the coast of Japan) Especially remarkable is the persistence of that biblical name Noah. And this is particularly so when you consider the ultimate language differences between peoples, and the extreme local distortions which (developed in flood legends. Yet the name survived virtually unchanged in such isolated places as Hawaii (where he was called Nu-u), the Sudan (Nuh), China (Nu-Wah), the Amazon region (Noa), Phrygia (Noe) and among the Hottentots (Noh and Hiagnoh). :

SUDDEN APPEARANCE

Are you aware that "ALL CULTURES BEGAN SUDDENLY" and were fully developed? A long preliminary period is not supported by archaeology. Before cities on earth, there was nothing. There was no transition whatsoever between the ancient civilizations and any primitive forebearers. They were at their peak from the beginning. :

...Great cities, enormous temples, pyramids of overwhelming size. Colossal statues

GIANTS ON THE EARTH

with tremendous expressive power. Luxurious tunnels and tombs. Splendid streets flanked by magnificent sculpture, perfect drainage systems. A decimal system at the very start. A ready-made writing, already perfected. A well established naming system (in which each Pharaoh had as many as five names). Society already divided into specialist classes. An army, civil service and hierarchy minutely organized. A court exhibiting all the indications of well-defined precedence and form. Egypt came from a clearly established civilization.

The only conclusions that can be drawn from the evidence is that, 1) Each of the first civilizations appeared suddenly, already fully developed. 2) That a connection existed between them. 3) Their footprints led back to the Middle East mountains where Noah and his family left the Ark.

The sudden appearance of civilization is itself a memorial to history's one great catastrophe. More importantly, the flood is a historical event of tremendous testimonial importance to modern man.

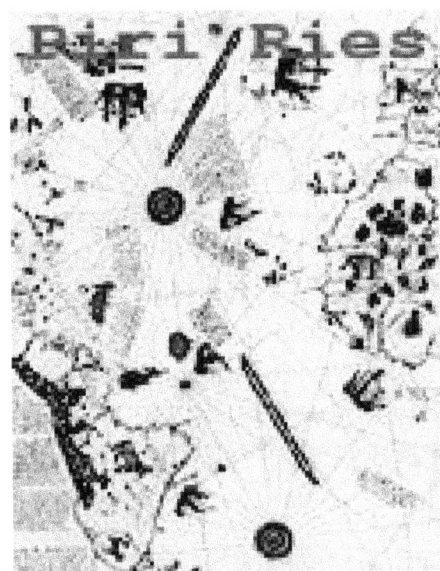

Ancient Maps

....hard evidence that shows the ancient's knowledge of planet earth as seen through their cartographers eyes was far more sophisticated than we have previously supposed. Their maps are surprisingly accurate and reveal knowledge of parts of the earth that were not known until very recently. They also show profound changes have taken place in man's lifetime since the flood, especially at the poles as you shall see.

Maps drawn from the 11th to the 17th century were obviously copied from maps probably drawn thousands of years before. Some maps show Greenland and Antarctica free of ice. (The Piri Reis Map from 1513 shows Antartica)

HAD TO BE COPIES

Obviously these maps..had to have been copied from earlier sources. They display a scientific achievement far surpassing the abilities of the navigators and map-makers of the Renaissance, Middle Ages, the Arab world, or any ancient geographers. THEY HAD TO BE THE PRODUCT OF AN UNKNOWN PEOPLE ANTEDATING RECOGNIZED HISTORY.–end of quote

"Science supports the Bible. That's just how it is. On the other hand, there's the theory of Evolution which is not science. What sustains it? FAITH! Science as Religion. One has to believe that all matter is self created, that this matter in turn created intelligence and, in spite of the fact that it has never been seen, that this inorganic self-creating matter then created life in opposition to observed science. All of this in violation of the 1st and 2nd law of Physics, probability theory, biogenesis and common sense.

This belief system necessitates extraordinary explanatory contortions, strange suppositions and sleight of hand. For example, since catastrophic events in our history would lend too much credence to the truth of the Flood of Noah event, those theories are avoided.

GIANTS ON THE EARTH

It is thought and promoted that man has evolved both physically and technologically from the primitive to the modern on a uniform basis.

Given that presupposition, what do you do as a scientist when you encounter ancient artifacts produced by antique high technology?

As a scientist, you"d better be careful what you say or risk ridicule and professional suicide. As a result one can wind up convincing oneself, other scientific disciplines and the public that these things can be explained by elbow grease or some other arcane theory which is best not examined too closely.(That's how items like true optical lenses get described as "worship artifacts"--because everyone knows the ancients didn't have optical lenses). See True Suppressions

If the Bible account is true, evidence in the form of archeological artifacts and the like should be occasionally found in the fossil and archeological record--and they are!

On subsequent pages we discuss some of the evidence that indicates that what we've been told by science may not be entirely accurate. One note of caution: this information comes from a variety of sources with a variety of beliefs and ideas behind them. Our viewpoint is that of Christians who believe that there is one God and that He created the universe at some time in the past-- nowhere near millions or billions of years ago. Exactly how long ago is besides the point. We believe that there was a worldwide flood and that evolution as an explanation for our existence is a fairy tale. If you believe differently perhaps we can at least agree that what we're being told about origins and the past is seriously flawed.

**The Human Skull in Ancient Rock
Right: Evolution Takes a Hit**

Scientists fear evidence that man is as old as coal
Photo Right:Hard evidence for hard hearts? Solid rock proof for hard heads? Smithsonian squelching evidence again?

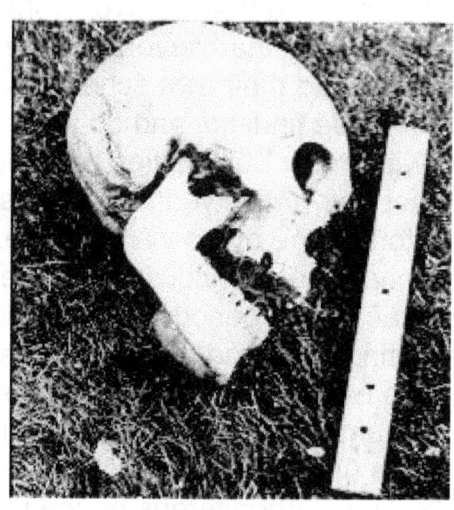

"Physical evidence currently exists that proves man inhabited the earth while coal was being formed, shaking the very foundations of who we really are and how we really got here. An assortment of human bones and soft organs, transformed to rock-like hardness, has been discovered between anthracite veins in Pennsylvania.

"Since one of the golden rules of geology is that coal was formed during the Carboniferous -- a minimum of 280 million years ago -- it means that man has existed multimillions of years before the ... insectivore from whom the evolutionists claim we eventually evolved.

"However, the scientific establishment has wielded its powerful disdainful influence—deceit, dishonesty, collusion and conspiracy—to prevent evidence of the most important discovery of the 20th century to be documented as fact and, therefore, keep us from learning a monumental truth about ourselves." ...Ed Conrad

Additional Info: Quoted from Anomalies and Enigmas Forum

"Aside from the evidence of bones, evidence of human occupation of this area in Car-

GIANTS ON THE EARTH

boniferous times included one particularly strange item: a petrified handle of some sort of a tool.

"This item was totally petrified and appeared almost to be made of coal; "coalified" might be a better term. Other than that, it appeared entirely similar to and entirely as well-made as any normal handle to an axe or sledge hammer of our own day and evinced a fairly high level of technology. The grain structure of a wooden handle was there.

"It appears that the bones in all cases were there first, that the shale formed up around the bones, and that the bone was then gradually replaced with minerals being carried into the cavities they left by water.

"The human femur bone we saw was very large; I would guess that its owner was eight or nine feet tall.(see "Giants" Page 6) Other than that it entirely resembled a normal femur bone from a man about my size which we had along with us for comparison in photos.

"Vine (an author) has also claimed that the American Indian was here in America from the beginning, his most recent book, "Red Earth, White Lies", strongly challenging the standard Bering land bridge thesis. I should think that what I saw would shatter the Bering land bridge thesis for anybody with lingering doubts.

"The experiences which Ed Conrad has had in trying to present these findings to scientists are entirely in line with what I would expect, given what experience has taught me about scientists in these fields. He has had several writeups in local and regional papers, including one in the Reding Eagle which indicates that all relevant tests have been done, and that all favor Conrad's claims.

"Conrad has had several prominent scientists agree to the validity of his claims, and yet these had their own schedules and projects and none were willing to attempt to take any of these findings and do anything with them, and attempts to deal with the Smithsonian and with major universities has been much like beating his head against a tree and, as of the last four or five years, he had simply given up. That, of course, was in the age just prior to the age of the WWW page...

"Conrad has previously assumed that his findings indicated man's presence on Earth in the accepted period of the Carboniferous age, i.e. almost 300 million years ago, and his writings in some of the documents noted here reflect that.

"The evidence seems to suggest one of three possibilities:

"1. humans/hominids were around in the Carboniferous period, conventionally dated to 300m (million) years ago.

"2. The Carboniferous period is vastly more recent than conventionally dated.

"3. The evidence is the result of an elaborate hoax.

"I rule possibility 3 out from my own direct observations; the femur bone embedded in shale along with other petrified bone embedded in shale boulders could not possibly be faked. Item 1 does not strike me as plausible for numerous reasons, not the least of which being that no complex species such as ours has ever lasted that long.

"I thus see the second possibility as the only viable one, and would recommend the section of Velikovsky's "Earth in Upheaval" titled "Collapsing Schemes" as a starting point for anybody seeking further information.

"It would appear that all of the dating schemes we are familiar with are simply FUBAR, standard army jargon meaning "Fouled Up Beyond Any Recognition". Either of possibili-

GIANTS ON THE EARTH

ties 1 and 2 above should cause major grief for evolutionists; the one requires man to be here long before monkeys or apes were, the other indicates there hasn't been time for evolution."--Endquote

1900: "There is nothing new to be discovered in physics now, All that remains is more and more precise measurement."... Kelvin

"So many centuries after the Creation, it is unlikely that anyone could find hitherto unknown lands of any value." - Spanish Royal Commission, rejecting Christopher Columbus' proposal to sail west

CREDIT: JON HUGHES/NARG; SMITHSONIAN INSTITUTION

Some fossils are rare, but this one recently unearthed in eastern Oregon may be positively mythic. In life, the 2-meter-long Jurassic seagoing crocodile (above), discovered by members of the North American Research Group, sported scales, needlelike teeth, and a fishtail. Some paleontologists, including Stanford University researcher Adrienne Mayor, think similar fossils may have inspired Native American representations of water monsters. Mayor notes the croc's "remarkable" resemblance, for example, to a 19th century Kiowa artist's drawing (inset) of a legendary water serpent....Science

Yeah, or they could have seen one! Maybe they weren't extinct millions of years ago! Don't be thrown by the antlers, they are fairly common in "sea monster" descriptions. It's much more likely that the Kiowa's actually saw this creature rather than that they assembled the bones like a paleoentologist and then painted the result! Don't forget that the experts have been known to put the wrong head on a dinosaur (brontosaurus) or place a bone on the wrong end...

There is something in every generation and perhaps every culture that causes it to feel that the sum of its knowledge and scientific sophistication is such that it can see the end of science... that everything worth knowing is pretty much known. If we now know everything, then those before us knew nothing.

Whatever else flows from this "hubris", one consequence is that historical scientific data and observations will probably be discounted.

If some prior generation reported on phenomena, particularly that which doesn't fit the current paradigm or mode of scientific thinking, such phenomena is easily discounted, even if dutifully reported by scientists and other learned men of that generation.

If we find hundreds of reports of men of giant stature found throughout parts of North, South and Central America, even in the scientific literature of the day, we might wonder why they couldn't have taken more care with measurements.

And if we find that there were hundreds of reports of "sea monster" sightings in the rivers, seas and oceans and washed upon beaches in bygone eras, be it printed in the popular press or in scientific jour-

Copyright Orkney Museum

GIANTS ON THE EARTH

nals, we marvel at their naiveté and superstitious beliefs, no matter the number and character of the eyewitnesses.

Of course, they likely had it coming, having taken the same condescending attitude towards the historical and eyewitness accounts of the generations that preceded them. How can we take seriously the accounts of such phenomena when we know that the scientists of bygone eras believed that vermin could spontaneously generate from old rags and filth?

Maybe because this generation of scientists believe that the entire universe spontaneously generated from…….nothing! How will future, presumably more enlightened generations evaluate our eyewitness accounts?

Notwithstanding the foregoing, a brief outline of certain articles of interest from the recent past follows. I'll have to admit at the outset that clearly the testimony of people who wore such funny hats, dresses and pants, and bathed maybe once or twice a week, has to be discounted.

Source: New York Times, 1925

We'd like to think we would have written something like this note Mr. Chambers wrote back in 1925. In the fall of 1924, Samuel Hubbard, curator of archaeology at the Oakland Museum, along with Charles Gilmore a paleontologist, led a scientific expedition to the Hava Supai Canyon in Arizona. In the course of their expedition, called the Doheny Expedition, after the oilman who funded the trip, they discovered several ancient drawings that stirred scientific controversy.

'The drawings included representations of dinosaurs and an elephant (which supposedly never lived in North America) . Responding to the Darwinist naysayers of his day, in this case a Dr. Wessil (no fooling, that was his name!) Mr. W.D. Tenbroeck dropped a little "dinosaurs, in literature, history and art" in a letter to the editor of the New York Times in April, 1925.

"Dr. Wessil seems unaware of similar drawings of dinosaurs, one of which was recently discovered at by W.L. Chambers at Grand Lake in the Colorado Rockies. Cuvier wrote in the last century in "Revolution du Globe":

""If anything can justify the hydra and other monsters, whose figures were so often repeated by medieval historians, it is incontestably the plesiosaurus.""

We read in the Memoire a l'Academie of the naïve astonishment of Geoffrey Saint-Hilaire when M. de Paravay showed to him in some old Chinese works and Babylonian tiles, dragons, saurians, ornithorynchuses and extinct animals which he thought unknown on earth till his own day.

These are but two of many similar quotations available. How could these ancients know anything of extinct monsters of the carboniferous or Mesozoic times, unless they had seen these monsters themselves or possessed descriptions of them in their traditions….."?

He goes on to mention other "ooparts" (out of place artifacts) such as the report of a gold thread embedded in rock reported in Scientific American as well as a piece of metal which had been shaped 'geometrically" and "frozen" in a lump of tertiary coal.

Giants in Those Days

"There were giants in the earth in those days; and also after that"…Genesis 6:4

Apparently, there were hundreds and perhaps thousands of reported discoveries of giant human remains in antiquity, in many parts of the world. It's not clear how men who

GIANTS ON THE EARTH

were clearly "modern" and yet "gigantic" fit into evolutionary theory, but their existence is clearly mentioned in the bible. The Bible also mentions that some of these giants of old had extra fingers and toes, a feature often noted in the antique reports that have come down to us.

I would note that sometimes skeletal remains as "short" as 6 feet 3 inches were reported as giants, which almost gets me in, cheapening the category somewhat. Here I present just a few of the many reported discoveries.

Hints Giant Ancestors
Dr. F. Weidenreich Tells of Java Jawbone and China Tooth
New York Times, July 1946

We don't know for sure what kind of giant primate was discovered by Dr. Weidenreich in 1946 but he seemed to believe that some of the remains were human. In my humble opinion and that of many, remains identified as primitive humans were actually simply the remains of apes, chimps or gorillas. Still, according to the bible, there really were giants in those days.

"Evidence that some of modern man's earliest ancestors might have been giants ranging up to twice the size of a male gorilla was disclosed today by Dr. Frantz Weidenreich, research associate of the Museum of Natural History.

"....It might not be too far from the truth if we suggest the Java giant was much bigger than any living gorilla and that the Chinese giant was correspondingly bigger than the Java giant-that is one and one half times as large as the Java giant and twice as large as a male gorilla, he said.

"He added that there were mere indications thus far that the giants were older than all other human types......"

Giants Survive the Age of Fable
New York Times, July 12, 1925

"An American engineer, driven to shelter in a storm in the mountains of Western Chihuahua found at hand a cavern and in its dimness, made out great bales wrapped in leather. He opened one and in the flicker of a torch discovered the skeleton of a man 12 feet tall.

"All around him there were others, skeletons of men so big that even in a sitting posture they rose six feet, like columns and in the clay of the cavern floor was a footprint 18 inches long".

The engineer who made the discovery was identified simply as Nesbitt and the 1925 article went on to suggest that plans were afoot to move the remains to a local museum for study. A follow-up article further details that there were eight skeletons between 10 and 12 feet in height and that a local museum was mounting an expedition to visit the site and return with artifacts. The area had a history of stories about giant former inhabitants.

Unearth the Bones of 10 Foot Giants.
Gold hunters Report the Discovery in Great Burial Mounds Southwest of Tepic, Mexico.
New York Times, May 14, 1926

GIANTS ON THE EARTH

Tepic, Mexico. "Discovery of the bones of a race of giants who towered more than 10 feet in height was reported here today by Captain by Captain D.W. Page, an American and Captain F.W. Devalda, an Englishman who returned from an unsuccessful search for legendary Spanish goldmines.

The two men said they made their discovery in the great burial mounds in mountains southwest of here and that the state of preservation of the bones indicated that the giant race lived in that section more that 500 years ago ...

A Race of Giants in Old Gaul
The London Globe, 1892

"In the year 1890 some human bones of enormous size, double the ordinary in fact were found in the tumulus of Castelnau, (Herault) and have since been carefully examined by Prof. Kiener, who while admitting that the bones were those of a very tall race, nevertheless finds them abnormal in dimensions and apparently of morbid growth."

It would seem that Prof Kiener, like many of his race (professors) is hedging his bets by claiming that an entire race of giants simply had a pituitary problem.

Reports Find of Bones of Men Eight Feet Tall
Mining Engineer Tells of Discovery in Sonora by Laborers Digging in a Cemetery.
New York Times, December 1930

Tucson, Arizona. "Discovery of apparent remains of a race of giants has been made a Sayopa, Sonora a mining town 300 miles south of the Mexican border J.E. Coker, a mining engineer reports that laborers clearing ranch land near the Yaqui River dug into an old cemetery where bones of men averaging eight feet in height were found buried tier on tier.

The heads of the skeletons Coker said, were especially large.

Bernard Brown, curator of the American Museum of Natural History sent out from Darwin Studios central casting said '"blah, blah, ..blah harrumph! Nope!" (paraphrased)

Giant Skeletons Found
Archeologists to Send Expedition to Explore Graveyards in New Mexico Where Bones were Unearthed
New York Times, Feb. 11, 1902

"Owing to the discovery of a race of giants in Guadalupe, New Mexico, antiquarians and archeologists are preparing an expedition further to explore that region".

The giant skeletons were reported to have been found near Mesa Rico, an area 200 miles southwest of Los Vegas, Nevada.

"Luiciana Quintana on whose ranch the ancient burial plot is located, discovered two stones that bore curious inscriptions and beneath these were found in shallow excavations the bones of a frame that could not be less than 12 feet in length.

The men who opened the grave said that the forearm was 4 feet long and that in a well preserved jaw, the teeth ranged in size from that of a hickory nut to that of the largest walnut in size.

The chest of the being is reported to have a circumference of 7 feet."

GIANTS ON THE EARTH

Skeleton of Giant Found
New York Times, November 1856
We note a trend here; no one seemed to be digging up their own giants in those days.

"A day or two since, workmen engaged in sub soiling the grounds of Sheriff Wickham at his vineyard in East Wheeling, came across a human skeleton."

"…. The impression made by the skeleton in the earth and the skeleton itself were measured by the sheriff and a brother of the craft locale, both of whom were ready to swear that it was 10 feet nine inches in length. It's bones and teeth were almost as large as those of a horse".

Find Skeleton of Giant
Idaho Road Men Dig Up Bones of Prehistoric Herbivorous Woman
New York Times, March 17, 1924

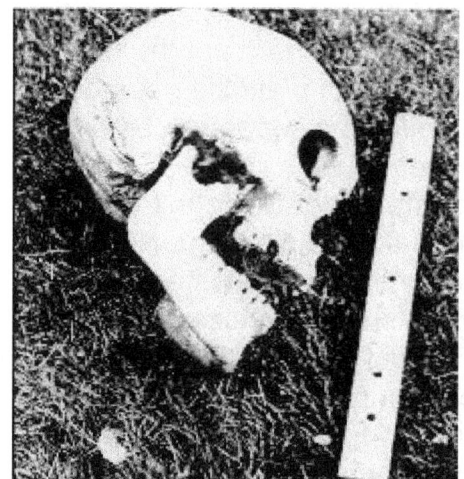

Lewiston, Idaho. "A huge skeleton, believed to be that of a prehistoric human being has been discovered in Salmon River Country by two members of the State Highway Dept., who brought their find to the City".

The bones were to be sent to the Smithsonian for study and were reported to have been found in a cliffside at a depth of 50 feet. Physicians thought that the skeleton which was largely intact was that of a woman and was more than eight feet long.

Photo: The "Lovelock Skull"
with yardstick for comparison

"Belief that the person was of an herbivorous race was expressed owing to the peculiar formation of the jaws and teeth. Both the upper and lower jaws each had only ten teeth, all of which were intact."

Chilean Fossil Man Seen
Skull, Believed to be that of Human Giant, Found Near Conception
New York Times, November 1941
Summary: A human skull found 60 feet underground during a coal mining operation was reported to be from a man judged to be from nine to ten feet tall. An examination by experts determined an ear to ear internal spread of nine inches and ten inches at the base of the cranium.

The Boneyards/MegaFauna
"The waters rose and covered the mountains to a depth of more than twenty feet. Every living thing that moved on the earth perished—birds, livestock, wild animals, all the creatures that swarm over the earth, and all mankind. Everything on dry land that had the breath of life in its nostrils died. Every living thing on the face of the earth was wiped out; men and animals and the creatures that move along the ground and the birds of the air were wiped from the earth. Only Noah was left, and those with him in the ark"….Genesis 7

GIANTS ON THE EARTH

Russians Report Finding Dinosaurs by the Million
New York Times, November 1948

Moscow— "Soviet scientists just returned from Mongolia said today that they discovered the bones of millions of dinosaurs and other prehistoric creatures in the southwestern Gobi desert.

The site is reportedly near an ancient river in the desert. The dinosaurs were found at a depth of between approximately 50 feet to 130 feet.

"Among the prize specimens Professor Yefremov said were a horned dinosaur 36 feet long, one of five such ever found and a 98 foot five inch dinosaur that walked on its hind legs."

Gigantic Fossils of Animals Found
East African Cites Sheep as Big as Horses, Hogs with Elephant like Tusks
New York Times May 11, 1956

Readers of s8int.com certainly and others will know that Dinosaurs were not the only giants of the past. Giant versions of many, many animals and even of plant life have been discovered over the years. Science often gives these mega animals a separate name within the species but typically they only differ from their smaller cousins in size.

Creationists tend to support the idea that these animals existed prior to the fall, when animals and plants lived under perfect conditions. According to this article in the New York Times, Darwinists suspect that they were caused by something in the water.

"The remains of gigantic animals have been found, including sheep the size of present-day cart horses, hogs with tusks like elephants have been dug out of an ancient gorge at Olduvai in East Africa. Two giant human teeth have also been found."

".....Specimens have been brought to London by the man who found them for comparative study. He is Dr. Louis S.B. Leakey, Director of the Coryndon Museum at Nairobi, Kenya......"

Along with the animal fossils, he has found according to the article, numerous stone tools and implements of a group of people who he calls Chellean man and which he suggests are either extremely large or of average stature with very large teeth!

Again quoting from the article;

"Dr. Leakey has found the complete skeleton of a Pleistocene sheep with a horn-span of fourteen feet. He also unearthwed wild hogs the size of a rhinoceros with elephant sized tusks. He has found a giant sized giraffe, baboons as big as modern gorillas, massive zebras and antelopes."

(A special note to chicken, cattle and turkey ranchers follows)

"....The Olduvaian animals of 400,000 years ago probably lived in the delta of a big river in Dr. Leakey's estimation. As the erosion or breakdown of the rocks in pluvial times was two or three times what it is today, vital salts known as trace-elements collected in unusually large quantities and were taken up by the vegetation there. The vegetation, in turn was eaten by the delta haunting animals which grew to abnormal size...."

Eagles and Their Prey
From the Cornhill
New York Times, Dec. 24, 1899

GIANTS ON THE EARTH

"There is at the present moment in the museum of natural history, a model of a skull of a gigantic eagle so large that the imagination can scarce fit it into the life of this planet at all.

The whole head is larger than that of an ox, and the beak resembles a pair of hydraulic shears. Unlike most of the giant beasts, this eagle which inhabited Patagonia appears from its remains to have differed little from the existing species. Its size alone distinguishes it."

"…It could have killed and torn to piece creatures as large as a bison, and whirled up in the sky and dropped upon the rocks the gigantic carapaced animals of Patagonia as easily as the modern California eagles drops the tortoises upon which it feeds."

Dragons/Sea Monsters/Dinosaurs

"So God created the Great Dragons" …Genesis 1:21 The Latin Vulgate; 5th Century

---

Monster Unique in European Seas
Pictures and Measurements Taken Before Waves Break Carcass at Cherbourg
Covered with Fine Hair, Head Roughly Like That of a Camel
Link to Lock Ness Scouted
New York Times, March 1934

Cherbourg. "Nothing even remotely resembling the sea monster that was washed ashore at Querqueville, two miles west of here has ever been seen in this part of the world."

According to the article, the sea monster when discovered had been in one piece but the action of the waves and of scavengers soon broke the carcass into several pieces. In the interim however, photographs and measurements had been taken. The creature was measured at twenty five feet.

The article goes on;

"The skin was bluish grey and covered with white hairs. The tail and fins had the same hairy covering but in addition had white bristles described as like those of an elephant. The tail as it was seen yesterday was bifurcated like that of a seal but was far larger and enormously powerful. Two lateral fins at the shoulder seemed almost paddle shaped. The creature had also a dorsal fin.

br> What was most remarkable was the neck which was slightly more than three feet long, putting the monster definitely out of the class of whales…."

Details in the article include the fact that the liver was about 15 feet long.

A professor Corbiere who examined the creature said that it was certainly the first creature of its kind to wash ashore there. He opined that he didn't know that much but was certain that it was unrelated to the Loch Ness creature. He guessed that it was a hyperoodon, (beaked whale) even though they generally don't have necks.

A Sea Serpent in Iowa
The Monster who Startled Farmers and Fed on Their Hogs
New York Times, October 1893

"A prodigious serpent has been terrorizing residents near Scranton, Iowa this summer, is stated by a paper of that state. Whether it was a sea monster that had worked its

GIANTS ON THE EARTH

way up the Mississippi or the summer resort sea serpent attracted by the World's Fair has not been definitely settled".

According to the article reprinted by the Times, hog farmers of the general area had been losing hogs and devised several strategies to run down the culprit. A neighbor of farmer Jacob Black, while taking a short cut through his pasture encountered the culprit after hearing the squeal of a hog:

".....looking up he saw a hog that would weigh 200 pounds in the coil of a snake and the hog lifted seven or eight feet from the ground".

".....The snake seemed to pay no attention to the man but after smashing the life out of the hog very leisurely wended his way to the river and went over the bank into the same."

According to the report, a neighbor who saw the serpent said that it was surrounded by other little ones of about eight feet in length. He shot two of them and reported that they were covered in scales like a fish only coarser.

The story goes on to recount the hunt for the serpent near the river where they found burrows where the snake apparently hung out. Their shooting produced mostly anger and a shrill whistle from the sea serpent who departed by way of the river.

"They describe the monster as being at least 40 feet in length; they say its head was about the size of a calf's head and the body in the largest diameter about ten inches"

Find Huge Sea Monster
Scientists Unable to Name Creature Dead on Florida Coast
New York Times, Feb. 1921

"Scientists and deep-water fisherman here are puzzled of the finding of a huge sea monster off the coast of Soldier's Key, a few miles south of Miami, which they are unable to name. The body of the creature was found three weeks ago by Elmer. E Garretson of L.I.,N.Y who today towed part of the skull to Miami. This fragment is fifteen feet long, seven feet wide and weighed three tons".

Mr. Garretson said that he was unable to see the full length of the creature but that he did see that it was at a minimum, eighty feet long. At the time he saw the creature it was being eaten by many sharks.

A Mississippi Monster
New York Times, Sept. 1877

This "sea monster" described in this story bears a striking resemblance to the "Stronsay Beast" (above)one of several over the years seen near the Orkney Isands. This drawing was done after the Stronsay beast washed up on shore there in 1808, some 69 years prior to this sighting in Missippi.

"The Stronsay beast was first sighted on September 25, 1808, lying on rocks at Rothiesholm Head, in the south-east of the island.

There, John Peace, a local man fishing off the coast, was puzzled by the sight of sea-birds flocking around what looked like an animal's corpse on the rocks.

Turning his little boat, and watched by another Stronsay man, George Sherar, Peace made his way to the carcass. But what he found was unlike anything he had encountered before. Lying on the rocks was the remains of a serpent-like creature, with a long, eel-like neck and three pairs of legs.

GIANTS ON THE EARTH

.....The beast was described as serpentine, measuring exactly 55 feet long, with a neck measuring ten feet three inches long. The head was like that of a sheep, with eyes bigger than a seal's. Its skin was grey and rough to the touch. However, if stroked from the head down the back, it was said to be as "smooth as velvet".

Six "limbs" extended from the body and a bristly mane of long, wiry hair grew from the beast's shoulders down to its tail. These silver coloured bristles were said to glow eerily in the dark.

Source for quote and drawing, and the Complete Story Here: Orkneyjar, the Heritage of the Orkney Islands

"Mr. Jacob Erst....was riding along the bank of the river when he saw a monster of hideous mein lying on the sand.

Mr. Erst set off on horseback to secure some witnesses (according to the article) and returned with a few witnesses armed with shotguns.

"A more intricate animal has seldom if ever been seen outside the geographical area of cheap whiskey. A hasty survey was made of the monster....he was found to be seventy feet long.

His enormous body consisted principally of snake, with a variety of bird, beast and reptile attachments. The head was shaped like that of a dog with a long pelican's bill.....The bill in this instance was five feet long which is not out of proportion to the entire length of the monster.....

The animal's body was about the diameter of a flour barrel and was covered by large and brilliant scales. The neck was ornamented by a horse's main of great length.....In addition to six strong legs the monster also had fins of such immense size to more properly be called paddles."

The monster was reported to also have an intricate fan on the end of his tail and left the area when shot at via the river.

Sandy Hook Ship Sees Sea Monster
Scientists Hope to Classify "Transparent Creature" Which is 40 Feet Long
New Search Is Planned
Frogmen with Cameras Try to Verify Findings in Area Called "Mud Hole"
John Devlin, New York Times, Aug 20, 1963

"A 40 foot "what is it" that somewhat resembles a transparent serpent has been sighted 25 miles southeast of Times Square by Federal scientists in the ocean off Sandy Hook, New Jersey.

Dr. Lionel A. Wolford, Director of the United States Fish and Wildlife Research center....... saw the creature. He said it undulated near the surface in a manner resembling the storied sea serpents.

....It is an invertebrate. It looked like so much jelly. I could see no bones, eyes, nose or mouth......looking as though it were made of fluid glass."

There were several witnesses and the good doctor was unable to find a suitable suspect for the sighting in the literature. The sighting was made from the research vessel Challenger. Dr. Wolford was headed back out in 1963 to try to get photographs. Do you see any photos?

GIANTS ON THE EARTH

300 Foot Sea Monster Off Sandy Hook
Scientific American 1879

"Kittell was the first to see it. He says: 'I looked out and saw a large head and portions of the body of a most terrible looking monster. It was wriggling slowly along like a snake, the head and several portions of the body showing above the water.

It was not a whale, as there was not more than twelve feet of water where it was, and a whale as large as that would necessarily have been in view all the time.....

George Lohsen makes the following statement: 'I took the glasses and ran down to the water's edge and leveled the glasses at the monster's head. The front of the head was square, with a projection about two feet long extending from the top of the head.

The eye was seven or eight inches in diameter, of a shiny black, and it appeared bulged out considerable. There looked to be a white rim around it. The animal's length was at least 300 feet from the head to the tail, as seen by us, not making allowances for the crooks in the body.'

Harry Foster, another of the crew, says: 'I got up and looked out, and saw the devilshest looking fish I ever put my eyes on. It was moving along about as fast as a man could walk. I took a pair of strong glasses and followed it along the beach. It was not more than 300 yards from the shore. With the glasses the head looked as large as a hogshead.

The front of the head looked square, and was about three feet high, with a projection two feet long extending from the top of its head. The eye toward the shore was as large as the top of my hat, was shiny black and had a white edge. . . .

From the head to the tail it was at the least calculation 300 feet long. It was moving along the water the same as an eel. The head and several parts of the body was constantly out of the water. It was some species of serpent. . . . not a whale. . . . This thing did not spout, and showed no fins on any part of its body excepting on the tail, which was formed like that of an eel.'"

Source: Beard, Daniel C., The Sea Serpent Accounted For, Scientific American, p. 1 (Dec. 27, 1879)./Historicpelham.com

Flying Creatures

"Get your guns ready, the Devil is coming." Joseph Denton, quoted in the Plattsburgh Sentinel in 1894, after seeing a monstrous bird approaching with wings like "barn doors". Joseph and his fellow hunters were armed but declined to shoot at the huge bird for fear of making it angry.

West Virginia "Monster" is Sighted in Daylight.
New York Times, Nov 1966

One of the early mothman stories.

"The mysterious "monster" of Macon County" struck" again, this week in its first daylight appearance, pursuing an automobile at speeds up to 70 miles per hour".

Thomas Ury was the driver and the eyewitness who claimed to have been shook up by the encounter. Mr. Ury decribed the bird as being six feet tall with approximately a 10 foot wingspan. Ury said that the "bird" had buzzed his car and then circled and chased him at high speed having no problem keeping up with him. It flew at approximately 75 feet.

Authorities and experts were of the opinion that the monster was a sandhill crane.

GIANTS ON THE EARTH

Winged Sea Monster Reported in Levant
Currant Laden Felucca Sunk When Sailer Belts Reptile with Pomegranate
Has Eyes Like Sidelights
New York Times, Aug 13, 1922

This particular episode allegedly documents a dragon in every conceivable sense except for breathing fire.

Photo of dragons taken from an airplane above the Himalayas. (www.dajiyuan.com)

Photo: This "Tibet Dragon", most likely an optical illusion, was photographed from an airplane window over Tibet.

"After a long absence, the sea monster has appeared once more. According to reports just received from Constantinople and Smyrna, the elusive creature is disporting itself in the Mediterranean...."

The most thrilling story was brought here last week by officers of the Greek Liner Constantinople, who said that motor launches armed with one- pounder quick-firing guns were searching the sea of Marmora for a winged marine monster which had been circling Dog Island at great speed for three of four days".

....."When the commander of the fort fired a gun in the direction indicated by the scared sponge divers the serpent rose to an altitude of 5,000 feet and flew away......"

....."The head of the nautical reptile was fully 10 feet across, with two enormous reddish green eyes butting out on either bow like a ship's sidelights, while its immense flappers looked as if they weighed a ton each".

An eyewitness reported that the serpent had a "beam" down the middle of his back which was 15 feet high and the length of the monster was fully 50 feet.

Look, I might be gullible, but what kind of color is reddish green?

GIANTS ON THE EARTH

Antiquity of "Modern" Man
The Antiquity of Man
New York Times, April 23, 1873

The Miocene Epoch, which is mentioned prominently in this article brief, is currently described as spanning the time period from 5.3 million years ago to 23.8 million years ago. It, like the other "periods" gets moved around in time occasionally whenever evolutionists need to make something fit.

From an evolutionary perspective, modern man was not supposed to be around at that time. In fact, even primitive man wasn't supposed to be around yet.

From a Biblical perspective finding evidence of modern man as far back as you look is what we expect because the universe, the earth and man were all created in the same week. Anomalies like the ones mentioned in this 1873 article suggest to us that the scientific dating system is useless, especially for dates over 5,000 years or so.

The Levant Herald reported for this story that a Frank Calvert, an "experienced" geologist had made an "immense" find which was certain to contravene then current scientific beliefs concerning the age of man and move the existence of "modern man" back into the Miocene era, much further than had been previously thought by those influenced by Darwin.

"I have had the good fortune to discover in the vicinity of the Dardanelles conclusive proofs of the existence of man during the Miocene period of the Tertiary Age. From the face of a cliff composed of strata of that period, from a geological depth of 830 feet, I myself extracted a fragment of a joint of a bone of either a dinotherium or a mastodon, on the convex side of which is deeply incised the unmistakable figure of a horned quadruped with arched neck, lozenge shaped chest, long body, straight forelegs and broad feet.

There are also traces of seven or eight other figures.....The whole design encircles the exterior portion of the fragment, which measures 9 inches in diameter and five inches in thickness."

He also reports finding other bones nearby in the same strata containing bones which had been split for the purpose of getting to the marrow inside. Mr. Calvert reports that several other "prominents' scientists had agreed that the items had come from the Miocene strata. He also reports finding what some might quaintly refer to as "mega tools" weighing up to 9 pounds.

Find Ancient Bones Near Pittsburg
Scientists Declare 49 Skeletons are Those of Mound-Builders
Living 10,000 Years Ago
All Baked Before Burial
Bodies Were Interred in A Circle With Faces
Upward and Shelved Between 11 Layers of Stone
New York Times, Sept 1932

How does the current paradigm deal with unknown, "advanced cultures" in the Americas prior to the arrival of the Native Americans? Not so well. They seem to be personas non grata. One reason is that certain scientists don't want the timeline for the arrival of peoples on this continent pushed too far back.

GIANTS ON THE EARTH

This story has giants, baked bodies and weird burial rites but I've really got to wrap it up, this article is getting too long. I mean, the title says; A Brief look! Is anybody still here? Please turn out the lights when you're finished reading.

"The unearthing of 49 bodies, 10,000 years old, focused the interest of scientists the world over on a wooded hill near Pittsburg.

.....They constitute one of the richest archaeological discoveries ever recorded in Pennsylvania, and tell the crude history of an ancient civilization.

One skeleton is of a giant nearly eight feet tall".

The discovery was made by a State Archeologist. The bodies were buried face up, on different levels between 11 layers of stone. Maybe it was an ancient space saver cemetery.

"Were one to picture the place as a huge earthen doughnut one would have noticed bodies side by side and head to toe around the periphery of the huge gouged ring.

Scientists were certain that the ancient people were completely separate and distinct from the "Native American" People.

Relics At UR Point to Pre-Flood Race
Religious Symbols Discovered Below 56-Foot Level of Shaft Traced to Prehistoric Era Pottery Factory Found
New York Times, February 24, 1930

"Special to The New York Times. Phil, Pa,. Feb 22—Religious symbols, the handiwork of peoples who existed in Southern Mesopotamia before the great flood described in Genesis, have been unearthed at the site of Ur of the Chaldees by the joint expedition of the University of Pennsylvania Museum and the British Museum, according to a report just received from C. Leonard Woolley, the Field director.

A complete prehistoric pottery factory and a copper figure of Rim-Sin, a Sumerian king who lived about 1900 B.C., were also uncovered.

As a result of the recent discoveries Mr. Woolley believes the expedition is able to trace the chronology of Southern Mesopotamia "from the time of man's first settlement in the marshes to the close of the Sargonid period, about 2600 B.C.""

Mr. Woolley went on to describe the dig; they had found levels of buildings representing 8 ages superimposed upon each other. They had taken the dig down to the 56-foot level at a date they estimated to be 3200 B.C.

Below the eighth level they found a pottery factory, represented by voluminous pottery shards and a large number of kilns. The kilns were buried on four levels testifying to the long span of time that the factory was in existence.

They discovered levels of graves and pottery. At one point the pottery was simple and almost primitive and yet below that the pottery technique color and style was high.

They reasoned that the high style pottery, below the level of the simple pottery and represented a pre-flood civilization. The primitive pottery above represented a people

GIANTS ON THE EARTH

A CORNER OF THE RUINED PALACE OF ASSUR-NAZIR-PAL

climbing back up to civilization after the flood.

"The upper graves marked the degeneration of the al'Ubaid period, the lower illustrated its zenith. In three of the latter we have found objects of a different sort, painted clay figurines of women grotesquely modeled on an archaic convention. Too delicate to be dolls, these queer slender figures, as also one of a painted bird with outspread wings, must be connected with the religion of the race which inhabited Ur before the flood.

"Already we have reached the levels that mark that disaster".

An undisturbed copper "idol" in the form of a king with a basket of mortar on his head and models of bricks at his feet they decided marked a building as a temple of Enki, the water-god and its restoration in 1900 B.C.

One of Woolley's many discoveries in the region was a "giant headress from Ur--at least claimed to be by some.... From the Royal Tombs of UR. Giant gold headress of Queen Puabi. This Gold headress is three times the size of a 'normal' human head....(various)

"Sir Leonard Woolley the famed British Archaeologist is credited with the discovery of the tomb of Pu-Abi, which was excavated along with some 1800 other graves at the "Royal Cemetery of Ur" by Woolley and his team between 1926 and 1932.

Pu-Abi's tomb was nearly unique among the other excavations not only because of the large amount of incredibly high quality and well preserved grave goods, but also because her tomb had been untouched by looters through the millennia. She was also buried with five soldiers and 23 "ladies in waiting for", retainers who had apparently poisoned themselves (or been poisoned by others) to serve their mistress in the next world.

The amount of grave goods that Woolley uncovered in Pu-abi's tomb were staggering: A magnificent, if heavy, golden headdress made of golden leaves, rings, and plates, a superb lyre, complete with the golden and lapis-lazuli encrusted bearded bulls head, a profusion of gold table ware, golden, carnelian, and lapis lazuli cylindrical beads for extravagant necklaces and belts, a chariot adorned with lioness' heads in silver, and an abundance of silver, lapis lazuli, and golden rings and bracelets....Wikipedia

Disputed Biblical Stories Get Support from Exhibition of Rare Ancient Relics
New York Times
December 22, 1953
One can't be sure that the Smithsonian would today sponsor an exhibit of 1,500 items calculated to support a "fundamentalist" view of the Bible but back in 1953, they did just

GIANTS ON THE EARTH

that. An article in the New York Times heralded and described the event.

"Washington, Dec 21 (UP)—The Smithsonian Institution is about to open to public view a collection of rare, archaeological finds tracing the history of mankind through 500 centuries. The exhibit provides material support for disputed stories in the Bible.

The ancient treasures—weapons, manuscripts, statuary, mosaics and religious relics—will be on display at the museum Jan. 10 through Jan.27.

Most of the items have been unearthed in the last two decades –a period that has revolutionized archaeological understanding of the Biblical era."

Reportedly, among the exhibits were; copper from King Solomon's mines, the "jawbone of an ass", as utilized by Samson in his battles with the Philistines and notably, a sling from the time of the epic battle between David and Goliath.

William Albright, an Archaeologist from Johns Hopkins University thought that the exhibits would "revolutionize our understanding of the Bible". He thought that the new data provided support for a fundamental understanding of Biblical events.

Among the conclusions reached by the exhibitors was that King Solomon was even more wealthy than he was depicted in scriptures.

FINDS NEAR BAGDAD: Ten Thousand Tablets in an Enormous Building— Possibly AnteDiluvian (Pre-Flood) Records
From the London Times
January 31, 1882

A Mr. Rassam reported to the Times of London on a monumental discovery he had made at a location approximately 15 miles outside of Bagdad in 1882.

"I met with an Arab who told me that he knew of an old ruined city, the remains of which were to be found within five hours of Bagdad—that is to say, taking the computation of three miles an hour, the place he knew was 15 miles from Bagdad.

As we were traveling along the route pointed out by the Arab, we came at a distance of four hours' journeying upon an old ruin that I had never seen before—a ruin of great magnitude—so large, indeed that it must be about three miles in circumference."

Later, while surveying the building they encountered among other things a layer of asphalt, which surprised them. They found a number of Assyrian artifacts including two cylinders, all of which were sent back to the London museum.

Mr. Rassam reported that this City was supposed to have been the oldest city in the world, founded by Noah, after the flood. By tradition, according to Mr. Rassam, Noah was supposed to have stored antediluvian records there in that city.

Subsequently, the team reportedly found 10,000 tablets covered with Assyrian style writing (antediluvian?) all of which were sent back to England.

The Three Stone Heads
Published Feb 18, 1871
New York Times

"Among other interesting relics lately found in Oregon, what are known as the "three stone heads" have attracted much attention, and are now being widely discussed.

These are heads of extinct animals, not men, and so can furnish only collateral data of an ethnological character.

GIANTS ON THE EARTH

They are, nevertheless, extremely interesting, and their discovery may prove of important service in constructing the history of American zoology.

The "Three Stone Heads" were found embedded in stone in the Cascade Range, near Mount Hood, in Eastern Oregon. They are pronounced by the best local authorities to be older than Mount Hood itself, to have been formerly fifteen hundred feet below the surface, and to have been uncovered by the slow action of a mountain ravine through which had flowed the freshets of thousands of years.

The heads belong to an extinct race, and appear to have been allied with a species now widely separated. They had the teeth of ruminants with tusks. One of them must have been something like the camel and something like the tapir and is said to be entirely new to science."

The article describes the second head as being similar to the first but very possibly an entirely different animal altogether and the third head as representing another extinct animal which was much larger than the other two and clearly of a different species.

The rocks from which the stone heads came were supposed to have been of the Miocene (thought by science to span 5.3 million to 23.8 million years ago) or mid Tertiary periods (1.8 million years to 65 million years ago). If the time period is correct, who was around before Mount Hood itelf and was sculpting stone heads of currently extinct creatures?

The author goes on to speculate on the impact such discoveries would have on Darwinism; "with the accumulation of material like these new-found relics, the resources of science will, of course, be increased for the determination of the stupendous problems connected with the origin of the species.

Whether the ancient view of distinct creation in each instance, the Darwinian view of the development of various types from the same original one, the theory of "evolution" through the unfolding of one species into another, or the theory of special providence – creating species for special fields—is to be sustained or exploded by the progress of discovery, we may conjecture but cannot decide."

Curious Relics from the Swiss Lakes
From the Hartford Times, Nov. 7 1866
Copyright New York Times

In 1854, the water level at Lake Zurich had fallen very low and the inhabitants of the lake area took the opportunity to make repairs on the banks. After digging down a foot and a half they began to find tools, and implements of stone, bronze, horn and iron as well as pottery shards.

The remains of piles, long poles driven into the bottom of the lake were found regularly spaced a few feet apart.

"Close examination by Dr. Keller, President of the Swiss Antiquarian Society, satisfied him that these piles had supported a raised platform; that on this platform huts had been raised; and that after being thus occupied, probably for centuries, the structure had been destroyed by fire.

The huts it would seem were for the most part circular in shape, measuring from 10 to 15 feet in diameter; they were of wattles plastered with clay, masses of which, hardened by fire, still bearing the marks received from the wattles when wet, have been recov-

GIANTS ON THE EARTH

ered from the beds of the lakes."

Further investigations have shown that most of the lakes of Europe have been thus inhabited. Up to 1864, 200 such pile villages have been found in Switzerland alone, and some of them of great size, containing not less than 100,000 piles."

The age of the pile villages at that time were estimated to be from three thousand to seven thousand years old or even older. So who were these ancient, unknown peoples with the technology to live above the lakes of Europe drawing their sustenance there from?

The artifacts found indicate that the inhabitants of the "pfahlbauten" ate the meat of the ox, cow and pig, and the now extinct auroch, raised wheat and barley, that their women knitted and made pottery, that of the fruits they ate raspberries, apples and elderberries and that they rode horses.

A strange "water nut", now unknown was found in a hermetically sealed glass tube.

Hunter Says He Saw Prehistoric Monster
Belgian Returns from Congo with a Story of Tracking Down a Brontosaurus
Copyright New York Times
December 13, 1919

London, December 12.—Details of the alleged discovery of a survivor of the prehistoric Brontosaurus are given in a relayed Rueter message from Bulawayo by the Belgian prospector and big game hunter, M. Gapelle, who has returned there from the interior of the Congo States.

He followed up strange footprints for twelve miles and at length, he says, sighted a beast of the rhinoceros order with large scales reaching far down its body."

Of course, there's no longer a dinosaur known as the brontosaurus; scientists had mistakenly placed the wrong head on the body of a sauropod. If M. Gapelle actually did see a dinosaur that day, it would be now called the diplodocus.

"In the 1960's, a leading jewel designer called Emanuel Staub was commissioned by the University of Pennsylvania...to produce replicas of a series of small gold weights obtained in Ghana. ...

So well crafted were they that the animals that they depicted could be instantly identified by zoologists--all but one, that is, which could not be satisfactorily reconciled with any known animal, until Staub saw it." (Shuker, Dr. Karl P.N., In Search of Prehistoric Survivors, 1995, p. 20.)

Originally photographed resting on its hind legs (as if bipedal), this enigmatic Ashanti gold figurine was difficult to identify. Once properly positioned, Staub noted that the mysterious artifact bears a striking resemblance to a dinosaur.

Perhaps this figurine was an attempt to model the sauropod Mokele-mbembe creature that is said to inhabit remote regions of equatorial Africa still today.

According to M. Gapelle, he did what any big game hunter would do when he comes upon a supposedly long extinct, possibly last surviving member of a species; he fired several shots at it whereupon it disappeared, perhaps forever into a swamp.

Mr. Gapelle further described the creature as having very thick, kangaroo like tail, a horn on is snout and a hump on its back.

According to the article the Smithsonian had a team of more than twenty persons in

GIANTS ON THE EARTH

the field at the same time hunting for the same creature and that a number of the Smithsonian team had been killed in a "rail accident."

The article goes on to quote a Dr. G.F. Harmer, zoologist and spoilsport from the British Museum, who doubted (while keeping an open mind) that "any of the race of dinosaurs had survived from so late an age".

Army of French Hunters Tracks "Dragon" with "Wolf Lieutenant" Leading Quest
By Associated Press
Published Sept 3, 1934 New York Times

"St. Gaudens, France, Sept 2.---The ancient wolf lore of this region within the shadow of the once savage Pyrenees was called into play today to track down a "monster with phosphorescent eyes" reported sighted here.

Despite storms sweeping the district, hundreds of hunters and sightseers headed by the St. Gaudens district's "wolf lieutenant" spent the week-end exploring Lake Camon, long regarded by geologists as the last trace of an ancient inland sea, in an effort to find the beast."

At one time in France there were 1,100 wolf lieutenants who acted as the official master of a pack of hounds whose purpose it was to protect communities from dangers such as wolves.

The" monster" in this case was described as "prehistoric", twenty five feet long and five feet thick. It was reportedly covered with scales and had "shining eyes". As of the time of the article, they had not yet found the creature.

Trail of Monster Seen in Scotland
Big-Game Hunter Finds Fresh Tracks of "Four-Fingered Sea Beast" at Loch Ness.
Reports are Reinforced
Many Reliable Residents of the Region Had Told of Seeing Animal 50 Feet Long.
December 22, 1933

Special Cable to the New York Times. London, Dec. 21---M.A Weatherell, Central American big game hunter, has found, according to the Daily Mail, a definite spoor of a huge amphibian n the shores of Loch Ness, the region from which stories of a remarkable "prehistoric sea monster" have emanated lately.

Mr. Weatherell described the creature as being twenty feet long, four fingered with evidence of claw marks or nails left on the bank. He further described the creature as "soft footed" with four pads, eight inches across.

It appeared from tracks and marks which were only "hours old" that the creature had attempted to climb a gravel bank of the Loch and fallen back.

Local eyewitnesses of which there seemed to be many were relieved that someone with some "expert" knowledge was backing there claims. They had chaffed a bit at the skepticism that there reports received.

The "sea monster" had first been reported the previous August and since that time many witnesses, even those of the "conservative type" the writer states had seen the "monster". By conservative, perhaps he meant; non-drinkers.

A Commander Gould, British Navy, retired, an author of a book on the subject, had interviewed 51 eyewitnesses and came to the conclusion that at least one creature in-

GIANTS ON THE EARTH

habited the Loch. Interviewing the 51 witnesses one by one and asking each either to draw or direct a drawing of what they had seen he reached the following conclusion;

The creature is at least 50 feet long with a maximum circumference of 5 feet. The creature tapered at the head and tail. It had four flippers or paddles. It was dark brown or dark grey in color and is able to raise its head quite a distance above the water.

It had a darker area that ran down the center of its back. It had small appendages, possibly gills where one might expect to see ears. It was quite flexible.

Commander Gould went on to speculate that it was simply an elongated form of the "common newt"?

Witnesses had put the speed of the creature at 15 knots (17.3 miles per hour).

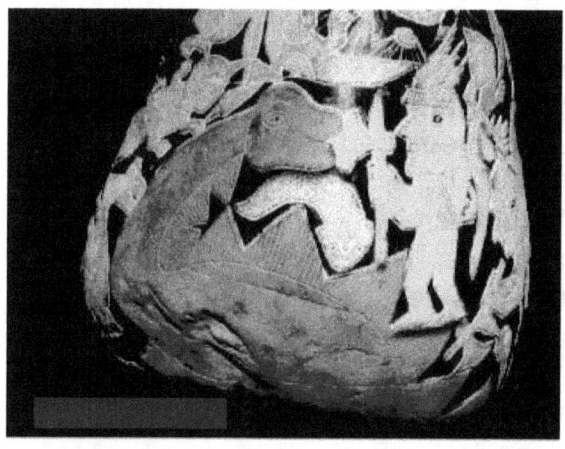

Another What is it?
Man Eaten by Dinosaur?
11/2/1877
Galveston News
From the Carthage (Mo.) Patriot.
One of the "Ica Stones" from Peru showing dinosaur and human interaction in antiquity.

Evolutionists often ask why if men and dinosaurs interacted, no evidence of their fossil remains having been found together exists. One of the aims of several sections of this website has been to show that such evidence exists in quantity, but that it has been lost, suppressed or ignored.

Any scientist who today announced for example that he had found evidence that a dinosaur bone showed evidence of having been butchered by man would not make a name for himself but would rather, end his scientific career.

Evidence supported by science has been discovered numerous times (such as the Doheny Expedition) and according to an article in the Galveston news, reprinted from the Carthage Patriot, another such an impossible interaction was discovered;

"Mr. Henry "Woodard owns a stock rancho in the Indian Territory, in the Peoria Nation, on which is situated the big sulfur spring. The spring is surrounded by a quagmire, which is very deep and " slushy," and so soft that it will not bear any considerable weight.

Mr. W. lately undertook to curb up the spring in order to get water more easily, and while working in the mire came upon what appeared to be an enormous bone. He at once began an examination which disclosed the fact that it was the head of some mammoth beast.

His curiosity was aroused, and, with the assistance of three other men, he began the work of excavation. For four days they worked, but did not succeed in bringing the monster to the surface. They threw off the marl, but could not lift the head of this golitic giant.

They found the skeleton well preserved, and the immense teeth still sat in the jaws. The jaws were both in place and the spinal column attached to the cranium. Tho earth was thrown off from the body to the length of twenty feet, but still the gigantic skeleton remained beneath".

GIANTS ON THE EARTH

The men finally managed to dislodge a number of the creature's ribs which according to the report, were eight feet in length. When the dirt was removed which was encircled by the ribs and bones, Mr. Woodard and the men with him got an even bigger surprise according to the article.

"There lay the skeleton of a human being, with one hundred and two flint arrow points and fifteen flint knives. The cranium indicated that it was the skeleton of an Indian. It would have been impossible for the man to be inside the animal without having been swallowed by him".

The skeleton of the man, it was reported was broken and smashed on its right hand side, providing support at least to the men on site that the injuries had been sustained in a confrontation with the creature.

The witnesses also believed that the creature was carnivorous based on the shape and size of a large molar and two incisors which still survived the passing of years in the upper jaw. There were also tusks on each side of the jaw.

The teeth were exhibited at the offices of the Carthage Patriot and weighed and measured there. The largest tooth weighed eight pounds and measured 8 inches by 4 inches.

" The article concludes with the following:

"All the bones indicate that they have lain buried for an incredibly long period, as they crumble rapidly when brought in contact with the atmosphere. Every circumstance goes to show that these are the largest animal remains ever resurrected, and the teeth, tusks, and structure of the head and jaws prove unmistakably that it was of the carnivorous class."

Plus it had a guy in its stomach?

A Strange Animal Discovered by Hunter in Screven County Swamp
The Queerest Freak on Record
The Hunter was paralyzed with fear and forgot his gun in the excitement
Atlanta Constitution
Feb 11, 1895

The pterosaur wasn't as well known in 1895 as it is today. There certainly was no internet, newspapers still printed few pictures and television was still years away. In the early 1800's scientists still thought the pterosaur was some kind of aquatic creature rather than a flying reptile. In our minds, assuming this report to be a true and accurate account, a sighting of a large pterosaur is the only animal that fits the description.

Sylvania, Ga. Feb 10. (Special) A Screven county hunter relates a thrilling story of a strange animal which he encountered in a swamp....

The hunter relates that he was standing, armed with a rifle behind a stand of trees and

GIANTS ON THE EARTH

was hoping to be able to take a shot at deer passing by. At that time he heard a fairly noisy call that caused his hair to stand on end because it was an unrecognizable and very strange animal sound. The hunter described the sound as being a combination of the sound of a "large duck" with that of a snake's hiss.

"The sound seemed to issue from a thick place surrounding a kind of lagoon. I kept my eyes fasted on the spot with cocked gun in hand...

In a few seconds I heard a kind of splashing in the water and peering through the bushes I saw, about a hundred yards away, what seemed the head of an enormous duck. But I thought surely it was the king of all ducks –for the bill was at least a foot long and as black as could be."

The hunter noted that the creature continued to make his duck/snake call and seemed to be either swimming or wading in the swamp.

"..The creature raised itself up a little and I saw the blackest, ugliest, most loathsome looking animal that ever inhabited this earth."

He described the body of the creature as being three or four feet long and black and he now thought that perhaps he was looking at an alligator because of the teeth and jaws. He continued to crouch behind his tree in fear and wonder and soon had an opportunity to more closely inspect the creature.

"..what I had thought was an alligator stepped up on this little elevation, and then I saw that it had only two feet. As near as I could judge, its legs were about a foot and a half long, and it stood there like some huge blackbird of the night, with its bill stuck downward...."

"It's body was rough and scaly, like an alligator's and the tail went off to a point. It had legs like a turkey or a duck only they were larger and stronger". The hunter reported that he was unable to see its eyes or its feet. Here's where figuring out what the creature was got even more difficult for the hunter.

As is often the case when things seem bad, they got a little worse for the hunter as he continued his observations. The hunter testified that during this period he remained extremely terrified of this unknown creature even though he was armed with a deer rifle.

"After a short while, that seemed an age, the creature gave a kind of spring from the ground, and before I could realize what it was doing it went up into a large tree and sat on the lowest limb. As it did so I could hardly believe my eyes when is saw two dark wings spread out from its side and strike the air with a heavy sound that made my heart sick. I had not noticed before that it had wings; but wings they certainly were although I could see no feathers."

The hunter reports that when the wings were drawn again close to his body, they could not really be seen. At that point, with the creature in the tree with its back to him, that he made his hasty retreat.

Wild Man of the Woods-
The Compiler, Gettysburg 1851

"A gigantic man of the woods has been discovered in Greene county, Arkansas, and a party has been organized to catch him.

When last seen he was pursuing a herd of cattle, who were flying in a state of great alarm, as if pursued by a dreaded enemy. On seeing the party who discovered him, he

GIANTS ON THE EARTH

looked at them deliberately for a short time, turned, and ran away with great speed, leaping from twelve to fourteen feet at a time.

His footprints, according to the article were about thirteen inches long. He was reported to have a gigantic build, to be covered from head to toe with hair. His hair was reported to have been particularly long at the head and shoulders.

An early bigfoot report or an early, unruly neighbor report?

Ocean-Bed Mystery
Soviet Report Trace of Unknown Animal
October 5, 1961
New York Times, October 5, 1961

The Research vessel Vityaz was built in 1939 as the German cargo ship Mars. After the WW2 it was transferred to Soviet Union as war reparation.. She was converted to research ship in 1947-48 and renamed Vityaz. From the early 1950's through the early 70's the ship was responsible for many deep sea discoveries.

Pravda published a photograph of the Ocean bed showing what it called "a gigantic trace of animal so far unknown to science".

"It said the photograph had been taken nearly 10,000 feet down by the staff of the Soviet research ship Vityaz. No further details were provided.

The New Scientist Magazine reprinted the photo and noted that the "gigantic tracks" had been photographed 9,700 feet down on the floor of the Indian Ocean.

Perhaps they are the tracks of leviathan. Perhaps they are artifacts of a pre-flood civilization. If anyone has access to New Scientist Magazine of 1961—the only details given, maybe they could give us a look at the photograph.

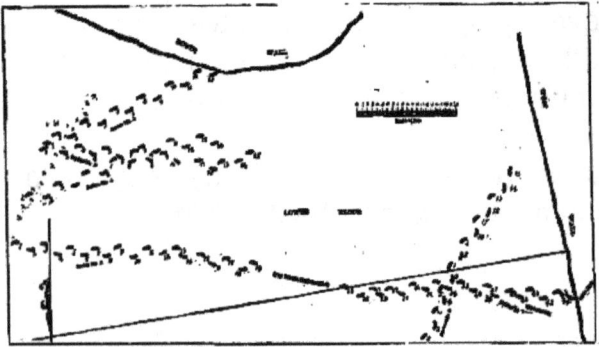

Weekly Nevada State Journal
April 7, 1883
Prehistoric Footprints (gigantic, in sandstone)

We have already written previously about the discovery of fossilized footprints at the Carson Nevada Prison site in 1883. 1883 was such a gentler time in the course of the Darwinist religion, because a number of scientists let themselves get involved with the site in the first place. These days, a report of "colossal human footprints" would be debunked by scientists without a visit to the site or examination of evidence and thus without any risk to career or challenge to the orthodoxy.

A size thirteen shoe is approximately 12 inches long. The sandaled footprints in Nevada were as long as 21.5 inches and eight inches wide. The tracks included those of the elephant, man, the horse, bird and deer, none of whom should have been found in North America at the time sandstone formed. Rocks, no matter what type, are supposed to have formed millions and billions of years

GIANTS ON THE EARTH

before 'complex" life evolved.

According to the article "The scientific world became greatly interested in these tracks, and several members of the California Academy of Science visited the quarry and inspected the tracks. Those who read papers on the subject at the Academy were Dr. H.W. Harkness, C.D. Gibbes, R.E. C. Stearns, Prof. Joseph Le Conte and J.R. Scupham."

Brave men all.

The tracks were laid out as shown in the accompanying diagram by C.D. Gibbes. The scientists surmised that the location of the tracks were near what had been the mouth of an ancient stream. The tracks had been overridden many times by modern riders and animals, but because they were locked in stone, they had not been obliterated.

"Clarence King in his geological survey of the fortieth parallel, the "Lower Quarternary". Referring to this region, he says it is composed of sandstones and clays worn down from the adjacent high mountains and deposited in the water and on the shores of a lake of many hundreds of miles in area…"

According to the 1883 report, the scientists went on to say: "presumably we stand on the shore of this ancient pond or lake, and as we look about us we see the footprints of a variety of animals, among which we recognize those of the mammoth, the deer, the wolf, of many birds, of a horse, and most important of all, the imprints of the sandaled foot of man.

There are six series of the tracks of man, each being represented by a number of footprints (from 8 to 17), in regular order, and each showing more or less plainly, the imprint of a sandal. Besides this, in one of the series the form of the sandal differs markedly from the others.

Each of the imprints furnishes us with evidence, as we believe, that the feet of the one making the tracks were protected by sandals. In no single impression do we find conclusive evidence of this fact, but when we study them as a whole we find that which is wanting in one is furnished by other which follow."

The distance between the left and right man tracks were twice that of current men although the stride proved to be about the same trending to slightly longer than the current average.

About the series of human tracks, scientist G.D. Gibbes' report included the following information:

"Series No. 2 consists of 13 human foot-prints 21 inches long, and 7 inches wide, going in a southwesterly direction until lost in the sandstone bluff at the south wall, which is 22 feet high at this point. This man had a very peculiar shaped foot, and may be said to have toed the mark, he walked as straight as a surveyor running a line……This series covers 40 feet.

Series No. 3 contains 15 human tracks, 18 inches long and 7 wide, going nearly west, with the toes turned out, and stopping rather irregular.

Series No. 4 has 14 tracks, 18 inches long, going nearly parallel to No 2 and crossing No. 3.

Series No. 5 covers 112 feet of ground….."

One might well strain a stomach muscle trying to pin down how old science believes sandstone is. There are various types, believed to have formed between 3 million and 250 million years ago—and even older. What are the implications of the footprints of

GIANTS ON THE EARTH

giant man, birds, wolfs, horses, elephants or mammoths, and deer locked in sandstone? Creatures who were there together before the sandstone formed and set?

Forget about seeing any of the foregoing in a geology or evolutionary textbook. Those scientists back in 1883 weren't writing for posterity.

GIANTS ON THE EARTH

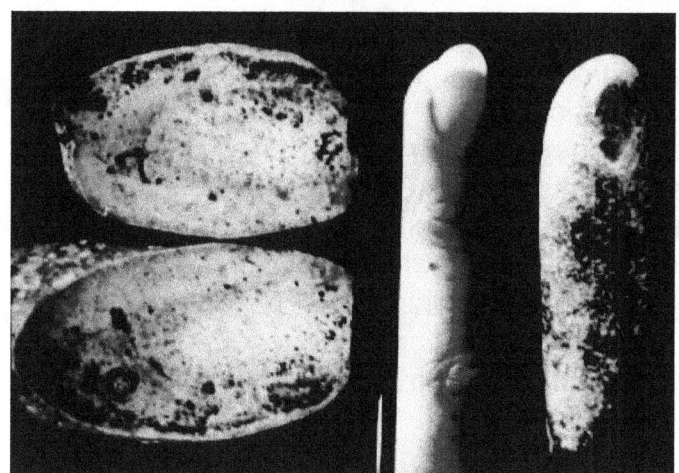
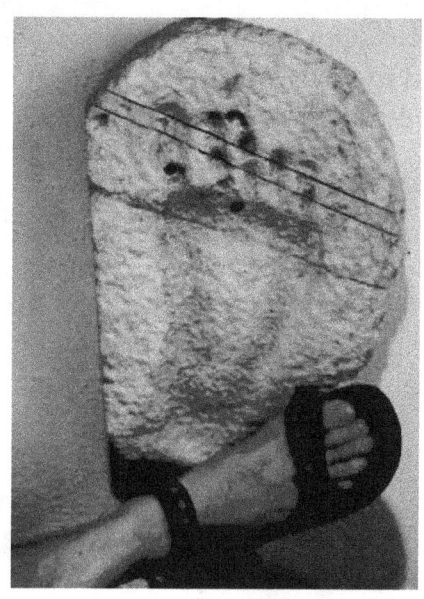

Giant Humans and Dinosaurs

A petrified finger found in cretaceous limestone, belonged to a "prehistoric" human. Broken short of the middle joint, it measures 7.6 cm (3 inches). At full length it would measure about 15 cm (6 inches). In the photo, it is compared to a regular full-length finger. Excavations of this limestone has also revealed a child's tooth and human hair.

Sectioning revealed the typical porous bone structure expected in a human finger.

Cat-scan and MRI identified joints and traced tendons throughout the length of the fossil.

Cat-scan showed dark areas interpreted as the interior of bones and marrow. Areas less dense than surrounding stones, easily pass X-rays, causing darkening of the image. Black area is caused by sectioning.

One dinosaur footprint in cretaceous limestone on the banks of the Paluxy River is approximately 30 cm (one foot) across, and located with similar tracks. Early excavations in this area revealed human footprints inside the dinosaur tracks leading to rumors that the human prints had claws–later excavations uncovered human footprints up to 64 cm long (25 inches) next to the dinosaur prints—this discounted the doubters. A human handprint was also found. This confirms that dinosaurs occupied the arbitrary and spurious "cretaceous" period of geological history. Human prints contemporary with dinosaurs contradict modern evolution theories stating mankind was not to evolve for another 75 to 100 million years.

One of many human footprints contemporary with dinosaurs taken from the Paluxy River located in Dinosaur Park near Glen Rose, Texas. Pictured with my foot, it exceeds 45 cm (18 inches) in length. The cross-sectional cuts determined by compression studies that it was a woman's footprint. Estimates indicate her stature approximately 305 cm (10 feet) and 454 kg (1,000 lbs). Several strata of human prints with dinosaur prints have been excavated in this park. According to Dr. Carl Baugh, the archeologist who coordinated the excavations, these strata were laid down during the first few days of Noah's flood when water levels were low enough to allow daily tidal changes to form layers of mud so fleeing creatures could seek higher ground—the upper strata showed no prints.

GIANTS ON THE EARTH

Obviously the people who lived contemporary with dinosaurs were intelligent, and the footprints indicate that they were quite human, as the large toe on primates is located close to the heel to facilitate clinging to branches.

Dr. Hilton Hinderliter of Apollo Campus Pennsylvania State University, studied the evidence presented at the Glen Rose, who excavations and stated: "I would have to say that the belief in evolution is in a state of terminal illness but its death will only be admitted by a new generation of scientists whose minds have not been prejudiced by the type of education now prevalent in the nation's public schools, an education which begins with the belief that evolution has happened, which interprets all evidence according to that faith and simply discards any evidence which cannot be fitted into the evolutionary framework" (Quoted from "Dinosaurs" by Dr. Carl E. Baugh, 1987. Promise Publishing Co., Orange, CA 92667.

This interesting photograph is of a hammer found in similar strata. It's iron head and wooden handle are solidified in sandstone. Metallurgical studies show that it was constructed of a type of iron that could not have been made under present atmospheric conditions. It is believed that before the flood our atmosphere was compressed to approximately twice its current density, and no ultraviolet radiation.

In June 1934, the Hahn family discovered a rock, sitting loose on a ledge beside a waterfall outside of London, Texas. The site primarily consists of 75-100 million years old cretaceous rock. Noticing this weathered rock had wood protruding from it, they cracked it open, exposing the hammer head. To verify that the hammer was made of metal, they cut into one of the beveled sides with a file. The bright metal in the nick is still there, with no detectable corrosion. The unusual metallurgy is 96% iron, 2.6% chlorine and 0.74% sulfur (no carbon). Density tests indicate exceptional casting quality.

The density of the iron in a central, cross-sectional plane shows the interior metal to be very pure, with no bubbles.

Modern industry cannot consistently produce iron castings with this quality, as evidenced by test results that show bubbles and density variations that have caused pump and valve bodies to break. The handle eye is partially coalifed with quartz and calcite crystalline inclusions, oval shaped, and roughly 1" x 1/2".

A Personal Testimony

Several years ago, I heard about human footprints being found alongside dinosaur tracks in a Cretaceous limestone in the vicinity of Glen Rose, Texas. There were newspaper accounts in both the Fort Worth Star-Telegram (June 17, 1982) and The Dallas Morning News. Also, Dallas area television stations Channel 5 and Channel 8 reported on the finds. I did not think much about this at the time but later, because of my extensive reading on the subject of evolution, I was reminded of it. In January, 1995, I made a trip to Glen Rose specifically to visit the Creation Evidences Museum and find out all I could about these footprints.

I discovered that the excavation work there is done for about two weeks in summer each year as the Paluxy River is too high in the other seasons. Also, the landowner allows the digging to proceed for only this limited time.

I visited the area of the river bank and observed for myself the large and clear left-right trails of dinosaur prints. Many are 6-10 inches deep, 2-3 feet across, and show

GIANTS ON THE EARTH

a three-toed foot. I decided to visit the museum and find out all I could about these footprints.

During a long conversation that afternoon at the museum, I learned that human tracks had been uncovered in this area since at least 1910. Geologist Clifford Burdick, Ph.D., verified human tracks here in the 1940's. The work of the individuals connected now with the museum began about 1982. Since then, 57 footprints of man have been found in excavations along the Paluxy River and in at least one other site in the same general area. During my visit, I was shown casts of some of the footprints found previously. One section of rock is displayed which was cut out of the river bed because it contains one of the clearest footprints found to date. A cross-sectioning of one of the best finds is also displayed. Pressure laminations consistent with a human footprint in mud are clearly shown.

During our visit, I was shown casts of some of the footprints found previously. One section of rock is displayed which was cut out of the river bed because it contains one of the clearest footprints found to date. A cross-sectioning of one of the best finds is also displayed. Pressure laminations consistent with a human footprint in mud are clearly shown.

Several well-credentialed scientists had witnessed and testified to the genuineness of the discoveries. Media from around the country had witnessed at least some of them. Evolutionists, however, dismissed the human footprints as carvings of Indians, the tracks of a sick dolphin, a case of misidentification, or even an outright fraud. One gentleman was so threatened by the discoveries that he actually took a hammer, went to the river, and broke up some of the footprints to make them useless for study.

Some of the human footprints have been found right next to those of a dinosaur. One was even found inside the animal track! The relatively soft limestone rock is subject to rapid weathering from exposure. The human tracks are shallow and look like a footprint made in mud or wet cement. Because of this the details of the human prints are lost within days of the time of exposure.

I knew that the human footprints, found side by side with dinosaur tracks, if genuine, destroyed the theory of evolution all by themselves. Still, I wanted to see for myself.

Along with two of my friends, Ted and Jorge Gomez, I went to Glen Rose to observe and participate in an excavation on June 19, 1995. We helped to remove the exposed rock ledge at the work site. This ledge covered the limestone layer in which the tracks had been previously discovered at other sites along the river. Each portion of the ledge we removed (approximately 50 sf.) weighed at least 2000 pounds. The removal of each piece took several men with sledge hammers and three heavy duty jacks; hours of heavy work to accomplish. No Indian had ever lifted and then replaced this covering rock to carve anything! A dinosaur track,but no human track, was discovered on our first day.

Jorge and I returned to work on another site on June 29, 1995. This site was about 150 feet down river from our earlier location. Both sites were chosen because previous findings indicated a trail of footprints might extend to them. Dr. Carl Baugh (Ph.D. Anthropology, M. Archeology), was in charge of the excavation. Several of the people there had been working for the entire two week period.

When we arrived Dr. Baugh was beginning to carefully excavate clay from a de-

GIANTS ON THE EARTH

pression in the target limestone. Several of us worked with hand trowels to remove the 3-4 inches of clay which overlay the fossil layer. This clay had been uncovered when the exposed covering rock had been removed the previous day. It was quite obvious that the clay layer had never been disturbed since its deposition. I worked within 3 feet of Dr. Baugh.

Once he suspected that the depression on which he was working could possibly be a human track, all other activity in the area ceased. Everyone then focused their attention on his work. Dr. Baugh removed the clay with utmost care and no chipping or sculpting occurred. Several of those in attendance testified to this on camera and that the site was previously unexposed or disturbed in any way. The rock ledge and clay had completely covered the depression until we removed them.

The depression in the limestone was clearly made by a large human foot. It was a right foot. The big toe and three rightmost toes made very clear impressions and rock ridges were found between the toe marks. The second toe made a lesser impression which is consistent with the way humans walk. There was a rock bump in front of each of the toes made when they pushed up the mud. The shape fit the arch and also the right side of a foot. The heel was not clear but looked as if the individual had slid in the mud. The depth of the impressions was consistent with the depth of tracks made by someone walking in mud. The toes were round and smooth. Everything was in the proper proportion.

Since I had the largest foot in attendance, size 13, my bare foot was used as a comparison for the extensive video tapes and photographs that documented the excavation. As my foot was both beside the footprint and in it for quite a while, I was able to examine it very closely.

Without any doubt, it was a human footprint.

I testify that everything I witnessed I have reported faithfully and without exaggeration.

M. Coppedge

Plaster casts of similar footprints found in Australia are in the possession of Rex Gilroy, together with many other interesting artifacts. In old river gravels near Bathurst, NSW, huge stone artifacts—clubs, pounders, adzes, chisels, knives and hand axes—all of tremendous weight, lie scattered over a wide area. These weigh anything from 8, 10, 15, to 21 and 25 pounds, implements which only men of tremendous proportions could possibly have made and used. Estimates for the actual size of these men range from 10 to 12 feet tall and over, weighing from 500 to 600 lbs.

A fossicker searching the Winburndale River north of Bathurst discovered a large quartzitised fossil human molar tooth, far too big for any normal modern man. A similar find was made near Dubbo, N.S.W.

Prospectors working in the Bathurst district in the 1930's frequently reported coming across numerous large human footprints fossilised in shoals of red jasper.

Even more impressive were fossil deposits found by naturalist Rex Gilroy around Bathurst. He excavated from a depth of 6 feet (2 m) below the surface a fossil lower back molar tooth measuring 67 min. in length by 50mm. x 42 mm. across the crown. If his

GIANTS ON THE EARTH

measurements are correct, the owner would have been at least 25 ft. tall, weighing well over 1,000 lbs!

At Gympie, Queensland, a farmer, Keith Walker, was ploughing his field when he turned up the large fragment of the back portion of a jaw which still possessed the hollow for a missing lower back molar tooth. This is now in Rex Gilroy's possession. The owner of the tooth would have stood at 10 feet tall.

In the Megalong Valley in the Blue Mountains NSW, a Mr P. Holman found in ironstone protruding from a creek bank the deeply impressed print of a large human-like foot. The print was that of the instep, with all 5 toes clearly shown. This footprint measures 7 inches across the toes. Had the footprint been complete it would have been at least 2 feet (60 cm in length, appropriate to a 12 foot human. However, the largest footprint found on the Blue Mountains must have belonged to a man 20 feet tall!

A set of 3 huge footprints was discovered near Mulgoa, south of Penrith, N.S.W. These prints, each measuring 2 ft long and 7 inches across the toes, are 6 ft. apart, indicating the stride of the 12 ft. giant who left them. These prints were preserved by volcanic lava and ash flows which "occurred millions of years" before man is supposed to have appeared on the Australian continent (if one is to believe the evolutionary theory):

Noel Reeves found monstrous footprints near Kempsey, N.S.W. in sandstone beds on the Upper Macleay River. One print shows a toe 4 inches (10cm) long and the total toe-span is 10 inches (25cm) — suggesting that the owner of the print may have been 17 feet tall.

It is certain the Aborigines were not the first to reach Australia. Anthropologists maintain mainland Aborigines are in fact quite recent arrivals who ate their predecessors who were akin to the New Guinea natives.

Aborigines themselves admit in their ancient folklore that this land was inhabited by several groups of men, as well as giants, before they settled here.

Fossilised human footprints have also been discovered in Sweden, and in Mexico.
Giant skeletons have been discovered throughout the United States.
Photos of giants from recent times.

An article from Strand magazine (December,1895) reprinted in "Traces of the Elder Faiths of Ireland" by W.G. Wood-Martin mentions this fossilized giant discovered during mining operations in County Antrim, Ireland: "Pre-eminent among the most extraordinary articles ever held by a railway company is the fossilized Irish giant, which is at this moment lying at the London and North-Western Railway Company's Broad street goods depot, and a photograph of which is reproduced here. . . This monstrous figure is reputed to have been dug up by a Mr. Dyer whilst prospecting for iron ore in County Antrim. The principal measurements are: entire length, 12ft. 2in.; girth of chest, 6ft. 6in.; and length of arms, 4ft. 6in. There are six toes on the right foot. The gross weight is 2 tons 15cwt.; so that it took half a dozen men and a powerful crane to place this article of lost property in position for the Strand magazine artist. Dyer, after showing the giant in Dublin, came to England with his queer find and exhibited it in Liverpool and Manchester at sixpence, sixpence a head, attracting scientific men as well as gaping sightseers".

GIANTS ON THE EARTH

But the Woman being deceived, was in the Transgression

The seed of the serpent produced Cain. If his daddy was a great big giant of a fellow, what would Cain be like? His daddy. And he went to the land of Nod and took one of his sisters. Only way he could, there were no other females. . .

Cain went to the land of Nod, and produced giants. They were smart educated, intelligent people. Is that right? They were builders, inventors, scientists: Not through the seed of the righteous, but through the seed of the serpent. They were scientists, builders, and great men, educators; the Scripture says so. They worked brass; they worked iron; they worked metals. They invented things. They tempered different metals and built houses.

The Scripture says one of those giants had fourteen inch fingers. Now, your finger is just as long as your closed hand. Open it up; that would be a twenty-eight inch hand.

And they were scoffers at the seed of the woman: Noah, the righteous. Jesus said, "As it was in the days of Noah, so will it be when the Son of man is revealed." That's today. And it is so. Genesis 6:1-4, "And it came to pass, when men began to multiply on the face of the earth, and daughters were born unto them, that the sons of God saw the daughters of men that they were fair; and they took them wives of all which they chose. And the LORD said, My spirit shall not always strive with man, for that he also is flesh: yet his days shall be an hundred and twenty years. There were giants in the earth in those days; and also after that, when the sons of God came in unto the daughters of men, and they bare them children who became mighty men which were of old, men of renown."

". . . daughters of man . . ." signifies the MORTALITY of the serpent seed in contrast to the immortality of the sons of God. Their EARTHLY origin is contrasted with the heavenly origin of the "Sons of God," created in the likeness of Father God by His spoken Word. The "daughters of man" are Cain's race, the earthly, carnal offspring of the Satan-incarnate Serpent, they are hybrid and not a spoken Word of God's creation.

The phrase, "came in unto" refers in this connection only to the male who visits a woman's quaters and describes the immorality of "free love" which has repeated in this day along with miscegenation between the descendants of Cain and the children of Adam as Jesus foretold and lauded as "multiculturalism" (Genesis 30:16; 38:16; Matthew 24:37; Luke 17:26-27).

"Men of renown" speaks of men with an enduring name. Genesis describes these people as great builders and engineers, musicians, inventors, craftsmen, unbelievers and scoffers at the righteous of Adam's race. The same race are renouned in these occupations today. Undaunted by the Flood their descendants declare " . . .let us make us a name . . ." and erect a tower in carnal defiance of the Lord God.

The Hebrew word "Nephilim" is rendered "giants" in our English Bibles, but the form of the word indicates a verbal adjective or noun of passive or neuter signification, from Naphal, "to fall" and means "the fallen ones," that is, the descendents of Cain. Afterwards the term is transferred to their offspring, the only other passage in which it occurs.

In their evil report of the land of Canaan, the ten spies say, "All the people we saw in it were men of great stature. And there we saw the Nephilim, the sons of Anak, descended from the Nephilim: and we seemed to ourselves as grasshoppers, and so did we to them" (Numbers 13:32-33).

It was doubtless the mention of the great stature of these men, together with the

GIANTS ON THE EARTH

Septuagint rendering that suggested our translation "giants." However the roots of the Greek word, have no reference to great stature and signify "earth-born". The meaning of "giants" in our sense of the term is secondary, arising from the fact that these beings of mixed birth are said to have displayed a monstrous growth and strength of body.

God commanded Moses to exterminate the whole race of these people from the Land of Canaan whom He said would corrupt their morals and pervert their heart to paganism if they intermarried or made agreements with them. Sadly, history, the Bible and telephone directories in every city record how the sons of Israel intermarried with daughters of men until today their identity and their land has been usurped by "men of renown"—clever inventers, actors, musicians, businessmen, singers, writers, traders, bankers and outright liars.

The Lord Jesus said, ". . . the children of this world are in their lineage wiser than the children of Light" (Luke 16:8).

Paul wrote, "Mortify therefore your members which are upon the earth; fornication, uncleanness, inordinate affection, evil concupiscence, and covetousness, which is idolatry: for which things' sake the wrath of God comes on the children of disobedience" (Colossians 3:5-6).

Immediately after the commission of the antediluvian sin, God pronounced the doom of the world. And prophecy assures us the present-day great rebellion will call forth the Lord Jesus in flaming Fire to take vengeance. Only those whose Names are written on the Lamb's Book of Life will not be deceived—the Bride of Christ manifesting the sons of God, and the 144,000 elect Israelites who are Israelites of the flesh and of the faith.

GIANTS ON THE EARTH

The title pages of the early county and pioneer history books often included phrases like "CAREFULLY WRITTEN AND COMPILED" and "LEST WE FORGET."

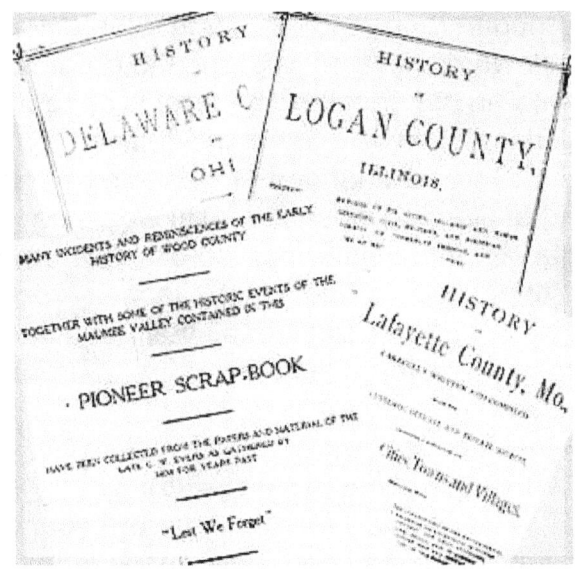

Holocaust of Giants
The Great Smithsonian Cover-up
(reprinted with permission)

Noted Native American author and professor of law emeritus, Vine Deloria, writes in a personal communication:

It's probably better that so few of the ruins and remains were tied in with the Smithsonian because they give good reason to believe the ending of the Indiana Jones movie—a great warehouse where the real secrets of earth history are buried.

Modern day archaeology and anthropology have nearly sealed the door on our imaginations, broadly interpreting the North American past as devoid of anything unusual in the way of great cultures characterized by a people of unusual demeanor. The great interloper of ancient burial grounds, the nineteenth century Smithsonian Institution, created a one-way portal, through which uncounted bones have been spirited. This door and the contents of its vault are virtually sealed off to anyone, but government officials. Among these bones may lay answers not even sought by these officials concerning the deep past.

The first hint we had about the possible existence of an actual race of tall, strong, and intellectually sophisticated people, was in researching old township and county records. Many of these were quoting from old diaries and letters that were combined, for posterity, in the 1800s from diaries going back to the 1700s. Says Vine in this understanding:

Some of these old county and regional history books contain real gems because the people were not subjected to a rigid indoctrination about evolution and were astonished about what they found and honestly reported it.

Some time before archaeology came to subscribe the general public to its view of prehistory—generations prior to Darwin's troublesome theory—the pioneers thought that some of the earthworks were as ancient as could be concurrent with human habitation in America. Some among the early settlers exercised their pens assured that the earthworks were not built by the direct ancestry of the native people living in the historical period, but rather were constructed in a more remote era encompassing a different

GIANTS ON THE EARTH

social order. They compared the "Mound Builders," with the "Indians," clearly discerning the former as belonging to an earlier time—possessing a different fate or destiny from the latter.

Evidence for the occupation of this region before the appearance of the red man and the white race is to be found in almost every part of the county, as well as through the northwest generally. In removing the gravel bluffs, which are numerous and deep, for the construction and repair of roads, and in excavating cellars, hundreds of human skeletons, some of them of giant form, have been found. A citizen of Marion County estimates that there were about as many human skeletons in the knolls of Marion County as there are white inhabitants at present!

The History of Marion County, Ohio
(complied from past accounts, published in 1883)

Mastodonic remains are occasionally unearthed, and, from time to time, discoveries of the remains of Indian settlements are indicated by the appearance of gigantic skeletons, with the high cheek bones, powerful jaws and massive frames peculiar of the red man, who left these as the only record with which to form a clew to the history of past ages.

The History of Brown County, Ohio
(complied from past accounts, published in 1883)

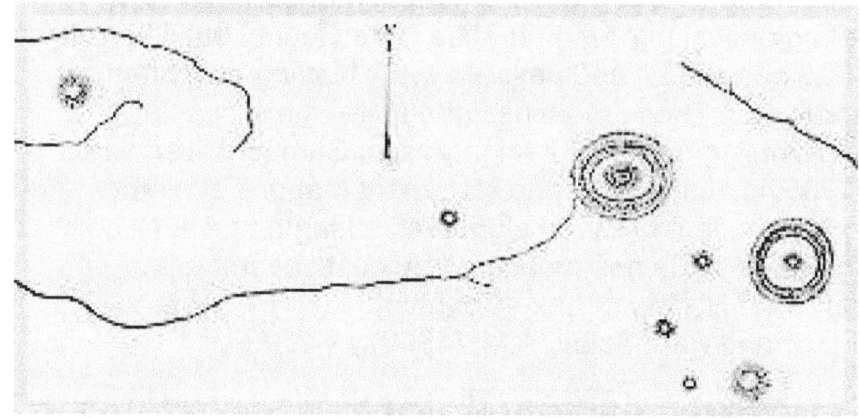

Group of Mounds in Brown County, Ohio.

She said also that three skeletons were found at the mouth of the Paw Paw Creek many years later, while Nim (Nimrod) Satterfield was justice of the peace. Jim Dean and some men were digging for a bridge foundation and found these bones at the lower end of the old buffalo wallow. She thought it was Dr. Kidwell, of Fairmont, who examined them and said they were very old, perhaps thousands of years old. She said that when the skeletons were exposed to the weather for a few days, their bones turned black and began to crumble, that Squire Satterfield had them buried in the Joliffe graveyard (Rivesville). All these skeletons, she said, were measured, and found to be about eight feet long.

Now and Long Ago-A History of the Marion County Area
by Glen Lough (1969)

Another of many examples, this one, collected by James Mooney (1861-1921), tells of the visit of very tall people from the west:

GIANTS ON THE EARTH

James Wafford, of the western Cherokee, who was born in Georgia in 1806, says that his grandmother, who must have been born about the middle of the last century, told him that she had heard from the old people that long before her time a party of giants had once come to visit the Cherokee. They were nearly twice as tall as common men, and had their eyes set slanting in their heads, so that the Cherokee called them Tsunil´ kalu´, "the Slant-eyed people," because they looked like the giant hunter Tsul´ kalu´. They said that these giants lived far away in the direction in which the sun goes down. The Cherokee received them as friends, and they stayed some time, and then returned to their home in the west...

Dancing Figures Found on a Copper Plate in Union County, Illinois.

This kind of recorded tradition did not start with Mooney, rather beginning early in American history. During the Colonial and post-Colonial era, the information seekers were keen on gathering as much knowledge of the forgotten past as feasible through native sources. Some of it was woven into romantic tales including verse, but the main of it went into records, which, like the accumulation of earth and debris over ancient village sites, became buried in the musty stacks of old libraries—considered to have no real "substance" in the emerging field of the white man's science.

Of the very early history of the region which now embraces Lake County but little can be written. The Mound Builders had occupied it and passed away, leaving no written language and but little even as tradition... These mounds were quite numerous... Excavations...have revealed the crumbling bones of a mighty race. Samuel Miller, who has resided in the county since 1835, is authority for the statement that one skeleton which he assisted in unearthing was a trifle more than eight feet in length, the skull being correspondingly large, while many other skeletons measured at least seven feet...

Historical Encyclopedia of Illinois and History of Lake County
Edited by Newton Bateman, LL.D. and Paul Selby, A.M. (1902)

From the outset of North American archaeology, no federally sponsored concern has researched and collected evidence specifically emphasizing the existence of unusually tall Native Americans in prehistoric, and even in historic times. There are reasons for this oversight, though in hindsight it has placed limits on our overview of prehistory. Because there were only occasional people of large stature born among the light-skinned, European races, numbers of giants were far from anticipated in America. Scientists in Europe, in case-by-case studies, declared their giants to have been victims of pituitary disorder. Another reason was that when the private citizenry in the U.S. unearthed the bones of very tall and strongly constructed people, and when these disinterments were recorded, rarely was any comparison made with sites of similar contents. It was still a sort of wilderness in many rural areas right until the middle 1800s. In this, each discovery was sort of "unique"—only to end up in the stacks of old township libraries to be

GIANTS ON THE EARTH

complied later as curiosities—if they survived at all. The following account originated around the year 1800:

There were mounds situated in the eastern part of the village of Conneaut and an extensive burying-ground near the Presbyterian church, which appear to have had no connection with the burying-places of the Indians. Among the human bones found in the mounds were some belonging to men of gigantic structure. Some of the skulls were of sufficient capacity to admit the head of an ordinary man, and jaw bones that might have been fitted on over the face with equal facility; the other bones were proportionately large. The burying-ground referred to contained about four acres, and with the exception of a slight angle in conformity with the natural contour of the ground was in the form of an oblong square. It appeared to have been accurately surveyed into lots running from north to south, and exhibited all the order and propriety of arrangement deemed necessary to constitute Christian burial...

Historical Collections of Ohio in Two Volumes
by Henry Howe, LL.D. (1888)

Although not regarded by the government as reliable, the oral traditions of the native people in the eastern U.S. aver of the existence of possibly two races of giants, one supplanting the other by violent means. Here we have the first inkling of some very remote prehistory preserved, through the tradition of the Chippewa, Sandusky, and Tawa tribes, (members of the Algonquin language group), the existence of giant, bearded men.

In this connection I would say that Mr. Jonathan Brooks, now living in town, stated to me, that his father, Benjamin Brooks, who lived with the Indians fourteen years, and was well-acquainted with their language and traditions, told him and others that it was a tradition of the Indians that the first tribe occupying this whole country, was a black-bearded race, very large in size, and subsequently a red bearded race or tribe came and killed or drove off all the black beards, as they called them.

The Firelands Pioneer (1858)

Offsetting the carefully recorded diaries of the rural folk, there were popular writers who creatively developed the more contemporary histories and folk legends, leaving to cursory treatment the deeper accounts of North American antiquities. These authors, while having captured the essence of the public perception of the noble native tradition, were not reconciled to the antique body of legend. The pens of James Fenimore Cooper (1789-1851) and Henry Wadsworth Longfellow (1807-1882) relate virtually nothing of the tall ones. Native Americans, as we know, were discouraged from writing, although some, such as David Cusick, circumvented the bias using Christian names. Fortunately, early missionary concerns gathered oral tradition from the tribal elders concerning men of giant stature.

But even the most informative or entertaining accounts could not instill enough respect for the native people to put an end to the further destruction of the sacred sites. The attitude of the white race in general toward the red race was an abomination, totally lacking in mercy and compassion. Many of the Native American skulls were compared with European skulls, but selectively so as to depict the current native populace as being of inferior intelligence. Almost without resistance, the black seeds of racial bias were

GIANTS ON THE EARTH

forming in the uncorrupted soil of prehistoric interpretation. Take for example the words of an important government official and popular writer, Henry Schoolcraft (1793-1864):

The Indian has a low, bushy brow, beneath which a dull, sleepy, half-closed eye seems to mark the ferocious passions that are dormant within. The acute angles of the eyes seldom present the obliquity so common in the Malays and the Mongolians. The color of the eye is almost uniformly a tint between black and grey; but even in young persons it seldom has the brightness, or expresses the vivacity, so common in the more civilized races.
Bureau of Indian Affairs (1852)

Schoolcraft, who himself married a half-Indian woman, was apparently predisposed to labeling the native people in general as inferior. This kind of ridiculous prejudice underscored the tone for the unbridled continuation of the earthwork debacle. The result of this is accurately reflected in how archaeology was organized more than one hundred years ago, and may be summed up in the policy of Joseph Henry, first secretary of the Smithsonian Institution. Says Henry in 1846: "The collection of data should precede theorizing..." Unfortunately, the collection of data seemed to have no end, and any subsequent theorizing was (and is) in a state of transience. The Smithsonian, playing a sort of leading role in the massive undertaking attempting to cast light on the inscrutable prehistory of the United States, inadvertently collected far too many relics to ever analyze in a comprehensive sense. Estimates of the number of moundworks in Ohio alone—at the end of the Colonial period—topped ten thousand. Today, less than one-twentieth of these exist, and, moreover, they exist in a reconstructed form. No quarter of special status was given to any earthwork, no matter how sacred or strategic to tribal lands. It was a holocaust of an unprecedented nature, for it undermined the very morale of the native people who understood the peace of their ancestors to be ruined.

Differing only in the professionalism somewhat absent from the previous seventy years of ghoulish quests, Henry's mandate dictated emphasis on the creation of an inclusive system of excavation, recording, and description. Any analysis that followed had to be based upon this criterion. But competent analysis of anomalies rarely (if ever) came from the Smithsonian and other institutions formally engaged in the practice of exhumation. Given this understanding, it is no wonder that the Smithsonian is believed by knowledgeable people to be actively stymieing research that would produce a more enlightened view of American prehistory.

There is, however, some compensation for this oversight in that the Smithsonian, like the Peabody, and the Carnegie shortly thereafter, faithfully upheld Henry's mandate to detail, as was feasible, their mound "explorations." However, the present-day inaccessibility of the bones and objects these people removed for future study is a reflection and symptom of the proposed "oversight." One thing that pleased us in this research effort was the fact that there were many skeletons of gigantic frame discovered and reported by the Smithsonian, boosting the validity and value of the old township diaries, as well as the native legends. Some of these are presented below.

GIANTS ON THE EARTH

A Brief History of the Museum

The Smithsonian Institution, easily the world's largest museum complex, began from the generous gift of James Smithson, an English scientist, in 1829. Believed born a bastard (especially in the eyes of his later detractors), Smithson was a "diligent young student," receiving a Master of Arts from Pembroke College, Oxford, in 1786. He became a distinguished scientist. The gentle man passed away in 1829, bequeathing his fortune to nephew James Henry Hungerford with the stipulation that if this man died without an heir, the remainder of the fortune would go to the United States. It seems he felt that the United States was the future of Britain. Perhaps Smithson saw the "New World" as fertile, worthy, intellectual territory.

Hungerford died in 1835. Although there was some controversy in the interim, the finding of the Smithsonian, based upon the more than a half million-dollar gift, took place officially in 1846. His legacy to the American people was, in his own words, "for the increase and diffusion of knowledge." Since that time, the museum's collections have increased considerably, with problems in the cataloging and location of stored finds developing due to changing standards of administrations over the last 150 years. Analogous to the Vatican with its antique cache of confiscated, problematic treasures, the booty of the Holy See may pale in comparison to the Smithsonian's boatload of diffuse evidence. Pity of it is that Smithson's request has gone into a different mode of interpretation. Instead of diffusing knowledge, it has unwittingly become confused with the problem of sprawling storage.

Powell and Thomas

Grave a, a stone sepulcher, $2\frac{1}{2}$ feet wide, 8 feet long, and 2 feet deep, was formed by placing steatite slabs on edge at the sides and ends, and others across the top. The bottom consisted simply of earth hardened by fire. It contained the remains of a single skeleton, lying on its back, with the head east. The frame was heavy and about seven feet long. The head rested on a thin copper plate ornamented with impressed figures...

12th Annual Report of the Bureau of Ethnology to the Secretary of the Smithsonian Institution 1890-1891

(published in 1894)

(Cyrus Thomas' investigations of Etowah)

In 1882, after some thirty-six years of growth and sound management, Smithsonian executive John Wesley Powell (of Grand Canyon exploration fame 1869-1872), hired Cyrus Thomas. Powell wanted this man to head up the fieldwork for the Smithsonian's newly created Bureau of Ethnology, specifically the Eastern Mound Division. Thomas was a minister and an entomologist whose broadened interests included archaeology. He was, inotherwords, a bible-advocating, insect-adept archaeologist who believed in the mystery of a lost race at the time of his being recruited. Powell, who was much in sympathy with the plight of Native Americans, having lived among them for a length of time, be-

GIANTS ON THE EARTH

lieved that there was no lost or mysterious race of mound builders. He desired to credit the downtrodden native people with the worthy and gentle arts associated with the ancient mound building societies. Subsequently, and in light of other politic considerations marking the era, Powell sought to enact these personal convictions through the instrumentality of Thomas. In spite of his personal beliefs, Thomas was not outspokenly resistant to accepting the position. Besides, Congress was allocating solid funding for this proposed ramble through the ancient landscape.

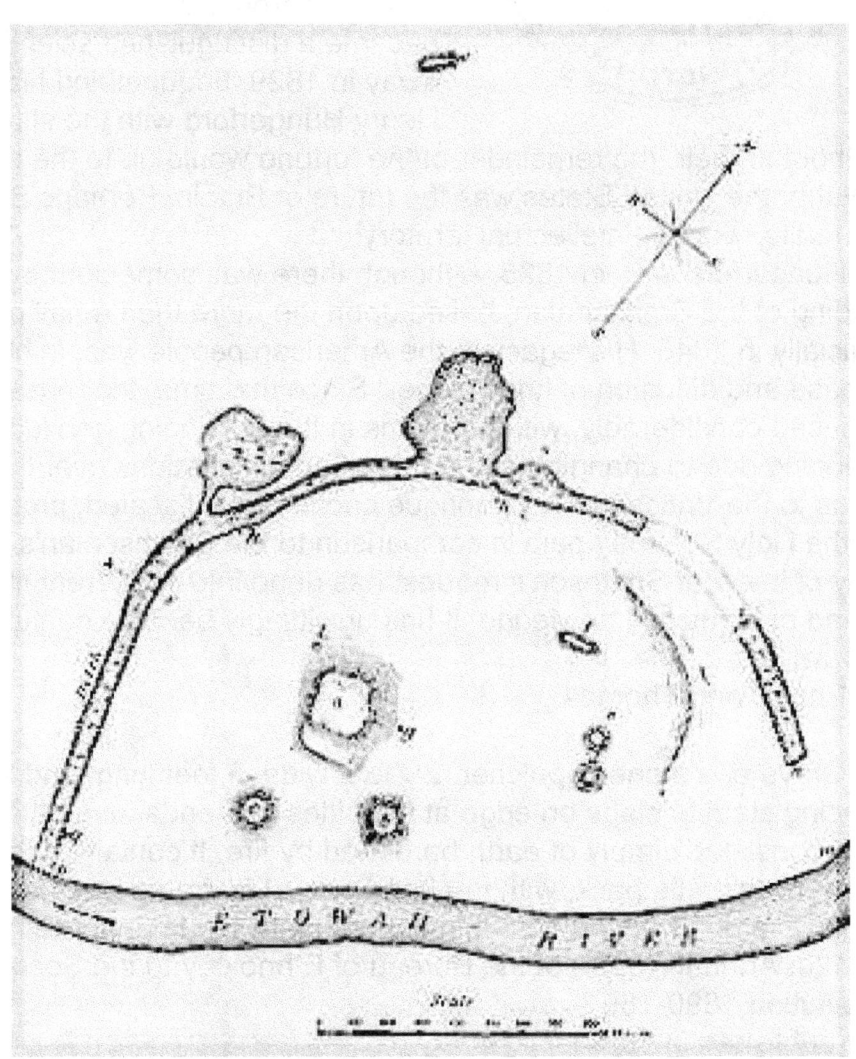

Plat of the Etowah Group, Bartow County, Georgia.

Grave A (found in the largest mound of the group) contained a seven-foot skeleton having a heavy frame.

There was apparently an important decision made at this time concerning the facilitation of an enveloping theory—so necessary to create order where chaos loomed. Before discharging a book, one logically creates an outline to guide one's thoughts. This was to become a hierarchical arrangement that would decide the angle of vision for the categorizing of the finds that would be made. On one hand, the belief that others discovered North America before Columbus (such as Phoenician, Egyptian, Hebraic, Greek, Roman, Celt, Scandinavian, or even Asian mariners) was explored.

On the other hand, the idea of the continent having been isolated from outside influences was put on the table. It was perhaps because of Powell's deference to the native kinship that the latter idea—i.e., screening out any extra-continental visitors—was adopted. Needless to say, this was an extraordinary assumption, and one that has affected decision-making right until the present day. On the positive side it viably linked the living factions of the Native American people with the more ancient mound building folk, and shortly thereafter was responsible for the faintly successful preservation of what remained of the mound builder's legacy. From this it may be understood how aspects of

GIANTS ON THE EARTH

Powell's work, such as analysis of the social order of the mound builders, was not a priority.

Powell's decision regarding isolation was in reality a two-edged sword. While it was a meaningful step that fostered a meager though important harmonic between the federal government and the native people, it was regrettably based upon a false notion. An example of its contradiction is found right in the 12th Annual Report itself. Again and again Thomas and his operatives came up with anomalous evidence directly questioning Powell's sweeping suppositions.

Cave burials occur in this district in the following counties: In Grayson, Hart, Edmonson, Barren, Warren, and Fayette counties; Kentucky; Smith, White, Warren, Giles, Marion, and Fentress counties, Tennessee, and Bartow county, Georgia. These localities lie mostly in a belt extending in a north and south direction through the center of the district.

In most of these caves, both in Kentucky and Tennessee, the bodies appear to have been laid on the floor of the cave, sometimes in beds of ashes, sometimes on a pavement of flat stones. There are, however, some instances in which the bodies have been found incased in stone slabs, and afterwards imbedded in clay or ashes. In Smith and Warren counties, Tennessee, and in Warren and Fayette counties, Kentucky, the flesh of the bodies was preserved and the hair was yellow and of fine texture. In some cases the bodies were enveloped in several thicknesses of coarse cloth with an outer wrapping of deer skin. Some of the bodies were wrapped in a kind of cloth made of bark fiber, into which feathers were woven in such a manner as to form a smooth surface. In two cases the bodies, placed in a sitting or squatting posture, were incased in baskets. In one of the caves in Smith county the body of a female is said to have been found, having about the waist a silver girdle, with marks resembling letters.

12th Annual Report of the Bureau of Ethnology to the Secretary of the Smithsonian Institution 1890-1891

(published in 1894)

(explorations in the Tennessee District)

Armed with a self-created doctrine powered by ample funding, and with a little help later from the one-way door to the Smithsonian's inaccessible catacombs, the years that followed saw Powell and his underling nearly succeed in the obliteration of the last notions of the legendary, mysterious, and antique class of mound building people, and for that matter, any people that didn't fit into the mold of his theory. Did Powell intentionally overlook some of the archaeology so as to focus on his own special agenda?

Powell and his associates at the Bureau were quite certain that people had arrived in the Americas only sometime after the first Egyptian dynasty—less than 4500 years ago! They also believed that the Mississippi Valley was sufficiently isolated from the Ohio Valley to warrant the simultaneous flourishing of quite distinct cultures over a long period. Since carbon dating was not yet discovered, Thomas used stratigraphic (after Lyell) analysis and, following the rest of the mandate, included detailed record keeping and documentation whenever appropriate. His findings were broadly accepted, and are still referenced.

Underneath the layer of shells the earth was very dark and appeared to be mixed with vegetable mold to the depth of 1 foot. At the bottom of this, resting on the original sur-

GIANTS ON THE EARTH

face of the ground, was a very large skeleton lying horizontally at full length. Although very soft, the bones were sufficiently distinct to allow of careful measurement before attempting to remove them. The length from the base of the skull to the bones of the toes was found to be 7 feet 3 inches. It is probable, therefore, that this individual when living was fully 7 1/2 feet high. At the head lay some small pieces of mica and a green substance, probably the oxide of copper, though no ornament or article of copper was discovered.

12th Annual Report of the Bureau of Ethnology to the Secretary of the Smithsonian Institution 1890-1891
(published in 1894)
(explorations in Roane County, Tennessee)

But Thomas' time was limited because of the large territory he was to explore. Under such working conditions, anomalies were put aside for future research—to be, as it has turned out, forgotten. Thomas was forced to rely on the accounts of operatives in many cases. Evidently, some of these people discerned between "Indian" burials and the burials of the Mound Builders, perhaps challenging the patience of Powell.

No. 5, the largest of the group was carefully examined. Two feet below the surface, near the apex, was a skeleton, doubtless an intrusive Indian burial... Near the original surface, 10 or 12 feet from the center, on the lower side, lying at full length on its back, was one of the largest skeletons discovered by the Bureau agents, the length as proved by actual measurement being between 7 and 8 feet. It was clearly traceable, but crumbled to pieces immediately after removal from the hard earth in which it was encased....

12th Annual Report of the Bureau of Ethnology to the Secretary of the Smithsonian Institution 1890-1891
(published in 1894)
(mounds at Dunleith, Illinois)

Mound Group, Dunleith, Illinois.

"Near the original surface, 10 or 12 feet from the center, on the lower side, lying at full length on its back, was one of the largest skeletons discovered by the Bureau agents, the length as proved by actual measurement being between 7 and 8 feet."

Regarding the problem of "intrusive" Indian burials, what kind of a time gap were these men looking at between the original burials and the later ones? As his agents uncovered the physical evidence for powerful men of towering stature, Thomas held the position that any and all skeletal remains represented the direct ancestry of the present day people. Was it not plausible to consider an extended "family" or hierarchical group of very tall folk who served with the people? Were they selective enough in their sexual associations to appear, overall, as a race with

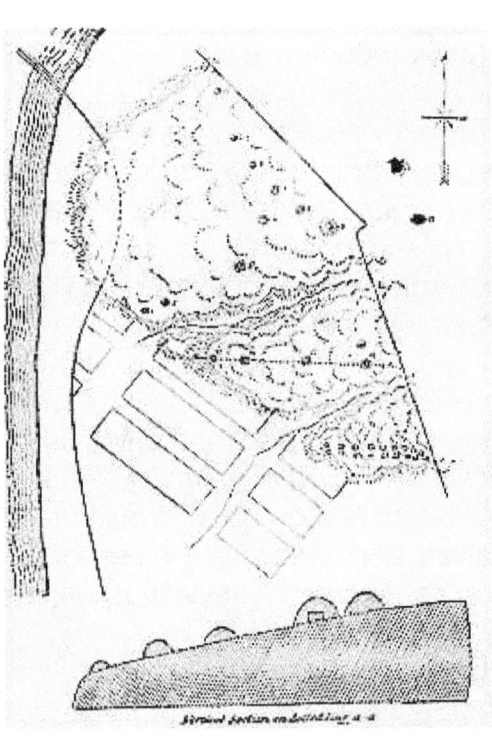

GIANTS ON THE EARTH

its own peculiarities and even physical characteristics? The findings that didn't fit in to the guideline established by his superior were summarily recorded and forgotten by Thomas—a legacy we have inherited today.

An old Indian mound has been opened on the farm of Harrison Robinson, four miles East of Jackson, Ohio, and two skeletons of extraordinary size and a great quantity of trinkets have been removed. Some years ago a party of relic hunters, supposed to have been sent out in the interest of the Archeological society visited the Robinson farm, and after a few days search removed a great collection of stone hatchets, beads and bracelets, which were packed and shipped to an Eastern institute, and until this recent accidental discovery it was supposed that everything had been removed by the relic hunters. It is thought by many that more relics are to be found and preparations are being made for a through investigation.

The Adair County News
January 5, 1897
(Kentucky)

What has become of all the evidence? Again and again, only a single long skeleton or two was found among those of normal size. The understanding of tall, ruling chiefs and their wives was not developed at all, as is evident in these examples.

The other, situated on the point of a commanding bluff, was also conical in form, 50 feet in diameter and about 8 feet high. The outer layer consisted in sandy soil, 2 feet thick, filled with slightly decayed skeletons, probably Indians of intrusive burials. The earth of the main portion of this mound was a very fine yellowish sand which shoveled like ashes and was everywhere, to a depth of 2 to 4 feet, as full of human skeletons as could be stowed away in it, even to two and three tiers. Among these were a number of bones not together as skeletons, but mingled in confusion and probably from scaffolds or other localities. Excepting one, which was rather more than 7 feet long, these skeletons appeared to be of medium size and many of them much decayed...

12th Annual Report of the Bureau of Ethnology to the Secretary of the Smithsonian Institution 1890-1891
(published in 1894)
(Pike County, Illinois)

No. 11 is now 35 by 40 feet at the base and 4 feet high. In the center, 3 feet below the surface, was a vault 8 feet long and 3 feet wide. In the bottom of this, among the decayed fragments of bark wrappings, lay a skeleton fully seven feet long, extended at full length on the back, head west. Lying in a circle above the hips were fifty-two perforated shell disks about an inch in diameter and one-eighth of an inch thick.

12th Annual Report of the Bureau of Ethnology to the Secretary of the Smithsonian Institution 1890-1891
(published in 1894)
(Kanawha County, West Virginia)

Spring Hill Inclosure, Kanawha County, West Virginia. In the bottom of Mound

GIANTS ON THE EARTH

11 (upper left) was found a skeleton "fully seven feet long."

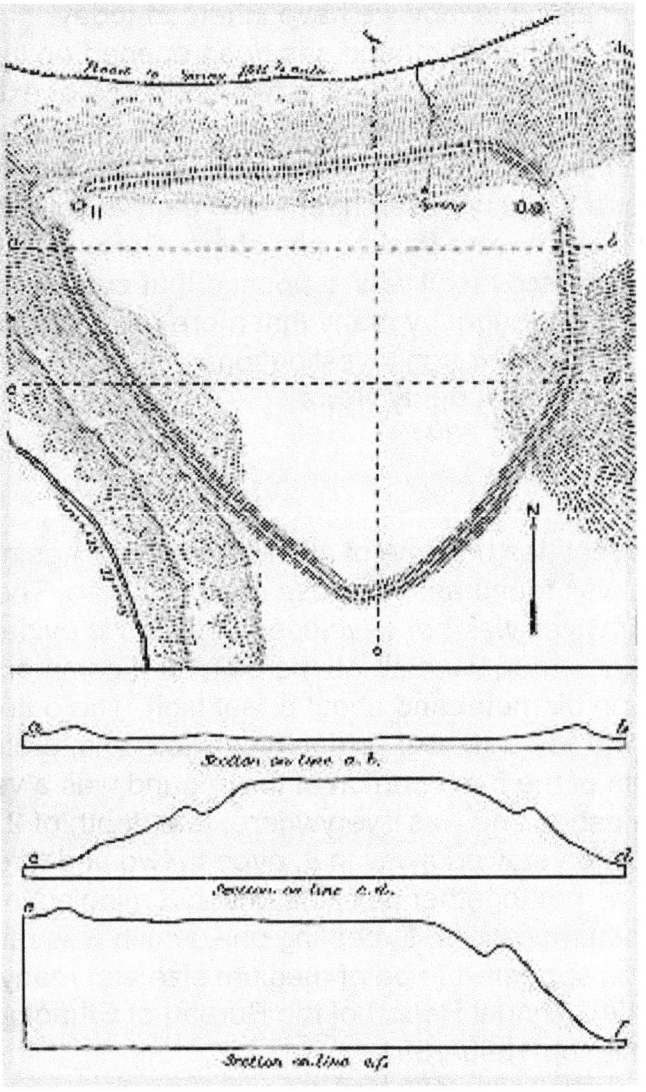

Largest in the collective series of mounds, the Great Smith Mound yielded at least two large skeletons, but at different levels of its deconstruction by Thomas' agents. It was 35 feet in height and 175 feet in diameter, and was constructed in at least two stages, according to the report. The larger of the two skeletons represented a man conceivably approaching eight feet in height when living.

At a depth of 14 feet, a rather large human skeleton was found, which was in a partially upright position with the back against a hard clay wall...All the bones were badly decayed, except those of the left wrist, which had been preserved by two heavy copper bracelets...

Nineteen feet from the top the bottom of this debris was reached, where, in the remains of a bark coffin, a skeleton measuring 7 1/2 feet in length and 19 inches across the shoulders, was discovered. It lay on the bottom of the vault stretched horizontally on the back, head east, arms by the sides... Each wrist was encircled by six heavy copper bracelets...Upon the breast was a copper gorget...length, 3 1/2 inches; greatest width 3 3/4 inches...

12th Annual Report of the Bureau of Ethnology to the Secretary of the Smithsonian Institution 1890-1891
(published in 1894)
(Kanawha County, West Virginia)
A Section of the Great Smith Mound, Kanawha County, West Virginia.

GIANTS ON THE EARTH

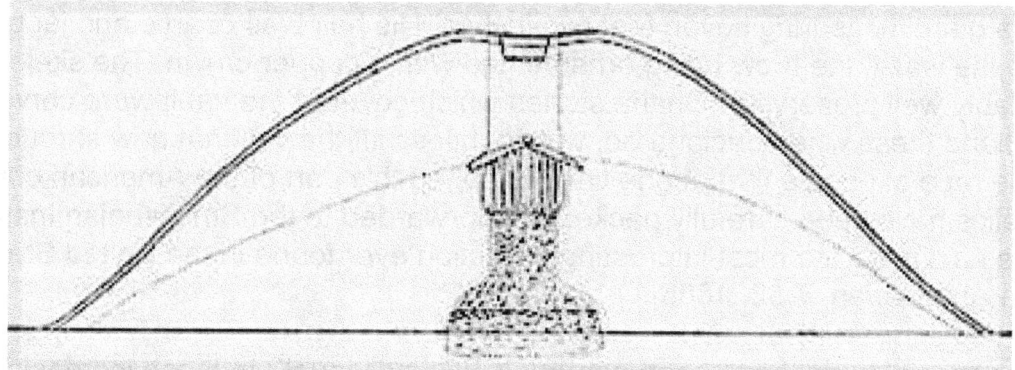

This cone-shaped mound rose 35 feet high and measured 175 feet in diameter at its base. The interior of the mound contained a vault made of timber measuring 12 feet by 13 feet. It was positioned within the mound 20 feet above surface level.

The pressure of the time schedule doubtless made it inconvenient to seriously consider the possibility of an ancient lineage of leaders taking the form of very tall people. The fact of gigantic stature never settled in as a clue to a greater mystery, and the evidences of very tall, ruggedly built men vanished—and often enough into the Smithsonian's temporary charnel house of pre-Columbian miscellany.

Three feet above...the skeleton of a large, strongly built man lay extended at full length with the face up, the head toward the east...The skull was obtained almost entire. Under it were thirteen water-worn quartz pebbles. The femur measured 18/inches...

12th Annual Report of the Bureau of Ethnology to the Secretary of the Smithsonian Institution 1890-1891
(published in 1894)

(Union County, Mississippi)
Group of mounds in Union County, Mississippi.

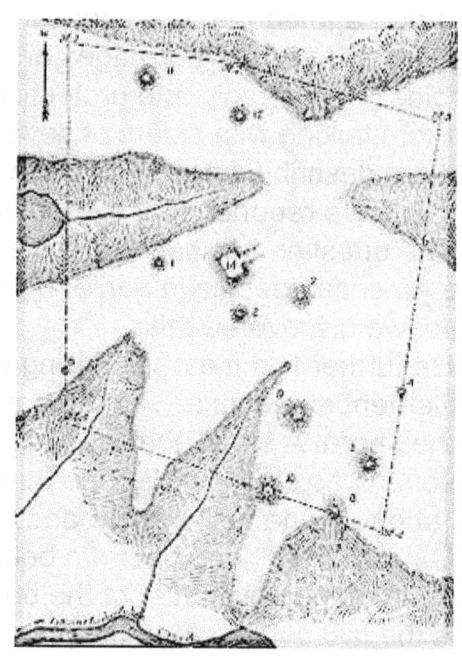

A femur (thigh bone) exceeding eighteen inches would indicate a man of very great height-easily over seven feet. Femurs exceeding twenty inches have been found however. Though hindsight is said to be 20/20, Thomas' methodology was little better than a government-sanctioned dissolution of the sacred burial places. He dismantled the sanctuaries and charnel houses with the fervor of a man whose first priority was to impress his employer. From Florida to Nebraska—including twenty-three states and Canada's Manitoba region—over the next seven years he and his agents worked like men possessed of a deadline.

A large Indian mound near the town of Gastersville, [Gastonville?—Ed.] Pa., has recently been opened and examined by a committee of scientists sent out from the Smithsonian Institute. At some depth from the surface a kind of vault was found in which was discovered the

GIANTS ON THE EARTH

skeleton of a giant measuring seven feet two inches. His hair was coarse and jet black, and hung to the waist, the brow being ornamented with a copper crown. The skeleton was remarkably well preserved...On the stones which covered the vault were carved inscriptions, and these when deciphered, will doubtless lift the veil that now shrouds the history of the race of people that at one time inhabited this part of the American continent. The relics have been carefully packed and forwarded to the Smithsonian Institute, and they are said to be the most interesting collection ever found in the United States.
American Antiquarian, 7:52, 1885

Could this special burial have been another kingly individual? In these increasingly hasty intrusions into the native burial grounds' inherent sanctity, the holocaust delivered its zenith under the officialdom action of former Union Major Powell. This man who in his youth had lived among the "Indians," somehow was insensitive to the sanctuary of their graveyards. But others came later to do a fair share of damage as well, all in the name of information gathering. The prehistory of eastern North America is not what we have been asked to accept from the efforts Cyrus Thomas, nor from the subsequent authorities who based so much of their work upon his, and the reason is worth repeating—many or most of the oldest mounds and subterranean burial acreages were promptly destroyed long before any focused "scientific" effort came on the scene.

Apart from the disregard of the settlers' records, the other part of the problem is the labyrinthine mausoleum that is the Smithsonian bone and artifact collection. In sum, we today are deprived of the real knowledge of the more ancient lineage. The early settlers observed that the giants of old may have passed on their grand stature to the later native people, for there were individuals among their later progression who were of a size and build that goes beyond our current notions of Native American physicality.

The Telling of the Bones

It is difficult not to understand the probability of an elite lineage of tall men and women who propagated their own genetic inheritance. These people lived, worked, and bred together. Were their marriages arranged to ensure the continuance of the grand stature in roles of leadership and protection? In his classic Red Earth, White Lies, Vine says:

From talking with elders of several tribes, my understanding is that the Indians were and are describing people of more than average height. In fact, some elders as a routine matter have reported that the Indians themselves were much larger and taller.

The question has been raised asking whether there was giant stature among the Native American people in earlier historic times. From Hardesty's History of Monroe County, Ohio, we discovered this:

He further told me of the killing of a big Indian at Buckchitawa, about the time of the settlement at Marietta. The Indians had a white prisoner whom they forced to decoy boats to the shore. A small boat was descending the river containing white people, when this prisoner was placed under the bank to tell those in the boat that he had escaped captivity, and to come to the shore and take him in. The Indians were concealed, but the big Indian stuck his head out from behind a large tree, when it was pierced by a bullet from the gun of the steersman of the boat. The Indians cried out Wetzel, Wetzel, and fled. This was the last ever seen of the prisoner. The Indians returned next day and buried the big

GIANTS ON THE EARTH

Indian, who, he said, was twenty inches taller than he was, and he was a tall man. When Chester Bishop was digging a cellar for Asahel Booth, at Clarington, many years ago, he came across a skeleton, the bones of which were removed carefully by Dr. Richard Kirkpatrick, and from his measurement the height of the man when living would have been 8 feet and 5 inches. It is probable that these were the bones of the big Indian of whom the Indian at Jackson's told me.

The Mound at Marietta Drawn by Henry Howe in 1846.

Howe stated this mound was "of a magnitude and height which strike the beholder with astonishment." It's base had a diameter of 115 feet; it's height reached up 30 feet. It was surrounded by a ditch four feet deep and fifteen feet wide.

And again this:

A large quantity of human bones was discovered in a fissure in the limestone near the United States Coast Guard lighthouse. A crude tomb of black stone slabs, of a formation not known on the island, was found many years ago beneath the roots of a huge stump. Eight skeletons were found, one measuring over seven feet in height.

Sketches and Stories of the Lake Erie Islands
by Theresa Thorndale, Sandusky (1898)

Some of the settlers and their descendents may have seen clearly, but the representatives of the Smithsonian and other sanctioned institutions, in spite of good intentions, lacked the kind of thoroughness in their analyses that included a broadened field of vision. We have felt heartily from the beginning of this research that the Smithsonian is the recipient of mandates put into place well over 100 years ago. It is virtually exempt from NAGPRA (Native American Graves Protection and Repatriation Act), for the reason (say they) of there being too much data to finish analyzing to prepare for repatriation.

Concealing evidence that conflicts with accepted theory is common scientific skull-

GIANTS ON THE EARTH

duggery. For years the Smithsonian Institution has been accused of hiding in storage vaults things it doesn't like. In 1968 two Neanderthal-like skulls with low foreheads and large brows were found in Minnesota. As for dating, University of Minnesota scientists said they were reluctant to destroy any of the material, although carbon-14 testing only requires the burning of one gram of bone. They were sent to the Smithsonian. Later Dr. Lawrence Angel, curator of physical anthropology at the institution, said he had no record of the skulls there, although he was sure they were not lost. We have a right to wonder whether some professional scientists mightn't find a really early date for the bones distressing.

American Indian Myths and Mysteries
Vincent H. Gaddis (1977)

Why distressing? Because no true Neanderthal remains have ever been recognized by any Federal authorities as originating on the North American continent, what to say of the Americas in general. Is there yet today a conflict between established theory and what has been physically discovered? Is the "ghost" of Powell yet haunting the halls of the Museum?

So what is the policy of the Smithsonian? Does the institution intentionally withhold information? Is the fact of a race of giant warriors and chieftains threatening to the closed, internal doctrine of American archaeology? That there was a race of men and women possessing an unusually tall and strong physicality living over an extensive area North America has become a forgotten fact.

There are other examples, and names like the Gungywamp Society of Connecticut, Ed Conrad, and others have bizarre stories to relate about the ineptitude or simple prejudice of the Smithsonian when dealing with their materials. In these examples, there is growing appreciation for an actual cover-up.

Another grotesque twist is the Army Medical Museum's collection. According to the ABC News special "Skeletons in the Closet," the United States government acquired a real interest in Indian corpses. The Surgeon General, in post-Civil War 1868, requested that the army collect the skulls, utensils, and weaponry of Native Americans "as far as you are able to procure them." According to the report, these were to be sent to Washington, D.C. as part of a program that studied the effects of modern bullets and other weaponry on human bodies. The collection of such remains, estimated at 4,000, was taken mostly from grave and battle sites. What was left over became part of the Smithsonian collection estimated at 18,000 individuals, and this by way of the Army Medical Museum.

The objects here collected which have not been given, or acquired by exchange, have been purchased for the use of the museum by order of the surgeon-general... There is a skeleton of a giant, who, in life, measured seven feet, prepared by Auzoux and mounted by Blanchêne's method, which, if I may use that term, is really a beauty. It is as white and clean as new fallen snow, and the brass joints and screws which keep it together are bright, and of the latest style and finish...

"The Army Medical Museum in Washington" by Louis Bagger
Appletons' Journal: A Magazine Of General Literature
Volume 9, Issue 206 (1873)

GIANTS ON THE EARTH

Today however, bones are no longer as good a source of information as they once were thought to be, and for several good reasons. Bone, while composed dominantly of the metallic calcium, yet is made up of organic molecules. Depending on moisture and temperature, it will decay, break down with time, and return to the condition of the soil after a certain number of centuries. Bone evidence has created over-emphasis on certain periods of prehistory, in this region the so-called "Hopewell" and "Fort Ancient" (Mississippian) people. Thus, a great proportion of the Archaic and early Adena bones discovered were decomposed beyond preservation. Due to a lack of skeletons other more antique periods have not received the same kind of recognition save from the better scholars affecting the interested public's view of the ancient world. Ironically, the holocaust of giants, while deadening our sense of the past, may well serve as a lesson for the future.

Recommended Reading:

Red Earth, White Lies, Native Americans and the Myth of Scientific Fact
by Vine Deloria, Jr. (Fulcrum Pub; ISBN: 1555913881; 1997)
www.knowledge.co.uk/xxx/cat/deloria

Dave Cain explores West Virginia
www.theaaca.com/biocain.htm

The Nephilim Giants

Who were the Nephilim? The heart of the matter lies in the ancient accounts of the Nephilim and their offspring—who and what they really were, what they did, where they are now, what their agenda is, and so on. Well over twenty years of research has led me to this conclusion. Those materials, as borne out by QUOTES from the book of Enoch in the Book of Jude, Revelation bear witness to this, as do the actual mentions in the original Old Testament of the Nephilim, Anakim (Anunna/Anunnaki), Rephaim, and Rapha—along with others descended from Nephilim forbears.

In fact, the TRADITIONAL HEBREW VIEW is that the "rapha," meaning, interchangeably, "irrevocably dead," "evil spirits," "demons," and GIANTS, are the spirits of the half-angelic Nephilim offspring that were killed in the great cataclysm we remember as the Flood. This is not a tall tale, but a truth of which Christ and his disciples were aware. This is why they quoted from the book of Enoch. The story can also be found in the books of Jasher, Jubilees, and the recently-found Dead Sea Scroll, the Book of Giants.

Angels have bodies. They can take a variety of forms, as well ("for Satan can appear even as an angel of light," etc.). There were two angelic rebellions, the first being the Luciferian rebellion that most are familiar with; this is the source of what Paul calls, in the sixth chapter of Ephesians, "Spirit wickedness in high places." This is why Jesus calls Satan "the prince of the powers of the air."

UFO researchers, take notice.

The second rebellion came much, much later, and is well known in Hebrew esoteric tradition. In fact, much of this knowledge is still intact in the Hebrew tradition. Many

GIANTS ON THE EARTH

books which were originally in the Bible—the books of Enoch, Jasher, Jubilees, and so on—contain the whole story of the fallen angels who rebelled in order to mate with human women. These beings were called the NEPHILIM, literally "those who came/fell down."

A recent dead-sea scroll find and translation, "the Book of Giants," also contains this story in great detail. Before you question the validity of the non-canonical books I mention, keep in mind that not only were they part of the original Old Testament, but many of them—particularly Enoch—were quoted from by the Apostles in the New Testament. Quotes from the book of Enoch can found in the books of Jude, Revelation, and several other places.

The book of Enoch pre-dated the time of Christ by around 300 years. In the Old Testament, Genesis tells us that "the sons of God looked upon the daughters of men and found them fair, and took of them wives as they chose."

The result of these unholy, unsanctioned unions were "the mighty men of old, the men of renown." The actual translation of this passage reads something like this: "The nephilim came and took human wives for themselves, as many as they wanted. Their children were the nephilim of old, the giants."

The books of Jasher, Jubilees, Enoch, and others contain the complete story of what happened in the pre-flood world. The Nephilim angels set themselves up as pagan "gods" to be worshipped, and their hybrid, genetically monstrous sons as "demigod" kings over the rest of humanity. These offspring were also called nephilim, and they were brutal, cruel, occultic and cannibalistic giants who treated ordinary human beings with contempt.

There were 300 original "Watchers" above the Earth, who rebelled and became the Nephilim. Their leader was named Semyaza. Through corrupt angelic knowledge, the pre-flood world was corrupted. The book of Enoch says that the Nephilim and their children "sinned against all flesh," creating HYBRID creatures which were part human, part beast, part fowl (or bird). Sound familiar?

The 300 fallen "watchers," whose original job had been to PROTECT humanity and the Earth, were utterly depraved. They taught mankind the arts of witchcraft, sorcery, drug abuse, and war. The gene-pool of the human race was tainted as well, almost beyond recovery. When you read the story of Noah and his family, it should be understood that he was not only selected to survive because of the quality of his character; Genesis states that, unlike the majority of the rest of humanity, Noah was "found perfect in all his generations." In other words, he and his family were UNTAINTED by the fallen angelic bloodline, which God had cursed to eternal damnation (in the Hebrew Old Testament, the word "rapha" means "the damned," the "eternally dead," "demon," "ghost," and GIANT, i.e., the spirit of one of the offspring of the Nephilim.

After the flood, when MOST but not all of the Nephilim offspring and hybrid mutations were destroyed, the 300 former "watchers" were confined inside the Earth, in a prison from which they can not escape. These are those who are referred to by Paul in Ephesians chapter 6 as "the rulers of the spiritual darkness of this world." Although imprisoned, they are still VERY powerful and can influence world events, particularly through their offspring and creations.

Jude refers to them, quoting directly from the book of Enoch, when he says "the an-

GIANTS ON THE EARTH

gels who are chained in eternal darkness, awaiting the judgement of the great day." This is NOT a reference to Lucifer/Satan and his angels, who still "wage war in heaven."

The more one learns about the ancient knowledge and traditions, the more it is seen that a spiritual yet physical and galactic war is behind all the myths, legends, religions and traditions of our world. This a very complex topic, but the information is out there if you want to look for it.... Regarding this passage from Genesis: Chapter 6:1

"And it came to pass, when men began to multiply on the face of the earth, and daughters were born unto them, 2 That the sons of God saw the daughters of men that they were fair; and they took them wives of all which they chose. 3 And the LORD said, My spirit shall not always strive with man, for that he also is flesh: yet his days shall be an hundred and twenty years. 4 There were giants [nephilim] in the earth in those days; and also after that, when the sons of God came in unto the daughters of men, and they bare children to them, the same became mighty men which were of old, men of renown. 5 And God saw that the wickedness of man was great in the earth, and that every imagination of the thoughts of his heart was only evil continually.

The passage "and also after that" refers to a time after the flood, when an unspecified form of Nephilim or fallen angels once again took an interest in human women. These are not the same as those nephilim who did this before the flood however, as they are imprisoned. The result of these later unions were the Canaanite and other "giants" of the Old Testament, such as those mentioned in the Book of Numbers and elsewhere: "'And there we saw the Nephilim (the sons of Anak, who come from the Nephilim); and we seemed to ourselves like grasshoppers, and so we seemed to them.' Then all the congregation raised a loud cry; and the people wept that night." (Numbers Chapter 13 verse 33) The Anakim or Children of Anak are synonymous with Zechariah Sitchin's Anunnaki, or Anunna. There was a specific reason that the Israelites were commanded to utterly wipe out these peoples, as this represented a new effort to undermine the planned destiny of humanity. The issue of technology, based on advanced scientific (fallen angelic) knowledge, comes into play in all of this as well. UFOs, particle beams, all types of advanced technology are described in both the Old and New Testament. This demonstrates that a physical presence is require by both sides in the ongoing conflict, and technology is required in order to function in our reality. UFOs and their relationship to predatory interlopers is made obvious in many places, particularly in the book of Zechariah. Apparently a certain amount of this activity was allowed or permitted by God, among those who followed the ways of the Nephilim who had set themselves up to be worshipped and emulated:

1 Zch5:1Then again I lifted up mine eyes, and saw, and behold a flying scroll. 2 And he said unto me: 'What seest thou?' And I answered: 'I see a flying scroll; the length thereof is twenty cubits, and the breadth thereof ten cubits.' 3 Then said he unto me: 'This is the curse that goeth forth over the face of the whole land; for every one that stealeth shall be swept away on the one side like it; and every one that sweareth shall be swept away on the other side like it. 4 I cause it to go forth, saith the LORD of hosts, and it shall enter into the house of the thief, and into the house of him that sweareth falsely by My name; and it shall abide in the midst of his house, and shall consume it with the timber thereof and the stones thereof.' 5 Then the angel that spoke with me went forth, and said unto me: 'Lift up now thine eyes, and see what is this that goeth forth.'

GIANTS ON THE EARTH

In ancient times, a "scroll" was one rolled-up piece of leather or parchment, tightly bound. In other words, this was a cylindrical flying object of some sort, one which moved with intent and purpose. When one considers the "cybernetic" aspects of many unknown creatures and entities—metallic hardness, metallic sounds, luminous eyes, and so on—it becomes apparent that we are dealing with an advanced and ancient technology, one which easily melds and utilizes genetic material and inert technology. These qualities have been noted in strange creatures for centuries, but recent beings with such qualities abound: Mothman, El Chupacabras, the Hopkinsville/Kelly Goblins, "El Diablito" (a super-dense, violent dwarf) in Argentina, and a variety of other creatures described as more or less impervious to machete or shovel-blows, pick-blows, vehicle impact, shotgun blasts, and handgun ammo.

Again, all of these things tie together to give us an overall bigger picture. Similar traditions exist in the Hindu Vedas and Puranas, Norse mythology, Greek mythology, and elsewhere. The Judeo-Christian tradition, in my opinion and after twenty-plus years of study, is the most accurate one in terms of painting a picture which may represent some sort of historical accuracy. The oldest written language which we know of is that of ancient Sumer (the biblical Shin'ar). Ur was a city in this region (later called Chaldea), and it was from Ur that Abram (later called Abraham) came. He was the son of a pagan priest. How do we know this? Because cuneiform tablets have been found which describe the leaving of Abram from Ur, along with his possessions, servants, family members, and so on! And these match the biblical account.

The oldest extant written story, tradition, or text that has been translated is the Epic of Gilgamesh, a half-human demigod who lamented his mortality, and who went on a journey (part of it below the ground, in the underworld) in search of immortality (like that of his father). An interesting observation: In the "Book of Giants" (4Q203, 1Q23, 2Q26, 4Q530-532, 6Q8), a Hebrew text, several giants, and their Nephilim fathers, are mentioned by name. One of them is Gilgamesh, the same Gilgamesh from the Sumerian tradition, a "mighty man" who is lamented his own impending death and damnation: 4Q530 Col. 2 1 concerns the death of our souls [. . .] and all his comrades, [and Oh]ya told them what Gilgamesh said to him 2[. . .] and it was said [. . .] "concerning [. . .] the leader has cursed the potentates" Enoch sends a tablet which pronounces the sentence of the flood, to the giants (who were rulers over men): 4Q530 Frag. 2 The scribe [Enoch . . .] 2[. . .] 3a copy of the second tablet that [Epoch] se[nt . . .] 4in the very handwriting of Enoch the noted scribe [. . . In the name of God the great] 5and holy one, to Shemihaza and all [his companions . . .] 6let it be known to you that not [. . .] 7and the things you have done, and that your wives [. . .] 8they and their sons and the wives of [their sons . . .] 9by your licentiousness on the earth, and there has been upon you [. . . and the land is crying out] 10and complaining about you and the deeds of your children [. . .] 11the harm that you have done to it. [. . .] 12until Raphael arrives, behold, destruction [is coming, a great flood, and it will destroy all living things] 13and whatever is in the deserts and the seas. And the meaning of the matter [. . .] 14upon you for evil. But now, loosen the bonds bi[nding you to evil . . .] l5and pray.

The hybrid beings mentioned in other books such as Enoch and Jubilees are also in the Giants Scroll: 4Q531 Frag. 2 [. . .] they defiled [. . .] 2[. . . they begot] giants and monsters [. . .] 3[. . .] they begot, and, behold, all [the earth was corrupted . . .] 4[. . .

GIANTS ON THE EARTH

] with its blood and by the hand of [. . .] 5[giant's] which did not suffice for them and [. . .] 6[. . .] and they were seeking to devour many [. . .] 7[. . .] 8[. . .] the monsters attacked it. 4Q532 Col. 2 Frags. 1 - 6 2[. . .] flesh [. . .] 3al[l . . .] monsters [. . .] will be [. . .] 4[. . .] they would arise [. . .] lacking in true knowledge [. . .] because [. . .] 5[. . .] the earth [grew corrupt . . .] mighty [. . .] 6[. . .] they were considering [. . .] 7[. . .] from the angels upon [. . .] 8[. . .] in the end it will perish and die [. . .] 9[. . .] they caused great corruption in the [earth . . .] [. . . this did not] suffice to [. . .] "they will be [. . .]

So the oldest written human tradition that we know of is reflected in the Hebrew tradition of the Nephilim and their hybrid children. The monumental task at hand is to deduce, if possible, where and how Mothman and other anomalous entities fit into this tradition. Additionally, there's an entire related tradition of the "pre-Adamic" or "pre-Adamite" world, which was peopled by humanoid beings of various types, along with other strange beings. These may be some of the same hominids that are represented in the fossil record; and some of these forms, as survivors and anachronisms, may explain some sightings of anomalous beings. Lilith may well have been of one of these races, and she fled into the wilderness, where she mated with subterranean "demons" and other beings, swearing that she and her children (the "Lilim") would always prey on human children, and seduce human beings into hybrid-producing sexual encounters.

Again, this is paralleled in nearly EVERY ancient tradition, from the Lamias of Greece, to the Huldre-folk and seductresses of Scandinavia and the Dragon-kings, queens, princes and princesses of China and Japan.

William Michael Mott
Author of Caverns, Cauldrons and Concealed Creatures and This Tragic Earth

www.ingramcontent.com/pod-product-compliance
Lightning Source LLC
Chambersburg PA
CBHW080358170426
43193CB00016B/2758